Praise for *1945: THE RECKONING*

'Phil Craig has produced a vivid and compelling narrative, one that is painted on a vast canvas yet remains focused on detail. As the war reaches its climax and the British Empire teeters, we are introduced to a colourful cast of protagonists who stride like giants through the pages of this book. Flawlessly researched and vividly written, *1945: The Reckoning* is history at its finest.'

– **Giles Milton, historian**

'Phil Craig's superb book is a timely reminder that the political and military trajectory of history is much more about the personal agency of single men and women working in unison, than it is about understanding this or that movement, or this or that ideology. In Craig's account, individuals matter. It's the only way, for example, to understand how an Indian army officer could want the independence of his country while simultaneously wanting to defend it from the depredations of a totalitarian enemy. Nuance matters, and Craig gives it to us in spades. This is a brilliant evocation of the best of the historian's art.'

– **Robert Lyman, historian**

'In this brilliant book, Phil Craig expands the narrative of the Second World War in this measured and objective masterpiece. A gripping narrative on Britain and the changing Imperial world.'

– **Helen Fry, historian**

'As the War in Asia ended, a new order emerged from the chaos of a broken British Empire. This fascinating book tells the story, paying close attention to the men and women on the spot who shaped that huge transition.'

– **Professor Tirthankar Roy, London School of Economics**

'*1945: The Reckoning* is written with a fluent command of research, and is packed with great characters, observations and affecting human details.'

– **Amanda Craig, novelist**

'I really enjoyed this and think it's the best popular history book I have read for a long time. Phil Craig paints an enormous canvas with real skill, beautifully employing vignettes of real personal experience, and his conclusions are nuanced, accurate and fair. There are details here that are new to me and stories that should be much more widely known. I hope that people from across the culture war spectrum will read this because all can learn a great deal from it.'
– **Professor Alan Lester, University of Sussex**

'If you have even passing interest in history, this is a must-read; fascinating and hugely informative, this is non-fiction with the narrative pull of fiction at its best, wearing its considerable learning with such ease it is genuinely hard to put down.'
– **Marika Cobbold, novelist**

'This is terrific history writing, erudite yet vivid, a truly fascinating new perspective on one of the most important periods of the 20th century.'
– **Laura Thompson, historian**

'A gripping account that makes the war in Asia central to the story. Amidst the clash of empires, consider afresh the Indian soldiers who fought for and against the Raj; the nurses and prisoners of war caught in the maelstrom; and the many motives of Britain's imperial authorities in their war against brutal Japanese occupations. The tales we most readily recall about the end of the Second World War are just part of a much bigger picture, one that looked very different in Asia.'
– **Dr Samir Puri, Associate Fellow, Royal Institute of International Affairs**

'I love how *1945: The Reckoning* gives me perspectives on the Second World War that I have never accessed before, and the personal stories bring colonial history to life so engagingly. This book is a triumph!'
– **Jane Caro, broadcaster and writer**

'India's relationship with its Second World War involvement has always been somewhat ambivalent. India provided the largest all-volunteer force among the Allies (and earned a commensurate number of gallantry awards); but most Indians unequivocally wanted independence. Phil Craig's *1945: The Reckoning,* while telling the larger story of the war, manages almost uniquely to balance these competing narratives in Indian memory with real skill – as part of the larger, globe-straddling stories he assembles, of that era-defining war. I thoroughly enjoyed it.'

– **K. S. Nair, author of** *The Forgotten Few:*
The Indian Air Force in World War Two

'Britain's war against Germany and Japan in 1939–1945 was an imperial war, involving not only Canadians, Australians and New Zealanders, but also West Indians, Africans and, above all, Indians. That some tens of thousands of the latter should have chosen to fight with the Japanese against the British concurs with the cartoonish, black-against-white narrative of today's zealous anti-colonialists. But that millions more Indian volunteers – many of them nationalists – chose to fight in British uniform, both in Asia and in Europe, complicates the moral picture. This is one fascinating aspect of the nuanced story that Phil Craig tells so well.'

– **Nigel Biggar, Regius Professor Emeritus of Moral Theology, University of Oxford**

Also by Phil Craig

Finest Hour
End of the Beginning
Trafalgar: the Men, the Battle, the Storm
Diana, Story of a Princess

1945: The Reckoning

War, Empire and the Struggle for a New World

PHIL CRAIG

HODDER &
STOUGHTON

First published in Great Britain in 2025 by Hodder & Stoughton Limited
An Hachette UK company

The authorised representative in the EEA is Hachette Ireland, 8 Castlecourt Centre, Dublin 15, D15 XTP3, Ireland (email: info@hbgi.ie)

1

Copyright © Phil Craig 2025

The right of Phil Craig to be identified as the Author of the Work has been asserted by him in accordance with the Copyright, Designs and Patents Act 1988.

All rights reserved. No part of this publication may be reproduced, stored in a retrieval system, or transmitted, in any form or by any means without the prior written permission of the publisher, nor be otherwise circulated in any form of binding or cover other than that in which it is published and without a similar condition being imposed on the subsequent purchaser.

All reasonable attempts have been made to contact the copyright holders of all images. You are invited to contact the publisher if your image was used without correct identification or acknowledgment, and amendments can be made in further editions.

A CIP catalogue record for this title is available from the British Library

Hardback ISBN 978 1 399 71449 5
Trade Paperback ISBN 978 1 399 71450 1
ebook ISBN 978 1 399 71451 8

Typeset in Bembo MT by Hewer Text UK Ltd, Edinburgh
Printed and bound in Great Britain by Clays Ltd, Elcograf S.p.A.

Hodder & Stoughton policy is to use papers that are natural, renewable and recyclable products and made from wood grown in sustainable forests. The logging and manufacturing processes are expected to conform to the environmental regulations of the country of origin.

Hodder & Stoughton Limited
Carmelite House
50 Victoria Embankment
London EC4Y 0DZ

www.hodder.co.uk

For Jennifer, Tony and a really brusque doctor

Contents

Foreword by James Holland   xi
Introduction   xvii

SECTION ONE: SONS OF THE RAJ

1. The Soldier   3
2. The Rebel   21

SECTION TWO: RALLY 'ROUND THE FLAG

3. The Nurse   47
4. The Exile   67
5. The Prisoner   91
6. The Hunger   107
7. The Trailblazers   129
8. The Road to Delhi   151
9. The Condemned   165

SECTION THREE: EVERY SCRAP OF TERRITORY

10. The Great Game   189
11. The Secret Agents   213
12. The Doctor   233
13. The Laundry   251
14. The Surrender   271
15. The Martyr   291

16. The Horror	313
17. The Children	335
Acknowledgements	348
Picture Credits	353
Bibliography	355
Notes and Sources	359
Index	375
About the Author	381

Foreword by James Holland

The Second World War changed the world forever. It was not just the tens of millions that were dead as a result, nor the shattered cities, towns and villages. The maelstrom had affected peoples, cultures, societies and ways of life in so many other ways. Future misery in many parts of the globe was assured, the defeated had to try and emerge from the wreckage, while the victors had to adjust to a global order that had altered immeasurably. Revolution and civil war followed as borders changed, regimes were toppled and the old era of European-dominating imperialism drew to an end. Of the 'big three' victorious combatant nations, the United States was poised to become the dominating global superpower for the rest of the century, the Soviet Union had also grown in stature and power despite its horrific losses, while Britain had to come to terms with a complex new world in which the moral certitudes that had guided it through much of this long, bloody conflict now appeared far less clear.

The story of Britain's role in the changing world and the inevitable end of the largest empire in history has been the subject of much debate and discussion ever since – and it is also a narrative that has dramatically evolved as contemporary broader views about imperialism, colonialism and liberalism have changed. The old ideals of much of pre-war British society seem woefully outdated today, but in truth they appeared outdated to many by 1945 too; in recent years, however, a new post-imperial view of history has emerged that is mostly unhelpful and lopsided. Understanding the past is vital; history is the compass that guides us to the present and helps us to prepare for the future, which is why it is good to be as objective as possible rather than succumbing to viewing history through a prism of social trends that reflect the present rather than the past.

The rich and incredibly nuanced views, hopes and aims of those emerging from the world at war require, and deserve, an equally nuanced and considered appreciation by those looking back on such extraordinary times today; it is something Phil Craig has achieved with a deft hand in this book, but which all too often has been lacking in the past. I was first introduced to his work a quarter of a century ago – from the time of writing this – when I read, utterly captivated, *Finest Hour*, which he co-wrote with Tim Clayton, and which accompanied a major BBC television series about the tumultuous summer of 1940. They were among the very first to shatter the myth that Britain had been all alone, a plucky amateur defying the mighty moloch of Nazi Germany when all around them had already succumbed. Rather, they rightly showed that Britain still had much in its favour following the retreat from Dunkirk and the fall of France, and not least its immense global reach with its Dominions and empire.

More importantly, they wrote with immense energy, vividness and originality, creating a compelling, page-turning narrative that was rooted in the extraordinary human drama of that incredible first summer of the war. This cut to the heart of what remains most people's essential interest in the war: that this conflict, more so than others, was fundamentally about ordinary people caught up in extraordinary events. The Second World War was arguably the greatest period of human drama in our history; certainly, for all the major combatant nations, it affected every man, woman and child more directly than any other conflict in history. *Finest Hour* combined exciting and fresh historical research and perspectives with a very well-defined cast of characters who were the readers' conduit through those dramatic summer months of 1940 – and all relayed with a reportage-style narrative that was both accessible and genuinely compellingly written. Walking this very

FOREWORD BY JAMES HOLLAND

narrow ridgeline between academic authority and narrative flair is exceptionally difficult and achieved by few writers. Slip too far down the slopes of academia and the prose can swiftly become dry; but veer too heavily towards the side of the novelist's prose and authority is swiftly lost.

Phil Craig and Tim Clayton skilfully managed to stick to the ridge in *Finest Hour*, a book that dramatically changed the course of my life. Reading it, I realised they had discovered the ideal formula for writing popular narrative history: a defined cast of characters, flawless research and an exciting writing style that ensured both readability and authority. It was after reading this that I sat down to write my first history book and I cannot overstate the influence *Finest Hour* had on my own approach to writing and the career I have had as a historian ever since.

Phil Craig has now written an altogether more challenging book about Britain and the changing imperial world that emerged in 1945. Threading through the narrative is another fascinating cast of characters, which has enabled him to view Britain and those countries inextricably bound to her through a wide range of perspectives. Along the journey, the reader heads to the jungle of Burma, the horrors of Belsen, the back lanes of Devon, to the headhunting tribes of Borneo and to that vast, melting pot of different peoples and creeds, India. No writer has yet provided a more balanced and objective take of the fascinating Subhas Chandra Bose, for example, freedom fighter but also founder and leader of the Indian National Army, the INA. The mythology around Bose still runs deep – Kolkata's international airport bears his name – yet he was also a man who sided with the monstrous Imperial Japanese regime and courted Hitler. He was a man who has always divided opinion yet here Craig paints him in a much more even-handed and rounded light. And he emerges as a far more, not less, fascinating and complex figure as a result.

And while there is Bose, a man prepared to take many profound choices in his quest to rid India of British rule, there is also Kodandera Subayya Thimayya, the first Indian officer to command a brigade in the Indian Army, who fought against the INA as well as the Japanese and later, as a general, found himself caught up in the terrible civil war of post-Indian independence of 1947. Thimayya, or 'Colonel Timmy' as he was known, is as interesting a character as Bose and while a proud Indian nationalist, also provides a fascinating counter-point to the more revolutionary INA leader.

This, though, is a book that crosses the globe from Britain to Germany and from India to Indonesia. It is not especially lengthy but is nonetheless ambitious, deeply thought-provoking and, as with all the very best history, compellingly told. There are surprises here, episodes that prompt not only a sense of wonder and admiration but also shame. And there is that rich cast of characters, expertly chosen, and whose lives, hopes, disappointments, moments of fear and joy, shock, horror, relief and wonder so vividly frame this endlessly fascinating and profoundly compelling story. The past is a complex place, but we rely on those directing the compass to steer us through the difficult waters. Lives are not black or white nor lived in straight lines, as Phil Craig shows us in this highly original and finely judged book.

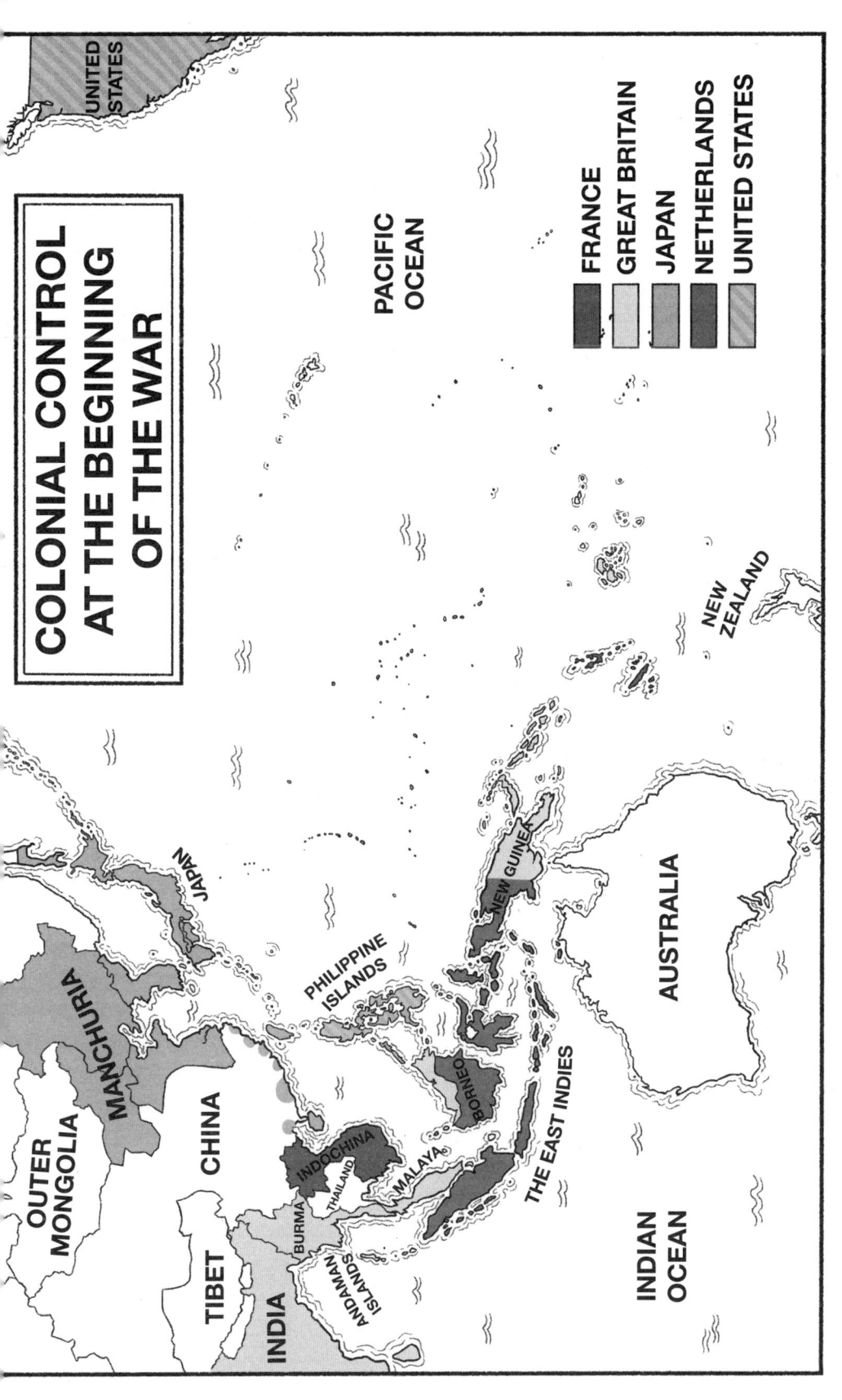

Introduction

This is the third book I've written about Britain in the Second World War. For 1940 the Battle of Britain was front and centre and for 1942 it was the campaign in the North African desert. Here the focus is India, Burma and the fate of the British and other empires.

As I researched the end of the war, I was drawn time and again to the words that historian Robin Prior chose to open *Conquer We Must,* his superb account of British strategy across the two great conflicts of the twentieth century:

> It fell to Britain to confront a number of regimes which represented a threat to the civilised world . . . And, given the nature of the powers it was fighting, it was essential that any chance of a liberal world order (however imperfect) emerging with peace, depended on Britain being on the winning side.

I share this fundamentally positive view, yet how to square it with some of the less pleasant and certainly less *liberal* things that the British state actually did as the war came to an end? In that regard I found another quote most helpful, from historian David Olusoga:

> History is not there to make us feel good, proud or comforted. It's simply there to be fully understood in all its wonder, pain and, yes, its cruelties and injustices.

INTRODUCTION

Many things have changed since the first book was published in 1999, and there's a sharper focus in publishing and in public life on questions of colonialism and race. Discovering what really happened in some of the old European colonies during 1945 — what I call 'imperial muscle memory' — can be surprising and confronting. But it's necessary, I would argue, for anyone who wants the warts and all version of how the war was won.

There's much more about the people who helped me write this book at the end, but I do here want to thank one historian from Australia who has been especially valuable and generous. After years of research — and carrying out dozens of unique interviews — Christine Helliwell wrote *Semut*, a book I have plundered extensively for quotes and insights for my account of 1945 in Borneo. It's one of the most exciting and original things I've read in a long time — a radical blend of anthropology, military history and personal memento — and I recommend it to anyone.

When we wrote *Finest Hour*, Tim Clayton and I set out to sweep away decades of myth-making about 1940, and we always planned to do the same for 1945. Tim has gone on to write a number of excellent books by himself, but I like to think that there's a little of his insight and cleverness lingering in these pages. *1945: A Reckoning* does have one important thing in common with *Finest Hour*, though. The bulk of the story is told through the experiences and the words of people most readers will find unfamiliar and, I hope, intriguing. They range widely in geography and biography. Some can truly be called history makers; others, people to whom history just happened. Or perhaps people who experienced history happening to them and were sometimes able, in some small but important ways, to give it a little shove.

SECTION ONE

Sons of the Raj

'We could only control India through force of arms, but force was useless against a people who didn't fight back; because you couldn't kill people like that without killing a part of yourself too.'

— Abir Mukherjee, *Smoke and Ashes*

1

The Soldier

Burma, 1945

The imposing young officer striding purposefully on board HMS *Phoebe* was known affectionately to his friends as 'Timmy' and more respectfully – or downright nervously – to the men of 8/19 Hyderabad as 'Colonel Timmy'. Or, rather, 'Colonel Timmy . . . Sir!'

He might have died a few days before reaching Akyab, the tiny Burmese port where his men were now crowding onto the big Royal Navy cruiser. As it was, when his jeep triggered the Japanese land mine the only fatality was a soldier standing close by. It was an upsetting end to a successful battle but so far they'd taken few losses and the experience of commanding troops in combat – only the second time he had ever done so – had been exhilarating. He'd spent years preparing for just this sort of campaign, and faced many painful choices along the way, but he felt happy and confident now, about himself and about the course of the war. After years of failure and disappointment, with some of the worst of it taking place in this region, there was a real sense of momentum in the army and something else that had once been missing – professionalism. As they risked their lives clearing out Japanese positions, the Hyderabadis had come to depend upon things that had been, at best, haphazard in the past: the right supplies in the right place, reliable air cover, medical care where it was needed and, especially during the last month, some highly accurate supporting fire from a group of

Australian, Indian and British warships that had shadowed them down the north Burma coast.

Tired to the point of exhaustion, Timmy was at first most reluctant to leave his bunk when *Phoebe*'s captain requested — somewhat peremptorily — that he join him in what he called the 'Admiral's cabin'. The British and their arcane rituals could be trying. Why waste valuable rest just to shake some old duffer's hand? But in fact he wasn't being ordered to shake a hand or exchange a salute; he was being invited to enjoy his own luxury suite, beautifully decorated with an enormous bed and a private bathroom complete with a huge porcelain tub. It was everything he'd dreamed of during his long slog through the stinking Burmese jungle, sleeping in tents, fending off suicidal Japanese soldiers and trying to avoid the voracious wildlife that lurked in every thicket. And, luxury of luxuries, there was even a private bar. Timmy's life thus far had been defined by his willingness — or not — to conform to British ideas and British traditions. But the generous amount of quality booze in His Majesty's warships was one custom he never challenged. Pouring himself a large whisky, he stretched out luxuriously into his hot, deep bath and thought about the battle to come.

This amphibious coastal-hopping operation in the Arakan region of Burma was a key part of the army's offensive plans for 1945. It had gone well enough so far but the biggest challenge was now only hours away, which is why Timmy and the troops he commanded were sailing south on HMS *Phoebe* in varying degrees of comfort. They were about to land in territory that the Indian Army hadn't set foot in since early 1942. British commandos were to lead the way, taking an initial bridgehead and then heading for the village of Kangaw, but their main support was to be a brigade of the 25th Indian Division that was currently being led by Timmy in an 'acting' capacity. He was the first non-white soldier ever to be given the command of a brigade of the Indian Army and this brought a mixture of pride and pressure. He knew that many eyes would soon be upon him and that, after a few vocal disagreements in the recent past, his ability to work alongside other senior officers would be subject to particular scrutiny.

The plan — which everyone knew was ambitious — called for the Indian troops and the commandos to force the Japanese away from the coast and into a trap between themselves and two West African divisions that were simultaneously advancing down the valley of the Kaladan River. All of this was to support the imminent invasion of northern Burma by General Bill Slim's 14th Army, divide Japanese forces still remaining in the country and set the scene for a rapid and, it was hoped, decisive drive to the capital Rangoon before the monsoon struck in late May. Yes, there was now professionalism, a proper plan, some decent leadership and a warming whisky.

The next day, just before the commandos headed for the coast, Timmy had a brief conversation with their leader, Brigadier Campbell Hardy. Over another glass or two the Englishman was relaxed and confident and when Timmy asked if there were any final orders he simply said, 'Orders? There are no orders as such.' Impressed by the bravado but slightly concerned about the practicalities, Timmy took out his map and invited Hardy to show him where he wanted the Indian companies to land and what their initial objectives should be. 'No use worrying about details now,' the Brigadier replied, 'this operation is a bit of a shot in the dark. We don't know what we'll find. We'll figure out what you should do when you get to the beaches.'

Unlike the whisky, the operation did not go down smoothly or quickly, and Campbell Hardy sent word back to HMS *Phoebe* that his commandos were facing dogged opposition in the thickly covered hillsides and needed Timmy's men — and their recent experience of jungle warfare — as soon as possible. But even getting ashore was fraught with danger. The designated landing zone was under continual shellfire and the men steering the

Indians troops towards it soon began losing their nerve. One frightened young pilot tried to persuade Timmy that his soldiers should disembark in a mangrove swamp a safe distance from the beach. But to heavily laden infantrymen, being tangled in submerged tree trunks and tormented by sea snakes was almost as dangerous as enemy artillery and would put them nowhere near the comrades they had promised to help. Despite his relaxing bath, Timmy's temper was short, his blood was up and soon his pistol was in his hand.

> You will recover your courage and deposit my men at the appointed place, young man, or else be assured we'll find somebody on this boat to replace you and you'll be up on a charge of cowardice in the face of the enemy.

They rushed through what he called 'a solid wall of flying steel' and hurled themselves into the undergrowth, preferring the company of tics and leeches to that of Japanese shrapnel. Timmy had never experienced fire this intense before, but he had faith in the steadiness of his men, many of whom he'd known for years.

> Not far inland we came upon the commandos' artillery support. These men also had been taking a terrific shelling. Obviously the enemy guns were so well dug in that they could not be blasted out. The British gunners were slithering around in the mud and their aim was poor. Their morale was low; many of them already had been killed.

He could clearly see a feature that the planners called 'Hill 170'. The commandos had already taken it, but the Japanese seemed determined to grab it straight back, firing upon the men who were pinned down there relentlessly from the nearby hills. It was immediately obvious to Timmy that this 'shot in the dark' was turning into a major battle and that days of hard fighting lay ahead. Scrambling through the vegetation, he located Brigadier Hardy and, along with hundreds of others, they spent a deeply uncomfortable few hours hunkering down against the shellfire. Then a patrol of Hyderabadis came back from another contested hill called 'Pinna' saying that they could only get halfway to the top but were close enough to hear the cries of wounded commandos.

I took two companies and hurried to 'Pinna' and discovered that the commandos had no tools with which to dig themselves in. Moreover, the Japanese used shells that exploded among the trees, raining death on the unprotected men below.

The scene on that hilltop in the misty dawn was horrible beyond description. Dismembered bodies were everywhere. My men and I had to step over arms, legs, heads, and unrecognizable parts of human anatomy. The pitiful screams from the badly wounded were now less — because only about thirty of the commandos were still alive. A hundred men had been killed here.

Timmy's men took care of the wounded as best they could while he planned a night attack on a nearby hill from which the Japanese were firing. Two companies — perhaps 250 men in all — crept uphill in the dark before facing a ferocious onslaught from what appeared to be at least a thousand enemy soldiers. Eventually Timmy ordered a bayonet charge that cleared most of them away. It was brutal fighting but they were now slowly making progress, assisted by the Sherman tanks of the 19th Lancers and the welcome supporting fire coming in from *Phoebe* and the other warships. Sensing this, the Japanese commander ordered a final mass assault on Hill 170. 'I had a perfect view of the action. I saw the Japanese officers pointing out the way, with swords, to their men. The commandos put up a devastating fire, but the Japanese still came on.'

The Japanese were so desperate to drive their enemies back into the sea that some of them launched suicide attacks, running from behind trees right at the British tanks, wielding tin boxes packed with explosives at the end of short bamboo poles. Vehicles erupted in flames as their crews struggled to escape. But the commandos matched their enemy in determination and had better weapons. Lieutenant George Knowland stood outside his trench firing first a Bren light machine gun and then, astonishingly, a two-inch mortar straight from his hip before he was shot down and killed, winning a Victoria Cross in the process. From the next hillside, Timmy and his Hyderabadis saw it all.

> Then the commandos, yelling wildly, charged ... fighting the Japanese hand to hand. I signalled, offering to help. I was refused but I simply could not resist. I ordered our mortars to open on the closely grouped enemy. It was pure slaughter. I saw the Japanese being killed by the hundreds. The commandos made another charge. This time the enemy broke and before dark the entire attacking force was wiped out.

Next day his own men joined the frenzy in the assault on the last defended hill, called 'Perth'.

> They leapt from their cover and charged up the hill right into the enemy guns. They threw grenades, and I could see the flashing of their kukris. The enemy were demoralised. They left their posts and ran. A lance corporal and his men chased the whole enemy force from the hilltop! I saw him plant the regimental flag on top and then crumple with three bullets in his leg. I was with him soon after, when he was put on a stretcher, still hysterical with delight at having captured the hill. He was later decorated and awarded five acres of land.

One of the commandos who fought alongside Timmy's men that day, Colonel Peter Young, had never seen a battlefield like it.

> The *Bosch* could not have stood five hours of it. The Japanese tactic was sheer brute force and ignorance and their dead were

very bunched. They had to be most thoroughly slain, most with two or three wounds, any one fatal. Heads off, legs like sponges were very common. One of their officers was killed on one of our tanks; another was blown up by his own pole charge. They mostly had their long clumsy rifles, like spears with their long French-style bayonets. Their dwarf-like figures under their mediaeval helmets, with glasses and many with gold teeth, looked like creatures from another world.

With the fall of 'Perth', the battle for Kangaw was over. The British and Indian troops – with critical help from the navy – had seized some key territory and were ready to meet the enemy's main force if and when it retreated down the roads from the north. It was another in a series of small but important victories that displayed what was being called the 'New Indian Army' at its best. It was also an example of something else: the deep bonds of trust that now existed within what was a truly diverse military force. The commandos and the Indian infantry battalions that had fought alongside them celebrated together and a grateful Brigadier Hardy handed Timmy one of his unit's famous green berets, symbolising that he considered the Indian soldier, ubiquitously known as a *jawan*, to be as good as any commando. It came with a handwritten note stating, 'We cannot buy anything here but we would like you to accept this as a token of our great admiration for the bravery and achievement of your battalion.' Timmy was moved by the gesture and decided to reciprocate.

> We invited the commandos to dine. They brought their own food. Some of it must have been beef or ham. Nevertheless, our chaps did not hesitate to take bites of the English food while they gave the guests bites of theirs. At the huge banquet the two units were seated with one of the commandos alternating with one of the *jawans*; I was touched to see these men who came from such different backgrounds but who had grown so close together in shared experience. After dinner, rum was passed

around and then some of our men performed their colourful hill dances.

Timmy received a Distinguished Service Order for his leadership under fire at Kangaw and soon his position was confirmed when he was made the first Indian-born brigadier in the history of the Indian Army.

Stories of volunteer soldiers from all around the world fighting willingly alongside the British in a great cause are naturally exciting and romantic. Alongside the many thousands of Indian troops in Burma, men and women from modern-day Nigeria, Sierra Leone, Kenya, Uganda, Zimbabwe, Gambia and Ghana played critical roles in a campaign that was distinguished by things that were not always associated with the British in the Second World War: inspiring leadership, trust between units and the imaginative use of high technology. General William 'Bill' Slim, the presiding genius of 14th Army, believed that he commanded 'the greatest volunteer army the world has ever known . . . an army in which all races, all castes, all Regiments, all men are equal and have freely volunteered to rid the world of a tyranny'. A Kenyan soldier called Waruhui Itote, fighting under Slim's command in the valley nearby, agreed wholeheartedly.

> Among the shells and bullets there had been no pride, no air of superiority from our European comrades-in-arms. We drank the same tea, used the same water and lavatories, and shared the same jokes. There were no racial insults . . . the white heat of battle left only our common humanity.

While Timmy helped drive the Japanese back in Arakan, British and Indian military engineers threw a 1,100-foot-long Bailey bridge across the Chindwin River to help Slim push into northern Burma.

It was the longest such bridge ever constructed and the men manoeuvring its sections into position faced strafing runs from Japanese fighter planes. 'I had asked for the impossible,' Slim said, 'and got it.' The confidence and momentum of 14th Army at the beginning of 1945 was down to a stunning all-hands effort that threw up new barracks, depots, roads, railways, pipelines, airfields and hospitals at astonishing speed. All of this took the enthusiastic collaboration of hundreds and thousands of men and women, the coloniser and the colonised, the white, the black and the brown.

But that's not the complete story of Burma in 1945.

Tens of thousands of Indian soldiers would soon stand on the banks of the Irrawaddy, the great river that bisects central Burma, all poised to fight. However, not all of them took their orders from Bill Slim. A substantial number were members of the INA, the Indian National Army, and they were there to risk their lives for the cause of a free India in alliance with the Japanese. The nation in which they were fighting also contained many thousands of people who had volunteered to resist the British in the hope of creating an independent Burma, and this was itself a microcosm of a region in which popular sympathies were very much divided. Millions of Burmese, Malays, Javanese, Borneans, Sumatrans and others had been delighted to see the Japanese sweep the British and other colonial powers out of their lives a few years earlier. The cruel stupidity of the Japanese army had by early 1945 alienated a large proportion of them, and indeed as Timmy fought in Arakan the key Burmese nationalist group was poised to swing back to the British side. But that did not mean that a reconquest of the old colonies would be in any way welcome or popular. Even some of the volunteers who had travelled halfway around the world to fight for their King were dreaming of a life after empire. Waruhui Itote — so impressed with the racial harmony he experienced in Arakan — was soon to become a leading agitator for Kenyan independence and would one day use the military experience he gained under General Slim to attack British colonial authorities as a member of the Mau Mau.

One of the victorious British commandos at Kangaw had cause to reflect on the tangled politics of it all. During the fighting, Private Victor Ralph came upon a local family that had tried to find shelter in the jungle, including

> a young Burmese girl, 17 or 18 years old, and her baby — only a month old. They were lying in a pool of blood with her stomach torn out. And the thought occurred to me: was it our shelling that did that, or was it when we were attacking and the Japs mortared us? Then it occurred to me it didn't matter very much. She was in her homeland and here were two foreign powers fighting, and she and her baby had died because of that.

For all his pride in his men, for all his comradeship with Brigadier Hardy's commandos and for all the whisky and warm baths of the Royal Navy, Timmy knew these things better than most. That is why *his* perspectives — and the choices that he made — are so interesting. His real name, his *Indian* name, was Kodandera Subayya Thimayya and throughout his military career he was a committed nationalist and fierce critic of British imperialism. He almost resigned from the army over the issue of independence, he swore that he would never order his men to shoot their fellow Indians when they took to the streets in protest, he was close to the nationalist Nehru dynasty and he saw the turmoil of the war years tear his own family apart. As Timmy's loyal Hyderabadis were killing Japanese soldiers in Arakan, his own much-loved brother Ponnappa was digging in on the Japanese-occupied side of the Irrawaddy River preparing to fight and die for the INA. In fact, by early 1945 both brothers believed that they were fighting for a free India, just differing violently over the means, the route and the men they chose to stand alongside. It was a complicated, messy situation and it was not the only one, especially in this region and especially in this year.

THE SOLDIER

India, 1945–1946

The collapse of the Red Fort trial — about a year after Timmy's heroics in Kangaw — is an irresistible story and that's why so many accounts of India during the Second World War begin and end here. Three men of the Indian National Army stood in the dock: a Sikh, a Muslim and a Hindu. Men who had fought bravely for their nation's independence yet who'd killed members of the official Indian army, *Timmy's* army.

Prem Kumar Sahgal, Gurbaksh Singh Dhillon and Shah Nawaz Khan were determined to end almost two hundred years of imperial rule from London, with its periodic acts of cruelty, oppression and carelessness for the plight of its subjects. Yet they'd chosen to fight on behalf — and partially under the command — of a rising new empire run from Tokyo, in which cruelty and oppression reached levels rarely if ever seen before. The trial was meant to shore up British authority in India, yet it resulted in popular protests so vast and uncontrollable, bringing onto the streets men who had risked their own lives in combat against the INA, that it served only to underline the fact that British rule had lost moral authority, popular support and now had just months left to run.

Few outside India know much about the INA or its charismatic leader, Subhas Chandra Bose, the warrior-prophet, the widely acclaimed *Netaji*, or 'most respected leader'. Even fewer know that in today's India he is studied, revered and, truth be told, near-worshipped as much if not more than the original heroes of independence, Mahatma Gandhi and Jawaharlal Nehru. His choice of anthem, 'Jana Gana Mana' ('Thou art the ruler of the minds of all people'), is now India's national song and his rousing cry of *Jai Hind* is ubiquitous, particularly among the soldiers of the army that once fought him. Indian politicians, especially Hindu nationalists, raise statues of Bose, open schools named for Bose and regularly invoke Bose's long struggle for freedom. Any mention of India and the Second World War in an online forum rapidly evolves into a debate about his importance then and now, with Bose's many young fans prominent, adulatory and loud.

One person who would definitely *not* be surprised at his modern-day fame is Bose himself, since he was never one to underestimate his own historical significance. But even he might be shocked to see how quickly his invasion of his own country — one that quickly turned into a military disaster by any standards — transformed him into a mainstream folk hero.

At the Red Fort trial all three of the men who had pledged their loyalty and their lives to Bose were found guilty and sentenced to deportation. But the reason they were reprieved and sent out into wildly celebrating crowds in the streets of Old Delhi, was that the case was pushing India to the point of revolution. This debacle was something that the supposedly clever men who organised the trial might have anticipated. Either way, they clearly didn't give much thought to symbolism. Firstly, the Red Fort stood for British power and had done so ever since the bloodbath of 1857, the first great Indian uprising against the crown. Putting Indians on trial here was as clear a provocation to nationalist sentiment as could be imagined. Secondly, Bose — whatever his moral or tactical failings — consistently attempted to bind India's religious communities together and so to prosecute a Sikh, a Muslim and a Hindu side by side was near-guaranteed to unify millions against the authorities. Finally, all three accused men were from the Punjab, for generations the loyal heartland of the British Indian Army, which made the decision to prosecute them look even more insensitive. Sensing the mood on the streets, even the Congress Party, which Bose had rejected (although once led) fell in behind the INA defendants and Jawaharlal Nehru himself, the party's most prominent leader and one of finest legal minds in the subcontinent, volunteered to represent them in court.

As the trial progressed, the Indian military — transformed into a tough, efficient and truly national fighting force by the pressures of war — began to fracture. When twenty thousand sailors declared their support for the men of the Red Fort, senior officers feared that mutiny might sweep the country. Demonstrators were everywhere with *Jai Hind* and 'Save the Patriots' prominent among their slogans. The Hindu-dominated Congress joined with the Muslim League in protest. In Calcutta, Bose's original stronghold, pro-INA boycotts and sit-ins caused chaos and the police resorted to their guns, killing almost a hundred men and women. Sir Claude Auchinleck was Commander-in-Chief of the Indian Army. It had just won a historic victory, perhaps the greatest of all victories against the Japanese army in the Second World War, and yet it looked to be on the point of collapse. Understanding that the once fearsome imperial state was daily losing its power to command, he intervened to get the sentences commuted and the men released.

Officials grumbled into their gin, calling the scenes across India the hero-worship of traitors, but worshipped they were. Millions of pamphlets and flags celebrated their courage and dignity in the face of what looked like a classic case of tone-deaf, out-of-date colonial coercion. Indian's many newspapers and radio stations, newly released from wartime censorship, reported their triumphant progress around the country with a fascination verging on rapture, and as an unmistakable sign that the nation was now poised for historic change.

How did this happen? How at a moment of glory and celebration did the British Empire's most treasured possession move irrevocably towards independence?

Addressing that prompts a deeper question: was the persistence of British rule during this time based on loyalty, on apathy or on fear? Any honest answer will sit uneasily in an online post or a documentary sound bite. It will, in fact, be as complicated and as messy as the choices that faced both Subhas Chandra Bose and Kodandera Subayya Thimayya throughout their turbulent and interconnected lives.

India, 1906–1920s

If an ambitious young man wanted to make his way in the world, he had to adapt to the British and their peculiar customs and that's all there was to it. In the case of Kodandera Subayya Thimayya that process began with his own name. According to the perfectly sensible system of the Coorg people of southern India, 'Kodandera' represented his clan, 'Thimayya' was his father's name and tucked neatly in the middle was his specific or personal name: 'Subayya'. But at young Subayya's first school in the Coonoor hill station the British teachers thought it confusing and illogical to refer to a child by some odd middle name and so, through a process that was never quite clear to him or his family, he became known simply as Thimayya, or, rather, the anglicised 'Timmy' for short. A single word that doubled up as a given and a family name. After a while he accepted and even began to enjoy this early concession to the king.

But there were limits. Timmy discovered one of them during his first days as a student in the brand-new Prince of Wales Royal Indian Military College at Dehra Dun, in the beautiful Himalaya foothills. He had travelled there all the way from his southern homeland for a course of study that, if all went well, would send him on to the most prestigious military academy in the world: Sandhurst in England. And he had brought with him various important items.

'You, boy. Where are you going with that teapot?'

That was the voice of his new teacher, Mr Kittermaster, who then added, 'Why don't you share it, boy?' Gripping his *lotha* tightly, Timmy politely explained that this was no ordinary teapot, and something that was very much *not* made for sharing. This was the personal water carrier – complete with a most helpful spout – which he, like millions of other Indians, took into the latrine for cleansing. When paper of the type used by the British was offered as an alternative he gripped on even more tightly, explaining to his increasingly embarrassed teacher that this was simply not the way that people in India behaved. He left out the word 'civilised' before the word 'people' so as not to cause offence. But privately the boys, like pretty much every other Indian, took regular and incredulous pleasure at the barbarous bathroom habits of the British. Scraping at themselves ineffectually with rough pieces of paper when they could instead be properly washed and rinsed, and then wondering why their newspapers were full of advertisements for haemorrhoid creams and the dogs sniffed at them in the street.

Kittermaster had not taught Indians before and he laughed off this moment of cultural confusion, but some of Timmy's other early encounters with the British were markedly less pleasant. A few years earlier, at the Bishop Cotton School in Bangalore, considered one of the best in southern India, whites and mixed-race Anglo-Indians dominated the classrooms. While he and his older brother Ponnappa waited in the playground for their parents to complete the entry paperwork, some older boys gathered around them and one cried out, 'God, man! What is the school coming to when they have started taking ni**ers into it?' Ponnappa immediately launched himself at the offending boy and Timmy joined in the resulting melee enthusiastically. But whether it was his capacity for self-defence or his aptitude for all kinds of sport, Timmy mostly enjoyed his education and thrived in all of the schools he attended. He especially stood out in hockey, football, cricket and tennis teams, and quickly rose through the ranks of both the Boy Scouts and the military cadets.

Despite the occasional offensive remark, he came to understand the British better and sometimes even admired them. His dormitory at Bishop Cottons overlooked the Bangalore United Services Club. Every Saturday night it hosted grand parties that he found utterly captivating. The fairy lights in the trees, the music, the games on the immaculately tended lawns, the laughing and dancing of the men in smart uniforms and the women in their beautiful gowns, this was a life he very much wanted for himself.

Such a world was not entirely closed to him in the 1920s. In Coorg well-to-do Indians like his parents, from a family of successful coffee planters, did regularly socialise with their white neighbours, some of whom owed them money. But in the more populous north of India examples of egalitarianism like this were much harder to find. Timmy would often feel the unfairness of his situation keenly but rather than protest about it in the streets he resolved to turn himself into the kind of man who *would* be welcome at the grand polo picnics, the exclusive clubrooms of the racing tracks and the fanciest kind of ballroom.

The Indian Army was the obvious route to such a life and that's largely what led him from Bishops Cotton to the Military College at Dehra Dun. It had been opened to help prepare a new generation of officers, some of whom — and Timmy desperately wanted to be in this group — would also be allowed to go on to Sandhurst. By this time he was physically hard, confident, an excellent athlete and he spoke English well enough to decipher the broad Durham accent of Sergeant Major Gorman, one of those charged with getting the best cadets ready for the intimidating Sandhurst entrance procedure.

'Blimey are you tryin to 'av relations with that wooden horse? Don't try to go *into* it. Jump over it!'

'Come on, Mr Timmy, don't look at the ground now. You won't find yer commission lying down there. Look up for your star, son!'

Although the school commandant believed that Timmy was 'probably the best all round cadet we have at the college', competition for Sandhurst was intense and a long series of technical and personal questions lay before him. That included an interview with the Chief of the Indian General Staff and, finally, when he was so close to his goal he could almost touch it, a meeting with Lord Reading himself, the Viceroy of India, in his grand office. As it transpired that was the easiest part of the whole process. Timmy, fortified by a glass of port, launched into a lucid and confident description of his home community that instantly endeared him to the imposing English lord, who claimed to be a great enthusiast for the region and the Coorg people. After this the Viceroy turned his attention to the part of Timmy's curriculum vitae that was almost perfect.

'Hockey, cricket, football, tennis and squash?'

'Indeed, sir.'

'Good, then I hope you enjoy Sandhurst.'

In the anteroom, he let out a small cheer and was rewarded by the Viceroy's assistant with another and rather larger glass of port. He would be going to the ball after all.

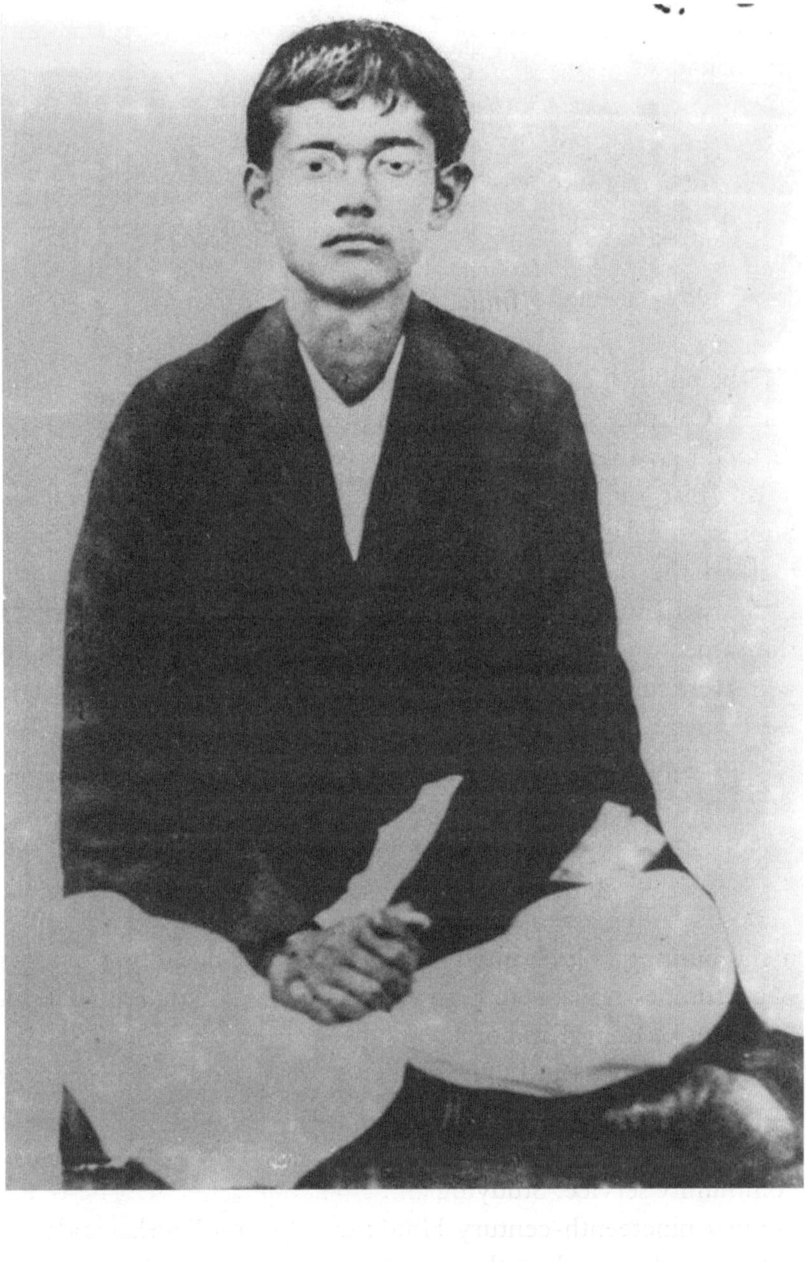

2

The Rebel

India, 1897–1920s

The public life of Subhas Chandra Bose began with a scuffle in a Calcutta school corridor and a history teacher he transformed into a verb.

In 1897, while his parents celebrated the arrival of baby Subhas, the land that he would one day attempt to liberate marked the diamond jubilee of Queen Victoria, Empress of India, with vast — and vastly expensive — public ceremony. At the same time officials struggled to provide relief to millions who were suffering and dying from severe food shortages. These were portrayed in pro-colonial circles as a natural disaster or the sad consequence of overpopulation, but in radical and nationalist ones as the result of a system that drained the country of wealth and resources and prevented Indians from solving their own problems.

Bose's father was a successful lawyer with substantial government business. He wanted his gifted son to benefit from the opportunities available to high-ranking families like his own, both in his native Bengal and one day, he hoped, in the famous universities of England. But by his teens Bose was already moving away from the attitudes that underpinned his father's life, becoming deeply, even obsessively, interested in politics, religion and community service. Studying and emulating his earliest hero, the popular nineteenth-century Hindu sage Swami Vivekananda, he volunteered to work in the poorest regions of Bengal.

His family enrolled him into the prestigious Presidency College in Calcutta, a hothouse for Indian boys destined for high office. Here he immediately stood out as both a rebel and a natural leader of rebels, finding himself at the forefront of a group of like-minded, serious and studious teenagers. All believed that India was at the point of an historic spiritual and political awakening and destined to be rid of the British in the decades to come. With his friends Bose travelled into rural communities where bare subsistence farming was the norm. Here he got 'a picture of the real India, the India of the villages, where poverty stalks the land, men die like flies and illiteracy is the prevailing order'.

Such images and ideas were surely at the forefront of the young radical's mind when, at the age of nineteen, he had his fateful confrontation with Edward Farley Oaten. And the contradictory way that this incident was reported and remembered set the scene for the rest of Bose's life.

The daily indignities of living in a racially divided society cut Subhas Chandra Bose deeply. It was impossible for him to travel to and from his school, or even walk along its corridors, without witnessing displays of casual arrogance from people who had grown so used to controlling Indian lives. This made a compassionate young man, who believed so strongly in fairness and justice, quietly seethe with anger.	One of the most popular teachers at Presidency College, Mr Oaten's life was defined by a love for India and for Indians. He taught with sensitivity and flair, becoming almost fluent in Bengali. Believed to be a quiet supporter of independence, he was devoted to his classes and regarded his pupils as the future leaders of their nation.
When he heard of Mr Oaten's rough language and manhandling of a young boy, Bose knew immediately that the moment had come for him to stand up for the ordinary Indian.	Unfortunately, one day a group of permanently difficult students led by the recalcitrant Subhas Chandra Bose picked up some schoolyard gossip about him and exaggerated it wildly.

Although traduced by the usual lickspittle commentators in the Calcutta press, Bose knew that most Indians would instinctively sympathise with someone who experienced everyday colonial insults and proudly cried 'No more!'

Bose took no part in what was a brief, though amply justified, physical confrontation with Mr Oaten (which lasted thirty seconds at most) but he did witness it.

Showing the mix of loyalty and determination that would from that day mark him out as an inspirational leader, a true *Netaji*, Subhas Chandra Bose refused to name the boys who had laid their hands upon Mr Oaten, even though he knew that this honourable silence would only draw more punishment.

Oaten had recently asked some boys loitering noisily in a corridor to lower their voices and, as he did so, he'd ushered one of them towards his classroom with a gentle push on the shoulder. But Bose's group characterised this as some kind of physical attack upon a weak child. They stirred up so much trouble that a pupil's strike was organised, which then spread to other schools around the city, drawing in yet more troublemakers.

Although the injustice of this cut him deeply, Oaten offered a qualified apology and things calmed down for a few weeks until yet another unfounded rumour, this time about him actually beating a boy, raced around the school – almost certainly at the behest of the Bose gang. This resulted in a frightening physical attack. He was putting up the weekly cricket notices when he was jumped upon from behind and beaten most severely, leaving him dazed and badly bruised.

An orderly quickly identified Bose as one of the attackers and, as the city's more sensible newspapers rightly condemned this appalling act of violence, the boy was suspended and named 'the most troublesome man in the college'. But the damage had been done, and in numerous other schools teachers found themselves 'Oatenised', set upon by mobs of angry children, in violent solidarity with the assailants of Presidency College.

Teachers like Oaten, who spoke of the 'civilising mission' of an empire that allowed millions to die of avoidable hunger and disease, would now walk less comfortably through the schools of this city, and every report of a teacher being 'Oatenised' brought Bose much satisfaction.

The decision to suspend him from all education in the city was a typical example of colonial spite, throwing his whole family into despair. His father's dream of seeing him travel to a British university appeared to be over.

Bose would not be allowed to study anywhere in the city for at least a year, a slight punishment indeed considering the offence and the short-tempered character of a boy who was – as Oaten happily acknowledged – clearly talented in numerous other ways.

Despite these shocking and undeserved indignities, Oaten continued to be a highly successful and much-loved teacher and – showing a generosity of spirit so sadly lacking in his accusers – wished Bose well. Indeed, many years later he wrote an affectionate poem about his chief tormentor.

There's something in 'Oatenisation' that brings to mind E. M. Forster's *A Passage to India*. A series of misread signals, the instinct to ascribe the worst possible motives to the actions of a member of a separate group or race, a confused encounter between people in contested circumstances – all coming together to spark a personal and political crisis.

Teenage rebellion versus imperial arrogance is an easy story to tell and most of us rush to take sides on issues such as this, then and now. Bose, never one to choose the *less* dramatic phrase, spoke of this period as his baptism of fire, his first experience of martyrdom, his first understanding of the personal price that the call to leadership would demand of him. But for all that he was hardly nailed to a cross. Behind the scenes strings were pulled and family influence peddled and within a year the young radical was back in education, a semi-detached member of upper-class Bengali society once again, studying philosophy at the Scottish Church College in Calcutta. And within two more years he did after all set out for England, to take up a much-coveted place at Cambridge University.

India, 1920s

British India was generally known as the British Raj, or simply 'the Raj'. As they sat in their splendid palaces and grand bungalows, the men who administered it liked to boast that they ran the place with just a few thousand imported officials and a handful of filing cabinets full of clever local alliances. Given the scale of India – multiple climatic and geographical regions, over 310 million people drawn from numerous ethnic and religious backgrounds, and hundreds of quasi-independent 'Princely States' – this was some achievement. They also liked to claim that, apart from a minority of agitators and troublemakers like Subhas Chandra Bose, the great mass of people across all these disparate communities were content to live under the beneficent rule of the crown. There was some truth in this as well. The sheer number of Indians would have quickly made the nation ungovernable without some kind of consensus that, although imperfect, the Raj still made sense. But that consensus was fraying and would fray even more in the 1920s and 1930s as a pro-independence protest movement, whose most prominent leader was the internationally renowned Mahatma Gandhi, challenged authority and drew millions onto the streets, along with periodic outbreaks of rioting and a persistent but low level of armed resistance.

Whenever such resistance reached a point deemed dangerous it had, for a long time, been efficiently and ruthlessly suppressed. The men in charge had at their disposal an impressive modern police force, British-led but mostly Indian-staffed, supported by the Indian Army as and when required, most notoriously at Amritsar in 1919. There was also a shadowy cohort of secret policemen operating on the fringes of or quietly beyond the law, with violent interrogations overlooked by incurious judges, suspensions of civil liberties and long terms of house arrest or incarceration in distant fortress prisons. But whatever their private feelings, many of India's cleverest students – young men like Bose and Timmy — continued to compete for jobs in the army and the Indian Civil Service. The latter was widely described as honest and capable, although the nationalist leader Jawaharlal Nehru, channelling Voltaire on the Holy Roman Empire, famously called it 'neither Indian, nor civil nor a service'.

We focus today on the hierarchies of race in the British Empire yet, in India at least, the complex and ancient gradings of *class* were at least as important. The caste system and a long tradition of autocratic rule in the Princely States meant that the most common form of oppression experienced in colonial India was that of poorer Indians by much richer ones. Some of the excesses and eccentricities of the numerous *nawabs*, *emirs* and *maharajas* in the more than five hundred quasi-independent regions made the Raj look positively enlightened: rapacious tax collection, justice delivered on the whim of a local princeling, and with minimal right of appeal to higher authority, *droit de seigneur* exercised over young women and concubines collected by the score. Gandhi himself was known to defend the caste system — in which he personally sat near the top — and had opinions about race relations, especially those between Asians and Africans, that shocked his liberal supporters in Europe and America.

The Raj could be flexible, too. The 1919 Government of India Act brought limited local self-government, which would be much expanded in 1935. This allowed politicians in London and high officials in India alike to present themselves as agents of change. The changes might be slow but they clearly led towards devolution of certain powers and a widening franchise. Perhaps surprisingly, some leading nationalists agreed — or half agreed — with this analysis. The prominent social reformer B. R. Ambedkar, like most of his peers, wanted to see the end of the Raj but he openly acknowledged that it was only the power of the British that gave long-oppressed groups, such as the so-called 'untouchable' class, the hope of a better future. If radicals like Bose saw India as an ancient and cultured civilisation repressed by foreign rule, Ambedkar saw it as a flawed and sometimes brutal society that the British could help improve before they left.

With all this in mind, perhaps the word 'consensus' doesn't quite capture why the Raj remained popular enough to survive. It might be more accurate to say that, as more and more voices were raised for independence, it managed to present itself as the *safe* form of modernisation, and one that stood apart from India's many class and religious conflicts. Historian Zareer Masani highlights the 'promotion of liberal values, the rule of law, a professional civil service and parliamentary institutions across almost all its territories' as a real achievement of the Raj, and the principal reason for its longevity.

If the debate between reformers *within* India could be fraught and complex, the outside world mostly saw it as a simple case of outdated imperial domination. Through the interwar decades, Gandhi, Nehru and then Bose himself found a growing international audience for their arguments, particularly in the United States, and independence for India became one of the great progressive causes of the age. It was an issue for left-leaning Britons as well, especially in the colleges where many of the leaders of the independence movement received their education, before or even *between* bouts of official harassment and arrest. Yet the administrators of the Raj did not feel they were struggling to keep a lid on an imminent revolution. Students and lawyers might protest from time to time but the great mass of the people seemed if not loyal then at least acquiescent, and there was no shortage of smart young recruits to keep filing cabinets filled and regimental ranks swollen. Few, even among the most passionate campaigners against British rule, truly believed that it would all disappear completely in their lifetime.

Cambridge and India, 1920s–1930s

Just weeks after Bose began his studies at Cambridge, troops under the command of General Reginald Dyer murdered hundreds of Indian protestors in the Jallianwala Bagh atrocity, better known in Britain as the Amritsar massacre. Somewhere between four hundred and a thousand people died when Dyer, panicking over a demonstration that he feared might turn towards insurrection, issued his command to open fire. The general was condemned in the British press and on all sides of the House of Commons. Minister of War Winston Churchill, an imperialist to his very core, described Amritsar as 'an event of an entirely different order from any of those tragical occurrences which take place when troops are brought into collision with the civil population. It is an extraordinary event, a monstrous event.' Novelist Abir Mukherjee was not the first to grasp that killing unarmed demonstrators killed something in the British as well, undermining the core justification of the Raj. The Secretary of State for India himself, Edwin Montagu, demanded of those who tried to defend Dyer: 'Are you going to keep hold of India by terrorism, racial humiliation and subordination, and frightfulness . . . or are you going to rest it upon the goodwill, and the growing goodwill, of the people of your Indian Empire?'

Bose spent most of his time at Cambridge with students and teachers — both Indian and British — who were passionate anti-imperialists. But as he read speeches from men like Churchill and Montagu, he surely noted that even the loudest defenders of empire could feel shame at its excesses, and also clearly state in public that the 'goodwill', or at the very least the tolerance, of the massive Indian population was an essential, inescapable, component of the Raj. The obvious implication was that if and when such goodwill dissipated then British rule would end, however many soldiers might be sent onto Indian streets.

Bose sat the challenging entrance examination for the Indian Civil Service, as his family had long wished, and although he passed with some ease his political principles made him hesitate. He explained his dilemma in a letter to his brother.

> I don't know whether I have gained anything really substantial by passing the Indian Civil Service examination but it is a great pleasure to think that the news has pleased so many, and especially that it has delighted father and mother ... A nice flat income with a good pension in after life I will surely get. Perhaps I may become a Commissioner if I stoop to make myself servile enough ... But for a man of my temperament who has been feeding on ideas which might be called eccentric, the line of least resistance is not the best line to follow.
> In short, national and spiritual aspirations are not compatible with obedience to Civil Service conditions.

No, Bose would not serve the British in his homeland; he would dedicate his life to replacing them. Soon back in Calcutta, he began building a following that extended far beyond university graduates, forging alliances with grass-roots campaigners for reform in numerous towns and villages, and growing ever more radical. He was drawn to protest groups and secret societies, some underground and illegal. Although he publicly admired Gandhi's commitment to non-violent protest, he would not condemn those who did resort to bombings, robberies and assassinations. One of his closest friends was the brother of Gopinath Saha, who attempted to shoot the police commissioner of Calcutta but killed another man by mistake. When Saha was executed, Bose offered condolences to his family at the gates of the prison. All this inevitably drew the attention of the police and in 1924 he was arrested for the first time, under an ancient law that allowed the authorities to detain anyone indefinitely without trial or even a published charge, solely on the basis of the testimony from anonymous witnesses.

The authorities thought Bose a dangerous agitator or perhaps even a violent Bolshevik, but it was more complex than that. Peaceful change through negotiation remained Bose's stated preference and yet he could not ignore what had just happened in Ireland, nor the argument, widely discussed in the circles in which he moved, that the surest way to bring politicians in London to a negotiation was to ensure that British rule became too expensive in terms of money, casualties or both.

For three years he suffered inside a forbidding, damp and draughty prison in distant Mandalay, far from his friends and family. Here his health, never strong, deteriorated and he began to show signs of the respiratory, abdominal and gallbladder ailments that would plague him for the rest of his life. He was allowed books and read Bertrand Russell and other British liberals, along with Nietzsche, stories of Ireland's long struggle for independence and serious Russian novels. He was also allowed to write letters to comrades old and new and these helped to spread his name and fame all around the country. Soon millions of ordinary Indians recognised Bose as one of the leading voices of nationalism, his idealism and capacity for self-sacrifice amply demonstrated by his incarceration. He refused the offer of an exile in Europe, which could have markedly improved his health, and chose instead to remain as a martyr in his gloomy prison cell, where he seemed set to languish for many more years until a new and more liberal governor of Bengal unexpectedly set him free in 1927. His fame and flair for self-promotion guaranteed him an important voice in the Congress Party and he was arrested once again during the civil disobedience campaigns of the early 1930s. The Raj was evidently unsure how to handle this irritating but popular young agitator and he experienced phases of official harassment punctuated by months of relative tolerance. In 1933 officials permitted him to travel from India to Europe for medical treatment but suggested that they may not allow him to return.

By now he was known far beyond the shores of India and wherever he went a string of prominent politicians, writers and celebrities queued up to meet him and be photographed alongside him. In 1935 he published a book destined to be one of the most influential of the decade. Called *The Indian Struggle*, it was an important statement about the future of the British and other European empires. It received excellent reviews in London literary magazines and the more serious British newspapers, but back home the colonial authorities quickly banned it, thus turning every smuggled copy into a very hot property. The justification for the ban was that Bose encouraged 'direct action' in the book and so might stir up violence, but in fact it was a rather measured work, containing fresh ideas about how a future independent India might govern and reform itself, some of which would come into practice just thirteen years later. One of its admirers was Irish Prime Minister Éamon de Valera, who invited Bose to visit his newly independent nation, and there Bose discussed anti-imperial tactics with men who'd recently taken their freedom by carrying rifles rather than writing books. His rapturous reception in Dublin was matched in numerous other European capitals, including Paris and Rome.

He personally handed a copy of his anti-imperialist book to Italian dictator Benito Mussolini, then engaged in building an empire in North and East Africa. Back in India the Congress Party could not decide how to respond to the men that had recently taken charge in Germany, the Soviet Union and Italy, men who were transforming their nations but at the price of militarism and repression. Jawaharlal Nehru was instinctively opposed to such authoritarianism but Bose was less certain. Although still considering himself a democrat, he was drawn to the idea that, to make the sweeping changes India needed, a strong governing party imposing a military style of discipline might be necessary. 'Nothing less than a dictator is needed to put our social customs right,' he explained in a private letter, and it wasn't hard to guess who he already had in mind for the role.

He was hardly the only young politician in the mid-1930s to think like this. Many people, disenchanted with capitalism and dismayed by the global economic slump, looked at what was happening in Germany, Italy and the Soviet Union with open admiration. Stalin's ability to transform a backward, mostly agrarian society into an industrial powerhouse within a single generation was of obvious interest to nationalist leaders from poor nations currently living under the control of Europeans. Stalin's men, and his sympathisers in Europe and the USA, did a good job of downplaying the sinister side of his rule — the show trials, the gulags and the man-made famines — and much use was made at this time of phrases involving the making of omelettes and the breaking of eggs. There was also an undeniable glamour to the dictators of this decade, whether communist or fascist: the mass rallies, the ranks of strutting soldiers, the burning torches and the 'Triumph of the Will' rhetoric. Bose had yet to don a uniform or address a military parade, but did he already imagine himself in just such a role: the 'Father of his People' at the head of a transformative paramilitary state?

Sandhurst and India, 1920s–1930s

Perhaps consider it like this. You're playing rugby and you fall straight into a pile of dog shit. It's all over your hands, maybe your face. So what do you do? Grab some newspaper, wipe yourself a little and carry on. Or do you run for the nearest water tap as fast as you can? Now, if you treat your hands like that then why not your precious British arses?

It was largely pointless but the small number of Indian cadets at Sandhurst did from time to time attempt to spread the benefits of their culture and, lavatory habits apart, Timmy was pleasantly surprised at how much his fellow students were open to foreigners and their ideas. He experienced little trouble on account of his race — certainly far less than he'd seen at schools in India — and instead found that it made him stand out as somebody different and interesting. There was plenty of colour-blind brutality, though, and all endorsed by the senior officers who ran the place. The first few weeks of relentless drilling 'on the square' marked out the new entrants for a range of cruel and ingenious after-hours punishments meted out by the older cadets. But Timmy was tough and hit back when he could, and once the 'square bashing' phase was over his status quickly began to rise as the curriculum focused on all the things that he was good at. There was strenuous outdoor physical exercise, intense body conditioning in the gymnasium, cricket, hockey, horse riding, rugby, football and a new enthusiasm – boxing. In between all of that there were lectures on weapons, tactics, styles of leadership and military history delivered by some of the cleverest men in the British Army and academics drafted in from the top universities. He was happy and popular during what he called eighteen of the best months of his life. He even spent a blissful few weeks in Switzerland with a group of friends mastering winter sports.

The only time being a 'colonial' seemed to count against him was when he won his 'spurs' by excelling on an equestrian course. This should have entitled him to the formal award of a 'College Blue' but it never arrived. The rumour mill told him that Gandhi's well-publicised agitation was causing a few of the senior lecturers to question the loyalty of their Indian students but he was never given a proper explanation. Posted back to India as a newly qualified lieutenant in the 2nd battalion of the Highland Light Infantry, he would soon witness political demonstrations first-hand. He'd also experience some of the notoriously 'loose' behaviour of the white officers of the Indian Army, behaviour that had long offended conservative and religious Indians. There's a good sense of this – and of the openly promiscuous culture of many interwar regiments – in the written examination questions that the army set for its own officers in the 1920s.

You are Capt. P. O. de L. FAKER, 1st. Bn. THE ROYAL THRUSTERS (Henry the Eighth's own) and you are a rival to your C.O., Lieut-Col E. M. BRACER in the affections of the frail and fascinating Mrs. I.

LOVETT. The lady has informed you that her husband is in RAZMAK for the summer, while she will be in MUSSOOIRE.

Lieut-Col BRACER is:-

(a) Of a somewhat brutal nature.
(b) Furiously jealous of your success with the lady.
(c) Acquainted with her movements.
(d) Convinced that you are a rotten officer.
(e) Aware that you have already had more than your share of leave.

REQUIRED FOR EXAM.

A letter applying for two months leave to MUSSOOIRE.

Men such as the gallant Captain 'Poodle-Faker', nineteenth-century slang for a young seducer, and his rival E. M. Bracer, were common in Timmy's new regiment. The white officers pursued each other's wives, brought local girls to their rooms and openly visited prostitutes. Timmy found all of this shocking, but it passed almost without comment in an officers' mess where the phrase 'sowing one's wild oats' was often spoken. This perhaps explained the constant absence of officers and men alike due to venereal disease. Most of the supposed 'Highlanders' under his command actually came from in and around Glasgow. They were tough men and heavy drinkers, too. Fights were common and they were not above taking a swing at an officer, even one as physically intimidating as Timmy. He discovered that they responded well to firm leadership, tough language and sometimes his fists, but there were some unavoidably comic communication issues. When he accused one soldier of being drunk on duty the man replied, 'I don't mind it, Sir.' 'Well, you bloody well should mind it,' Timmy exploded, 'and you should mind your insolence even more because I'm taking you up before the company commander on both charges.' Later the commander gently explained to him that 'I don't mind it' in Glasgow dialect means 'I don't remember it'. He never came upon any open prejudice on account of his colour, but he couldn't help noticing the strong animosity towards any English officer who found himself in command of the Glaswegians.

The Indian Army consisted of battalions from Indian and Gurkha regiments (and their mostly white British officers) mixed in with a minority of all-British battalions such as the Highland Light Infantry. The Scots rated Timmy a promising young officer but he longed for the chance to command real Indian troops. That eventually brought a transfer to the regiment that would become his military and perhaps even his spiritual home for the rest of his life — the 19th Hyderabad. Most of the white officers in his new base of Allahabad were pleasant enough but some clearly resented the wave of Indians rising through the ranks, especially at a time of continuing political strife when they might be called out into the streets at any time. Timmy's new commander, Colonel Hamilton-Britton, worked hard to smooth out any tensions and even arranged for his Indian officers to join the kind of smart colonial clubs that Timmy had long admired, most of which had only recently begun to accept non-whites.

Indian soldiers took time to adjust to officers who looked as they did. For as long as anyone could remember most of them had seen the British as in some way natural commanders and internalised colonial prejudices about their fellow countrymen: that they were poor decision-makers; that they would abandon their men in a crisis; that they would be corrupt. But it didn't take long for Timmy to receive letters from the relatives of his *jawans* thanking him for what he was doing and revealing that the soldiers he commanded were actually bragging about being under Indian officers when they visited their home communities on leave. This made him feel intensely proud and helped him develop a belief that a fully *Indian* Indian army was not only inevitable but would be the key to independence. His political ideas deepened when he made a very important new friend. A mutual acquaintance introduced him to none other than Motilal Nehru, one of the grand old men of Indian politics and father of the famous Jawaharlal Nehru. On their first meeting Nehru asked Timmy a most uncomfortable question, demanding to know why he had willingly chosen to wear the uniform of a coloniser and an oppressor. Answering bluntly, Timmy did not seek to defend the Raj as an institution, but he did speak up for the Indian Army and explained his belief that it would one day be an essential part of a free nation. Pleased with this answer, Nehru made Timmy a regular guest.

One day a Hyderabad battalion team was playing a hockey match in Allahabad against the police when a large crowd gathered in the nearby park waving Congress flags, ahead of an address from Gandhi himself. One of the white police officers let slip that 'we are going to cut off the electricity so that no one will hear the speech'. The Indian soldiers quietly passed word to the organisers of the rally who then carefully arranged the audience and placed 'sub speakers' every fifty yards or so, allowing Gandhi's words to pass quickly through the crowd. Timmy listened to every one of them. Nationalist protests like this could turn ugly and he feared what might happen if his men were ordered to suppress one. After a series of graffiti attacks and vandalism in the area around Allahabad he was told to organise a 'flag march', literally a way of showing the flag and demonstrating military force. He was to lead an armed battalion through the countryside to remind people that the authorities were still firmly in control. He thought of resigning over this, but Motilal Nehru changed his mind during a conversation that revealed much about the complexity of Indian politics and protest at this time.

> First nothing would please the British more than your resignation. For thirty years we've fought for army 'Indianisation'. We're now winning the fight. If you give up, we shall have lost it. But that's not the most important reason you must continue. We're going to win independence. Perhaps not this year or the next, but sooner or later the British will be driven out. When

that happens, India will stand alone. We will have no one to protect us but ourselves. It is then that our survival will depend upon men like you.

India, 1930s

Bose returned home in the spring of 1936, a leader in waiting. Familiar games of catch and release immediately recommenced. He was arrested within hours of disembarking from his ship, but this time allowed to live in relative comfort and granted 'walking privileges', so he could exercise outside the bungalow in which he was confined. But even under lock and key he posed a problem. In 1937 Congress was due to elect a new leader and Bose was the outstanding candidate. Did high officials in New Delhi really want the man at the apex of India's independence movement, one publicly committed to non-violent means, to be sitting in one of their prisons? Once again Bose's poor health provided a good excuse to let him go, and the tens of thousands who attended huge rallies to hear their hero speak immediately acclaimed him.

Bose was working on a second book, called *Indian Pilgrim*, an autobiography that blended political vision with religious and philosophical insight, covering everything from love, sexual relations and 'the idea of the self'. Much of this had been prompted by a passionate romance with an Austrian woman called Emilie Schenkl, who had worked as his secretary while he wrote *The Indian Struggle*.

Bose's unfinished autobiography revealed his desire to blend political with spiritual leadership, a belief that he could become – and perhaps already was – a mystic, or even a guru, as well as a president in waiting. His politics, every bit as much as his belief in the power of love, flowed from 'yogic perception' and trying to grasp 'the essence of the Universe'. But before he could become India's new philosopher-king, Bose had to navigate his way through the more mundane world of politics. Another high-profile visit to Britain saw him warmly and widely welcomed by politicians from Clement Attlee, a future Labour prime minister, to the 'conservative's conservative' Lord Halifax, a previous Viceroy of India and a future foreign secretary under Chamberlain and Churchill. He spoke at Cambridge and was called 'India's de Valera' in the press. He met with the real de Valera for a second time, too, and once again their conversations focused on the question of when to fight and when to talk when it came to dealing with the British. On a visit to Austria he married Emilie in a private Hindu ceremony, although neither of them publicly spoke of it and it was not registered with any civic authority.

In January 1938, as expected, he was chosen to be the new President of the Indian National Congress, the high point of his political life, or at least the part of it that took place within the mainstream of constitutional politics. He'd been in and out of prison and subject to a range of judicial sanctions that had probably taken years off his life and yet, at this point, it very much looked as if he was embarking on a transition that prefigured that of numerous other post-colonial leaders. He'd impressed the British, and not only those on the left. He'd met with government insiders and top civil servants. He was clearly someone the London establishment thought it could work with, if not now then soon.

Bose's first great speech as the President of Congress was markedly moderate, and much of it anticipated and predicted the commonwealth-style relationship that exists between Britain and India today. He spoke warmly of the ordinary British people he had met, people who shared his hope for a freer, fairer world. He paid tribute to Gandhi and his doctrine of *satyagraha*, too, praising 'active resistance . . . of a non-violent character'. As if to reinforce this evolutionary approach he appeared on the cover of *Time* magazine in March 1938, described as a man of the future. But signs of a different Bose continued to emerge. The other Congress leaders found him arrogant and irascible. The word 'demagogue' was whispered and even Gandhi began to intrigue against him. In return Bose alleged that moderates in the party were secretly talking to British agents behind his back. Perhaps to counter this, Bose arranged a private meeting of his own with Nazi party officials in Bombay. No records were kept but it was unlikely to have gone well. At this stage Hitler was making no secret of his admiration for the British Empire and had stated that he would 'far rather see India under British domination than under that of any other nation'.

As relations with his comrades in Congress gradually worsened, an imminent European war reignited Bose's revolutionary spirit. It also generated more signs of his positive, or at least ambivalent, feelings about Hitler's Germany. When uniformed men from the kind of militias and youth movements that interested Bose ran riot during *Kristallnacht* in November 1938, destroying Jewish property and violently attacking its owners, the scale of the threat facing Europe's Jews become frighteningly clear. In India some Hindu journals printed strikingly anti-Semitic arguments defending the Germans. Most leaders of Congress disagreed and said so, but Bose opposed this position and refused to support a motion offering Jews refuge in India. At this time many other nations were also being hard-hearted towards Jewish refugees, and long dormant anti-Semitic feelings were being aired all around the world. Nevertheless, as Hitler steered his nation towards a war of conquest and extermination, it was an early indication that Bose would not overconcern himself with the suffering of the Führer's principal victims.

The North West Frontier, 1930s

By the mid-1930s Timmy was based in Quetta, serving on the famous North West Frontier, the region that porously divided India and Afghanistan. It was a classic imperial policing role and here, in-between dealing with bands of tribal warriors, he witnessed the Indian Army engaging in one of its favourite pastimes – sexual scandal. A friend of Timmy's from a Sikh regiment, another newly 'Indianised' unit, was caught having an affair with the wife of a fellow officer. She was white and he was not, which led to much grumbling in the clubs and the officers' mess. The grumbling had nothing to do with sex. There were plenty of enthusiastic 'E. M. Bracers' and 'I. Lovetts' active in the military community. In fact, a group of officers and their wives were openly organising events that today we'd call swinger parties and nobody seemed to care very much about that. And Timmy's own commanding officer, when a captain, had deserted his wife to live with the wife of a junior officer, who had himself then moved in with the captain's abandoned partner. The four of them still remained in the base enjoying these unconventional relationships, although the women would sometimes 'snarl' at one other after a heavy night in the club. No: the problem with the 'Sikh affair' was that in this case love, or at least lust, had for the first time broken through the colour bar. Timmy looked on with a mixture of disapproval and sly pleasure.

> We were amused by the flap it caused among the British. Some of us, including me, were delighted that one of our group had outridden all the British hunters and 'won the brush of the prettiest vixen in the field'. But other brother officers feared that our position might be jeopardised by such a juicy scandal.

When he spoke about this many years later Timmy said that, if anything, it smoothed relations between the races in his unit. Indian politicians and agitators tended to speak in pseudo-religious tones that the British loved to parody as sanctimonious. So a little red-blooded wickedness from a fellow Indian officer made them all seem a lot more human, and certainly a lot more British. Timmy fell in love himself at this time, but in a much more traditional way. In a marriage more or less arranged by the two families, and after a single short meeting, he agreed to wed eighteen-year-old Nina Cariappa, a distant relative from his own Coorg community. Despite their very different life experiences, and an eleven-year age gap, the relationship was a great success from the start. Nina, who had been educated partly in Europe, was confident, stylish and spoke perfect French. Unlike some of the other Indian Army wives she neither wanted nor expected to live any part of her life in *purdah*, socially secluded from men, and she soon became an enthusiastic and much prized member of the very active Quetta social scene. One of the first invitation cards she received came from Sir Norman Cater, the head of the Quetta district and a former Chief Commissioner of Coorg where he had known both Timmy and Nina's families well. The district military commander General Sir Henry Karslake and his family also became close friends of 'the Timmys', as they became known, and he had coffee with them most days after his morning horse ride.

Timmy's experiences on the frontier strongly reinforced his view that the army would be key to independence. Whether British- or Indian-led, he had no doubt that a substantial and well-run military force would be required to control the fierce, vendetta-ridden and rapacious Pathan tribes of this isolated region. British political agents, backed up by the Indian Army, had spent years perfecting a mixture of bribery and brute force that managed to keep the settled population living down in the valleys mostly safe from predation. But in 1935 it almost broke down completely when a disastrous earthquake shattered Quetta and towns for hundreds of miles around. With all roads closed and only a limited number of planes and airfields available to bring in aid, it fell to the army and the police to organise search and rescue, provide medical care, place the homeless in tents, ration and administer whatever food could be secured and, most pressingly of all, deal with the swarm of merciless looters that immediately descended from the hills.

No amount of military training could have prepared Timmy for what he experienced here. His men and their families, Nina included, worked until they were sick with fatigue, using picks, shovels and even their bare hands to pull people from under the tons of tangled wreckage that had once been a city. But they could not reach everyone crying out from under the rubble in time. Vultures fought over the corpses in the street. Jackals and rats tried to eat the wounded and the dead alike. But worst of all were the human scavengers who stole and killed without pity. Dead bodies were stripped of anything of value and left naked in the street and Timmy's men even found injured survivors, sometimes still half buried in the ruins of their own homes, with ears and fingers cut off so the looters could more easily steal their jewellery. Back in Allahabad Timmy had vowed never to give an order to shoot his fellow countrymen, but he enthusiastically did so here. His troops also tied captured tribesmen to trees and lashed them in public in the vain hope that news of such humiliation might stop the frenzy.

Nina took up smoking cigarettes to help cover the stench of death hanging over the city and helped nurse twenty survivors inside her and Timmy's own home. She later received a national award for her heroism during this overwhelming emergency. More than 60,000 people died but that number would undoubtedly have been much higher without the efforts of Timmy's men and the other military units deployed in and around the city. He was forever proud of what the Indian Army did here and it showed that the Raj system could still deliver security and decent governance under pressure.

Timmy was now a captain and pressing for admittance to the Indian Army's Staff College, an essential step for anyone who dreamed of commanding brigades, divisions or even entire armies. His own uncle Bonappa Thimayya had been one of the first Indian-born officers to take the course. But before he could make the move Britain, and so therefore India, was at war.

SECTION TWO

Rally 'Round the Flag

'He did not realise that "white" has no more to do with a colour than "God save the King" with a god, and that it is the height of impropriety to consider what it does connote.'
— E. M. Forster, *A Passage to India*

EASTERN INDIA AND BURMA

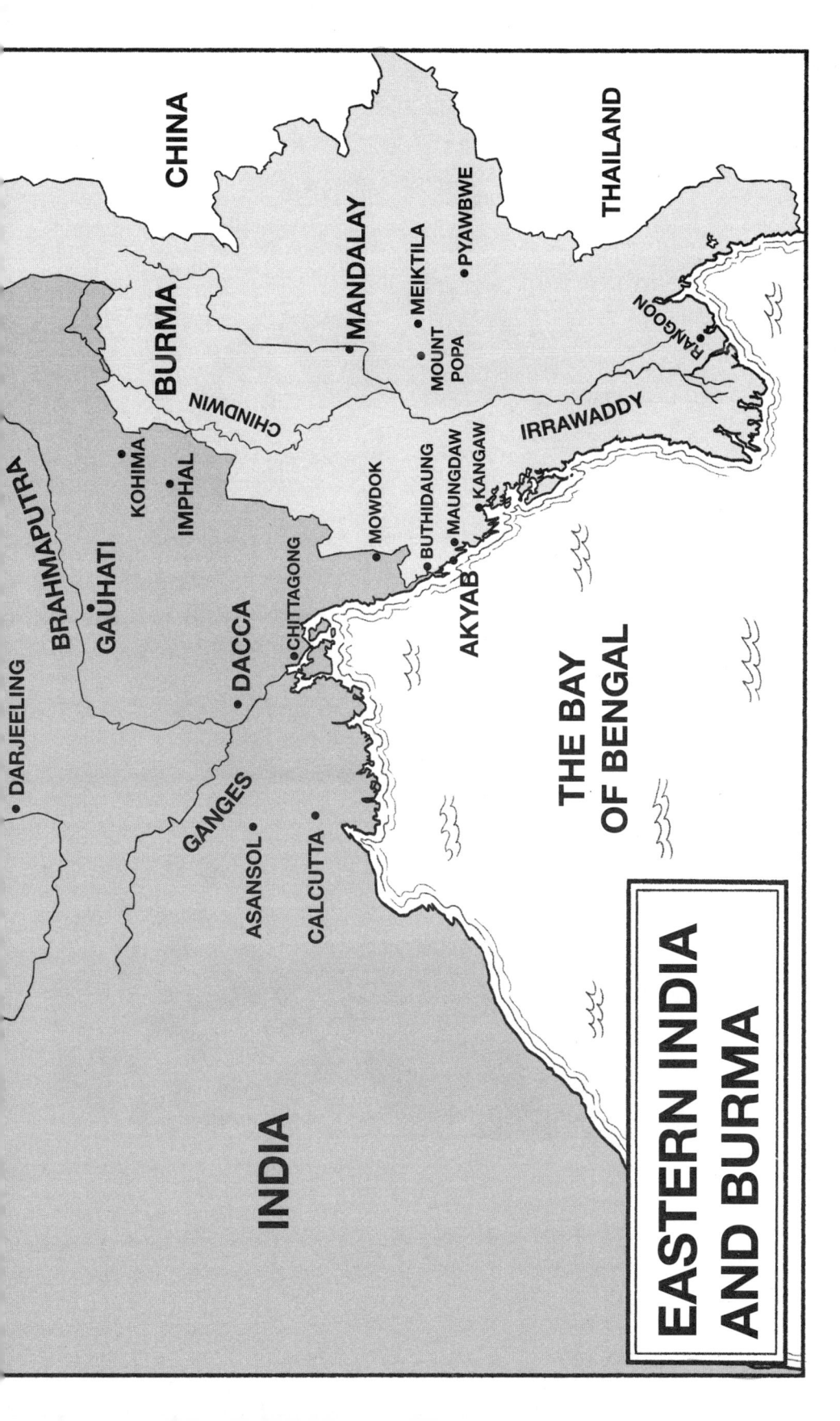

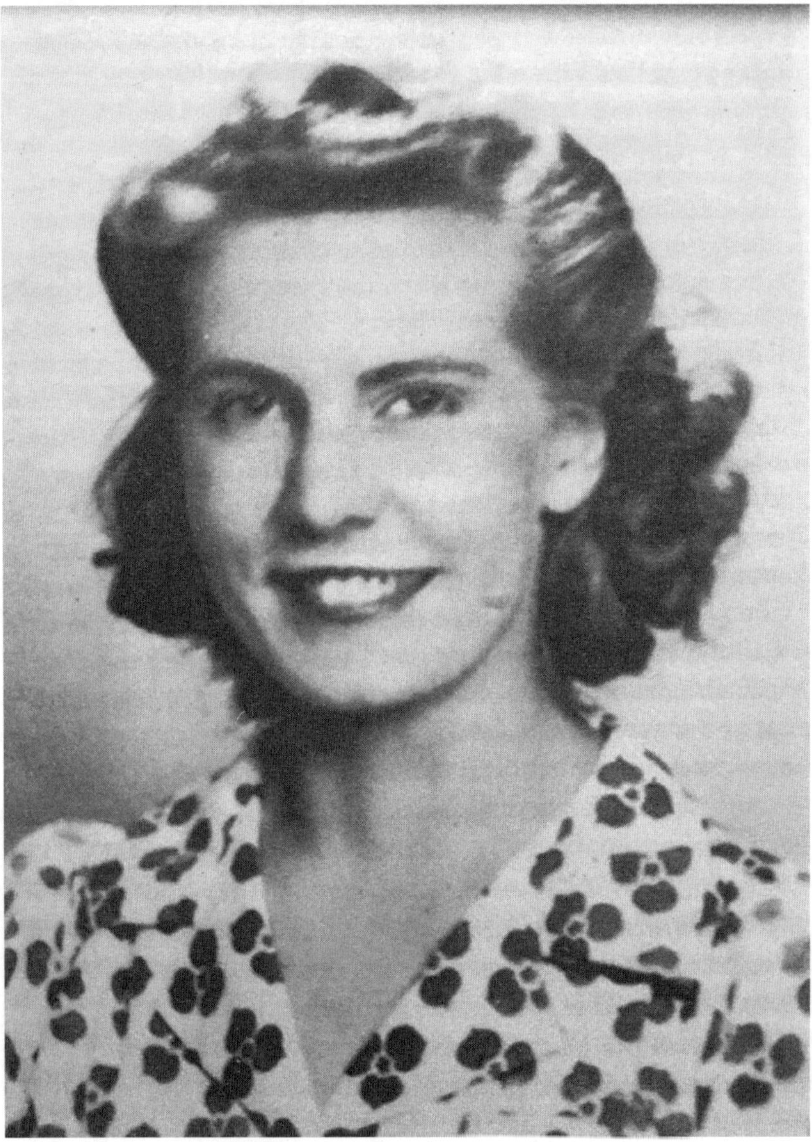

3

The Nurse

Britain and India, 1940–1941

There can't be many amusing anecdotes about dysentery, but soldier-turned-comedian Spike Milligan had one of the very best. In some dusty colonial encampment a scabby looking private is charged with defecating upon the perfectly manicured parade ground, defiling the British Army's holiest of holies. In mitigation he claims a dose of uncontrollable 'squits'. A mildly disinterested junior lieutenant sits in judgement and asks the sergeant major for his opinion on the matter. In a stentorian tone he gravely responds: 'I had the opportunity to inspect the offending item, Sir, and in my opinion it was produced' – he pauses for the full dramatic effect – 'with an *effort!*'

Dysentery and other digestive ailments, along with malaria and 'scrub typhus', were among the biggest challenges facing soldiers during the war in the East. At one stage the Indian Army reported 120 men sick for every one wounded. But with rigorous prevention and more effective treatment this ratio fell quickly. Such state-assisted bowel control, a strategic drive to make sure that every visit to the latrine did indeed require 'an effort', was central to British hopes in the region. Enemy soldiers, squatting and squitting miserably in their dugouts, would enjoy no such improvements.

Nurse Angela Noblet was destined to play a full part in this medical and lavatorial revolution and, based on the diary that she kept constantly tucked into her uniform pocket, she would have enjoyed Milligan's story very much. These diaries began in her final year at the minor Catholic boarding school in Lancashire to which she was sent when her mother died, and they open with an honest self-portrait.

> My Faults: Obstinacy. Dislike of criticism. Caring too much about other people's opinions.
> My Ambitions: To travel abroad. To marry a poet. To write a book.

Angela's father discouraged her from attempting a career in journalism and instead steered her towards something he thought more appropriate for a young lady − nursing. She qualified aged twenty-two, in the spring of 1940, just in time to live and work in a south London hospital during the Blitz. She clearly still felt the urge to write and her diary reveals a real talent for capturing the world around her, along with kindness, empathy, a sense of cheeky fun and some genuine courage. One night incendiary bombs landed in the grounds of the hospital dormitory, spluttering and spitting dangerously, and she rushed outside with a bucket of sand just like a proper Air Raid Warden. She also admitted to feeling an illicit thrill as she sat up late at night watching searchlights flashing over the night sky seeking targets for the guns: 'I couldn't help feeling excited when the black shape of a German bomber was outlined in their pencil beams for a few seconds. I could imagine the pilot's feelings as he twisted and turned, frantically trying to escape the probing fingers of light.'

She didn't meet a poet − at least not yet − but amorous thoughts were never far away. She spent one evening in London during the blackout, watching a film and half enjoying the attention of a young Canadian officer who she managed to fend off before taking a darkened train back to the suburbs. 'Blinds Must Be Kept Down At All Times' read the posters in her carriage and she laughed when she noticed that on one of them someone had changed the word 'Blinds' to 'Blondes'.

Her ambition to travel was fulfilled sooner than expected. She took a course as a 'Fever Nurse' and then, when she saw a newspaper advertisement for specialists in tropical medicine, looking for young women who might like to join the Queen Alexandra's Imperial Military Nursing Service, she was immediately interested. Soon she was in Liverpool stepping on board a magnificent liner called the *Monarch of Bermuda* with sixty other nurses and more than a thousand troops. 'We shall set sail shortly for an unknown destination,' she wrote expectantly as a convoy formed around them in the Mersey estuary. This was the start of a long, dangerous but intensely exciting journey down the coast of Africa, around the Cape of Good Hope and into the Indian Ocean. Surrounded by her new friends she loved to sit out at night watching storms rolling over the horizon, the shimmering phosphorescence on the water and flying fishes darting through the liner's silvery wake. The nurses were invited to dinners and drinks parties almost every evening, along with 'improving' talks and exercise classes, carefully screened off so that the men couldn't stare. They also performed enthusiastically in amateur concerts, where a 'Three Sisters' sketch soon became a firm favourite with the cheering and, if truth be told, also leering soldiers. After a while she admitted that she quite enjoyed all the attention: 'The spiral stairway leading to the dining saloon is wide and thickly carpeted. If you are late for a meal and have to hurry you are liable to run straight into the arms of a young naval officer, which is quite a pleasant experience.'

Although 'well brought up women are meant to be proper and my convent education makes me more proper than most', that didn't stop her weighing up her options.

Introduced to handsome Geoffrey Lavers, the assistant adjutant, who has made a vow not to dance with anyone until he returns home to his wife. Talked to Charles, the schoolmaster, about poetry. Charles is very thin and dark, tall and slightly stooping, the quietest of the four, self-effacing, serious but whimsical; probably the most mature. Dick is a nice ordinary chap, predictable and ideal for a shipboard friendship — after all no one wants to get involved emotionally at this stage of the war. Eric attracts me more — he's a great reader — but he is spoken for. Mitch is beautiful; calm, thoughtful and detached. I think he is newly-wed so must be feeling miserable.

She asked herself via the diary whether she was becoming 'frivolous and self-centred' but also admitted to a feeling of exhilaration that 'at any moment I could meet someone very special indeed'. And it wasn't only men and women who were sizing each other up. She heard and recorded some scandalous gossip about late-night misbehaviour involving the cabin stewards and various lonely soldiers who, as she put it delicately, 'might in their deprivation feel that a little titillating excitement was better than nothing at all'. There was more cheeky gossip when the stewards — with something of a knowing grin — handed out what they called 'Dutch husbands'. These long, firm, rectangular pillows were meant to help them find a comfortable sleeping position in the oppressive tropical heat, by giving them something to drape their legs around, all of which immediately became the source, 'of much burgeoning innuendo and suggestive talk on board the ship'.

They were constantly on the alert for U-boats, with regular lifeboat drills and spotter planes coming and going from the carrier HMS *Formidable*, part of their escort. Then one day she watched as a plane failed to make it back and crashed into the sea. 'The cold certainty that there were no survivors shocked us into silence.' Whether it was the sudden proximity of death or the continuing pleasures of warm evenings out on deck, she soon found herself enjoying the company of a particularly good-looking officer. As they retired for the night, hands touched and lips brushed against cheeks, only for her to discover the next morning that he was married. Mortified, she decided never to be alone with him again.

The stewards brought more than upholstered husbands and racy gossip. Soon one let slip that their destination was to be India, which is exactly what Angela was hoping. She had packed numerous books about the place and written in her diary with animated anticipation about how she yearned to experience

> the scarlet thread of glamour and romance . . . an exotic world peopled with princes from the Arabian Nights in jewelled turbans, riding on elephants hung with priceless Kashmir rugs; and sari-clad ladies with gems in their nostrils feeding rose petals and sherbet to snow-white does.

The books in Angela Noblet's trunk were an interesting mix. There was plenty of Kipling, of course, *The Jungle Book* and *Just So Stories*, and other classic imperial tales, but she'd already read *A Passage to India*, E. M. Forster's withering critique of the hypocrisies and prejudices of British India, and she'd brought that along with her, too. She was also well aware of Gandhi and the struggle he was leading for Indian independence, remembering that the great man had visited her home county when she was a teenager in 1931 and received a warm welcome from workers in cotton mills that had long relied upon raw materials from British-owned farms in India.

Angela's on-board popularity was sealed at a lavish St George's Day dinner off the coast of South Africa, where she was impressively 'wined and dined' by the officers of 340 Artillery Battery. After everyone raised several toasts to the great English Saint – with generously filled glasses of the great French wine of Nuits-Saint-Georges – the battery's commanding officer Col Kenneth Hargreaves announced that he would henceforth rename his unit 'Angela's Own' and install her as its Honorary Colonel. In this happy spirit he signed her menu with thanks for all of her 'good influence' on his men and she sat delighted 'as all the other officers signed with suitable (gentlemanly!) comments'. It was a glorious evening and a boost to the confidence of a young woman who did not always feel as self-assured as she appeared.

Calcutta was a shock to the senses, with fewer jewelled turbans and rather more diseased beggars than ever featured in her picture books. But she revelled in its strangeness. And although she took advantage of numerous offers to visit the privileged side of the city – exclusive clubs with swimming pools and tennis courts, and restaurants where the only Indian faces seen were of those carrying trays or working the ceiling fans – she regularly ventured out into

> the dusty excremental streets where the heat blasts you with its foetid breath . . . bicycle bells ring constantly as their owners try to break through the solid phalanx of overloaded buses manoeuvring around cows chewing their cud, women with baskets on their heads and children swarming around for your attention, offering to do all manner of chores for you until a khaki-clad policeman raises his baton. You sense the dung from the fires, spices from the stalls and an all-pervading sweet coconut scent, fruit covered in flies, the same that land on the faces of the sick children begging in the street, bright red spittle on every surface, the result of chewing 'pan', a sticky mixture of areca nut and betel leaf.

Some of the men she'd befriended on the voyage quickly slipped into a set of attitudes that didn't please her at all, becoming overbearing towards the Indians and dismissive of the idea that these people could ever govern themselves. Not insulting exactly but 'as though the Indians were part of the *décor*, not really human beings at all'. As she prepared to deploy out of Calcutta, she confided her hopes and fears to her diary once again. She was feeling strong, less fragile than she'd been back home, when a word of criticism from a doctor or a stern ward matron could cut her deeply, and ready to take on anything, even the realities of a military hospital in a region bracing itself for war.

There is little talk of discipline here, but an unspoken presumption that one is a mature and professionally trained person . . . In my training days I felt like I was regarded as useful but expendable, but now I have a greater confidence in myself and my work even when the task ahead seems daunting.

Angela Noblet was clearly more tolerant, more interested in the people of India and more supportive of the independence movement than many other British men and women of her time. And she was soon to receive a profound, and indeed *daunting*, education in all of that and more.

India and Germany, 1940–1941

Indians had fought in dozens of Britain's wars. In the lifetime of the new occupant of 10 Downing Street that included the struggle against the Mahdi in Sudan (during which a young Winston Churchill of the 4th Queen's Own Hussars charged into battle at Omdurman); the Boxer Rebellion in China; colonial conflicts in Afghanistan and Tibet; the Great War in Europe, Turkey, Egypt, Sudan, Mesopotamia, Aden and Persia; and various campaigns and 'police actions' in the 1920s and 1930s against enemies as varied as Iraqi tribesmen and the mysterious 'Faqir of Ipi' in Waziristan. But none of these conflicts brought about changes as profound as those triggered by the Second World War.

Subhas Chandra Bose imagined that a European or Soviet-style strongman might modernise his homeland, but it was the pressure of 1940s mechanised warfare that truly transformed it. The Indian Army, Navy and Air Force expanded rapidly to become the largest all-volunteer military force in history, over two and half million-strong by the end. And as the armed forces grew they started to look more like the real India, promoting locally born officers like Timmy and seeking recruits beyond the traditionally loyal or so-called 'martial' races and regions. In the past Muslims and Sikhs, especially from the Punjab, supplemented by regiments of Nepalese Gurkhas, had made up the bulk of India's fighting force. The authorities had long been wary of the majority Hindu population. According to stereotypes popular with the British and many Indians, too, Hindus did not make for good or reliable fighters and, ever since the great rebellion of 1857, they were seen to be of questionable loyalty to the crown. But now they flowed into the military in huge numbers. And the ever-expanding number of front-line troops created a need for yet more volunteers in the numerous support services that modern war demanded: technicians and mechanics; doctors, drivers and nurses; cooks, carpenters, builders and quartermasters.

No doubt some of the people who joined were coerced by local princes and landlords, or attracted by the idea of steady money and reliable food in a land that was often short of both, but that in no way explains the overwhelming numbers. Today the idea that a colonised people would willingly serve the power that had colonised them — and serve with great pride — might seem archaic. It didn't seem so then. The timeless appeal of travel, adventure and glory accounted for some of it. Young men from poor villages or crumbling slums hoped to better themselves and win the praise of their peers. Men aspired to be warriors and gained status from being so. That is the way it had always been, and not only in India. And yet we cannot discount the role of simple patriotism either. Despite the best efforts of Gandhi, Nehru, Bose and others, a large number of ordinary Indians in the early 1940s clearly did regard themselves as a part, and not merely the *subjects*, of the British Empire. So naturally they wanted to defend that empire when its homeland — and within two years their own homeland — came under attack. If we want to understand the people of the past and how they acted, we need to factor in the influence of older values and older ways of thinking. And when we do that it becomes obvious that, for the first two years of war at least, flag waving in the traditional style was as important to many Indians as it was to the volunteering white men and women of Australia, Canada and New Zealand. And there were certainly romantic echoes of the nineteenth-century imperial heyday in the way the first victories of the Indian Army against the Italians in Eritrea were celebrated. Churchill himself wrote to the Viceroy that

> the story of the ardour and the perseverance with which they scaled and finally conquered the arduous heights of Keren recalls memories of the North West Frontier of long years ago and it is as one who has had the honour to serve in the field with Indian soldiers from all parts of Hindustan, as well as in the name of His Majesty's Government, that I ask your Excellency to convey to them and to the whole Indian army the pride and admiration with which we have followed their heroic exploits.

Heroic exploits in Eritrea, and the earlier triumphs of Indian troops in North Africa, were celebrated widely across the subcontinent. Schools, shops and government offices closed, military parades filed through flag-waving crowds, children collected cigarette cards of their favourite heroes, audiences cheered newsreels projected onto factory walls and the sides of village temples, and veterans returned home to show off their medals. All this drove more young men and women into the recruiting booths. But despite all the flag waving, Congress immediately saw the war as an opportunity, suggesting that the authorities create a 'Constituent Assembly' so that Indians could effectively share power and, by implication, prepare governing structures suitable for independence. Subhas Chandra Bose, already on bad terms with the party he'd recently led, thought this idea was shockingly weak and unworthy of the moment.

> Is not this the time to remind our British rulers that east of the Suez Canal there is a land inhabited by an ancient and cultured

people who have been deprived of their birth right of liberty and have been groaning under the British yoke? And is this not the time to tell the British people and their government that those who are slaves at home cannot fight for the freedom of others?

Bose told a student conference in Delhi in 1940 that 'freedom comes to those who dare and act' and not to those who compromise with imperialists every bit as menacing to the cause of liberty as the totalitarian regimes they were fighting. 'If we hate totalitarianism we hate imperialism more,' he said. Like the Irish rebels of 1916, Indians should exploit the fact that war will weaken their colonial masters and immediately demand — indeed declare — independence and then be prepared to fight for it if necessary.

At this point Bose led no mass movement of his own. And even if he had it seems unlikely that, amid such popular enthusiasm for the war, he could have backed up an Irish-style declaration of independence with any real force. And so, for the moment, the men he disparaged as 'compromise-wallahs' took back control of Congress and independence remained on hold. Bose next suggested that the Hindu-dominated Congress and the Muslim League combine to create joint Citizen Defence Corps outside the control of New Delhi. But the idea went nowhere and the mainstream Congress leadership still supported the war effort, albeit in lukewarm language. Seeing his fellow nationalists hold back at such a moment brought Bose's frustration with the 'old guard' to boiling point and soon he was openly lambasting what he called the 'sanctimonious hypocrisy' of 'Gandhi-ism'. 'What interest,' he asked, 'can we have in fighting for the perpetuation of our own slavery?' Language like this was in flagrant breach of new wartime regulations and by the summer of 1940 the authorities were ready to pounce once again upon their most resolute enemy. Although far from being the end of his political career, 2 July 1940 was Bose's last day living as a free man in India. The clever but troublesome student from Presidency College was locked away on the other side of Calcutta in the austere Presidency Jail. By November he was so angry about the tough conditions there that he wrote to the governor of Bengal declaring that he would starve himself to death unless released, in a statement couched in the kind of quasi-spiritual language he had made his own:

> Today I must die, so that India may live and may win freedom and glory . . . What greater solace can there be than the feeling that one has lived and died for a principle? What higher satisfaction can a man possess than the knowledge that his spirit will beget kindred spirits to carry on his unfinished tasks . . . What higher consummation can life attain than peaceful self-immolation at the altar of one's Cause?

After watching the already unhealthy Bose refuse food, and fearing that his death would trigger a crisis, the government relented. He was released into a form of house arrest inside his old family compound in the city, his movements and visitors carefully monitored and the area around his home swamped by police. And yet, despite all this, he was able to plan an escape that played out like an exciting episode in a John Buchan novel. Sending coded messages through a network of couriers, Bose obtained a disguise good enough to deceive all his many guards. Then, with the help of his supporters, he managed to travel for days by train, in private cars and on foot across many thousands of miles of northern and then north-western India with half the country's police out looking for him. Such ingenuity and courage, from a man weakened by a long history of illness, turned Bose into even more of a hero among the believers in his cause, and generated furious official cables that bounced ineffectually back and forth between the police, the governor of Bengal, the Viceroy and Westminster.

Bose's great escape was a sensation. Excited speculation about where he might be, along with news of numerous fake sightings, raced around the world. Had he already secretly flown to Europe? Had he been smuggled onto an ocean liner inside a trunk? Was he about to lead a revolutionary army even now gathering in some remote mountain pass? In fact, he avoided the searching police and intensified border controls by trekking on foot along high mountain tracks and then hitchhiking along rough Afghan roads until he arrived safely in neutral Kabul in early 1941. There he made the most fateful decision of his life. He contacted diplomats from the German and Italian embassies and asked for their help to travel to the very centre of the struggle against the British Empire – Berlin. Only there, he believed, could he best represent the interests of India to Britain's most potent enemy. In the heart of Germany he would plan a revolution and help bring down an empire, accepting help from his oppressor's foes just as the Irish freedom fighters had done in 1916. And he would begin by recruiting an anti-British military force from the thousands of Indian prisoners of war now sitting in German and Italian prison camps.

An elaborate plan formed to help Bose escape to Europe, involving not only Italian and German spies but also the local representatives of the Soviet Union. The British, who had plenty of their own agents in Afghanistan, learned of Bose's new location through deciphered cables and immediately planned to assassinate him, a sure sign of how important he had become. London picked up word of a scheme to transport him to Europe through Turkey but instead he went north, using a fake Italian passport and yet another disguise. Evading all the British spies in the border towns, he entered the southern outpost of the Soviet Union, passing through Samarkand on his way to Moscow and then flying from there straight to Berlin on 2 April 1941.

Although Operation Barbarossa was only eleven weeks away, Stalin remained formally tied to Hitler through the Molotov–Ribbentrop pact of 1939, and this fact was very useful to Bose and his supporters. If the Soviets still saw fit to deal with Nazi Germany,

THE NURSE

why shouldn't he? He wrote that his enemies in Congress 'conveniently forget the imperialist character of Britain's war and also the fact that the greatest revolutionary force in the world, the Soviet Union, has entered into a solemn pact with the Nazi government'.

At this stage of the war the British Empire was still very much fighting alone, with only limited economic support from the United States. Hitler's armies dominated Europe and were chasing thousands of British and Commonwealth soldiers out of Greece. Meanwhile his panzers besieged Tobruk in North Africa, his air force pounded British cities nightly, his U-boats menaced the Atlantic and he appeared still to be in lockstep with Stalin. So it's easy to understand why Bose assumed a German victory to be inevitable, and why, too, in that scenario, he would want to be part of the negotiations about India that would inevitably result. And there was a very personal reason for him to be in Germany – a reunion with his secret wife Emilie.

The Nazi High Command welcomed Bose but initially showed little enthusiasm for his plan to recruit Indian prisoners. Hitler's Foreign Ministry worried that this well-known anti-imperialist might be unhappy about what was about to unfold in the East. Files discovered after the war recount how German diplomats regarded him as being too much under the influence of the global revolution rhetoric of the Soviets and the Communist International organisation known as the Comintern. Germany's massive invasion of the Soviet Union did indeed come as a shock to Bose, but he quickly shrugged it off. If the Soviet Union was to collapse quickly, which appeared more than likely in the spectacular early weeks of Barbarossa, he knew that Hitler's troops would soon be approaching the northern borders of the Raj and so he urged his contacts in Berlin to make Indian independence a formal German war aim. He could, however, no longer use the Soviet alliance with Hitler as a justification for his presence in Germany. Instead he cited the experiences of Lenin during the Great War, a true revolutionary who had worked with the Kaiser's men to help bring much-needed change to the world. Perhaps appreciating this great flexibility of thought, the Nazi hierarchy began to warm to Bose and his plans for the future.

The Atlantic Charter, 1941

When he first read the eight-point joint declaration agreed by President Roosevelt and Prime Minister Churchill on 14 August 1941, a document that would soon become known simply as the Atlantic Charter, Britain's Secretary of State for India and Burma, Leo Amery, was not overly impressed: 'We shall no doubt pay dearly in the end for all this fluffy flapdoodle.'

Words, fluffy or otherwise, can change history. And few words have ever exercised as much influence as those carefully chosen to fill the single page of this document. In it Churchill and Roosevelt announced to the world that they

> deem it right to make known certain common principles in the national policies of their respective countries on which they base their hopes for a better future of the world.
>
> First, their countries seek no aggrandizement, territorial or other;
>
> Second, they desire to see no territorial changes that do not accord with the freely expressed wishes of the peoples concerned;
>
> Third, they respect the right of all peoples to choose the form of government under which they will live; and they wish to see sovereign rights and self-government restored to those who have been forcibly deprived of them.

Employing language that would directly shape the United Nations Declaration in January 1942 and then its charter in June 1945, these principles did not simply clarify Anglo-American war aims. They suggested a future unrecognisable from the colonial past, setting a benchmark against which all future Allied actions could and would be judged. And yet they were not primarily chosen with an eye to the future at all, but to solve the urgent political and strategic problems of two very different leaders.

In mid-1941 America was neither in the war nor intending to be in the war. Helping Britain resist Europe's tyrants was very much Roosevelt's intention but, as he had discovered the previous year, this was not an easy sell to his party or his nation. Anti-war, anti-British and anti-colonial feelings were strong in America and there were powerful groups — notably the many voters of Irish, German and Italian descent — who did not easily give their support to Winston Churchill and the nation he led. During 1940, Roosevelt had extracted some valuable real estate in return for US aid through the 'destroyers-for-bases' deal. But in 1941 he needed — and got — much more, this written promise that the age of imperialism was coming to an end.

That, however, wasn't quite how Churchill interpreted it. His policy — and it had been so since he first came to power — was to say anything to bind the Americans close then argue afterwards about what it all really meant. The charter was drafted with Europe under Hitler's feet and German tanks racing towards Moscow. All that mattered was to secure a guarantee of long-term US aid and send a signal to the wider world that America stood behind Britain politically and economically in its — then — still lonely and painful confrontation with Nazi Germany and Fascist Italy. And although the American press did indeed claim that it was a clear sign of a future without empires, the charter's preamble could be interpreted (and was so in London) to suggest that the whole 'flapdoodle' was aimed primarily at the places conquered by Adolf Hitler rather than those administered by the likes of Leo Amery and the British Colonial Office.

> The President and the Prime Minister have had several conferences. They have considered the dangers to world civilization arising from the policies of military domination by conquest upon which the Hitlerite government of Germany and other governments associated therewith have embarked, and have made clear the steps which their countries are respectively taking for their safety in the face of these dangers.

Even while negotiating the charter, Churchill had cabled members of his War Cabinet using language that he doubtless did not deploy in front of Roosevelt, writing, 'We must regard this as an interim and partial statement of war aims designed to reassure all countries of our righteous purpose and not the complete structure which we should build after victory.'

When he attempted to calm nervous Conservative MPs in the House of Commons he was able to identify several areas of what everyone called 'wriggle room'. As he'd crafted the document with Roosevelt, he claimed, they primarily 'had in mind . . . the States and nations of Europe now under the Nazi yoke', which he determined 'quite a separate problem from the progressive evolution' of Britain's colonial subjects. He also wrote directly to Leo Amery about the difficult third pledge, perhaps the fluffiest flapdoodle of them all, saying that its apparent promise of self-determination 'would only arise in such cases where transference of territory or sovereignty arose'. It was not, he insisted, intended 'that the natives of Nigeria or of East Africa could by a majority vote choose the form of Government under which they live' since 'prior obligations require to be considered and respected' and 'circumstances alter cases'.

But the 'natives' themselves saw things very differently. What might have read like a holding statement open to endless reinterpretation in London was, to most nationalist leaders, a clear and thrilling promise of change. Messages from the colonies immediately poured into London in numerous languages but with one common theme – 'That sounds good so when do we start?' The Prime Minister of Burma, U Saw, elected through a system that already gave some limited democratic rights to his people, came straight to London in a confident mood to press his case for independence, openly referring to the joint declaration as 'a charter of liberties for all peoples of the world'. 'The Burmese people,' he said:

> cannot help but conclude from the universality of the expressions used in the Declaration ... that the principles declared thereby must have application to the people of Burma and that their acceptance by [the] Democracies must of necessity lead Burma to attainment of national freedom.

U Saw met with Churchill and his senior ministers, and was entertained by King George VI. But the most that the prime minister would promise in person was that 'when Britain won the war, and only then, liberal ideas would prevail on the lines of the Atlantic Charter'. Churchill also reminded him that the charter 'was a unilateral declaration which His Majesty's Government must hold itself free to interpret'. U Saw was unsatisfied by that statement, and it does indeed deserve to be described by one of Churchill's own favourite words – 'weaselly'. Key members of the British War Cabinet were disappointed, too. Labour leader Clement Attlee, a core member of the group that had put and kept Churchill in power in 1940, addressed confusion about the true remit of the Charter when speaking to an audience of students, telling them that 'you will find [the charter's] principles will apply, I believe, to all the peoples of the world'.

While Churchill attempted to wriggle away from the idea that 'all the peoples of the world' had the right to self-government, Roosevelt told his own party that he'd secured a template for post-war Anglo-American cooperation on international security in a global community free of both dictators and empires. In a radio talk in early 1942 he asserted boldly that 'the Atlantic Charter applies not only to the parts of the world that border the Atlantic but to the whole world', especially its reference to the 'self-determination of nations and peoples'.

For two allies to have a different interpretation of their war aims was hardly surprising, especially when one of them wasn't even *at war* when the aims were drawn up. But we should resist the simplistic idea that Britain was full of reactionary imperialists while the people running America were all passionately anti-colonial. The US government had taken the Philippines from the Spanish at the end of the last century, after a war that caused Kipling to write of Americans picking up 'the white man's burden'. By the late 1930s US officials administered its many islands in a style reminiscent of Leo Amery's Colonial Office, although the Filipinos had been promised independence by the mid-1940s (a process that was soon to be interrupted by war). As recently as 1906 rebellious communities there had been crushed by US troops amid battles that a furious Mark Twain condemned as 'one-sided massacres':

> [American] General Wood was present and looking on. His order had been. 'Kill or capture those savages.' Apparently our little army considered that the 'or' left them authorized to kill or capture according to taste, and that their taste had remained what it has been for eight years, in our army out there — the taste of Christian butchers ... Our uniformed assassins have not upheld the honor of the American flag, but have done as they have been doing continuously for eight years in the Philippines — that is to say, they have dishonored it.

Tensions over the fate of colonies would indeed dog the UK–US relationship in the years after the Atlantic Charter was signed, but Roosevelt himself would begin to back away from some key elements of it. And his successor would take decisions that even an old-school British imperialist might have called reactionary, especially when America found itself conquering strategically valuable territory it was in no great hurry to vacate.

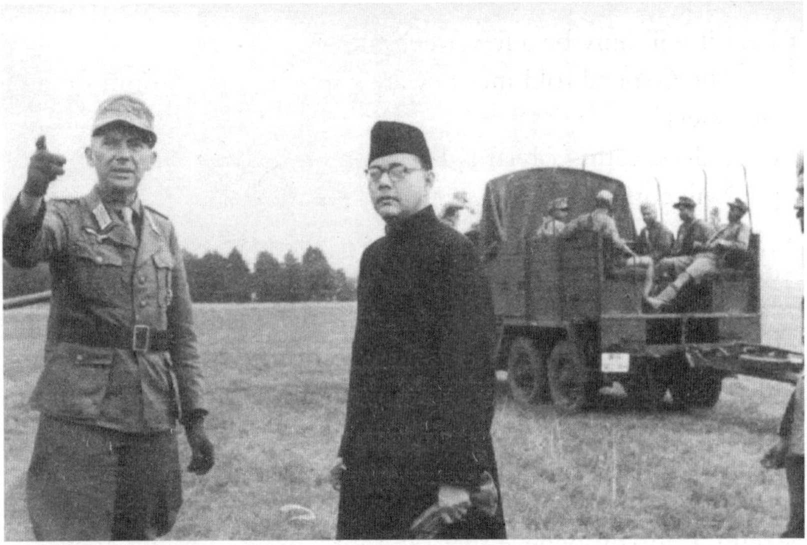

4

The Exile

Berlin, 1941–1942

'I hear it will only be a few weeks now.'

'The General told me they are running out of room for all the prisoners.'

'We'll all be eating caviar at the Kremlin before Christmas. Do say you will come visit us, Your Excellency.'

It must have been a magical time for Bose. His epic escape to freedom, now the talk of newspapers and magazines all around the world; his reunion with Emilie in their beautiful new home in Berlin's elegant Charlottenburg, a generous gift from his hosts complete with a cook and a butler; and access to the most important people at a hinge moment in history, people who really knew what was going on and who everyday were telling him things like this: 'The rumour is that Stalin is going to flee to London at the weekend. Can you believe that old fool Churchill might actually welcome him?'

At the many official functions he attended in that glowingly confident Berlin summer of 1941 the talk was of victory and the creation of a new international order. And Bose was treated as if he was already the representative of an independent country ready to take its place in a world remade, and addressed with great formality as 'Your Excellency'. His open relationship with Emilie was in flagrant breach of Germany's tough racial laws but the authorities were happy to look the other way. The couple sat in their pleasant garden receiving a stream of high-ranking visitors from various ministries and entertaining a growing band of Indian émigrés attracted to Bose's new 'Free India Centre' and apt to call him *Netaji*. The former Prime Minister of Iraq, Rashid Aali al-Gaylani, and Hajj Amin al-Husayni, the exiled Grand Mufti of Jerusalem, gravitated towards him, too, along with many of the other nationalist and anti-British figures who had found their way to Berlin hoping to win support. But as Bose happily talked about the coming collapse of the British Empire other conversations were quietly taking place in the city he now called home: 'Perhaps he had too much to drink but my cousin told me yesterday that in many cases the locals have "taken care" of the . . . you know . . . "population problems" even before our men get there.'

Throughout Bose's life the moral judgements made about him – and the ones he made about himself, for he was nothing if not self-aware – all came down to priorities. If liberating a subcontinent from an empire that had subjugated it for centuries was the focus of your life, then that was all that mattered. Clarity and focus was all. Any unpleasant whispers you might hear about what your new allies are doing to some other people in some other place must necessarily take second place.

Bose makes for a soft target now. It's easy to contrast him at a gossipy drinks party with what was happening at the exact same moment in town squares, forest clearings and isolated quarries across Poland, Ukraine and the Baltic provinces of the Soviet Union. Places from where stories of the 'difficult work' being done by specialised military units, and their often enthusiastic local assistants, did indeed make their way back to Berlin that summer and autumn. But, his many defenders would argue, how can any of that horror be allowed to discredit Bose's pursuit of his dream of independence for India and a better world for all humanity? How can it gainsay his deep and proven commitment to communal coexistence and racial tolerance? A man doing a great thing in a bad world is still doing a great thing, is he not? If troops representing the men calling you 'Excellency' and serving you strudel are massacring Jewish women and children thousands of miles away, and you half know and half don't know about it, then why should that stop you pursuing a very different and decent policy of your own? It's just that you need the help of these dangerous people to bring a better world to fruition. Look what Lenin had to do. Remember all those guns shipped into Dublin during the last war.

Eventually Bose had to process a more exact understanding of what began that summer, alongside other crimes committed by soldiers from a second alliance he deemed necessary to secure his destiny and his dream. There's no reason to think that he knew any firm details of the worst atrocities during his time in Berlin but it's also impossible to believe he didn't notice the scale of persecution, exclusion and then gradual removal of Jews from public life in Germany and Austria during the many months he lived there. And yet of all the memos, articles, speeches, telegrams and letters he produced while living amid the leading men and women of Hitler's Reich, not one expressed concern for the plight of Germany's or Europe's Jews.

And anyway he had many other things to worry about. Although he had now received permission from the German military to recruit prisoners of war, there seemed little enthusiasm for him to do anything with them. He spent a lot of time writing position papers for the German Foreign Office and trying to understand the reasoning of his generous but still slightly suspicious hosts. One cause of the standoffishness was obvious. Most of the men and women flocking to his side had the sort of radical left-wing background that merited a long stint in a prison camp (or a bullet in the back of the head) in Hitler's Germany. And then there was Bose's famous and implacable anti-imperialism. It was a useful propaganda tool to help undermine British power, but it was not the most obvious ideology for the Nazis to support, given their strenuous efforts to occupy and colonise large parts of Europe and northern Asia themselves. Explaining this to a friend who was uncomfortable about some of his statements in Berlin, Bose settled on a formula he would use time and again: 'We won't say anything either in favour of or against the Germans, for what they do in Europe does not strictly concern us.'

Until suddenly the Germans knew exactly what Bose should do, and so did he. As soon as Japan entered the war discussions began about the possibility of another secret journey, one that would be even more dangerous, dramatic and fateful than his escape from Calcutta.

India, 1941–1942

Thermometer, forceps, Wellington boots, tea-infuser, tin kettle, Beatrice stove, folding lantern, enamel plate and mug; knife, fork and spoon; and the flat iron which comes in very useful as a door stop.

Angela Noblet was packing for a new life at the 65th Combined Military Hospital in West Bengal, and for a war that had started very badly. Ever a diligent correspondent, she wrote to a handful of the men she had met on the *Monarch of Bermuda* with details of her journey to Asansol, which she described as 'the Crewe of West Bengal', a bustling railway junction and industrial town with 'chimneys belching smoke and steam with steel for the war effort flowing from the furnaces and rolling mills to the trains at Asansol Junction'. While their husbands managed steel plants and coal mines, the local white *memsahibs* spent their days writing letters to family in Britain, running charity committees and playing tennis or bridge. So they had plenty of time to fuss over the new arrivals, pressing them to come for tea, swim in their club pool, deliver every scrap of news and gossip from home, and ideally hand over a modish dress pattern or two.

Angela shared a large, modern bungalow with another nurse, Mary McNally, and they both delighted in its pristine bathroom, hot running water, 'finest white gauze mosquito curtains' and comfortable beds. A 'turbaned bearer' brought them tea and arrowroot biscuits to enjoy every morning, but that was as far as their life of luxury went. At the hospital things were anything but easy as Angela came face to face with war for the first time, treating troops 'depressed by defeat, hungry and fever ridden'. 'My heart sinks when I see another casualty brought in. The majority suffering from malaria. All these deaths are having a bad effect on the morale of the rest of the patients.'

Many of the sickest men were suffering from a combination of malaria and heatstroke, a fatal mixture she'd never witnessed before. 'The dramatic treatment of wringing out sheets in a tin bath of ice water and wrapping them around the patient in full view of everyone . . . must be having a depressing effect on the others as it is frequently followed by the death of the patient.'

Heatstroke is a dramatic surge in temperature caused when extreme sweating flushes the body of salt and other chemicals essential to regulate core functions. Angela took time to study its symptoms and treatment. Only days later a letter arrived from one of the friends she'd made on the liner informing her that the 'beautiful, thoughtful but married Mitch' had recently died of just this condition. It's possible that this was the man with whom she'd enjoyed that moment of moonlit romance. 'I lie awake in the stuffy darkness in anger and distress, mourning a man I'd considered a brother, knowing that had I been there I would have spotted the first symptoms and may have saved him.'

She was soon experiencing the full physical challenge of nursing in the tropics. 'The sun burns like copper in a cobalt sky and even though the Indian coolies and sepoy orderlies assist us, our clothes are soaked with sweat merely in the process of organising everything.' The hospital was run entirely by British doctors and nurses, along with some of Anglo-Indian birth, but she did note a kind of rough equality among the patients. 'British, Indian and Gurkha troops, distinguished solely by the identity disks around their necks, share a brotherhood of emaciated raggedness,' she wrote in her diary. At the end of her first week she was exhausted but cheered by the sight of one of the friendly Indian assistants bringing in sprigs of bougainvillea for each of the newly arrived nurses.

Angela's own health suffered from the heat, the insects and the food, with bouts of fever, heat rash, laryngitis and diarrhoea. But she bounced back quickly from them all, feeling energised and able, and soon her life acquired a rhythm that she rather enjoyed: the daily walk to the hospital from the neat, whitewashed bungalow; the familiar ward routine of injections, thermometers, bedpans and strip washes, punctuated by sudden crises as sick or injured men arrived needing urgent treatment or a visit to the operating theatre. Then calmer afternoons distributing chilled lime juice or boiling sheets to kill off the blood-sucking insects that plagued patients and staff alike. Some days they took a gramophone outside and the 'walking wounded' sang along or attempted an unsteady dance to Fred Astaire or Bing Crosby. A croaky rendition of 'South of the Border (Down Mexico Way)' sounded less ridiculous in the pre-monsoon heat of West Bengal than in chilly old England.

From a mixture of newspaper accounts and army gossip, the nurses soon learned that Japanese soldiers were raping and murdering women as they swept through Asia and that the red crosses on their uniforms would offer them no protection. Asansol felt like a safe distance away, but it was rumoured that women in hospitals nearer the front line were allowed to carry a fatal dose of poison, just in case.

Evenings were for keeping up with her many correspondents, visits for dinner with the local ladies or reading a book on her terrace as egrets and cormorants swooped through the banyan and devil's trees. With Mary and her other new friends she ate mangoes with sugar and delicious chilled cream from the hospital fridge, hoping to avoid any lurking cobras as she carried the precious bounty back to the bungalow. On such evenings she often came across the hospital's commanding officer, Major Edward Lossing, a rather impressive, good-looking if slightly reserved man. He was a reassuring sight, leading ad hoc hunting parties to eradicate the armies of stray dogs that constantly threatened to invade the hospital. He obviously noticed her, too. While walking her home from a dinner party he casually suggested that she might like to join him for another dinner soon, this time *à deux*. Next morning, like a dutiful military nurse, Angela asked her Matron whether such a thing would be proper. Smiling, the older woman said that since other nurses had begun 'walking out' with various doctors and local businessmen it hardly seemed fair to deprive the poor CO of female company. But, turning stern, she reminded Angela that any off-duty relationship must be kept completely separate from whatever happened while she was at work and serving under a strict military hierarchy, with him at its apex. Intriguingly, she wrote nothing of their first evening together but then, a few weeks later, she revealed that

> I have been out quite often with Teddy. Although his name is Edward I have decided to call him that. Dr and Mrs Niblock joined us after tea, when we went to fish in what we call the tank – an artificial pond of water about one hundred yards long, rectangular and surrounded by banks of earth – but all we caught was a bony mudfish. It was a perfect evening; the sky was lemon and eggshell blue with smoky clouds. The new moon rose at six o'clock and later the sky was thick with huge stars, some of them shooting across the sky.

Whether it was the effect of a blossoming romance or simply relief at the breaking of an energy-sapping heat wave, she was equally lyrical a few days later.

> Today the rains came in the small hours. First I heard a distant whispering like the sound the sweeper makes when he uses a broom of grasses to sweep the loggia then a susurration as though a hundred trees were blowing together and finally there came a deluge whose sound drowned every note in the universe. You could hear, see, smell and feel nothing but rain! I felt drunk on rain and as there was nobody about I ran outside, letting it sluice down my body shouting for joy as loud as I could because

nobody could hear anything above the steady, rolling, drum beat of the rain.

Rain brought relief, but problems of its own: mould, mildew, and myriad insects all determined to get inside every part of the bungalow, the hospital wards, her cupboards and her clothes. There were flying ants in her hair, frogs in her wash basin and centipedes in her dressing gown, but she loved to see the dripping wet trees and all the swelling, succulent tropical fruits. She was granted a long weekend in Calcutta where she visited Mitch's friends and heard of his final days. These men had yet to see any fighting, apart from that against India's many diseases. They also talked about politics, Indian independence and an infamous man who was in in a tearing hurry to pull down the curtain on the British Raj.

> It was good to talk to Charles again and I was interested in what he had to say about the arch-villain (from the British point of view) Subhas Chandra Bose. He is far more impatient than Gandhi and wants independence straight away even if he has to foment trouble amongst the population and side with the Japanese to put pressure on the British.

She left the city in a rather sour mood, reflecting on the many unpleasant things she had seen there.

> What a relief to leave the smells and sights of Calcutta. The other thing that concerned me was the plight of those rickshaw wallahs. Charles said that they had very short lives because they work on so little food and are riddled with diseases such as hookworm and tuberculosis. I saw both Indians and Europeans kick out at puny little men who pull them along in rickshaws to make them go faster. It would give me great pleasure to put such bullies between the shafts and drive them for miles through the crowded streets.

Back in Asansol she was detached from the military hospital to cover an Indian civilian ward where, for the first time, she was exposed to another reality of Indian life – illnesses rarely if ever experienced by people like her, people on the right side of a system in which even disease was split on racial lines.

> The Indian wards are a revelation to me. I came face to face with strange diseases I had never heard of. Infestation with guinea worm, the oldest known human parasite, which the orderlies twist round a small stick as it issues from the muscle of the leg, is quite common, as is elephantiasis, caused by another parasitic worm carried by mosquitoes. This is rarer but devastating in its later stages. The affected part – usually the foot – grows to enormous proportions and resembles the leg of an elephant. Tuberculosis is rife too. I turned the pillow of a terminal case and found a lump of black putty-like material. The Indian orderly said laconically, 'Opium, Sister Sahib, so he die happy.' I quietly put it back below his pillow.

To reach the wards she was guided through the dark by night watchmen carrying lanterns and brooms to swish any nocturnal snakes out of the way, alert for jackals or even the tigers that were said to prowl around the hospital grounds. One day someone escaped from the Indian psychiatric hospital nearby, burst into her ward and came at her with a pickaxe. With great composure she squirted a can of fly spray into his face, stunning him until the pursuing orderlies could pounce.

The sympathetic interest Angela took in her Indian colleagues and patients feels wholly authentic. Learning of their struggles, their debts, their children dead too young, their sons away fighting for a distant king in a distant continent. And their politely expressed hopes that before them – and maybe soon – lay a future free from the control of people who looked like her.

Burma and India, 1942

The casualties arriving at Angela Noblet's hospital were the result of a series of startling Japanese victories that triggered a political and psychological earthquake. With phenomenal speed Hong Kong, Singapore, Jakarta, Manila, Kuala Lumpur and Rangoon all fell, as British, Dutch and American forces proved unable to stem the tide. Great battleships were sunk, famous armies surrendered and supposedly impregnable colonial citadels fell without a shot being fired. Soon Japanese columns were advancing through Burma and towards the border of India itself, while the mostly Indian troops facing them tried desperately to organise a fighting retreat and guide hundreds of thousands of refugees to safety.

Many of those refugees were Indian, too, part of a large expatriate community in Burma that was threatened by both the invaders and by Burmese nationalist groups that rushed to join the conflict on Japan's side. As inter-communal violence exploded, and armed men sought to steal from, or simply murder, groups of frightened refugees, the fighting in Burma quickly became the object of horrified fascination across the subcontinent. To anyone looking on from India it was soon obvious − and obviously infuriating − that those with money and influence, the elite plantation and mine owners and officials who were predominantly white, were escaping first. An American consular official witnessed Indian families being turned away from a steamer leaving Rangoon so that the British and Anglo-Indians could board it instead and his account was shared widely around the world. The Muslim League, which was generally more supportive of the Raj than Congress, complained about 'shameless discrimination' on the roads out of Burma and when the Viceroy, Lord Linlithgow, ordered his civil servants to look into the evacuation he decided against publishing what they discovered for fear of further inflaming the situation.

As Burmese Prime Minister U Saw had discovered during his frustrating conversations with Churchill over the Atlantic Charter, there had never been much serious discussion about self-rule for Burma. And so few people there believed that continued loyalty to London might ease the path to independence. Japan's promises made much more sense, especially with the soldiers of the old colonial powers fleeing in every direction. Nationalist leader Aung San and his Burmese Independence Army quickly attracted many thousands of fighting men. As allies of the Japanese these men clashed with the militias of the Karen tribal people, traditional friends of the British. Communities were soon turning on each other all over the shattered country. Armed groups of Buddhist monks also launched themselves against the colonial whites and the Chinese and Indians who were seen as their lackeys. Ethnically driven banditry and religiously sanctioned terror by red-robed fanatics was the result.

Nine-year-old Krishnan Gurumurthy's family was one of those denied access to a ship from Rangoon, so his parents' and grandparents' only option was to travel for weeks through a war-torn nation by train, by boat and finally on foot.

> The first day [of trekking] was the most arduous with unbearable strain as the mountain was steep with no down hills throughout. My mother and grandmother were the worst sufferers. Many unfortunate evacuees perished on the wayside. There was no one who cared to remove the corpses of the dead. One's mental attitude at that point of time was such that even if your own child or near or dear ones perished you would just walk on to save yourself. Quite a few did just that. No one even bothered to remove the small gold ornaments still on the body. I can vividly remember holding my father's hand and asking how far still to go. He used to point at some flickering light and say that was it. I, of course believed him.

Credible reports of well-fed white families being ushered onto relief boats while Indians struggled along sodden jungle tracks, menaced by bandits and innumerable mosquitos and leeches, made a powerful impression. Of the 600,000 Indian civilians who attempted to escape Burma it is believed that 80,000 died in the process. Inevitably their friends and families wondered whether more could have been done to help them. E. M. Forster had written that it was 'the height of impropriety' to consider what being white actually meant in India but on the roads out of Burma it was plain enough. One Indian officer struggling along with his family reported: 'Every day we saw that many cars or lorries and motor trucks overtook us and these were occupied by Europeans,' adding, with a measure of understatement that Forster would doubtless have appreciated, 'that this caused some annoyance.' The Gurumurthy family did finally reach the Indian border and was delighted to come across some official — but mostly *unofficial* — aid there.

> Our reception in India was in sharp contrast to our journey through Burma. Spontaneous relief and assistance was forthcoming from various non-Government organisations like the Indian National Congress, Marwari Relief Society etc. to make our life as comfortable as possible. There was an air of sympathy and fellow feeling all round. They arranged free food, accommodation, travel and medical care. In short, our Indian people regardless of caste, community or language welcomed us with open arms.

Assessing the evacuation, General Bill Slim did find some reasons for hope, largely because his army just about held together during what he described as 'a long jungle Dunkirk'. But across India those who had previously argued that the Raj, for all its faults, was at least organised and capable found themselves at a loss. A year earlier families had cheered newsreels of Indian troops waving happily from Egypt or Eritrea. But the patriotism of that moment now curdled into a kind of shocked disgust, a feeling summed up by Gandhi, who could not believe what he was seeing.

> Hundreds, if not thousands, on their way from Burma perish without food and drink, and the wretched discrimination stares even these miserable people in the face. One route for the whites, another for the blacks! Provision of food and shelter for the whites, none for the blacks . . . India is being ground down to dust and humiliated, even before the Japanese advent, not for India's defence – and no one knows for whose defence.'

Singapore, 1942

Japanese intelligence officers had long planned to use Britain's reputation as a colonial overlord against it and so Indian prisoners were quickly separated from British ones and given favourable treatment. After hearing Japanese lectures on the future of Asia, Captain Mohan Singh, an officer of the Indian Army who had been captured in Malaya, offered to lead a force of prisoners prepared to fight alongside Japan and thousands of other Indian prisoners soon volunteered to join him. Although he would eventually part company with his new allies, Singh's initial enthusiasm is instructive. He had long felt uneasy wearing a British uniform and by 1942 that had hardened into a sense of shame.

> An old Irish adage – 'Those under bonds will put others under bonds' – truly sums up the basic aspect of slavery. We had not only meekly submitted to an evil, which a nation ought to fight to the last, but had become the standard bearer of the pestilence of servitude in several foreign lands . . . In contrast to the Japanese propaganda the British had not even given us an empty promise of freedom after the war.

I felt that if I approached the Japanese and succeeded in obtaining their help to start a movement for Indian's independence, I was bound to attract a number of soldiers . . . It would cut deep at the roots of the British policy of exploiting Indians for their wars all over the world . . . This would ultimately force the British statesmen, shrewd as they were, always preferring to bend than to break, to acknowledge India's irrefutable right to independence.

Thus the Indian National Army was born and 'Asia for Asians' was one of its earliest slogans. Enlisting clearly made sense to some of Indian prisoners, both ideologically and pragmatically. As every new story coming out of Burma confirmed, Britain was now a busted flush, a ragged and wrinkly old lion well past its prime. In its place a new Asia of independent nations would rise under the benign protection of the brave, unstoppable young warriors of Japan. Perhaps asking why so many Indian prisoners volunteered for the INA is the wrong way to look at this. Given everything that was happening, and that the alternative was a Japanese POW camp, surely a better question is: why did so many refuse?

Perhaps one reason is that, even as Captain Singh began to drill his INA volunteers, the men who had 'educated' him about pan-Asian liberation continued to reveal their savage side. In the months after the fall of Singapore a pre-planned massacre of 'anti-Japanese' elements in the city — and in neighbouring regions of Malaya — took the lives of tens of thousands of mostly Chinese Singaporeans and refugees. The purge was intended to remove political activists and other such potential troublemakers but, such was the bloodlust of the occupying army, there were numerous mass shootings of Chinese men for no reason other than their race.

Berlin, 1942

Bose first broadcast to India less than a week after the Japanese walked unopposed into Singapore and the fighting reached Burma.

> This is Subhas Chandra Bose speaking to you over the Azad Hind [Free India] Radio network. To arms, to arms the heavens ring with the clarion call to freedom's fray. Our cause is just!
>
> The fall of Singapore . . . means the collapse of the British Empire, the end of the iniquitous regime which it has symbolised and the dawn of a new era in Indian history.

Bose knew the Japanese ambassador and military attaché in Berlin very well, but he was not forewarned about Pearl Harbor (an ignorance he shared with Hitler). Hearing the extraordinary news was one of the most exciting moments of his life. His tortuously argued decision to ally himself with the Axis powers had proved to be both correct and far-sighted. The Wehrmacht's advance towards Moscow had paused for the winter but the colonialists of the Indo-Pacific — Bose's real enemies — were either on the run or looking nervously to the north and east. Could there be any doubt that he had chosen the winning side?

> Through India's liberation Asia and the world will move forward towards the larger goal of human emancipation.

No less an expert on propaganda than Joseph Goebbels was delighted by Bose's broadcasts which, he confided to his diary, 'have made a deep impression on world public opinion', adding that 'the crisis in India can no longer be denied and we are doing everything possible to pour oil on the fire. In London there is boundless wrath about the appeal of Bose.' To celebrate the radio talks Goebbels invited the entire staff of Bose's Free India Centre to a private tea party at his Ministry of Public Enlightenment and

Propaganda. A German foreign office file from this time, striking a surprisingly progressive tone, stated that 'Germany, Italy and Japan are convinced that the Indian nation will break the political and economic bonds of British imperialism and then as master of its own fate will carry out a sweeping transformation of its national life for the lasting benefit of its own people and as contribution to the welfare and the peace of the world.'

Shaken by the fall of Singapore and other disasters, Churchill's government made an offer of Indian self-government. He dispatched Labour politician Stafford Cripps to Delhi to discuss a form of dominion status leading to full independence if that was India's post-war choice. Cripps made this offer to the mainstream nationalist leaders in return for their full cooperation for the duration of the war. Goebbels thought this was a telling sign of British weakness and 'a world sensation'. But Cripps was unable to make a breakthrough and Gandhi described the concessions on the table as 'a post-dated cheque on a crashing bank'. One problem was that Gandhi and others had heard similar promises before (in the years before the bank 'crashed') and just didn't trust British politicians to follow through when − or if − the pressure of war receded. Another was that they genuinely believed that Britain's continued presence in India would invite a Japanese invasion, and so immediate independence was the only way to keep their people safe. Back in London some close to Churchill worried that Cripps' offer contained too much 'wriggle room' anyway, and that the prime minister's heart was not truly in it. According to his own Secretary of State for India and Burma, Leo Amery, Churchill's attitude towards the empire at the time of the Cripps mission was 'mid-Victorian in general' and, when it came to Indian independence, 'at the early Kipling stage'.

From Berlin, Bose dismissed any constitutional compromise, dominion status or delay to independence, arguing that no imaginable diplomatic effort could 'arrest the collapse and breakup of the empire'. And, in a phrase that might have been aimed directly at Timmy, he thundered that 'any Indian who now works for Britain acts against the best interests of his country and is a traitor to the cause of liberty'. He then asked Ribbentrop if the German navy could help him travel to the East, to lead a revolution in person. The request was discussed at the highest levels but someone very senior ruled against it. A debate was raging about the future direction of the war and the Japanese government was urging Hitler to downgrade his campaign in the Soviet Union and instead focus on a joint struggle to break the British and keep America at arm's length. Hitler wouldn't agree to this and so, for the moment, Bose was stuck in Berlin. British propaganda was painting him as a traitor and a dupe of Hitler, but he had a ready answer to that.

> If the Britishers, who are past masters in the art of diplomacy and political seduction, have in spite of their best efforts failed to tempt, corrupt or mislead me, no other power on earth can do so. All my life I have been a servant of India and till the last hour of my life I shall remain one . . . no matter in which part of the world I may live at a given time.

On 29 May 1942, Bose met Adolf Hitler for the first and only time. The Führer was in confident, expansive mood but explained to his Indian ally that, in the context of a global struggle, it was not yet strategically wise for his government to call for an uprising in India since German forces were not in a position to support it. Instead he urged Bose to work more closely with Japan and said that he was now ready to transport him to the East by submarine. Even though inwardly delighted, and perhaps realising that this meeting would always be used against him by his enemies, Bose didn't want to leave the room without challenging Hitler over statements in *Mein Kampf* that implied Indians were a subservient people. Dodging the question, Hitler said that he meant no disrespect to Bose's homeland and had only wanted to contrast his own muscular and aggressive philosophy with the passive resistance once championed by weak and foolish men such as Gandhi.

India, 1942

They called it 'The Great Flap', a nationwide panic about Japanese air attacks on the eastern coast and the threat of imminent invasion. Eighty-five per cent of the population of Madras fled into the hinterland during the retreat from Rangoon, encouraged to leave by officials peering nervously out into the Bay of Bengal. There was in fact no Japanese invasion fleet but that didn't stop the flapping. And so, after the many disasters in Burma, Cripps' abortive mission and now this widespread fear of war reaching Indian soil, Gandhi decided to act. 'One fine morning,' he wrote, 'I came to the decision to make this honest demand: "For Heaven's sake leave India alone!"'

Taking its cue from its most famous leader, the Congress Party toughened up its demands dramatically, launching a 'Quit India' campaign that brought millions onto the streets demanding immediate change. Gandhi argued that if the British announced they were leaving then Congress itself could negotiate a peace deal, stop the invasion and save many lives. Eager to support this analysis the government in Tokyo promised that it was fighting in the region only to give 'Burma to the Burmese and India to the Indians'. Amid massive protests, the Viceroy clamped down hard, arresting all the main leaders of Congress, Gandhi and Nehru included. Looking on from Berlin, Bose felt a surge of vindication. India's greatest nationalist hero had not supported him in recent years but, according to a friend who was allowed to see Gandhi while he was under house arrest, 'I found a change in his outlook. Many of his remarks convinced me that he admired the courage and resourcefulness Subhas Bose has displayed.'

'Quit India' convulsed the subcontinent and, with the older generation of leaders now in prison, it was the younger and more radical groups that set the pace. Everywhere there were boycotts of schools and colleges, strikes, marches and occupations. Only two of the sixteen daily papers in Calcutta were able to publish as journalists and print workers walked out in solidarity with the protestors on the streets. The Madras woollen mills that produced half the nation's khaki cloth shut down, as did the huge Tata iron and steel works at Jamshedpur. Agitators wrecked post offices, pulled down telegraph poles and uprooted railway tracks. In late August, Viceroy Linlithgow cabled Churchill to say, 'I am engaged here in meeting by far the most serious rebellion since that of 1857, the gravity and extent of which we have so far concealed from the world for reasons of military security . . . If we bungle this business we shall damage India irretrievably as a base for future allied operations.' And for a while it did feel like all order was collapsing. Two RAF men were pulled from a train, dismembered and drowned. A group of Indian policemen were doused with petrol and burned alive. A British officer wrote home boasting of how one day he had 'some jolly good fun shooting 24 ni**ers myself'.

A militant campaigner, Aruna Asaf Ali, saw her husband thrown into jail and responded by directing a campaign of sabotage, which soon brought a price upon her head. She targeted government property and the transport system and appeared to have sympathisers in the police and local newspapers. Officials leaked information to Ali and other saboteurs while some munitions workers damaged their own production. By continually evading arrest she soon became a cult figure, her image on tens of thousands of pamphlets and posters that proliferated much faster than the police could tear them down. The Viceroy was right: this was the largest revolt since 1857 and it cost over three thousand lives. After some fierce repression the movement did finally begin to wane — although Aruna Asaf Ali remained defiantly on the run — but it had truly shaken the Raj. And Berlin noticed, too. In the North African desert the Germans and Italians targeted Indian units with leaflets accusing the British of killing their friends and families back home, urging them to abandon their positions and join the fight for a free India. Few took up the offer, but it all helped build Bose's case that the nascent Indian National Army, now drilling in

Singapore, needed somebody with a global profile to lead it, namely himself. He also saw an opportunity to attack America, newly engaged in the conflict, mocking Roosevelt's stated case for war, and what he saw as Churchill's hypocritical embrace of the language of 'self-government'.

Behind the thick screen of gas, underneath the heavy blows of police batons, amid the continual whistle of bullets and the angry defiance of the injured and the dying, the soul of India asks 'Where are the Four Freedoms?'. The words float over the seven seas to all corners of the globe, but Washington does not reply. After a pause, the soul of India asks again, 'Where is the Atlantic Charter, which guaranteed to every nation its own Government?' This time Downing Street and the White House reply simultaneously – 'That charter was not meant for India.'

Singapore and India, 1942

Timmy's battalion had been in Singapore shortly before the war with Japan began and he was shocked and demoralised by what he saw there. Rampant racketeering, officials and soldiers drinking all day, a network of brothels operating beyond the law, their owners openly paying off the police. Narcotic addicts lay around in a stupor, even in the more fashionable neighbourhoods, and there were rancorously bad relations between different units of the army, leading to verbal and physical confrontations breaking out on national and religious lines.

Under the pressure of war the British High Command pulled off the difficult trick of being uninterested in serious problems but obsessed with phantom ones. The suspicion that Indian troops might become disloyal was strong, with suggestions that officers in battalions such as Timmy's were eager to send information all the way to Berlin. On top of all this, supplies were irregular and officials high-handed and soon the anger became so universal that some of his soldiers decided to go on hunger strike.

'The sympathy of the Indian officers was with the mutineers. Our anti-British feelings were intense. The war in Europe was going badly for the Allies, and most of us greeted the news of a British defeat with delight.'

In Quetta and on the frontier he'd seen an empire that still functioned but here in Singapore it appeared to be exhausted, inefficient and rapidly falling apart, with substandard leadership and little apparent will to correct the drift and decay. And yet, it was a sign of his continuing faith in the Indian Army — and perhaps his desperation to escape Singapore — that he agreed to return to India to help raise new battalions for the 19th Hyderabad regiment, and he was doing just that in Agra when the war erupted. Such was the reputation of Britain and its military that the initial wave of Japanese success came as an unwelcome surprise to many Indians, but Timmy was hardly shocked when he heard of Japan's easy progress through Malaya, its rapid conquest of Singapore and the chaotic retreat through Burma. He was heart-broken, though, to discover how many of his Hyderabadis had been killed or captured.

'Quit India' put Timmy in a familiar dilemma. Amid mass civil disobedience troops were frequently called onto the streets to keep a lid on things. In Agra Timmy was in charge of half-trained recruits, many of whom were the friends or even relatives of the people shouting for independence in the streets. 'Our recruits often played games with them. The idea of taking reprisals against these lads was abhorrent to us.' Ever since the horrors of Amritsar, when panicking troops sprayed thousands of bullets into the crowd, the use of force by the Indian Army had been tightly controlled. After a number of warnings a single bullet would be issued to an individual marksman who was told to aim at a ring-leader. If that didn't work, another bullet was issued and another target chosen. But when Timmy was inevitably called out to face a furious mob, including men who had been beaten bloody by the local police, he did his best to keep the bullets in their box. 'I tried to act calm, but I was shaky as I waved for silence. I gave them three minutes to disperse and they did. This happened on six occasions and no shots were ever fired.'

When Timmy first learned of the Indian National Army he was sympathetic to the men volunteering to follow Bose, some of whom were prisoners taken in Singapore from units he knew well, including Hyderabadis. 'It was difficult for us to view this action as anything but patriotic. But if we accepted these INA men as patriots, however, then we who served with the British must be traitors. This was especially difficult for me because I heard that my own older brother had gone into the INA.'

It was true. Kodandera Ponnappa Thimayya, captured in Singapore, was one of those who had decided to break his oath of loyalty to the King and fight for independence alongside the Japanese. Timmy said little about how this affected him personally apart from recording that it was 'difficult', but the prospect of one day going into combat against his own flesh and blood must have tormented him. As boys they had fought side by side against prejudiced playground bullies, standing up together for the dignity of their people, and now this. At this precise moment, and with impeccably bad timing, the Indian Army High Command almost triggered a mutiny. Just when British military prestige was slipping to an all-time low, Indian-born officers were required to sign a pledge stating that they rejected the Congress Party and would use force, if necessary, to defend the Raj.

> The younger Indian officers especially were incensed. We had heated discussions on the matter. I remembered the instructions that Motilal Nehru had given me, and I saw that this was one of the tempting situations he had predicted. I told the younger men what I had been told, and, before long, they were convinced as well. In the end we all signed the paper. Refusing to sign it would have had little political significance. But signing the paper, carrying on with our duties, and supporting the

British by force meant that we could learn the proper use of force. Who else could teach us? And when the time came to fight for our country, we would be able to fight effectively.

We'll never know how close Timmy came to following his brother's lead but it's clear that a deep suspicion of Japanese motives was one powerful factor. Did he really want to build a new India out of Japanese bayonets? He certainly listened to some of the copious propaganda aimed at India but in the end he judged the messages coming from Tokyo — and from Bose — to be fundamentally insincere. They spoke of freedom but how much freedom did the peoples recently liberated by Japan have in reality? And he found it impossible to forget or forgive how the Japanese army had treated the Chinese in the 1930s. 'The consensus [of men like me] was that we should help the British defeat the Axis powers and deal with the British afterward. I also felt that to sign on with the British, to learn from them and then to go over to their enemy was reprehensible; I doubt if I could have done it.'

Honour and pragmatism alike required him to stay with the devil he knew. It was obvious to anyone who could read a newspaper that, faced with extreme military peril, the British were now in a mood to offer concessions. After the war they would surely be on their way. And again, at the heart of all his thinking, there was the army, *his* army. It was a British creation and the best things about it came from British traditions and leadership. It could be bad but when it was good it was exceptional. It is what he knew and loved and developing it, evolving it, incorporating the best of it into something truly Indian, *that* was his vision and his life's work.

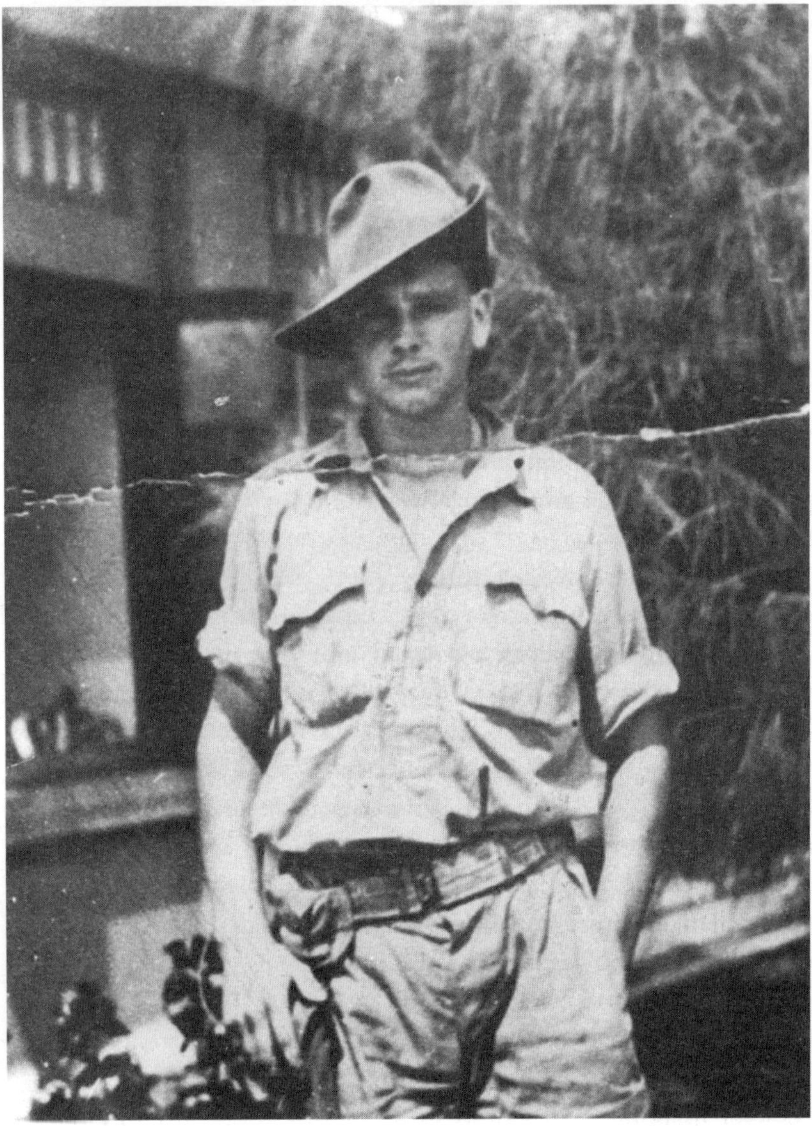

5

The Prisoner

South China Sea and Formosa, 1942–1943

'Hold on tight to your bum, chum!'

A soldier will make a joke about anything, even the prospect of explosive diarrhoea flying towards the top of his head. And on this subject Signalman Arthur Titherington had lost any squeamishness long before his daily climb up and down the ladders of the *England Maru*.

'Squeeze tight lads and think of the poor sod coming up behind!'

Fifteen minutes on deck a day was all they got, and everyone was in a hurry to make the most of it, to breathe fresh sea air and escape the stinking, overcrowded holds below. The Japanese had pushed them all into a pool of disinfectant back in Singapore, like so many sheep going through a dip, but that hadn't stopped the rampant dysentery. Down below it was wobbly buckets only and so those with any kind of control rushed to the wooden box toilets balanced precariously on the side of the ship. As the old steamer shuddered unsteadily through the South China Sea, seasickness and food poisoning – from the slop they were served once a day – only added to the misery and the stench. But Arthur discovered that his own constitution was stronger than he'd ever imagined. He could stomach just about anything and made a point of filling his belly every chance he got, even as his mates were noisily purging theirs. And it was here, surrounded by groaning comrades and overflowing toilet buckets, that he first started whispering to himself: 'Just another day, one more day, focus on that, ignore all else.'

Arthur and his friends were more fortunate than they realised. Other ships were on the move, as the Japanese redistributed huge numbers of people around the region. Many, like the *England Maru* itself, carried a mix of prisoners of war and Japanese troops and, as far as the American submarine captains knew, they were all legitimate military targets. On *Lisbon Maru* eight hundred British prisoners died when the torpedoes struck, some locked into their holds by their jailers and others shot while attempting to abandon ship.

As he travelled to an unknown fate, Arthur Titherington had plenty of time to reflect upon his life. He'd volunteered young at the recruiting centre in Birmingham in 1940, illegally young, in fact, which led to his angry mother writing to the commanding officer and a short but embarrassing delay to his military career. Like many teenagers from poor backgrounds he was attracted by the adventure, the chance to travel and cartoon tales of imperial glory set in exotic, far-flung lands. Handed a pith helmet and hot-weather uniform he was soon on his way 'out East' for his own taste of it. En route to Singapore he stopped off at the fabled old ports – Sierra Leone, Durban, Bombay and Colombo – and listened to endless lectures on hygiene, tropical diseases and the dangerous temptations of the brothel. By September 1941 he was a dispatch rider in northern Malaya, inside a camp surrounded by the British-owned rubber plantations he was there to protect. There were Indian servants to do all the cooking and cleaning, good food, the occasional beer, lots of sunshine and the only thing that made life unpleasant was the occasional heat rash.

> I was fast becoming [a] colonial soldier. Life was very interesting and, at times, quite exciting. Yet there were times when it troubled me greatly to think of all the folks at home, with all their trials and tribulations, the war on their doorstep and their

homes being bombed . . . and here I was surrounded by peace and plenty.

Neither peace nor plenty lasted for long. In early December the Japanese were in Malaya and Arthur was immediately caught up in chaotic battles and shambolic retreats. And he quickly discovered that many of the people he'd been living alongside were as likely to help the invaders as the British Army. He witnessed one possible reason for this when an Australian soldier he'd fallen in with stole some food from a shop and shot its owner dead when he complained. With stories of 'fifth columnists' aiding the enemy, the idyllic colonial lifestyle he'd briefly enjoyed in the plantations was replaced by an ugly campaign of ambushes, betrayals and massacres. For two frightening months his job was running dispatches along jungle tracks or between paddy fields, as his commanders struggled to make sense of a fast-moving war that they'd never expected, against a determined enemy that moved on bicycles, was supported by light tanks and fought under skies dominated by its own aircraft. The campaign stretched across hundreds of miles of jungle, mudflats, rice fields and plantations. He saw Japanese air raids, dead civilians, looted shops and burning warehouses. After the disastrous Battle of Muar River he learned that 150 Australian and Indian prisoners had been murdered by the triumphant Japanese and soon, after numerous close calls, including being blown off his motorbike by an exploding shell, he was feeling exhausted and despondent.

> Our campaign was a series of retreats, the hardest type of war to fight. Each time we thought we might be able to settle, or prepare for a push forward, word came that we were to move back once again. Time and again we were outflanked by the enemy . . . I was a little older and considerably wiser than the child who thought the whole thing was a *Boy's Own* type of adventure . . . and felt the whole of the Japanese army was making the war a personal matter between me and them.

He reached Singapore not long before it fell. As he was being marched into captivity he saw beheaded and bayoneted civilians lying in the streets. He learned of the massacres at the hospitals where Japanese troops had run riot, killing patients, doctors and nurses alike. His friends feared they would be next but life in Changi prison camp was reasonable at first. The guards left them alone for much of the time, they got a decent food ration and they even had the time and the energy to play the odd game of 'camp cricket' against some Australians. Things got more difficult when officers of the new Indian National Army started patrolling around their huts. The British prisoners were told to salute these men at all times. One who refused was beaten to the ground and an INA man punched Titherington in the face over some trivial misunderstanding of camp rules. Next he caught dengue fever, which prevented him joining a large group of prisoners who were being sent to Burma to help build a new railway line there. Not knowing what this meant, he counted himself unlucky. He would miss his mates, who at least would be allowed to spend time outside a prison camp. Instead, it was the *England Maru* and a long miserable journey to the north and east.

After a few weeks on board the dysentery below deck was supplemented by an outbreak of diphtheria and yet, despite all of this, only two prisoners died during the voyage. Finally, one morning he woke to hear someone calling, 'Come on, Tithy, we're there. You know what, I think it's Formosa.' Despite his own reasonable health he found it hard to stand when they were all mustered on the dockside under cold winter rain. With the guards yelling, '*Hayaku, hayaku*', they were arranged into a ragged column about five hundred strong and told to march to the nearby railway station. After a short ride to the base of some steep looking mountains there was more '*Hayaku, hayaku*' – or 'Speedo, speedo' in what they would soon come to call 'Guard English' – as they were once again cajoled and prodded into line and told to start walking.

Before long the rough terrain began to take its toll. The side of the track became littered with abandoned kit, dumped in a desperate effort to keep up with the column. To be a tail-ender was to invite the unwelcome attention of the guards. Men now began to fall with exhaustion. The reply was to kick them or jab them with a bayonet until in desperation the men would haul themselves to their feet, only to fall soon again.

Arthur helped some of them back to their feet and saw one soldier, close to exhaustion himself, trying to carry his friend over his shoulders. They walked through a small hamlet where 'members of the local population stood, silent and impassive, as we passed'. As a weak sun replaced the rain, under his breath he whispered over and over again, 'Just another step, just another day.'

Late in the afternoon they reached a plateau overlooking a deep mountain gorge: this was Kinkaseki Camp. An impeccably dressed officer he would soon come to know as Captain Wakiyama stepped forward and addressed them in Japanese, poorly translated by a guard. After listing a long stream of his nation's glorious victories, Wakiyama promised that 'bread and meat will be available soon after we have taken Australia which will be announced imminently'. Then he turned to the rules.

> From now on you will show proper respect for Nippon and the Nipponese. No longer will the words Jap or Japan be used. Anyone who disrespects or laughs at the great nation of Nippon will bring great punishment upon himself. You are here to work and work diligently. If you do that, then your life will be all right and you will be provided for all your human needs. Work and work diligently and there will be food! Be diligent and there will be food.

Those who had barely survived the uphill march went straight to the camp hospital, where ten of them would be dead within a month. The rest were taken in groups of thirty to a series of low wooden buildings that would be their new home. There they were given blankets, water and some bread. Arthur lay on his bunk and repeated inside his head, 'All that matters now is getting though this, acclimating myself to discomfort and living as far as I am able every day, one day at a time,' but in seconds, like everyone else, he was lost to sleep.

The Greater East Asia Co-Prosperity Sphere, 1942–1943

The sensational Japanese victories generated a feeling across Asia and the Pacific that it is difficult, certainly in Britain, to acknowledge or discuss today. That feeling was pleasure, an exhilarating, thrilling pleasure that was felt by millions of people whose families had long lived under British, French, Dutch and sometimes American control as if that was the natural, immutable way that the world was ordered. And now suddenly, surprisingly, the white men were being driven away in humiliation, and driven away by people who looked a lot like themselves. Remembering the army that had chased Arthur Titherington out of his country, Malay politician Raja Nong Chik Raja Ishak wrote, 'We cheered Japanese troops marching on the Malay peninsula. When we saw the defeated and fleeing UK troops, we felt the excitement we had never felt before.'

This is complicated territory. We know how cruel the Japanese were during this war, and that some of those who celebrated their freedom from European colonialism would soon experience the darker side of rule from Tokyo. Yet that doesn't mean that their initial thrill wasn't real or important. The jaw-dropping success of Japan demonstrated once and for all that Asian societies no longer needed outside help or control to run a sophisticated state, build a modern military or create a world-class economy, if they ever had in the first place. Japan's propaganda chiefs cleverly presented their nation as a liberating force, the 'Light of Asia', and that message was extremely effective in 1942. In the Dutch East Indies huge numbers took to the streets to cheer the newly arrived troops. Nationalist politicians who, as in India, had struggled to build a popular movement strong enough to break away from foreign domination were amazed and delighted to see it shattered so quickly and very much attracted by all the promises of a 'Greater East Asian Co-Prosperity Sphere' emanating from Japan.

Some of the joy that these newly liberated people felt was expressed with an outpouring of patriotic pride. But it was also a chance to vent long-suppressed anger at the colonists or, more simply, to grab their property and possessions. Attacks upon the soldiers and civilians of the defeated empires were common. As the Japanese advanced in the East Indies, armed groups of locals hunted down and killed Dutch men, women and children, or let the Japanese know where they could be found. In the notorious 'pig basket' murders dozens of captured Australian and, some sources say, Dutch troops were trussed up inside bamboo crates normally used for transporting animals. Carried into public places and displayed in the hot sun for the locals to see, the men were abused, refused water and finally thrown into the sea to drown. The daughter of one eyewitness later wrote that 'my father told me the trucks were driven through the town as a show to the Indonesians for the utter humiliation of the white race, finally being dumped into the harbour'.

The only parts of India that Japan managed to seize during its initial surge were the Andaman and Nicobar islands, off the southern coast of Burma. The largest town in the islands, Port Blair, was home to a notorious penal colony that the British had long used to incarcerate the most troublesome prisoners of the Raj. The small garrison force offered no resistance and the mostly Sikh soldiers there were well treated by the Japanese officers who took charge, which is perhaps why many of them volunteered to serve in the Indian National Army. The white British officers had sent their wives and children away just in time but the boat that was meant to return for them never arrived. Most were shipped to prison camps in Singapore but the Deputy Commissioner, Major Alfred Bird, was singled out for a different fate.

The Japanese had released all the prisoners and one of them, an Indian man called Pushkar Bakshi, was a sworn enemy of Major Bird. Bakshi told the Japanese commander that Bird was secretly working as a spy. It was alleged by local witnesses that he then persuaded another prisoner with a grudge, a man called Sarup Ram, to lie about Bird and plant wireless radio parts at the home in which he was imprisoned. There's no reliable way to find out what really happened here but Bird is one of those Oatenesque figures of imperial authority whose story is told according to what the teller thinks of the war and the British Empire. He was either a cruel martinet who enjoyed exercising arbitrary power over darker skinned people and now faced some rough-but understandable justice. Or else he was a sympathetic, deeply Christian man who spoke the local language and was admired by the many Indian friends he made during twenty years living on the Islands. One of those friends was Dr Dirwan Singh, a firm believer in Indian independence who volunteered to work with the Japanese in the hope that their rule would be benign.

In the face of Bakshi's accusations, Dr Singh could do little to stop the inevitable, although he did try. The people of Port Blair were summoned to witness a 'trial' and Bird was made to stand in front of a trench while Bakshi listed his alleged crimes against the new occupying authority. Before Bird was able to speak in his own defence, Bakshi declared to the Japanese officer standing in judgement that death was the only acceptable punishment in this case. Soldiers then immediately stepped forward, beating Bird and systematically breaking his arms and his legs with iron bars, leaving him in a twisted, agonised heap upon the ground. He begged for water and someone in the crowd came forward to help. But before Bird could drink anything the Japanese officer in command seized the bottle, poured the water over his sword and then cut through Bird's neck, shouting in English that 'an enemy must be killed like this'. Singh took the body of his friend away and attempted to bury it in the island's Christian cemetery, but the same officer insisted that it be burned. For his part in this sickening spectacle Pushkar Bakshi received an award. According to the local newspaper, 'Pushkar Bakshi was decorated with a medal for his valuable services rendered to the Imperial Japanese Forces, on the occasion of the Birthday of His Imperial Majesty the Emperor of Japan.'

Australian nurses marched into the sea and machine-gunned to death. Hospital patients dragged from their beds and used for bayonet practice. Civilians from the races that the Japanese did not like – Europeans and Chinese especially – relentlessly tortured, raped and brutalised in every imaginable way or else forced to live as 'comfort women'. And, as with the pig basket killings or poor Major Bird, some of these events staged as public spectacle. Long before anyone learned of the horrors of its prisoner-of-war camps, biological warfare experiments, death railways and forced marches, all of this was part of the Japanese way of war. A desire to display the subservience and powerlessness of the old masters in the cruellest and most humiliating way possible was no doubt due to the indoctrination given to the soldiers of the emperor. But it was also a performance for the benefit of those masters' former subjects, and at least some of them wanted to see it.

Berlin and the Indian Ocean, 1942–1943

Months passed and, despite Adolf Hitler's personal promise, Bose's travel plans kept running into logistical problems. Were the Germans still unsure about the wisdom of unleashing his anti-imperial energy upon the world? Were the Japanese reluctant to accept his help? It's not clear. But during the latter part of 1942 Bose continued broadcasting to India and made plans to expand and lead the INA. At the inaugural meeting of his

German—India society Bose heard the Hamburg Radio Symphony Orchestra play 'Jana Gana Mana' as the new national anthem of free India. He was also present when Emilie gave birth to their daughter Anita. Finally, in January 1943, all sides approved an elaborate and highly secret scheme to take him to Japan. He threw a party for his family and closest associates to celebrate his forty-sixth birthday and recorded a number of speeches to be broadcast while he travelled. In one of them he once again mixed politics and spirituality and, perhaps thinking of his newborn child and how she might never know her father, suggested that he may soon have to sacrifice his life for the cause:

> To us, life is one long unending wave. It is God manifesting himself in creation. It is an eternal play of forces . . . There is not only joy, but there is also sorrow. There is not only a rise, but there is also a fall. If we do not lose faith in ourselves and in our divinity, we shall move on through darkness, sorrow and degradation towards renewed sunshine, joy and progress.

Bose and his key aide Abid Hasan stepped on board *U-180* in the port of Kiel on 8 February 1943. British intelligence discovered that, once again, one of their most implacable enemies was on the move but they did not know where or how. In London keeping Bose away from India was seen as a strategic priority. The crisis of 1942 had abated and the men running the Raj were feeling more confident, buoyed up by Soviet success at Stalingrad and the defeat of Rommel at Alamein. It would be a huge problem if Bose somehow reappeared to stir everything up once again.

Life on *U-180* was far from easy, as Abid Hasan recalled:

> It was a small room where the entire crew, the doctors and us all sat together. We sat up all 24 hours. There was no elbow-room at all. We felt cramped. The moment we got up, we found ourselves in the way of somebody or the other. It was like solitary confinement. Even in jail the living conditions

would be better. Such then was our life, and I felt concerned about *Netaji*'s health. He had been losing weight.

On board the submarine Bose dictated an updated version of *The Indian Struggle* along with numerous speeches and essays to Hasan. Together, in their cramped, airless cabin, they practised the arguments that Bose planned to deploy with the Japanese High Command, with Hasan playing the role of Prime Minister Hideki Tojo. Mohan Singh, the original leader of the INA, had disagreed with the Japanese over access to weapons and training, and how his movement would be commanded in combat, and he was now back in a prison camp. With Tojo's help Bose wanted to inherit the role and build the INA into a truly revolutionary army backed by a proper Indian government-in-exile. But, as Hasan recalled, he knew it would be a complex negotiation:

> *Netaji* would think aloud. He asked me to imagine I was Tojo and then put questions to him, or he would take the role of Tojo and asked me to reply as Subhas Chandra Bose. He used to go into great details and examine all possible points that might arise. He had gone through all the questions one could think of, including, for instance, the future of Indians in South Africa. The future of the Andamans was also discussed. We must take them!

But before they could meet Tojo, Bose and Hasan got their first taste of war. *U-180* rounded the Cape and entered the Indian Ocean where, off the coast of South Africa, it came upon a lone British tanker, SS *Corbis* of the Anglo-Saxon Petroleum Company. Despite his important passenger, Captain Werner Musenberg was permitted to attack targets of opportunity and this he did. In his account of the incident Hasan wrote that, as the British ship went down into a flaming sea, the Indian and Malaysian sailors on board were put into lightweight, second-rate rafts while the white officers took the only proper lifeboat for themselves.

This is quite a claim. The attack took place just before 4 a.m., and from a distance of approximately two hundred yards. Was Hasan on the conning tower or watching through a periscope? It seems unlikely. Could he, or indeed anyone on the U-boat, see in detail what was happening as the oil tanker burst into flames and its crew desperately tried to escape with their lives? Available naval records, plans and photographs indicate that the tanker had a decent allocation of normal lifeboats and so would have no need to deploy cruder rafts. And who on board *U-180* wanted to loiter on the surface to monitor the evacuation procedures of their victims when British destroyers might be about? Or take the time to work out the difference between a real lifeboat and a flimsy raft? Or determine – in the dark, from a distance, and from a moving submarine – the ethnicity of men trying to avoid death? Despite such obvious questions, when recounting this anecdote one of Bose's more sympathetic biographers could not resist drawing a conclusion from this story: the sinking of the *Corbis* proved that 'the colour line was as ubiquitous as the Equator'.

In recent decades, enthusiasts have gathered together as much evidence as they can about the U-boat campaign. Based upon access to surviving German naval records, this is what one popular website has to say about that night:

> At 03.56 hours on 18 April 1943 the unescorted *Corbis* (Master Stanley Wilfred Appleton) was hit by two torpedoes from U-180 about 500 miles east-southeast of Port Elizabeth, South Africa. At 04.10 hours, the U-boat fired a coup de grâce at the stopped tanker, which evaded by reversing. A second coup de grâce fired six minutes later hit the foreship, set the ship on fire and caused her to sink in a short time. The Germans observed four lifeboats at the sinking position, but three of them were swamped. The master, 47 crew members and two gunners were lost. Four crew members and six gunners were rescued after drifting thirteen days in an open boat by a South African Air Force 'crash launch' and landed at East London.

So before they fled the scene the U-boat crew saw four lifeboats launched and not the solitary 'whites only' boat later recalled by Hasan. This strongly suggests that almost everyone on board did make it into a lifeboat initially, before three of them foundered. The same amateur historians also found the list of the men serving on SS *Corbis* that night. There are about a dozen British names on it, men like Thomas Simpson and Charles Tripp, and the master, too, Stanley Appleton. White British men like these formed the officer class of the merchant navy. In many parts of the world the bulk of the crews serving under them were known as 'lascars', common sailors and junior engineers recruited in India, Malaysia and port cities across the Far East. But looking at the list of lascars known to be on board *Corbis* the day it sank produces a surprise. There's Ong Ah Tiew, Sui Tip, Chaing Pai and Chow Yit Ching. But what there are *not* are any obviously Indian or Malayan names. It seems that the crew was entirely British and Chinese, the latter probably recruited in Hong Kong. Men like quartermaster Teng Yong had risen to a position of some seniority but there were no Chinese officers, as would be typical in the merchant navy of the time. As for the unfortunate Indian and Malayan sailors, cruelly forced into second-rate life rafts and sent to their deaths by their brutal white officers, they seem only to have ever existed in the imaginations of Hasan and Bose.

Here's another way of looking at it. Bose and Hasan had allied themselves with Nazi Germany for reasons many could understand but not everyone could accept. Although hardly short of self-belief, Bose himself struggled from time to time to rationalise what he was doing but, whatever his qualms, he could not and would not allow them to stand between him and his destiny. And yet now the men carrying him towards that destiny had suddenly forced him to confront certain inescapable truths, one of which was that dead Indians would be an inevitable part of the bargain he had struck. The moment he and Hasan learned that there were casualties they naturally *assumed* that would include Indians, since they knew that Indian-born lascars made up a large proportion of the crews of British merchant vessels in these waters.

As the crew of *U-180* celebrated, what did Bose feel, believing that he was now intimately connected to the death of people he had sworn to liberate? At such a difficult moment it would be natural to focus instead on how truly terrible his enemies were. The soothing power of what we'd now call 'confirmation bias' could then easily take care of the rest. 'Oh, *Netaji* did you hear that . . .' 'The man watching from the bridge is certain that he saw . . .' 'That's so typical of them, isn't it? . . .'

A colour bar certainly did operate in the British merchant navy, and in many other places in the 1940s. The existence of such inequality was why Bose, ever since he had walked the corridors of Presidency College, believed so fervently in *his* form of change. But there was something else operating on SS *Corbis* that night, and also within the fuselages of Allied bombers and on the floors of desert shell scrapes – a comradeship between men and women of different races in the face of enemies so terrible that they threatened the very idea of civilisation itself. The tanker went down with the loss of more than fifty lives, Chinese and British. Master Stanley Appleton was one of them and it's fair to assume he didn't spend his final minutes conducting a race audit.

A few days later there was a dramatic maritime rendezvous close to Madagascar that produced an iconic photograph. Bose was transferred through stormy seas from *U-180* to submarine *I-29* of the Imperial Japanese Navy, where he received a greeting that Hasan recalled being 'something akin to a home-coming'. The Japanese took him around the southern tip of India and dropped him in Sabang, a quiet inlet off the coast of Sumatra. He left the crew a heartfelt and optimistic message: 'It was a great pleasure to sail aboard the submarine. I believe this will mark a milestone in our fight for victory and peace.' Flying up through Malaya, Indochina and Formosa, he arrived in the Japanese capital and was installed in grand style in a new home just opposite the Imperial Palace. He was back in Asia and ready to shape all the institutions necessary to liberate his homeland, just as one of the most shocking and tragic events in the history of British India was about to unfold.

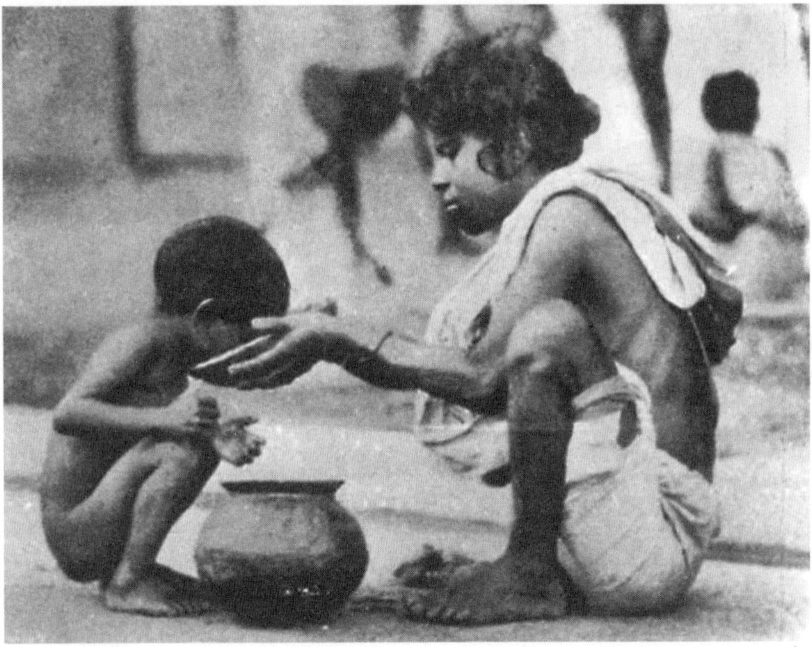

6

The Hunger

Bengal, 1943

Angela Noblet was in love. A love which, just as Matron had commanded, she kept carefully separate from her hospital duties, where she remained under the command of her *amour*, the newly promoted Lieutenant Colonel Edward Lossing. She and Teddy walked and picnicked, dined and danced. At the local concert hall they watched the latest American films together — *Blood and Sand* with Tyrone Power was a favourite — their feet crunching on half-chewed betel nuts as they stood to sing 'God Save the King'. Then they strolled back to the hospital arm in arm, alert for snakes and jackals, passing by the naked, grey-bearded sadhu (holy man) as he recited his hypnotic evening prayers. And soon the lovers even had a song.

> We took a truck to the river Damodar, a mile or so away from Asansol, taking along a wind-up gramophone, some records and a rug to lounge on. There for the first time I heard a recording of the great cellist Pablo Casals playing Après Un Rêve by Fauré, an experience that made such an impression on me that when I hear that plaintive melody so many years afterwards I am wafted back to a moonlit river bank, with a vista of distant mountains and romantic memories of my first real love affair.
>
> But in India one always swings between the earth and the stars. As I closed the lid of the gramophone I saw the busy scarab beetle rolling its ball of dung along the ground.

Angela shared nothing of the physical side of this relationship with her diary, but the couple were close enough to travel on leave together, although she did carefully note that separate bedrooms were in use at all times. One day, after leaving Asansol on a slow train journey towards a lake resort called Bhimtal, they suddenly ground to a halt alongside a goods train.

'What's that noise, darling? That tapping.'

'I can see some people under the other train, I think. Hundreds of them'

'What are they doing?'

'It's sticks, they have sticks and little bowls.'

'Good God, the poor wretches must be desperate.'

Angela had never shied away from the harsher side of life in British India but now, peering through the grimy window of the carriage, her eyes slowly adjusting to the dark, she was suddenly face to face with something horrific, something that today many people consider a war crime or even a genocide. Creeping along the tracks underneath the goods train were dozens of men and women pushing bamboo spikes up into the slatted floor of the wagons, in the hope of puncturing a sack of grain. A thin trickle of wheat was their reward, which they caught in small bowls. The driver knew they were there and did nothing to stop them. When the time came to move on, he let off a loud whistle to give them a moment to escape from under his wheels. Angela wondered aloud about people like this being not so sympathetically treated elsewhere, parents maimed or killed in their desperation to find food for their families. A sergeant who had joined her at the window said that half the grain would be gone by the time that train reached Calcutta.

After an uncomfortable night made more so by what she had witnessed, and by the hard beds of the ladies' rest room at Bareilly station, they took another train up into the mountains. Once again the troubles of wartime India interrupted the journey. An elderly Indian man started up a political conversation, asking what they thought of Gandhi, his 'iniquitous imprisonment' as a result of the 'Quit India' campaign and the fact that Indians under British rule were starving to death in Bengal.

> We told him about the plundering of the goods train. He remarked severely that, because of the Japanese invasion, there was no rice coming in from Burma and asked us when we were going to 'drive those fellows' out. We were suitably apologetic but explained that we could not manage without Gandhi's cooperation. He demanded to know how the Mahatma could help us when we had put him in jail. This seemed rather a circular argument so we sat and smiled at him. He beamed back expansively through his large spectacles, salaaming affectionately when we left the train.

This polite but firm disagreement on a train to a beautiful village, where food was plentiful, tourists lounged on the verandas of splendid hotels and spent lazy days fishing by the lake, captures perfectly a sense present in many sources from this time, both Indian and British. Anger mixed with fatalism. An understanding that, yes, of course, war had made famine relief more difficult than ever before but, alongside that, a bubbling fury that Indians *themselves*, while risking their lives in huge numbers all around the world, were not in a position to help their starving compatriots. And always close to the surface there was another feeling, no less powerful for never being tested in the real world, that *however* hard the authorities tried to help, and try many of them did, they would surely, inevitably, have done more had the food run short in Surrey, Manitoba, the Western Cape, New South Wales or North Island.

The calamity unfolding in Bengal further accelerated momentum towards independence and left an abiding stain on the reputation of the Raj. Nobody knows how many died in the great famine but it is probably between two and three million. That these deaths took place at a time of exploding economic activity in

India — and even in other parts of Bengal such as Asansol — only reinforced the shock and the outrage.

Rice was the staple food of Bengal's poorer communities. The year-long crisis began when a combination of a rare plant disease and a tropical cyclone in late 1942 destroyed much of the crop and sent prices soaring. Some traders hoarded what they could in the anticipation of even higher prices to come. Local officials did little to stop this. Those who could pay did so, but soon Calcutta and the larger regional towns were filling with people who could not afford the new prices and were forced to look for food elsewhere. Because of the intense fear of invasion, a policy known as 'denial' also played a tragic part. Boats and food supplies had been confiscated from border regions to prevent the Japanese from seizing them. As a result villages that had relied upon fishing began to struggle to feed themselves, farmers were no longer able to travel upstream to their paddy fields and it became much harder to move what rice supplies there were to the places that needed them most.

Soon entire families, weak with hunger, began to succumb to disease and corpses appeared on the streets. In Calcutta emaciated figures begged for scraps outside grand hotels where well-dressed and mostly white guests still enjoyed their gala dinners and Saturday night balls. The authorities attempted to organise relief camps and bring in fresh supplies of food, but the many pressures of war, the shortage of merchant ships and some bad flooding later in 1943 disrupted everything still further. Help was always late and inadequate and soon the scale of the misery was overwhelming. Letters reached Indian soldiers in North Africa and Italy revealing the desperation in their home villages, causing such anxiety that their officers pressed the authorities to do more. Clive Branson, a veteran of the Spanish Civil War, was now serving in India and what he saw appalled him: 'It is all very well to parade members of the 4th Indian Division around England but the sincerity of that praise wears a bit thin if those men's relatives are dying of hunger in the villages of Bengal.'

'I thought I was a sophisticated hard-boiled egg and could take a detached view of things,' wrote Satyen Basu, a doctor in the

Newspaper account of the Kangaw operation in English and Urdu, stressing the tenacity of British and Indian troops on the Arakan front in January 1945.

Royal Marines land on Cheduba Island in January 1945, as part of the Allied amphibious campaign along the Burmese coast.

Admiral Lord Louis Mountbatten congratulates some of the engineers who had built a Bailey Bridge over the River Chindwin, the longest ever attempted

'Hockey, cricket, football, tennis and squash?' Kodandera Subayya Thimayya, aka 'Timmy', as a young man.

'Indianisation' in action. British and Indian officers and their wives attend a typical regimental dinner, with typical wall hangings, during the 1920s.

A view of Quetta, Baluchistan, after the 1935 earthquake.

The Atlantic Charter

The President of The United States of America and the Prime Minister, Mr. *Churchill*, representing His Majesty's Government in The United Kingdom, being met together, deem it right to make known certain common principles in the national policies of their respective countries on which they base their hopes for a better future for the world.

1. *Their countries seek no aggrandizement, territorial or other.*

2. *They desire to see no territorial changes that do not accord with the freely expressed wishes of the peoples concerned.*

3. *They respect the right of all peoples to choose the form of government under which they will live; and they wish to see sovereign rights and self-government restored to those who have been forcibly deprived of them.*

4. *They will endeavor, with due respect for their existing obligations, to further the enjoyment by all States, great or small, victor or vanquished, of access, on equal terms, to the trade and to the raw materials of the world which are needed for their economic prosperity.*

5. *They desire to bring about the fullest collaboration between all nations in the economic field with the object of securing, for all, improved labor standards, economic advancement and social security.*

6. *After the final destruction of the Nazi tyranny, they hope to see established a peace which will afford to all nations the means of dwelling in safety within their own boundaries, and which will afford assurance that all the men in all the lands may live out their lives in freedom from fear and want.*

7. *Such a peace should enable all men to traverse the high seas and oceans without hindrance.*

8. *They believe that all of the nations of the world, for realistic as well as spiritual reasons, must come to the abandonment of the use of force. Since no future peace can be maintained if land, sea or air armaments continue to be employed by nations which threaten, or may threaten, aggression outside of their frontiers, they believe, pending the establishment of a wider and permanent system of general security, that the disarmament of such nations is essential. They will likewise aid and encourage all other practicable measures which will lighten for peace-loving peoples the crushing burden of armaments.*

Franklin D. Roosevelt

Winston S. Churchill

August 14, 1941

The Atlantic Charter: A bold vision of a world remade, August 1941.

'What they do in Europe does not strictly concern us.' Subhas Chandra Bose with Heinrich Himmler in Germany in the summer of 1942.

Hideki Tojo, Prime Minister of Japan (centre), meets leaders of the Great East Asia Co-Prosperity Sphere, including Bose (far right) in November 1943.

Japanese soldiers execute prisoners, likely Indian or Chinese, after taking Singapore.

Drawings and photographs of life in Kinkaseki camp and the nearby copper mine: A driller at work, a final letter home, prisoners' graves on the hillside.

> Signalman. G. Barber
> 2335228.
>
> Dear. Mam Dad & Family,
> Here's just to say I am safe and feeling quite well. Please try not to worry as I am keeping my chin up and patiently waiting the great day when we can be all together again. My love to Annie, Dith and baby. Tell Madge I love her and I am waiting to get home and be married tell her not to worry. Well this is all for now so cheerio
> From Your Everloving and Devoted Son.
> Gerard

new approach to jungle warfare. Australian troops use a light tank to attack Japanese positions in the battle for Buna, New Guinea, in early 1943.

'Apres Un Reve.'
Nurse Angela Noblet watches Lt Col Edward Lossing play chess with a patient.

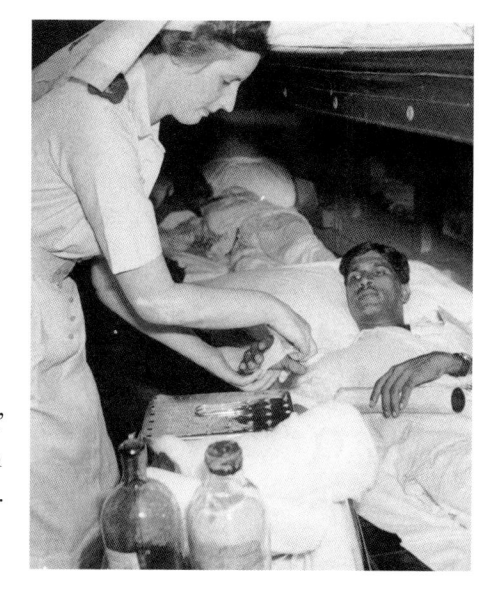

'A brotherhood of emaciated raggedness.' A New Zealand nurse treats an Indian patient on an ambulance train.

Subhas Chandra Bose between U-180 and Japanese submarine I-29 somewhere near Madagascar in April 1943.

Bose visits the Andaman Islands in December 1943.

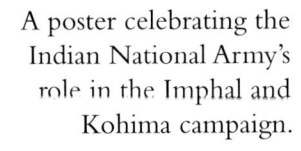

A poster celebrating the Indian National Army's role in the Imphal and Kohima campaign.

Indian Army, 'but witness a baby barely two years old lying in the lap of his brother of about six, both so devitalised that they are not able even to move from the street corner and biding their time to be shifted by somebody, sometime, alive or dead.'

Burma and Malaya had traditionally supplied rice to Bengal but, as Angela Noblet's fellow passenger had rightly pointed out, the Japanese had stopped all that. In the past so-called 'Famine Codes' had picked up early signs of distress and triggered official action. But as the crisis deepened during the first half of 1943 everything seemed to happen in slow motion, in glaring contrast to the intense activity in the war economy. Neighbouring regions did not rush food to Bengal for fear of running short themselves or – so it was whispered – because politically connected merchants wanted to keep the price up. Churchill's government did try to help but the issue took months to reach the top of the relevant in-trays in London. Hundreds of thousands of tons of grain then arrived in Bengal despite intense pressure on maritime resources and the threat of Japanese submarines. However, amid a general lack of urgency and 'grip', some of that food got caught up for weeks in bottlenecks at the ports and railway hubs. And still the people died. Churchill even appealed directly to Roosevelt for help with relief aid but the President said that he could not spare the shipping. Again, amid so many other priorities, the starvation of poor Bengalis never quite made it to the top of anyone's list.

The men who ran British India have received much furious criticism for the famine. But one of the least effective arms of the state was the democratically elected (albeit on a limited franchise) Bengali government of Khwaja Nizamuddin. Another Cambridge-educated politician, Nizamuddin would one day become Prime Minister of Pakistan. But in 1943 his administration was slow to transport food from areas of surplus into the worst affected parts of his region. After the war the celebrated Indian economist Amartya Sen studied all the available data about food production and storage in Bengal and other parts of the country in 1943. He concluded that there should have been enough in northern India to feed Bengal, but speculation, inflation and hoarding exposed the poorest class of people to fatal danger, and then officialdom didn't react decisively until it was much too late. Such was the dysfunction that India continued to *export* rice even as Bengalis starved. In charting the economic forces that shaped the Second World War historian Richard Overy also considered what happened in Bengal to be avoidable, an example of administrative oversight when faced with a familiar case of 'market distortion and uneven distribution' of a staple foodstuff. Food surpluses elsewhere in India — some lying tantalisingly close by — were not mobilised in time to do any good.

One key insight into the official British mindset comes from the letters of the governor of Bengal, John Herbert, a much more powerful man than Khwaja Nizamuddin. Herbert first played down the crisis, complaining about the 'bad press' it was generating and worrying that the huge number of wretched people trying to find a means to survive posed a security threat and a 'particular nuisance in areas where troops are concentrated'. Reading official communications such as Herbert's it is possible to see something else lying behind the tardiness — an ingrained acceptance of poverty and inequality as just 'an Indian thing', something natural, something baked into how the people in charge regarded life and death here. One day, perhaps just after riding in his official car through streets full of desperate human beings, Herbert wrote this:

> I hope we can get out some effective propaganda to counteract the present unhelpful tales of horror in the press which manifests itself largely in photographs which might have been taken in Calcutta at anytime during the last ten years.

You did not have to be a follower of Subhas Chandra Bose to recoil at such an attitude. And the obvious question that such comments prompted quickly appeared on a million lips: 'Does anyone doubt, were the victims white, that more would be done to help them?' All this horror unfolded a year after the chaotic retreat from Burma and just months after the 'Quit India' campaign had revealed the depth of support for independence — a triple catastrophe for the Raj. This was well understood by Archibald Wavell who took over as Viceroy in October 1943. He injected new energy into the relief effort and used the army to transport food into Bengal from areas of surplus, but the fight he had to get help from London depressed and infuriated him:

> I feel that the vital problems of India are being treated by His Majesty's Government with neglect, even sometimes with hostility and contempt . . . [the famine] is one of the greatest disasters that has befallen any people under British rule and damage to our reputation both among Indians and foreigners in India is incalculable.

There are some today who will tell you that Winston Churchill hated Indians and wanted them to die, actively *choosing* to starve Bengal out of sheer malice or as a twisted kind of revenge for the 'Quit India' campaign. Just about everything Churchill ever said was written down somewhere, along with lots of things that he might or might not have said. You can find ample evidence of his romantic, paternalistic love for India and plenty of his furious anger towards Indian nationalists and rebels. One day when particularly enraged about Gandhi, in a drunken snarl he infamously called Hinduism 'a beastly religion'. There are numerous examples, too, of how very old-fashioned views of India and Indians affected his thinking. At one point, he exploded with 'Muslims are warriors and Hindus are windbags'.

Churchill did not want Indians to starve but in the end it did come down to priorities. When describing his role in the famine the more sympathetic writers point to the unprecedented *scale* of the war effort being managed from London. Churchill's team had to organise supply convoys upon every ocean and numerous great campaigns on land, sea and air across multiple continents. Amid all of this — and with the future of the world in the balance — why would suffering in Bengal suddenly trump all other considerations? But now and again you can hear something else, something that lurked at the margin of this subject like an unwelcome spirit. It was the subtext of many conversations about the famine in both London and India and it went something like this:

> It's India. Famines happen there. There are too many people and a lot of them live on the margin of starvation even at the best of times. We are not heartless men. We do what we can and we do it better than anyone else. But we can't do everything. Oh, and there is a war on, don't you know?

When told of the need to rush food supplies to Greece in 1944 Churchill revealed a hierarchy of concern that was clearly based upon both racial prejudice and a caricature of Indians as helpless peasants: 'The starvation of anyway underfed Bengalis matters less than that of sturdy Greeks.' Indians didn't have to hear private conversations like that to know how the men at the top of the empire could sometimes dismiss their most pressing concerns. When released from house arrest and able to speak in public again, Gandhi immediately called what happened in Bengal 'a man-made famine'. Sucheta Kripalani, a future Congresswoman, damned 'the utter callousness with which the government behaved . . . perhaps one of the reasons that really drove iron into our souls'. Because if the British could not or would not manage the country primarily in the interest of Indians then they should stand down and let Indians themselves take their turn (and it is indeed worth noting here that there were no serious famines ever recorded in India after independence, although one did take place in Bangladesh in 1974).

Whether callous, careless or both, it was hard to deny the moral force of all this, especially if you claimed the right to govern this place based upon your ability to organise the essentials of life better than the people you ruled. A century earlier, when another natural disaster led to a nation-changing famine in rural Ireland, the British state was condemned both for a lack of action and for allowing prejudices about the rural Catholic Irish to undermine what limited action it did take. A famously angry leader column in the *Galway Vindicator*, written on New Year's Eve 1846, thundered that the London government's refusal to interfere in 'the market' of food

> puts to blush every feeling of humanity and libels the very name of Christian . . . It is, we repeat it, nothing less than the murder of the people . . . Even now [the authorities] seem inhumanly apathetic. Good God, was there ever such cruelty perpetrated before by any Government calling itself either civilised or Christian? Again we ask 'Must the people starve?'

Britain's reputation in Ireland is to this day affected by the way that question was answered. The long-term impact of the Bengal famine, and the way it was addressed, was not very much different. Because when the question 'must the people starve?' was asked once again the answer that came back was bleakly and sadly familiar.

Formosa, 1943

It mattered a very great deal to Captain Wakiyama that all of the prisoners under his control at Kinkaseki Camp came to understand the superiority of what he called 'Nippon culture'. So he required that they learn six words of Japanese every day. Given the importance of the morning roll call, Arthur Titherington decided to start with counting: *Ichi, ni, san, shi, go, roku, shichi* . . . and his own camp number, 466, or *yon roku roku*. After their first opportunity to practise these new words the men discovered what they were doing here high in the hills of north-eastern Formosa. They were to be copper miners. Issued with rubber-soled boots, cardboard helmets, shirts, shorts and miners' lamps, they were led out of the camp for the first time, apart from those still too weak from exhaustion, dysentery or diphtheria to leave the hospital hut. They walked in single file up a steep hill behind the camp from which they could see the Pacific Ocean stretching away from them towards the east. They then began a long, slow descent towards the mine entrance, following a line of rough stone steps. In time they would come to know these steps very well, and someone would go to the trouble of counting all 1,186 of them, in both English *and* Japanese.

At the entrance to the mine they were sent along a thousand-yard tunnel, illuminated by spluttering electric lights, walking on unstable boards that split and twisted underfoot, causing numerous sprained ankles and bruised knees, along with a familiar Anglo-Saxon curse repeatedly echoing in the darkness: 'Oh, fucking hell!' From this passage they descended a series of crude steps leading to numerous small chambers, which is where the bulk of their work would be done. Civilian 'blasters' came and went, setting off small explosions. The prisoners' job was to shovel and scoop the resulting rubble into bamboo baskets, drop it down a chute into small, wheeled bogies and then push the bogies out to a checkpoint to be counted against their day's quota. It was hot, the work was hard and their food consisted of two balls of cold rice contained in small wooden boxes, which they carried from the camp every morning. Once in their working 'holes' they were largely left to their own company. Their main worry was bad air in the depths of the mine, although they were alerted to this danger when their lamps began to splutter.

After a long climb back up the 1,186 steps and a final glimpse of the Pacific they settled in for their evening meal, lights out and the 'night watch', a system of self-guarding with one prisoner on duty at all times, for an hour each man. The guards checked in on them from time to time but there was never any thought of escape. Formosa had been a Japanese colony for many decades and as far as they knew most of the locals were perfectly happy with that. Certainly enough of them were employed in the mine. And even if a local family might help an escapee, where would they go? The nearest friendly base was thousands of miles across the ocean. Furthermore, Captain Wakiyama had made it very clear that if anyone escaped, or if anyone harmed a guard, the other prisoners would suffer for it.

The mine was hot and the men worked almost naked, but back at the camp it was usually cold and damp. They were supervised, endlessly counted and ordered to learn more Japanese. It was possible to go weeks without being mistreated, but then violence would flare up unexpectedly. A minor infringement of the rules, a failure to address someone correctly, a 'night watchman' caught asleep at his post and the face slapping would begin, generally followed by rifle butts or bamboo poles. Sometimes there was no obvious reason for the assaults, except perhaps the guards' heavy drinking. A door would suddenly fly open and they would rush in, hit as many men as possible then move on elsewhere. Arthur learned to roll with the punches. One day a Captain Sewell was attacked by a group of guards, apparently at random. He dared to complain to Wakiyama directly and to everyone's amazement – perhaps because Sewell was an officer – eight shamefaced Japanese men were brought before him, told to bow low and formally apologise.

Violence was endemic in the mine as well. The supervisors set quotas of ore to be extracted daily and if the men fell behind they were beaten with mining hammers. Some of the toughest supervisors were local Formosans. One of them, called 'the Eagle' by the prisoners, came upon Arthur one day resting on a pile of rubble. He used his poor Japanese to explain that the air was too bad to shovel rubble, but he was struck several times in reply. Others who failed to fulfil their quotas or who had been insufficiently grovelling in front of the supervisors were sent on 'punishment runs' up and down the hills. Two men subjected to this – Gunner Black and Lance Corporal Peterson – died shortly afterwards, two of at least fifty men that Titherington believed were killed directly by abuse in his first year at the camp. Others succumbed to mining accidents: one of his friends was hit by a falling rock that broke his back. Still more sustained cuts and fractures along 'Fucking Hell Tunnel' or when they fell down a ladder in the permanent gloom of the deep mine, injuries that could easily become infected. The camp hospital had few if any drugs with which to treat them.

Prisoners accused of small misdemeanours, already shattered by a day down the mine, were ordered to stand outside the guardroom holding weights until they collapsed, only to be beaten back to their feet again. Others were punished by being handcuffed to each other for days, meaning sleep became almost impossible, especially if one of them had 'the squits'. Arthur also saw men sent to the tiny 'ice box' to sit cross-legged and barely fed for days in an agony of cramp. When conditions at the mine deteriorated further the British officers complained that their work there was in flagrant breach of the rules of war. Wakiyama imprisoned them all on starvation rations for seventeen days until they publicly apologised in front of the entire camp, and accepted in writing that their treatment was fair and reasonable. They then had to sign a long, rambling letter in English full of praise for the camp commander and his men:

> We now see showing ourselves totally lacking consciousness and insulting Nippon and her soldiers . . . We are ashamed and feel sorry for Nippon and Nippon army and the Commander and forgetting the teaching he has generously given to us. We must now restore our honour. All mistakes in the past have been our fault and we now request clean slate after such an unpleasant incident.

Another of the commander's furious outbursts occurred when a prisoner rested a broom on the large map of Japanese military conquests painted on a wall. For this 'disrespect to Nippon', Wakiyama beat the man to the ground, sent him to the ice box and then insisted that every other prisoner stood before the map, saluting it and bowing low. The idea that Japan was replacing Britain as the 'top dog' in Asia obsessed him. In another of his many speeches he said: 'All time England say Nippon coolie. Now you all coolie and will work like coolie. You will be punished like coolie.' It seemed very important to him that the men under his control were not only submissive but also permanently grateful, no matter how badly they were treated: 'You must stop complaining about your food and losing your weight. You are prisoners because you have lost the war and you are not here for recreation. You should think yourselves lucky your lives are assured in this camp.'

Arthur Titherington spent much of the rest of his life thinking about cruelty and control, and why the men who dominated his life at Kinkaseki were not only so arbitrarily brutal but also so completely *strange* about it. The cliché of the Samurai spirit, and its famous disdain for any man who surrenders in combat, didn't explain it to his satisfaction. Most of the Japanese he encountered, including Wakiyama himself, were hardly Samurai warriors, more like the scrapings of the military reject pile with their bad teeth, poor eyesight and puny bodies. He came to believe that Japan was led by totalitarian fanatics who believed their moment had come to build an empire on the humiliated bodies of those who had once ruled the East. Perhaps they had conveyed this passion for subjugation to everyone in the chain of command. That made more sense to him and explained some of what he experienced. But some of the cruellest overseers were not even Japanese, they were local Formosans, and they could be almost as savage to each other as they were to the prisoners, with any disobedience, disrespect or even a sign of original thinking receiving instant punishment.

> Even the average Japanese soldier was frightened, bullied and humiliated by his superiors. We just happened to be at the end of a vicious line, just like thousands of Chinese, Koreans and others ... it wasn't a single sadistic NCO we were up against but a system, men who didn't seem to have any sense of their own individuality, maturity or independence of mind.

The men that he studied — even as they held the power of life and death over him — were all intensely *unstable*, permanently on the brink of an emotional or violent outburst like angry teenagers, and driven by a passion for 'saving face' in all circumstances by taking out their frustrations and rage on the next person below them in the hierarchy. And prisoners like Arthur were at the very base of it.

The Palm and the Pine

Subhas Chandra Bose was not the only rebel to benefit from a world-class education offered by this empire to those it ruled. Many of the people who went on to govern India after independence spent their formative years in Britain and it was in British universities that an ideology of decolonisation began to flourish, ideas that also inspired a generation of leaders across Africa. For every Curzon or Kipling there was a Keynes, a Bertrand Russell or an H. G. Wells, and even Kipling saw the darker side of imperialism by the end. Indian prime ministers Jawaharlal Nehru and his daughter Indira (later Indira Gandhi) attended Cambridge and Oxford respectively (and Nehru went to the highly exclusive Harrow public school before that) while Pakistan's first Governor General, Mohammed Ali Jinnah, studied law at London's Lincoln's Inn. Arguably the ancient colleges of Oxbridge, at the heart of the power structure of imperial Britain, contributed more to the decolonisations of the twentieth century than did the revolutionary agenda of the Communist International.

Even in Queen Victoria's time, critics of empire were almost as numerous as romantic cheerleaders, and they crossed pens in the 'culture wars' of their day. By the time *Pax Britannica* reached its Edwardian heyday its defenders felt they had to justify themselves — in arguments that still echo today — by claiming that this great enterprise was about much more than power and wealth. That it was a true *exchange* between the governors and the governed, a civilising mission that built railway stations, municipal palaces and fine libraries, imposed liberal values and fair-minded judges, and educated the brightest young subjects of the King-Emperor. And in some places colonial government could indeed mean the creation of an effective and secure civic society and a life free from aggressive despots – for those prepared to accept the white man's rule. Bose's story reveals much about the British style of repression at this time. Some very harsh things were done to him but alongside that there was always an invitation to talk, the first step to that 'seduction' he denounced in his broadcasts from Berlin. The men running India were more than willing to hang radical young Indians who turned to violence, and had done much more brutal things in the nineteenth and eighteenth centuries, but the coercion was sporadic and certainly in no way comparable to what happened in Nazi Germany or Stalin's Russia where a troublemaker like Bose would have been in a grave not at an ancient university. Of course, 'Not being as bad as Hitler or Stalin' hardly justifies hundreds of years of British rule in India, but it is surely a factor in how we judge the 1940s there, and the choices that independence-minded Indians like Timmy and Bose had to make.

But there's a real complacency, too, in some of the more positive British commentary on this subject. As if the generally warm relationship between the United Kingdom of the twenty-first century and its former colonies proves that *our* kind of imperialism was better than everyone else's. There's a telling episode of the classic documentary series *End of Empire* about Iran and the coup of 1953, filmed in the early 1980s when most of the powerful men of that era were still lucid, frank and surprisingly brazen. It's easily found online. What shines through are cold calculation and smooth ruthlessness. Promises are broken and lives are sacrificed thanks to a blend of old-school imperial swagger, the need to guarantee energy security at an uncertain moment and, of course, profits for the oil companies. In these voices it's easy to hear a rather chilling tone, the sly realpolitik that Britain was known for in many parts of the world and which, from time to time, also characterised its colonial policies towards the end of the Second World War.

All this matters because Subhas Chandra Bose wasn't the only person who saw Britain like this. Much of the rest of the world did so, too, however much they liked to play cricket and however many of their children they sent to Oxford and Cambridge. Many British people are so in love with the 'underdog' version of the Second World War – Dunkirk, rationing, the Blitz and 'the Few' – that they fail to understand that much of the planet never once looked at their country in that way, and for good reason. Britain was more often seen as the *over*-dog, and a bully to be feared. It was the cynical political agent, the secret policeman and the squaddie putting his size ten boot through your front door. A superpower with interests to be defended with battleships, bayonets and vast global resources. Any fair reckoning of this empire or this war needs to accommodate that. Military doctor Captain Harry Walker, who served in both India and Burma wrote:

> we were so very pious and holy – holding up our hands in horror at the things the Nazis did. Yet all the time we had India in a perfect grip. People were thrown into jail in their thousands without trial, for merely holding some political views the government disliked.

The widespread dislike of Britain explains why Japan's initial victories came as such a thrill to millions of colonial subjects. It also endlessly complicated Churchill's relationship with Roosevelt's America, the America of the New Deal and the Four Freedoms, something that Subhas Chandra Bose understood very well. Back in 1940 the mostly liberal and progressive American writers flocking to London did not feel much natural sympathy for Britain, nor saw it as necessarily superior in a moral sense to Hitler's Germany or Mussolini's Italy, no matter how shocking that may sound to us today. 'New Dealers' of the type that backed Roosevelt blamed Britain for oppressing half the world and for helping usher in the Great Depression with selfish imperial trade policies. That changed when reporters, politicians and the wider American public swung decisively towards Britain as it struggled on alone against Hitler, seeing it now as a plucky fighter against fascist terror bombing and Nazi tyranny rather than a tough imperial overlord. In truth, though, it was always both.

Tokyo, Singapore and Nanking, 1943

From his new office in Tokyo, Subhas Chandra Bose was busy planning a revolution. By the middle of 1943, Allied troops were in Sicily and the US Navy had the upper hand in the Pacific, but Japan's hold on South East Asia felt secure for a while longer, and maybe a while is all the time Bose needed. Between Singapore and Calcutta lived some two to three million Indian expatriates, many of whom Bose believed could be drawn to his cause. Some were prisoners of war but there were also business people, farm and factory workers, shopkeepers, traders and technicians who had stayed on when the Japanese took charge and who were, by and large, living unmolested lives. Many of them had supported Indian independence before the war or were in parties that were linked to Bose himself, and all had heard of him and his many adventures. He now wanted them to join — or at least *fund* — his new version of the Indian National Army and help him liberate India itself. One glorious display of bravery, he fervently believed, was all it would take to ignite a national rebellion right across their homeland.

The extended underwater rehearsals on board *U-180* paid off and Bose's meeting with Tojo was a great success. He told the Japanese leader that he should never underestimate the desire of the ordinary Indian to be free, and to use that as a lever to destroy British power in the region. He promised that a joint INA–Japanese military operation on the India–Burma border would not only be a clever way to damage their mutual enemy but would also burnish Japan's image throughout the world. He continued to broadcast to India every few days, urging millions listening to illicit radio stations to prepare for a critical moment when 'every patriotic Indian must advance towards the field of battle ... for only when the blood of freedom-loving Indians begins to flow will India attain her freedom.'

More recruits flocked to his cause and on 5 July 1943 he was able to stand before twelve thousand of them, all wearing the uniform of the INA, outside Singapore's Supreme Court, one of the British Empire's grandest buildings. They marched with a precision that would have impressed Sandhurst's toughest drill sergeants and then Bose told them that from this day forward they were no longer volunteers, prisoners or civilians but *citizens* of a brand-new nation, serving in the first true army that India had possessed since the eighteenth century. He promised that they would soon go into battle under Indian leadership making decisions based upon Indian priorities. This wasn't entirely what the Japanese military understood the relationship to be, for Bose had to rely on others for weapons, transport and much more besides, but on this exhilarating day nobody was going to challenge him on the details. Instead, a full-throated cheer rang out over this former imperial fortress, as Bose introduced his men to their new battle cry: *Chalo Delhi* – 'Onwards to Delhi!' – and then made a solemn promise: 'If you follow me in life and in death – as I am confident that you will – I shall lead you to victory and freedom.'

It must have been intoxicating, the culmination of a life of sacrifice and struggle. Bose the warrior-prophet finally standing before the ranks of his army, behind which now stood an impressive political and social movement stretching across thousands of miles and dozens of territories. Shah Nawaz Khan, who would become one of the Red Fort defendants, was there and recalled that 'I was hypnotised by his personality and his speeches. He placed the true picture of India before us, and for the first time in my life I saw India through the eyes of an Indian.' By August 1943 the INA could call on some 60,000 fighting men, supported by thousands of branches of Bose's Indian Independence League that were springing up across Japanese-occupied South East Asia. Of his troops about two-thirds were ex-prisoners who had rescinded their vows of loyalty to the British crown and these men set about teaching the 20,000 civilian volunteers the rudiments of modern war. He had an intelligence division, a female-only volunteer force, the famous Rani of Jhansi Regiment, named for a warrior-queen from the 1857 uprising, and his own press and broadcast departments. The INA would add real combat power to any attack on the British-led troops guarding the India–Burma border and, critically, Bose was convinced, it would lend it an irresistible *moral* force as well. He predicted that the troops of the official Indian Army would be most reluctant to fight against their brothers – sometimes, as with Timmy, their *actual* brothers – in the INA and he expected mass desertions to his cause to begin the moment battle commenced.

Bose's organisation clearly had some fascistic overtones, but it contained other and more attractive elements, too. He continually looked to boost female representation in public life and, unlike other mainstream politicians operating in India itself, his commitment to non-sectarianism was consistent and impressive. It's not hard to see why he was so popular with Indian émigrés. Indeed, sympathy for Bose and his army ran so deep in the civilian population inside Japanese-occupied Burma that one INA officer discovered that 'if you did not greet local Indians with *Jai Hind* they would not accept you as an Indian and would treat you as a foreigner'.

To further ratchet up support, Bose travelled across the region without pause, identifying Malaya, Thailand and Indochina, all with large and successful Indian expatriate communities, as important sources of recruits and finance. He spoke to and recruited Indians from the Philippines and East Indies, too, and then attended a formal ceremony marking Burmese independence (albeit an independence under Japanese military protection). There he proclaimed how thrilling it was to breathe the air of an independent country that had until recently been suffering under British rule, as his own still did. Finally, in October 1943, on behalf of what he called the Provisional Government of Free India, Bose took the final step, officially declaring that this new nation was at war with both the United Kingdom and the United States. He had previously tried to avoid any open conflict with the Americans, but the US Army Air Force was now in India (largely as a transit route to the campaign in China) and it was likely that any border campaign would lead to American air attacks on INA units. Bose's new government was immediately recognised by Germany, Japan, Italy and all the other Axis powers of Eastern Europe and he received a telegram of congratulation from his old friend Éamon de Valera in Dublin. In front of an even larger crowd in Singapore he promised to 'set foot on the holy soil of India before the end of this year'. He encouraged Indians from anywhere in the world to register as citizens of his new state and many hundreds of thousands did just that, swearing an oath to both Indian freedom and the leadership of Bose. The parades, the flags, the war cries, the cult of personality – it wasn't hard to see a model. But he was a man in a hurry who'd chosen his allies and there could be no going back now.

As if to emphasise that, he decided to visit the Chinese city of Nanking as a guest of some pro-Japanese militia leaders there, and while in this city he spoke of Asian unity and universal Asian values. It was an astonishing thing for him to do. Everyone who could read a newspaper or a magazine in the late 1930s – let alone be on the cover of one, as Bose had been – knew what the Japanese army had done in that city during a six-week rampage that went down in infamy as the Nanking Massacre or, more accurately, the Rape of Nanking. Finding themselves in complete control of a civilian enemy population, the soldiers of Emperor Hirohito indulged in crimes that even now are too upsetting to recount in detail. Coming from a society renowned then and now for its discipline and decorum, something truly bestial took hold of these men as they targeted young and old, and especially women and children, and inflicted upon them acts of sexual violence on a scale as spectacular as it was stomach-turning. Burying people alive, rape with sword and broken bottle, disembowelment, the torture of children, mass drownings . . .

there is nothing vicious and vile that the human mind can imagine that wasn't done in this city, and done with a celebratory relish. Some Japanese officers even competed to get the highest kill scores. And these atrocities took place not in the initial 'hot blood' of victory but slowly and systematically during weeks of intense and unrestrained sadism. That Asian men did all of this to other Asians in Nanking made Bose's decision to speak about unity and shared values there all the more remarkable.

In December the Japanese took him to Port Blair in the Andaman Islands, where for the first time he hoisted the flag of an independent India over territory that had been freed from British rule. The flagpole wasn't far from the spot where Major Bird had been executed. Bose is now so integrated into the story of Indian independence that, in 2023, the *Times of India* published an article celebrating the eightieth anniversary of this ceremony:

> Netaji Subhas Chandra Bose, being the relentless freedom fighter that he was, hoisted the Indian flag in Port Blair in 1943, long before India won independence. This was done to declare Port Blair free from British rule. If that was not one of the most incredible acts of defiance during the Indian freedom struggle, we don't know what was.

It was certainly an act of defiance, but it was also — inescapably — a propaganda effort on behalf of the empire that had replaced the British on these islands. And their rule was to be every bit as brutal and arbitrary as the Raj at its worst. Just a month after Bose's visit forty-four Indian civilians were shot without trial by the Japanese army in what was called the Homfreyganj massacre. Most of them were members of Bose's own Indian Independence League but the nominal governor he had appointed could do nothing to save them. It's one of many hundreds of examples of extra-judicial killings and torture that took place on the Andaman Islands, even though, as far as the outside word was told, they were now formally under the flag of a free India.

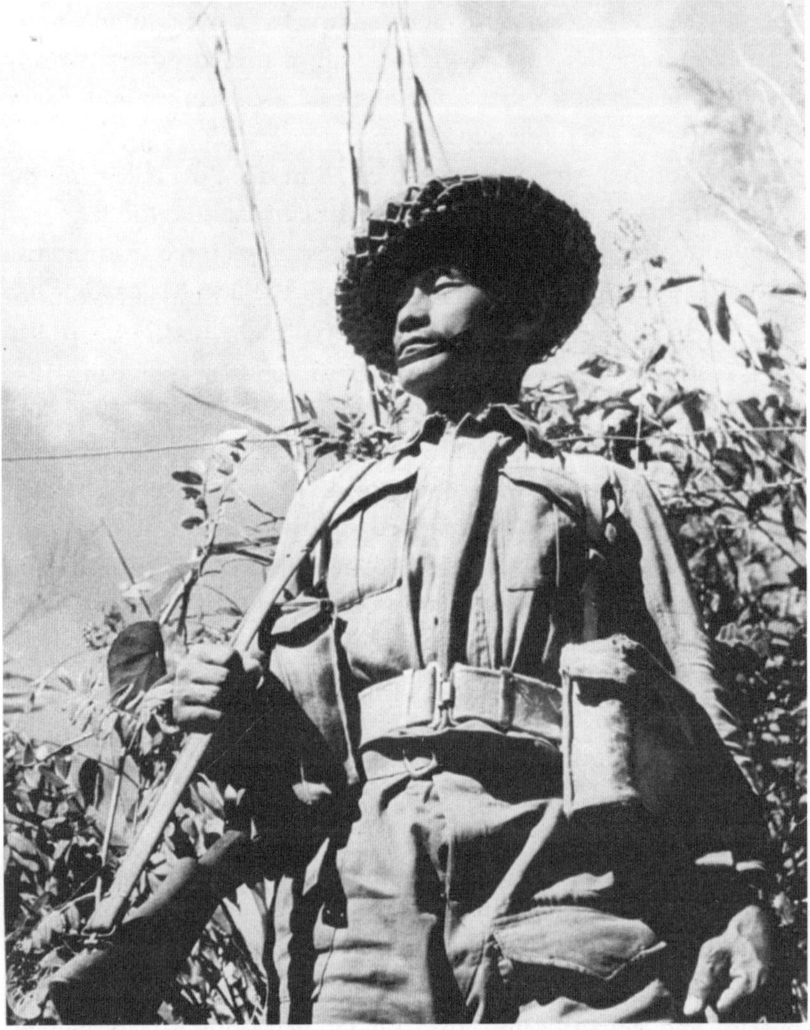

7

The Trailblazers

Australia, 1943–1944

Even as famine devastated Bengal a military revolution began to transform the Indian Army and at the heart of it was Australia. Along the Kokoda Track in New Guinea in 1942 and then at 'Bloody Buna' at the beginning of 1943, the Australian Army fought and defeated the kind of determined Japanese troops who had driven all before them at the start of the war. The Australians learned many painful but important lessons and immediately tried to pass them on through what would become the most famous jungle warfare school in the world. Thousands of men trained in the green, wet, mountainous hinterland of Queensland around the Beechmont Plateau, honing survival and fighting skills in an environment that closely resembled New Guinea. Experts from the school travelled widely and British and Indian troops soon benefited from their experience.

It was as much about attitude adjustment as learning new survival or fighting skills. British- and Australian-born commanders had come to fear fighting in the jungle, as if nature itself was in some kind of strange alliance with the enemy. During the disastrous Malaya and Burma campaigns, whenever Japanese soldiers infiltrated through static defensive lines they immediately spread panic. Being attacked unexpectedly from all sides at once was a frightening and disorienting experience for officers who had learned their war-fighting skills on Salisbury Plain. Decent and defensible positions were abandoned time and time again in search of the psychological comfort of a new line, one that would quickly, in its turn, be bypassed by a fast-moving enemy. And British commanders felt a constant need for a permanent physical link to their support bases in the rear and so would generally send a column back from every new position. Their Japanese opposite numbers quickly learned to exploit this habit, manoeuvring silently onto the route then waiting, armed and ready, for the Indian Army trucks to appear. All this fed into a deepening spiral of defeatism as the idea spread that the Japanese had produced a race of irresistible super-soldiers. But what if the Allies could develop a style of warfare that turned the realities of the jungle to their *own* advantage and left the Japanese to deal with its harsher side?

In New Guinea the Japanese were beaten partly as a result of the changing balance of supply. Australia was close and Japan very far away. But confident forward patrolling, better radios, improved medical care, the use of light tanks and portable artillery, more effective airborne reconnaissance and an ever-increasing number of Allied fighter-bombers and supply aircraft all added to a new 'jungle toolkit'. Especially important was changing everyone's ideas about what the term 'front line' actually meant. A Japanese unit that moved beyond your position was not necessarily a fatal threat. In fact, if you had a reasonable quantity of supplies – and could perhaps be 'topped up' from above – then the force that had just gone around you was the one that was now cut off. It would at some point have to go somewhere else in search of supplies of its own or, if it didn't move, then it would quickly fall victim to the jungle itself, through the many diseases and infections that endlessly threatened both sides. Major General John 'Tubby' Lethbridge, who was to become Slim's Chief of Staff in 1944, toured Queensland and was excited by what he saw there.

> The Australians have seen more fighting against the Japanese than anybody else, and are morally absolutely on top. They

are confident, man for man, they can beat the Japanese anywhere, and at any time. Their ideas on training are eminently sound, and they have all facilities for training large numbers. I am convinced that very serious consideration should be given to using existing Australian experiences and facilities for training British instructors for British troops in jungle warfare.

British and Indian junior officers travelled to Queensland, too, and were equally impressed, while the Indian Army High Command tried to get six hundred experienced Australians transferred to India, not for combat but simply for lecturing. It only ever received 168 of them but they proved to be a huge asset, helping the army develop its new mantra of 'Training, Training and More Training'. All of the many new Indian recruits did a nine-month basic course and then eight more weeks of enhanced 'battlefield inoculation' with a focus on combined operations in dense jungle: fighting in 'close terrain', aggressive patrolling, ambush preparation, navigation, hygiene, bivouacking, forward air control – in short, everything that could make the combat zone feel less alien. The Indians then opened two new specialist schools of their own, very much run on the Australian model. Claude Auchinleck, the Indian Army's new Commander-in-Chief, pushed these changes through with great energy and personally rewrote the training syllabus taught to all newly volunteering *jawans*. If the Australians had first challenged the Japanese army's aura of invincibility, Auchinleck was convinced that his men would be the ones to destroy it forever.

The 'Chindit' expeditions by 14th Army deep behind Japanese lines also helped build confidence and knowledge. General Slim was never convinced that missions like these would be enough to retake Burma but they did demonstrate that columns of Allied troops could live, travel and fight in hostile territory. And, just as happened with the Australians, important details were quickly tabulated and shared, such as the need to cut the vocal cords of any transport mules that travelled with the army, lest their braying alert the enemy. Slowly but surely the British, Indians and Australians started to see themselves as fighting in tune with the jungle, while the Japanese began to fear it.

India and Burma, 1943

'You're Timmy, aren't you? Well, thank God you've come!'

It was good to feel wanted and the colonel's greeting was warm and sincere. Timmy was now a major although already 'acting' as a lieutenant colonel. He was also fresh out of Staff College and ready to help lead the 25th Division of the Indian Army into Burma. Both officers and men needed more training, but it was immediately clear to Timmy that morale and organisation had improved dramatically since the miserable early months of the war.

> I had never seen military activity on such a vast scale . . . The prospect of having responsibility for this chaos was terrifying. Long lines of lorries, columns of troops, and masses of unfamiliar equipment were moving frantically in every direction . . . But I learned that the traffic, far from being confused, was moving with a miraculous efficiency.

At 25th Division 'efficiency' was the watchword. Timmy and the other senior officers practised manoeuvres with thousands of men, carefully ticking all the many boxes that a successful operation on this scale required: artillery transport, supplies for the mobile cookhouse, water purification, latrine digging, ammunition for the rifles and morphine for the medics. The daily routine of every unit was scheduled as near to perfection as military science allowed. They fought mock battles against another division, practised forced marches, jungle bivouacs, 'shoot-and-scoot' ambushes and methods of calling in air support. Timmy was soon on excellent terms with the other officers – the usual mix of Indian and British – and felt confident about the challenge ahead. The only issue was his immediate superior, General 'Taffy' Davies. Timmy soon discovered that he had not been the general's first choice for this post and, as the weeks progressed, he suspected that this was the reason his work was attracting such a high level of scrutiny.

Personal vendettas were traditional in the Indian Army, as much part of its unique culture as playing polo, shooting tigers, amateur dramatics and adultery. So much so that one of the questions in the interwar exams directly addressed the problem, challenging would-be staff officers to summon up all the tact, diplomacy and ingenuity they could muster when dealing with a difficult superior.

You are 2Lt A. BRICK-DROPPER, 14th Rumbelbellypore Light Infantry (the Bengal Bewaqufs).

On August 9th last you were Orderly Officer and therefore not allowed to leave barracks.

Nevertheless, on that day, during the absence of your commanding officer Lieut-Col. Currey-Puff, OBE, you without his permission took out hunting his very valuable horse named Threelegs. Unfortunately in attempting an ambitious fence, you brought down the horse and broke its leg. It has since been destroyed.

Your C.O. :-

(a) Dislikes you intensely.
(b) Values the horse highly.
(c) Knows you are heavily in debt.

REQUIRED FOR EXAM.

A letter informing Lieut-Col Currey-Puff of the occurrence.

Always a stickler for hard work and detail, and an officer who drove himself as hard as he ever drove his men, Timmy was no brick-dropper. But still he felt that whatever he did for General Davies was never quite good enough, and he couldn't help wondering why, in the words of the staff exam, he disliked him so intensely. Was it because he was the older man's second or third choice, or was it really all about the colour of his skin? Timmy respected the hierarchies of rank as much as the next officer, but he was also more than capable of making his feelings known when he didn't think that something was right — and soon his own bristling animosity towards his commander was evident to one and all. The simmering tension between the two men came to a head when the general's driver became confused during one of their training exercises and his jeep took a wrong turn. Flying into a rage, Davies immediately decided to blame Timmy's team for producing a set of incorrectly marked maps. It wasn't true, as all the other officers present knew very well, but the momentary confusion gave the general an opportunity to berate Timmy in public and he took it with some relish and at some volume. Stung by the unfairness of the criticism, Timmy withdrew with an angry and obvious scowl. A few hours later, as he wondered whether his time at 25th Division might already be up, he received a most unexpected invitation to join Davies for a nightcap.

'Timmy, I understand you were upset about what happened this morning.'
'Yes Sir, so much so that I do not want to stay here and I'm prepared to chuck my commission. What happened this morning was not my fault, Sir, quite frankly, it was yours. If you don't

want an Indian on your staff, that's okay with me, I'll leave, and no I do not want a Scotch!'

'Look Timmy, I've served my whole life in the Indian Army. I've got nothing either for or against Indian officers. You have an inflated opinion of yourself and you're too damned sensitive. You fancy you can lead this division better than I. When you find you can't your tender little feelings are hurt. You want to run off and hide. But I know you're a good officer and I'll be happy if you stay.'

It wasn't exactly an apology but it was said with a smile that was almost avuncular. And, now that his temper had subsided a little, Timmy did recognise an element of truth in the older man's words. However unkind his treatment, had he perhaps been prickly and over-sensitive in return? And did he really want to be the kind of officer who stormed off in a 'huff' when the going got tough? Not so much a Lt BRICK-DROPPER as a Lieut-Col FOOT-STAMPER.

Almost without realising it, he found himself smiling back at his general, and then slowly extending his hand towards the proffered whisky glass.

India, 1943–1944

For Angela Noblet the thrill of first love was quickly followed by the agony of first separation.

> Seated in the corner of a two-berth sleeper of the Darjeeling mail train on the way to Gauhati, a sense of isolation and depression swept through me and I burst into a torrent of tears, to the consternation of the middle-aged Jewish woman who shared the compartment with me. Asansol has become my home, the abode of the first person I have truly loved and who has loved

me in return. Now I am destined to travel, friendless and alone, to a new life in a strange country called Assam, six hundred miles away.

The order for her to move closer to the front line was a sign that her Matron thought she was a high-quality nurse suitable for the most intense duties. There was nothing that her commanding officer could do to keep them together and it would have been against the rules that governed both their lives for him even to try. Although very much missing Teddy, Angela's morale quickly improved when she met the other nursing staff at Gauhati. There was her friend Mary King, who she had thought the most beautiful girl on the *Monarch of Bermuda*, although also the shyest, and several others she had grown close to on board the ship. Their hair now bleached by the sun, they called themselves 'the Blondes' or, when feeling flirtatious, 'the Harem'. They all volunteered to perform in a revue at the local theatre in front of resting troops, which included a most salacious dance that Angela called 'delightfully shocking'. It featured a prim and proper-looking nurse (unnamed in the diary) parading modestly around the stage to the words:

She was such a shy maiden, her looks were downcast,
With an innocent air, like a maid from the past.
A sweet girlie like that was a pleasure to find . . .
. . . but what a naughty young lady she was round behind!

At this final line she spun around, raised her skirt and revealed bright scarlet underwear, as the audience stamped and cheered its approval.

Letters flew between Gauhati and Teddy's various new postings along the Burmese border. They were able to meet at least once before Angela, after a close encounter with an outbreak of smallpox, and then an emergency vaccination against that terrifying disease, was struck with dengue fever for the second time, laying her low for weeks. When she recovered she was soon back working in wards that were growing busier as the tempo of fighting increased. At Asansol she'd tended to serious battlefield wounds but, being so far from the front line, she had rarely faced the immediate trauma of casualty evacuation. It was different here.

'Can you take these dressing trays to the basha right now?'

'There are no day reports written yet, it's all on the hoof tonight with more coming in. There's an officer going into theatre right now, can you assist?'

'Captain Magid, both his legs blown off but they think they might save his arms. Can you hold him while I do the injections? Steady, steady, hold tight I need to find a vein.'

'I think he's gone, sister.'

And it was not only the wounds that were fresher here. So, too, was the shock.

'My mate copped it. Please write to my mother and tell her I was brave.'

'Sarge had his top half blown off in that lot. His jaw just flew off his face.'

Nurse Mary King played a full part in these nerve-shredding days. And she was also keeping a diary, one that began with sentiments not unlike the ones at the opening of Angela Noblet's own journal.

I resolve:
To write decent letters
To be 'sensible' about George
To get slimmer, or rather less fat (exercise etc.) and fit.

Mary's style was much more 'note form' than Angela's but there's the same mixture of gritty medical detail, romantic entanglements and sheer exhaustion.

Sunday:
I must be changing – I'm thinking quite seriously about marrying Murray. Asked Leader and Carter if they thought it ridiculous to marry someone so young. Read afternoon.
Tuesday:
Night duty . . .
Pretty busy. Casualties. One boy frightfully ill.
Wednesday:
Beastly day – shopped – bought white shoes.
Monday:
Didn't sleep much . . .
Very busy night – Roger died at 11ish. 'Last offices.'
Felt awfully tired.
Friday:
17 patients today – it's going to be hard work.
Col. very polite and helpful – he is awfully attractive!
Not a minute to breathe all night – slept all day.

But then both women witnessed a miracle. A soldier came in with a deep bacterial infection of his wounded leg, resistant to all their normal sulphonamides. It looked like an amputation case but then a surgeon called Major Niblock announced that he was going to try a new drug that had arrived at the hospital just that week; it was called 'penicillin'. Within three hours Angela could see an improvement and by the end of the day all 'the Blondes' gathered around to inspect the recovering patient, astonished that a dangerous, raging infection like that could ever recede so quickly. Five days later a man who would have certainly lost his leg the week before was cheerfully walking around the hospital grounds with a stick, thanking every doctor and nurse he met. More penicillin arrived but they were advised to limit it to only the most serious cases.

Angela was proud of her nursing in this high-pressure hospital. One day she spotted a tiny tick, the size of a lentil, embedded in the armpit of a mysteriously sick soldier she was bathing, and correctly delivered a diagnosis of scrub typhus, getting him the prompt treatment which probably saved his life. Later she had the great pleasure of writing to the man's mother to tell her that her son was recovering well. But the pressure was relentless, and telling. With the wards once again all but overwhelmed with seriously injured men, she got into an argument with an Indian orderly who was refusing to help carry a patient assigned to another man. In a sudden fury, she slapped him hard across the face. A shouting match erupted and then they both stormed out of the hospital.

> I was too ashamed to tell my colleagues what I had done and as soon as I was off duty I went to see the man's sergeant major and told him the whole story. 'Sister sahib do not apologise,' he admonished me, 'You English always apologising. You must say nothing. I will move him to another ward but please do not go alone around the camp for a few weeks.' He made a movement as though he held a dagger in his hand. 'It is a great disgrace for a man to be struck by a woman.'

Thinking about the incident made her realise that she had no way of communicating with Indian people except in English, which may have contributed to her confrontation on the ward. She resolved to learn some Urdu.

Outraged orderlies were not the only reason to fear the dark. Rumours swirled about men loyal to Subhas Chandra Bose out looking for British men and women to murder or take hostage. At night she was sure to grasp her surgical scissors firmly in case she suddenly needed to defend herself. A much-discussed but frustratingly unsolved murder of a British nurse at another military hospital in Assam only heightened the tension. Relief came with a chance to visit the Himalayas with Teddy, staying at the famous Lopchu Tea Estate between the beautiful towns of Darjeeling and Kalimpong. The air, she wrote, 'tasted like wine' and they rekindled their romance amid beautiful gardens, long healthy hill walks and views of the magnificent, unconquered Everest in the distance. Teddy was showing signs of strain, she noted, and looked painfully thin. 'The responsibility of setting up two large hospitals during the campaigning has taken a toll of his health.'

Here she gained another insight into colonial life. They met a friendly tea plantation manager, a Mr Creas from Scotland, who had recently married a local young woman called Jeti despite the fact that she was nineteen and he was over sixty. The age difference alone might have prompted criticism but what made Angela furious was the reaction of all the other white women she met. An affair with a young girl, she discovered, was considered completely natural, as would be 'keeping' one of them as a live-in mistress. But actually marrying not only an Indian but an Indian who had once worked on a plantation picking tea, and then introducing her to the community as some kind of a social equal ... well that was considered so shocking that Jeti was being shunned by one and all.

Angela befriended Jeti and they travelled into town for a spoiling day at the cinema, hairdressers and beauty parlour. To her surprise she discovered that the teenager appeared happy and entirely devoted to her husband, content with her isolation and very conscious of the fact that she would one day inherit rather a lot of money, which caused Angela to smile. Indians might not be running their country yet, but she imagined that Jeti might soon be higher up the social ladder of Darjeeling than the white women who were presently refusing her tea and cake.

Burma, 1944

In early 1944 Timmy's 25th Division was ordered forward to Arakan on the north-west coast of Burma. They were there to replace the 5th Indian Division, which was being sent north to help block any Japanese advance towards Imphal and Kohima. The 5th had recently taken part in a campaign in Arakan that many hoped would mark a turning point, and Timmy was instructed to study it in great detail. During what was called the Battle of the Admin Box, the Indian Army had beaten off a substantial Japanese attack, employing the latest jungle warfare tactics, including the tanks of the 25th Dragoons and a much-improved system of air support and supply. It was the first substantial victory of a British-led army over the Japanese since the war had begun and it suggested that Timmy's opponents could now only sustain a relatively short period of intense combat before running short of ammunition, medicine and food. This was largely because Japan's air power was dwindling and its system of logistical and medical support was nothing like as comprehensive or efficient as that now enjoyed by every Indian division. The excellent Spitfire Mark Vs of the RAF did much damage to what remained of the Japanese air force above the Admin Box and with longer range P-51 Mustangs and P-38 Lightnings arriving from the USA during 1944, the British would soon have effective control of the skies over the key border battlegrounds and much of Burma, too. A note found on the body of a dead Japanese officer after the battle read: 'We see planes bringing butter, beer, cheese, jam, beef and eggs in great quantities to the enemy and meanwhile I am starving.' Japanese wounded were found lying untreated in their trenches while the Indian Army's casualties received high-quality battlefield attention or were on their way to clean, well-supplied hospitals staffed by the likes of Angela Noblet and Mary King within a few hours. There they might receive penicillin or any number of other new medical treatments and techniques.

All this meant that Timmy's men were in high spirits as they travelled by train and lorry to Maungdaw, a Burmese coastal town recently seized by the 5th Division. Here the road became an ill-defined jungle path as dust clogged their lungs and coated their uniforms. Looking east, they could see the Mayu Hills beyond which another Indian Division, the 26th, was moving south towards the valley town of Buthidaung. Their job was to keep up with that movement, travelling parallel along the coast. But the Japanese were still in Buthidaung and, despite their recent defeat, had dug themselves deeply into the steep hillsides all around. Timmy found himself sitting on some logs by a jungle track alongside General Davies — with whom he was now on rather better terms — when they both heard the scream of an incoming shell.

> I leapt into a trench with an alacrity that came from years of hockey playing. In my seventeen years of service, except for some sniping in the Fort Sandeman area [North West Frontier] I had never before been under fire. I had often wondered how I would react to it. I found now that my trench had another occupant. He was a *jawan* with a big grin and he seemed delighted to see senior officers being shot at and in the undignified position of scrambling for cover. The shells were falling faster now, and overhead the air seemed full of bursting metal. I hugged the wall of the trench. The *jawan* laughed. He told me that this shelling was nothing and that it happened all the time.

But not far away other *jawans* were in deeper trouble. Despite all their training and their high levels of confidence, most of the men running 25th Division had, like Timmy, never experienced actual combat or seen the Japanese fight up close. Hot and dusty after a patrol, a few hundred men were allowed to strip and bathe in a river and their officers didn't think to set up a system of sentries. A large Japanese force had silently infiltrated nearby and when it was clear that most of the Indians were unarmed and in the water they attacked with mortars, grenades, automatic weapons and rifle fire. The resulting bloodbath cost over a hundred lives and the loss of an important forward position. It took the expenditure of almost another hundred — in this case Timmy's own Hyderabadis — to drive the Japanese back the following day. Two hundred men dead for a swimming break, and another painful lesson learned.

Some weeks later General Davies, troubled by the nightly artillery strikes, decided to drive the Japanese away from the nearby hills. He tasked another unit to lead the attack but Timmy, who by now knew the area well, wanted to offer some help. A rather arrogant British voice on the telephone told him not to bother and so he had to watch as an operation played out with tactics that looked, to Timmy, more suited to a table-top war game than a Burmese jungle hillside. It began with a long artillery barrage, which Timmy suspected would have little effect on the enemy in their deep tunnels, except to give them advance warning of what was about to happen. True enough, the Indians found the Japanese poised and ready and were forced to withdraw, at the cost of dozens of casualties. Timmy's sadness at this turned to anger when General Davies called him up to reprimand him for badgering the other unit's commander with bad and unwanted advice.

Was the general picking on him unfairly yet again, or was Timmy a 'brick-dropper' after all? He could see only one way to salvage his reputation, even though it went against everything he had been taught all the way from the Deera Dun military school to the Indian Army Staff College. Without telling Davies anything about it, he quickly planned an attack of his own, using methods he considered more suitable. He began by ordering his men to approach the enemy silently in the dark with no preliminary barrage.

> In my judgement the hill could be taken cheaply. If I was wrong, I had to know it now; otherwise I would never be sure of myself again. If I did lack judgment, I deserved to be removed from command. In any case, my situation could not be worse than it was, and I decided to take the risk.

It was an impressive act of self-confident insubordination but, if it failed, Timmy knew that the military career he'd spent decades building would be in deep trouble. After a poor night's sleep he felt nervous and fearful. He tried to glimpse what was happening through the darkness, imagining his men climbing slowly and quietly through thick, steep jungle and silently praying that none of them fired a shot by accident or shouted out at the sight of a snake. But they reached the top exactly as he had hoped they would — completely undetected, pushing through the foliage until they could see the entrances to the enemy tunnels.

> The hands of my watch crept on, and I was beginning to panic. Still no sound came from the hill. Five o'clock passed, and the sky began to lighten. 'In God's name what is happening?' I thought.
>
> A few minutes later the silence was ripped apart by the scream of *Hanuman ki jai*, our battle cry, from several hundred throats. There followed the bursts of hand grenades. The shouting and explosions went on for half an hour. In my excitement, I climbed a tree to get a better view. Then three flares arched up: red-green-red, the success signal! My first question was 'How many men have we lost?' To my amazement, not one of our chaps had been killed. Two had received slight wounds, but they were not incapacitated. Everywhere I saw Japanese bodies.

With victory costing not a single Indian life, General Davies was quickly on the telephone once again.

> I got the call I had been dreading — one from General Davies at Division HQ. Despite the success, I had disobeyed orders, and the general might take a dim view but he said 'I'm coming out to congratulate you in person' and I could tell from his voice that everything would be all right. I was vindicated. I felt sick with relief.

After this our fear of the enemy disappeared. He was formidable only because he was willing to take so many losses but our men no longer doubted that they could kill enough Japanese to defeat them.

Another enemy was also close – the INA. Might that include his own brother, Timmy wondered to himself. Either way, he was convinced that he had made the right decision. He'd long believed that the Japanese were a poor choice of ally and now, as he surveyed the half-starved and poorly equipped corpses of the men he'd just defeated on that hill, he could tell that the emperor's army was a shadow of the all-conquering force of 1942. The INA, however, clearly had faith in their Japanese allies, as was clear from the many pamphlets they left for Timmy's *jawans* to discover, warning them of their fate if they didn't do their patriotic duty, switch sides and follow Bose. One of them read:

TO THE PRINCES: You are Indians. You are betraying your motherland by siding with Britain. This is a fight to the finish. If you stand with Britain, you will be treated as enemies and you cannot expect mercy. If you side with India, you will be treated as Indians, and will be able to retain your position.

TO TITLED MEN: You are selling your country to win Britain's favour. But remember Britain cannot save you now. You will go the way of all traitors, if you do not mend your ways at once.

TO COMMUNALISTS: There is no room for narrow sectarian faction fight. There is only one fight in India – that is against Britain for India's freedom. Britain is the real enemy. Remember Britain is the wirepuller behind communal strife. Fight Britain – stop fighting between yourselves: Posterity will curse you as the men who failed Mother India in her hour of peril.

> TO ANGLO-INDIANS: Remember you are Indians. The British will soon leave you in the lurch. You cannot now fight India and then ask for mercy. Follow the example of your brethren in Malaya and Burma.
>
> THIS IS YOUR HOUR OF TEST ... IF YOU FAIL YOU ARE DOOMED FOREVER.

Thankfully there was no direct combat with the INA this time and Timmy's only contact with them was through pamphlets and the daily radio propaganda coming from Rangoon; and few if any of his *jawans* seemed impressed by either. Perhaps one reason for that was that Timmy now offered his men things that their enemies could barely imagine. To help them cope with the physical strain of jungle combat he'd established a rest and rehabilitation centre safely in the rear, simple bamboo huts but with decent beds, mosquito nets, radios and, every tropical soldier's fantasy, hot showers.

> Thus, with plenty of soap and hot water the men could get themselves thoroughly clean and allow their sores and bites to heal. I saw to it that the beds were comfortable so that the men could sleep soundly. In the daytime, they could have non-strenuous games and read books. A gramophone and a radio were installed so they could hear good music and tune in on the radio to the 'Troop's Hour' from Delhi.

As they relaxed by their radios, Timmy's soldiers were reassured by the sight of friendly aircraft patrolling the skies of Arakan, ready to attack their enemy's strongpoints and transport. And a growing number of those planes were flown by members of India's own air force, such as Pilot Officer CGI Philip from 8 Squadron, led by a pioneer of the Indian Air Force, Niranjan Prasad, an Indian Army officer who had volunteered to fight in the skies instead.

He [Niranjan Prasad] said he always wanted to lead an Indian squadron. Our first sortie was to answer a call for six aircraft. The Army gave you the target, a gun position or something like that and our job was to neutralise that post.

Prasad and Philip were flying American-made fighter-bombers called the Vultee Vengeance. They were not exactly state-of-the-art, and the RAF considered them unsuitable for use in Europe, but they were reliable, rugged, generally easy to control, and – reassuringly for Philip – usually accompanied by Hurricanes or Spitfires in case any Japanese fighters came looking for trouble. However, the real danger for the pilots lay hidden beneath the canopy of trees below them.

We used to go up to between ten and twelve thousand feet. As far as possible, we needed that much space, to get into correct position for diving and releasing the bomb, and then we'd hug the ground. If there was tree cover, that suited us fine, because we flew low just over the tree-tops. But the Japanese gunners on the ground were good and they did some very clever things.

The weather was changeable at best, and some days Philip was ordered to attack even when the cloud base over his target was higher than normal release level. Diving through thick cloud, he'd release his bombs dangerously close to the ground, and all those 'clever' Japanese gunners.

We had a few losses. One I remember, because it happened right in front of me, was a chap called Dougherty, an RAF pilot. I remember him very well, because we played poker together and he owed me 23 rupees.

Dougherty was Canadian, one of the many non-Indians who were transferred into the Air Force squadrons to keep rosters filled while more Indian volunteers were being trained. In Number 8 squadron, after something of a rocky start, the different races co-existed effectively – most of the time.

> There was a man called Osborne. He was South African and the South Africans don't like blacks. They were always suspicious of the Indian airmen. Sometimes they used to point guns at our chaps and then start laughing.
>
> One day Osborne and some of his compatriots were using a jam tin balanced on a log for target practice, popping away with their service .38s, just outside the Ops Room, and not demonstrating particular accuracy. Me and my mate 'Mickey' Nerurkar stepped out of the Ops Room with our hands theatrically over our ears. As I walked past, I turned around and pulled out my own .38, and I was a keen shot in those days, and I fired at the South Africans' tin target and sent it flying. They kept quiet after that!

When he wasn't confronting South Africans, or dodging 'ack ack' fire in the treetops, Philip was happy that he was using his newly acquired skills to save his comrades' lives. And he served with distinction in a series of precise and highly choreographed operations during the Arakan campaign.

> Our bomb lines would sometimes be just 25 yards from where our troops were entrenched. We'd dive down and drop and we didn't carry all instantaneous bombs. The first pilot would have a bomb with a 1-minute delay, the second would have a bomb with a 30-second delay and then there was one with an 11-second delay. And the army commander, the captain on the ground, he knew all that. So each section or platoon used to advance according to this time. It was very well coordinated.

General Bill Slim considered these first victories in Arakan at the start of 1944 a turning point as decisive as El Alamein or even Stalingrad. A public sign that the tide was turning in the East just as it had turned in the West. The hard jungle training and new attitudes that Auchinleck, Slim and all their divisional generals prioritised, along with all that new armour, aircraft and medical support, were creating an army that knew how to win and wanted to win some more.

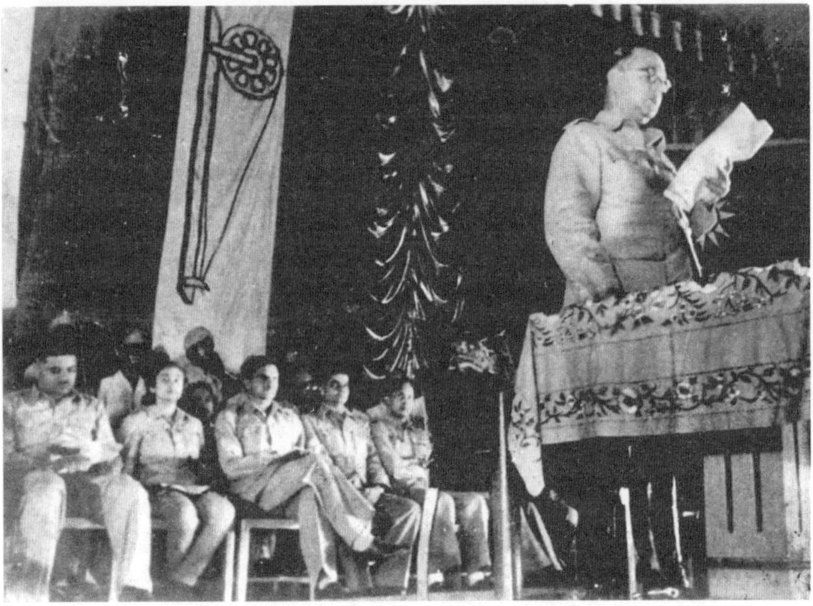

8

The Road to Delhi

Burma and India, 1944

Two powerful advocates for Indian independence, Kodandera Subayya Thimayya and Subhas Chandra Bose, now commanded thousands of Indian soldiers. They had chosen very different paths towards their goal and very different allies. Timmy's men had just won their first victories in Burma. Now it was the INA's turn to be tested in battle. By early 1944 Bose's army was well-organised, well-financed and bursting with confidence. In Rangoon he drew large crowds of Indians and Burmese, all loudly behind his anti-British agenda. The Japanese had developed plans for a joint invasion of India that included eight thousand of the INA's best soldiers. Bose had secured an agreement that his men would only fight under exclusively Indian command and serve in 'spearhead roles' because, as he said, a purely Japanese triumph in India would be 'meaningless if Indians themselves did not participate in it'. Bose also had an understanding that his army would administer all liberated areas and he put a huge amount of effort into planning every detail of how that would work, with ministers pre-appointed for key roles and even stamps and a new currency designed, printed and ready to go.

After the war Japanese documents revealed scepticism about the INA's fighting prowess, principally because most of the men in Bose's ranks had already surrendered once before. But Bose had no such doubts because this time his troops would be fighting for the dream of a free India rather than as the mercenaries of a dying empire. He also confidently predicted that tens of thousands of Indian Army soldiers would defect to his side as soon as the campaign began, joining their brothers in the INA and together liberating their homeland. He drew up an elaborate scheme to place these new recruits inside 'skeleton' divisions that would secure all the areas cleared of the British. Before sending his men to the border he gave them a final, stirring speech, a typically lyrical call to sacrifice:

There, there in the distance – beyond that river, beyond those jungles, beyond those hill lies the promised land – the soil from which we sprang – the land to which we shall now return. Hark India is calling. Blood is calling to blood. The road to Delhi is the road to freedom. *Chalo Delhi!*

The main thrust of the advance was to the north-east, targeting Imphal and Kohima, but the INA first went into action further south in Arakan, helping resist the British advances there, which included those recently made by Timmy's own troops. However it was not other Indians who first encountered the INA in battle; it was the West African volunteers of the 81st and 82nd Divisions. Although they failed to take much ground, one INA unit did triumph in some sharp skirmishes and managed to cross into a small corner of India itself. Amid great excitement, it took control of a handful of settlements, including the town of Mowdok, and raised the national flag. Those who revere Bose today like to share colourful and heroic stories about this historic moment.

Weeping soldiers prostrated themselves on the ground, according to such accounts, embracing the earth of their motherland – clear evidence that it was Bose who played the decisive role in the liberation of India. And when the Japanese forces alongside decided to withdraw, all of the INA officers flatly refused because their destination was Delhi and nothing could divert them from that aim, not even the fear of death. Moved by this act of courage and self-sacrifice, the Japanese left a platoon of their own men behind to serve under Indian command — so the legend goes — and later their Commander-in-Chief in Burma went to see Bose, bowed before him and said: 'Your Excellency, we were wrong. We misjudged the soldiers of the INA. We know now that they are no mercenaries, but real patriots.'

Mowdok was abandoned after three months when these few acres of liberated Indian soil became impossible to defend or supply. As for the inspiring words quoted above, it's entirely possible that they were spoken. It's entirely *certain* that they were what Bose wanted to hear. But if there ever was such a conversation between Bose and the Japanese Commander-in-Chief we can be sure that it did not reflect the *actual* behaviour and attitudes of the Japanese high command when it came to the INA, especially when combat began at Imphal and Kohima in March and April. Here, as at the Admin Box a few months earlier, General Slim's men dug in for a determined defence, combining this with aggressive patrolling to disrupt and damage their enemies and a vigorous air campaign. The Japanese air force, already weakened by the campaign in Arakan, was soon reduced to almost nothing and there were few if any new aircraft coming to reinforce it.

Airpower would influence but not determine the battles at Imphal and Kohima. What really mattered was determination, and in particular the determination of Indian soldiers faced, for the first time, by a substantial number of INA troops supported by a powerful Japanese army and relentless propaganda calling for their surrender or defection. Bose was convinced that this would prove to be the decisive moment for his cause but even before the fighting began in earnest the signs for him were far from hopeful. General Sato, commander of the Japanese 31st Division, led thousands of his men over the border, across rivers and over mountains, with all the skill and speed of the great advances of 1942. Then in the Naga hills he came upon the first outposts of the Indian Army, two companies of the Assam Regiment based at Jessami, about 80 miles to the east of Kohima. These young volunteers from the very fringes of British India had never seen action before but they stood their ground bravely for five days under the inspirational command of Colonel William Felix 'Bruno' Brown, even when surrounded by an overwhelming enemy force. By exploiting his own and his men's precise knowledge of the jungled hills and steep ravines, Brown managed to lead most of them out of their encirclement. They then embarked on an epic 77-mile march to Kohima that they completed – under fire and almost without rest – in just 39 hours, with Sato's troops no more than a few thousand yards behind them throughout. As they were about to reach their destination they experienced General Slim's growing air power in a most uncomfortable way, when patrolling fighters mistook them for the advancing Japanese and strafed their column. Despite all of this, Brown and 260 soldiers successfully reached Kohima, linking up with the garrison there and immediately digging in to join the defense of the town. It was a very good omen for Slim and a bad one for Bose and his patrons.

It was also, in its way, a microcosm of the wider campaign in these dangerous borderlands. It would have been easy and perhaps understandable had these young men from small hill villages decided not to risk their lives and instead accepted the promises of the INA. Their isolated communities had enjoyed little contact with or support from the Raj for many decades, and so there was no obvious reason for them to risk life and limb for a distant King-Emperor. But out of group loyalty, a well-founded fear of the Japanese or sheer cussedness, they continued to place their faith in a charismatic British officer, one who embodied some of the finest qualities of the Indian Army. As tough as they came, Brown also displayed a powerful almost loving devotion to the men under his command and consistently led fearlessly from the front – a trait that would cost him his life before the war was over.

The Battle of the Bungalow. Scraggy Hill. The Siege of the Tennis Court. The famous moments of this campaign reveal just how close and savage the fighting was, with attackers and defenders frequently at grenade-throwing distance. Although the numbers involved in no way matched Stalingrad, the intensity and intimacy of the combat does invite that comparison, and overall casualty rates were on a par with the largest British battles of the war, such as Alamein. Japanese troops at Kohima and Imphal may not have enjoyed the supply and medical advantages of 14th Army, but when not stricken by disease they fought as ferociously as ever. A young lieutenant in the Punjab Regiment, Robin Rowland, said it was 'the nearest I've come to hell'.

> It was war against nature: torrential rain, mist, bitterly cold early mornings, mud and blazing sun. It was also war against an implacable and ferocious enemy ... If men were brave in action, few witnessed it; if they had quit it would often have been unobserved. All depended on the soldier and how he bore himself, and each fighter had to conquer his own heart.

British doctor Harry Walker witnessed combat that resembled the trench warfare of the Great War. He saw wounded men under such intense fire that they could not be evacuated for days, meaning he had to treat them for maggot infestation and gas gangrene.

Following the new doctrine, the men commanding the Kohima 'box' ignored the fact that the ridges on which it stood were soon surrounded and let the enemy come to them. On 'Garrison Hill' the Japanese attacked every day and every night for two weeks, 15,000 soldiers repeatedly charging the lines of a mixed British and Indian force of just 2,500. Men from Assam, Nepal and Kent repelled every attack as the ground became littered with decomposing bodies that nobody was able to clear. At one point the medics dug a pit and covered it with a rough tarpaulin sheet for use as an improvised operating theatre. Even 14th Army's trump card of air supply failed to work here at one stage when the pocket was reduced to such a small size that parachuted cases of food, ammunition and medicine fell straight into the welcoming arms of the Japanese. RAF fighter-bombers and, finally, a relief column accompanied by tanks, saved the day but the level of casualties was horrendous. Of the 446 men of the Royal West Kent Regiment fighting at the start of the battle only 168 remained unharmed when the siege was over. In between the attacks the Indian troops were encouraged to surrender and join their 'true comrades' in the INA. It must have been tempting to do just that rather than face another night of terror in a muddy, stinking trench but almost no one did.

Bose's volunteers had some small victories. Fighting predominantly around Imphal, INA soldiers took the hilltop fortress of Klang Klang and a few dozen *jawans* did decide to join them. But Bose had promised that the invasion would trigger mass desertions, along with a general uprising across India, and it very clearly had not. In fact, one senior INA officer – Major B. J. S. Garewal – defected the other way to rejoin the British side, reporting that the Japanese were high-handed, only entrusted their Indian allies with light weapons and refused to consult with them on day-to-day tactics.

The RAF and the Indian Air Force continued to bombard their enemies incessantly, depriving them of rest and resupply. Bose's old friend Abid Hasan was serving as an officer in a front-line unit and was convinced that his men were a match for any British or Indian soldier. But they could do little when the main threat came from above.

> On foot [our enemy] was not prepared to meet us. He concentrated his efforts where his strength lay – in the air. His targets were our lines of communication. The bridges were destroyed and the roads and all that moved or crawled on them, even the humble bullock cart. The effects of this we began to feel at the front. Our supplies dwindled and then ceased.

Tortuously long logistical chains stretching back into Burma unravelled as British and Indian pilots relentlessly targeted lorries, carts, roads and bridges. And while their enemies started to run out of food, ammunition and medicine, the defenders of Kohima and Imphal were now getting regular supply drops.

British military intelligence drawn from intercepted front-line communications stated that the INA did fight well at Imphal but generally withdrew after a few hours, probably because of the mounting shortage of ammunition.

Initially, Bose was unaware of the problems. Japanese radio stations broadcast a non-stop stream of stories about great victories on the Indian border while his own commanders, perhaps not wanting to worry him, kept the worst of their struggles and doubts to themselves. Confidence in Rangoon was high long after the battle was effectively lost and Bose also toured Malaya to great acclaim, all the time working and reworking plans for the new ministries and agencies that India would soon need. In early July his supporters even put on a series of concerts, sports festivals and mock battles in Rangoon, celebrating what were, in fact, entirely phantom victories at Imphal and Kohima. Eventually disease and despondency began to spread through both Japanese and INA ranks and the reports reaching Bose turned from determination to recrimination. INA officers complained that their men were not receiving their fair share of supplies and were being used only as supporting forces. Always alert to any problems facing their allies, the Americans were watching and listening, too. The Office of Strategic Services (OSS) had a Research and Analysis Branch that was eavesdropping on Japanese and INA communications. In its secret report on the battle it stated that Bose's officers grew very unhappy very quickly.

> Often regarded with suspicion by the Japanese, INA forces were almost never employed as regular fighting units and were assigned inferior equipment . . . the British had been uncertain how much confusion Bose's Indians would cause but actual encounters proved that the Indian soldiers would fight the enemy whether he was Japanese or Indian . . . INA troops withdrew in very poor condition and Japanese officers were complaining about how they would no longer fight.

Even under the fiercest pressures, the Indian Army battalions employed in this critical battle remained well-motivated, well-led and well able to deal with the propaganda coming from the INA. Given the chaos of 1942 this was a sure sign that Slim's energetic leadership had indeed reignited confidence across all of his widely diverse units. And the behaviour of Bose's allies and patrons did little to encourage ordinary Indian soldiers to trust him. The murder of captured Indian doctors and hospital staff by Japanese troops during the Admin Box battle had become widely known and only made the *jawans* more eager to fight. Volunteers from what Bose liked to call a 'conquered people' would still go 'above and beyond the call of duty' in the service of a British king, which explains why Indian soldiers would go on to win twenty-two of the thirty-four Victoria and George Crosses awarded during the Burma campaign.

When the 1944 monsoon stopped all serious military action, the INA attempted to regroup and ready itself for the inevitable Allied offensive. There were still around 30,000 men prepared to fight for Bose and his top lieutenants, such as Gurbaksh Singh Dhillon, vigourously prepared to defend free Burma from what he saw as a British attempt to reconquer it. But the news reaching the INA headquarters in Rangoon and Singapore kept getting worse. The Allies were in Normandy and had taken Rome, US marines were poised to land on Saipan and Guam and, for the first time, B-29 Superfortress bombers appeared over mainland Japan. If it wasn't obvious before then it certainly was now. The tide wasn't just turning, it was running at full flood against the Axis powers in every theatre of the war. As he retreated from Imphal, Abid Hasan thought about the great plans he had discussed with Bose on board *U-180*. He still believed that the INA would one day liberate India but everywhere he looked he saw evidence of Britain's growing power.

> We marched sustained only by a great desire and a great longing. Chased by the enemy, open to attacks from the air . . . even the medical aid we had consisted of our lone doctor with the

medicines he could carry on his back. He too suffered as we did and later developed typhoid and had to be carried by us in turns along the way.

What Hasan and the other INA loyalists still had was pride, along with a belief that, whatever setbacks on the battlefield they suffered, they were doing something historic for India.

I felt proud and I feel more proud today that I belonged to [this army]. Baluchis were there among us and Assamese, Kashmiris and Malayalis, Pathans and Sikhs and Guajaratis, proud members of classes called the 'martial' and those till then denied reputation for martial valour but who proved in battle that they could by their deeds claim equal honour . . . we ceased belonging to groups like this because India became our goal.

The INA's role in the failed invasion of India cost the lives of about two thousand men who had put their faith in Bose. Only a quarter of them died in combat, the rest succumbing to diseases that the Japanese and INA medical services were unable to treat with anything like the techniques or quantity of medical supplies now available on the British side. And instead of welcoming a wave of *jawans*, it was the INA that was losing men. There were over seven hundred formal deserters and nearly a thousand captured, some of whom, despite the bravado of leaders like Abid Hasan, didn't seem to want to do any more fighting amid the chaos and disorganisation that came to define Bose's 'march on Delhi'. It was the bitterest disappointment of his life and British and American propaganda immediately redoubled its effort to denigrate him as a fascist agent, a Japanese puppet, or both. In public he reacted with characteristic bravado, blaming the temporary set-back on the early monsoon.

All preparations had been completed and the stage had been set for the final assault on Imphal when torrential rains overtook us, and to carry Imphal by an assault was rendered a tactical impossibility.

May the souls of those heroes who have fallen in this campaign inspire us to still nobler deeds of heroism and bravery in the next phase of India's War of Liberation.

In September he went into northern Burma and met some of the survivors. It was a chastening experience. Shah Nawaz told him of ten INA men under his command who had been tied to trees and bayoneted by out-of-control Japanese soldiers who thought they had been gathering intelligence for the British. In private Bose blamed Japanese High Command for not using his men properly and never grasping the true potential of Indian nationalism. And why was giving battle at Imphal and Kohima even necessary in the first place, he asked. A drive into the Brahmaputra Valley and East Bengal would have been a much better test of his belief that the people of India were ready to join his cause. It had long been the most anti-British region in the country, and the dreadful famine there had only deepened those feelings. As he pondered the many 'might have beens' of the invasion, he grew particularly bitter about the extensive logistical support that the Americans were now giving to 14th Army. He railed furiously at Roosevelt for not grasping what to him was so very obvious: that today's 'freedom fighters' in the East were little different from the Founding Fathers of the USA. From Tokyo he told his 'American friends':

Asia is surging with revolutionary fervour . . . you had an opportunity of helping us but you did not do so. Now Japan is offering us help and we have reason to trust her sincerity. This is why we have plunged into the struggle alongside of her. It is not Japan that we are helping by waging war on you and on our mortal enemy – England. We are helping ourselves. We are helping Asia.

But his choices of ally in Berlin and in Tokyo — and his easy faith in their 'sincerity' — meant that the days when Bose was on the cover of American magazines and the toast of Western intellectuals were now long gone.

Britain and Europe, 1944

During the first half of 1944 the Luftwaffe was shot from the skies of north-west Europe, primarily by swarms of P-51 Mustang fighters of the US Army Air Force operating from bases in eastern England. This was a hugely significant Allied victory, as important as 1943's great achievement, winning the Battle of the Atlantic. Bombing campaigns that had previously incurred frighteningly high casualty rates — such as the RAF's assault on Berlin or American daylight raids on German factories — were suddenly a great deal less painful. British, Commonwealth and American aircrew still suffered but at nothing like the same rate, while below them the economic, transport and urban infrastructure of their enemy was being systematically pounded with ever-increasing accuracy and ferocity. For RAF Bomber Command, under its remorseless leader Air Marshal Arthur 'Bomber' Harris, this meant a return to a strategy it had pioneered in the earlier and more difficult years of its war: 'area bombing' or, put more bluntly, the blasting and burning of every important German centre of industry, transport and population.

With little fighter opposition, new navigational systems to lead elite 'pathfinder' pilots to their targets in all weathers and an ingenious mixture of high explosives and incendiaries, the RAF became very good at this very quickly. On 14 October 1944 it dropped a greater weight of explosives on the city of Duisburg than the Luftwaffe had managed to unload on London during the entire war thus far. During two other October nights 1,800 heavy bombers struck Essen, in the heart of the Ruhr Valley. Only twelve were shot down while the city below, along with a railway marshalling yard that was supporting the German army's desperate attempt to defend the Reich, was smashed to pieces. The author J. R. R. Tolkien saw one of the Essen raids high above his garden heading eastwards, and was awestruck.

> I have just been out to look up: the noise is terrific: the biggest for a long time, a sky-wide Armada. I suppose it is all right to say so, as by the time that this reaches you somewhere will have ceased to exist and all the world will have known about it and already forgotten it.

These sky-wide armadas set out time and time again. Cologne was virtually depopulated as tens of thousands of refugees streamed into neighbouring towns and villages. Other industrial cities such as Gelsenkirchen, Nuremberg and Düsseldorf were similarly made almost uninhabitable. Although area bombing had always enjoyed his personal support, and for years was the only plausible way that Britain could inflict real harm on its main enemy, Churchill had his moments of doubt. 'Are we beasts?' he asked when presented with estimates of the civilian casualties that his bombers were causing.

As the war reached its final year there was 'beastly death' of all kinds, and the final months would be among the bloodiest of them all. But that's what Britain had become — an economy and a society finely tuned for modern war, manufacturing death for its enemies on a gigantic scale. There was even an upbeat popular song about it, sung by wartime superstar Gracie Fields.

> *I'm the girl that makes the thing that drills the hole that holds the ring,*
> *That drives the rod that turns the knob,*
> *That works the thingummy bob.*
> *It's a ticklish sort of job making a thing for a thingummy bob,*
> *Especially when you don't know what it's for.*
> *But it's the girl that makes the thing that drills the hole that holds the ring,*

That makes the thingummy bob that makes the engine roar.
And it's the girl that makes the thing that holds the oil that oils the ring,
That makes the thingummy bob that's going to win the war!

The Packard V-1650 Merlin, an American-made version of the Rolls-Royce engine that had helped the RAF triumph in 1940, powered many of the fighters that now dominated the skies, most notably the P-51 Mustang itself. And the rapid development of that engine epitomised some key changes in the years since the Battle of Britain. The technology had been improved, the systems of production had been expanded and streamlined, and all manner of lethal *thingummy bobs* were pouring out of the factories as a result. America's genius for mass production had also helped enormously, combining high quality with a *quantity* that was now overwhelming Britain and America's enemies in every theatre of the war. Like the Merlin engine, other British initiatives were also supercharged across the Atlantic. Bletchley Park's 'Bombes', machines to help decode enemy messages, were humming away in America in far greater numbers than they ever had in Britain, and a top-secret science initiative called Tube Alloys had metamorphosed into the Manhattan Project. Only a handful of people in Britain knew that ideas which had started life in a Birmingham university lay behind the biggest and most expensive industrial project in history, and absolutely *nobody* knew that an army of scientists and engineers in New Mexico was now just months away from trialling a wonder weapon.

Although nothing like the Manhattan Project could have been attempted back home, economically and militarily Britain was still a great power and wanted to act like one. But the strain was showing. A global naval effort, the nightly aerial onslaught on Germany and three major ground campaigns – north-west Europe, Italy and India – combined to put relentless pressure on personnel and logistics. And soon all that strain would begin to tell.

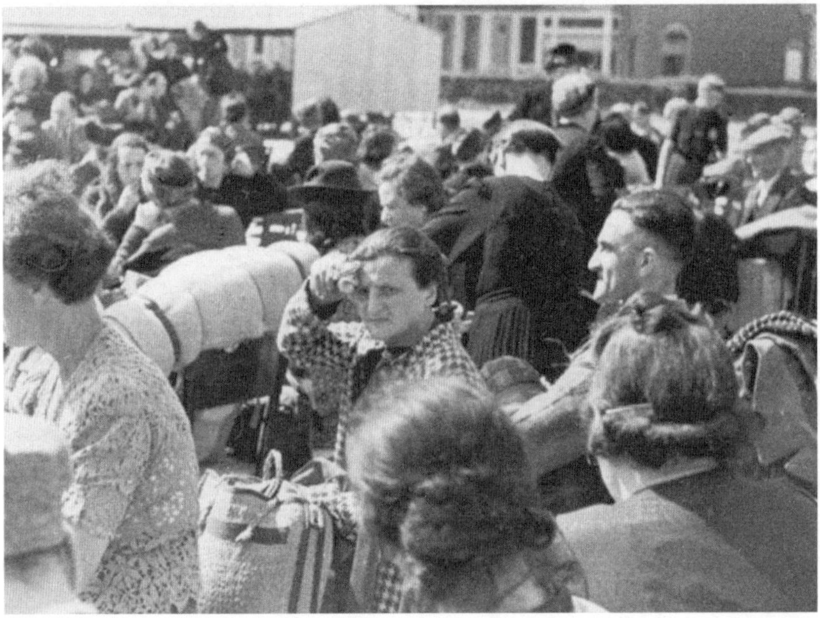

9

The Condemned

Occupied Europe, 1940–1944

Shortly before he left for Asia, Subhas Chandra Bose visited a concentration camp just south of Berlin. He was accompanied by some of the other exiles then living in Germany, including the Grand Mufti of Jerusalem, Hajj Amin al-Husayni, and by two of the most prominent architects of the Holocaust. One was Martin Luther, who had been the note taker at the Wannsee Conference in 1942, when plans for the mass extermination of European and Soviet Jews were formally approved. The other was the *Reichskommissar* of occupied Holland, Arthur Seyss-Inquart. One of Hitler's most trusted ministers, he had earlier supervised the *Anschluss* of Austria. The site this group inspected – in the town of Trebbin – was a forced labour rather than a death camp but those incarcerated there also suffered from the arbitrary violence that characterised the Nazi regime. Nobody ever recorded what Bose discussed with Luther or Seyss-Inquart on that day, but both men were already responsible for human suffering and murder on a phenomenal scale.

Holland had been neutral during the Great War and hoped to be so again, but Hitler had other ideas and the fighting lasted barely a week. By the time a compulsory registration began – the official separation of the Dutch from the non-Dutch – the country's large and long-established Jewish community knew that things were going to be hard. Soon new regulations would stop Jews from trading, from entering certain areas and from owning certain things. No one was quite sure yet what this all meant but, from the moment he became *Reichskommissar*, Seyss-Inquart was in no doubt about what was expected of him: readying 120,000 people for death. 'The Jews for us are not Dutchmen,' he wrote, 'they are those enemies with whom we can come neither to an armistice nor to a peace.'

There was no great history of anti-Semitism in nineteenth- or early twentieth-century Holland but Seyss-Inquart found many willing to help him from the outset. The Dutch government's own census bureau handed over the details of all the Jews known to reside in the country without demur, while other official agencies produced the special ID cards that Jews were soon required to carry around with them at all times. Holland's famously crowded towns and cities made it difficult for anyone to evade detection.

Early in 1941 some communists organised a protest about the treatment of their friends and neighbours, but the local police force quickly swept anyone making trouble from the streets and into the prisons. As newspapers and cinemas filled with Nazi propaganda the military recruiters were kept busy and, per head of population, Holland provided more non-German volunteers for the SS than any other occupied country in Western Europe.

Hans and Ruth Goslar had already tried to escape from the Nazis once, fleeing Berlin for Amsterdam in 1933, and their eldest daughter Hannah, known to all as Hanneli, went to school there with a girl of the same age, a girl whose story was to become synonymous with the Holocaust: Anne Frank. The first round-ups began in the summer of 1942. Families were told to attend their synagogues where they were picked up by the police and sent to a large camp in a place called Westerbork in the north-east of the country, close to the German border. They were allowed to take one suitcase each. There are some especially poignant photographs of families lining up in the street waiting to be collected, respectable people in good coats holding their cases while their children clutched a favourite toy, looking as if they were preparing for a nice weekend by the beach at Zandvoort. Some of those taking the photographs would soon be in the empty houses and apartments looking for fine china and expensive bedspreads, since everyone knew that Jews had money.

All went so easily in Holland that another key administrator of the Holocaust, Adolf Eichmann, remarked, 'The transports run so smoothly there that it is a pleasure to see.' Deportees were held for a few weeks at Westerbork before being dispatched to other locations in Eastern Europe. For the moment nobody knew what happened in these other places. The Jews who were sent to them were told they were to be resettled and found employment. In fact, most would be murdered within hours of arrival. During the course of the war 107,000 Dutch Jews were taken from their homes, held in Westerbork and then sent on like this, mostly to Auschwitz and Sobibor. Only 5,000 survived. It's believed to be the most efficient kill ratio achieved by the Nazis in any of the nations that they conquered.

The same policemen who had once cheerfully helped Hanneli Goslar and her friends cross the Raadhuisstraat or navigate Dam Square were now raiding locations where they thought Jews might be lying low, pulling families from their homes and pushing them into trucks in the middle of the night. Although they lasted longer than most, in June 1943 Hanneli, her father, her maternal grandparents, and her younger sister Gabi were all arrested and sent to Westerbork to await their fate. Some Jews, most famously the Frank family, went into hiding although Hanneli, like all of Anne's other friends, believed that they had somehow managed to escape. Others did try and mostly fail to reach England by boat. Until the United States entered the war thousands of people also appeared at the door of its consulate in Rotterdam hoping for an American visa, but hardly any were successful. The Jews of Holland, whether in the camps or hiding in attics, came to realise that they were non-Dutch, non-European, non-American and, to men like, Arthur Seyss-Inquart, not even properly human.

Formosa, 1944–1945

Whispered stories about the progress of the war gave faint hope to the despondent prisoners of Kinkaseki, stories brought in by the trickle of new arrivals or overheard from the guards. Arthur Titherington learned that the Allies had landed in France and were taking islands in the Pacific. But he also discovered that the growing pressure on Japan meant even harder work for him and his mates in the form of a new productivity drive at the copper mine. With fewer local people willing to work there, Arthur also received a most unwelcome promotion. He was handed a power drill and sticks of gelignite and given a crash course in one of the most dangerous underground jobs of them all. His friend Len Cullop was made a 'Blaster', too. One day Len was too slow getting away from the chamber where he'd set the explosives and was blown down one of the ladders. They carried him up all 1,186 steps and back to the camp, but he died two days later.

A Japanese guard called Sergeant Tashiro – known to all as 'Sanitary Sid' – controlled the camp hospital and was blamed by the prisoners for many deaths. Sid sent obviously sick and weak men back to work in the mine and would explode with rage at any hint of contradiction, hitting patients and orderlies alike and frequently beating the only British doctor, Captain Peter Seed. One of his more imaginative cruelties was requiring every prisoner to kill fifty flies a day as part of what he farcically called his 'camp health programme'. Sid counted each fly out with his fingers every evening and would smack any prisoner around the face if they fell even one insect short.

Captain Seed struggled tirelessly to treat men with minimal equipment and improvised drugs, burning wood into charcoal to make a powder that was their only hope of calming endless painful bouts of diarrhoea and dysentery. Arthur would be forever grateful to Seed for his ability to improvise: removing bad teeth with pliers, draining puss-filled boils by 'vacuum and heated glass' and cleaning up nasty looking cuts from the mine with a red-hot knife before they became infected. But despite the captain's best efforts, Arthur saw more of his friends die and felt the death of one of them, Corporal Jim Boughey, particularly keenly. The medical report stated 'malnutrition oedema with heart failure' but everyone knew it was just another case of overwork and mistreatment breaking what had been a strong young body. 'One day at a time,' Arthur said under his breath for the thousandth time.

When it rained – and it rained a great deal – their huts leaked spectacularly. The men worked together with string, bamboo and wood gathered from their daily walks to and from the mine to create elaborate drainage systems. These kept out some of the water but created perfect 'rat runs' for the rodents that bothered them every night. One day, with a cry of 'Hey, let go of my fucking gnashers' someone gave comic chase through the mud and puddles when he spotted a particularly large rat scurrying off with his false teeth.

As men fell sick and died, replacements were drafted in to work at the mine from other prison camps on Formosa. One day that brought some much-needed support for Captain Seed in the shape of a Canadian doctor, Major Ben Wheeler. In the secret diary he wrote at the camp, Wheeler described the men he came across at Kinkaseki as 'the walking dead'.

> Those in the mine who escape serious injury are racked with bronchitis and stained from constant exposure to the copper sulphate (formed by water interacting with the ore). Their sore cracked feet never heal. We lose them so often. One today, called Smith, has beriberi, starvation, mental depression or what-have-you. Just gave up, and who can blame him? Only 37 but he was wasted away and his hair had gone white, he looked at least 67.

Hoping he could succeed where Captain Seed had failed, Wheeler wrote polite notes to the commandant asking for better equipment and more drugs. But they led to an angry orderly — almost certainly Sanitary Sid himself — marching into the hospital with a sword and showing Wheeler how he proposed to remove his head if he questioned the established order once again. And so, like Peter Seed before him, the Canadian learned to improvise. Seed later wrote:

> Ben wouldn't say a problem was impossible, instead he would smile and say 'There must be an answer' and then worry at it until he came up with a solution. One man was covered in festering sores. Wheeler wrapped them in lichen he'd picked around the camp, saying 'there must be iodine and iron in those plants' and the sores vanished. Many prisoners suffered from jungle ulcers on their legs, which could quickly turn gangrenous. Wheeler seared them with a hot poker — almost as painful for him as for the patients — but it cured scores of men.

Arthur watched as Wheeler attempted the impossible day after day. A man wracked by pneumonia was clearly close to death. Operating without anaesthetic, Wheeler used the only surgical tool available to him — an old shaving razor — to cut deep into the man's chest cavity and release the fluid that was slowly drowning him, draining it out with an improvised rubber catheter that had been part of an old bicycle tyre half an hour earlier. Another patient, a man called Docherty, was carried in paralysed from the chest down after a rockfall at the mine. Under Wheeler's direction they built an improvised cradle out of wood scavenged from the huts, packed it with sand and laid him inside it. For weeks Wheeler and the others took turns to massage his damaged body until they could see his toes beginning to move. In the days that followed Wheeler designed and built a crude exercise bike with concrete blocks and rope around a simple seat and pedals. After using it every day for a month, Docherty began to walk again. But not every medical story at Kinkaseki had such a happy ending.

'He's escaped in his sleep, Sergeant.'

'What did he die of, Major?'

'Sergeant, he died of dysentery, malnutrition, famine oedema – but most of all he died of *disclinitis*.'

'What's that, sir?'

'That's no more inclination to live. And that's the most important disease in this camp.'

In December 1944 Major Wheeler wrote in his diary about the Canadian Christmas his family would be looking forward to in Alberta, their third without him:

> I tried to picture the tree I know Nell must have for the boys, and what presents I would like to give them all. Next year surely! Christmas dinner too – I could do a lot to one but I shouldn't complain. We had rice and boiled vegetable as usual, but also four oranges and a piece of battered pork today.

And in a letter to his wife he didn't hold back on the realities of his life in the camp:

> Three deaths [this week] from dysentery, two more cannot last more than a day, another three just touch and go. All have oedema and they develop an acute watery diarrhoea, absorb practically no food, are continually chilled in temperatures of 50–60 degrees F and absolutely no reserve. It is heart breaking to watch them. We have blankets to use on them but they are continually wet and a Herculean task to try to wash them. No soap, no brush, no hot water, and even more difficult to dry them. Men die on bare and open boards. Man after man is going off food completely, partly mental I'm afraid, because so many felt we were near the end [of the war] yet now things go on unchanged. Darling, I pray God all is well with this day, with our boys, with all the family. How I would like to have helped you fill the stockings. Still I must not dwell on such things too much, the only way to get through this is to be as near animal as possible and live from meal to meal. Good night, my love.

Wheeler never knew if his letters even left Formosa but every so often the prisoners were allowed to write short postcards that the Red Cross promised to deliver. One of Arthur Titherington's friends named Gerard Barber did so during Christmas 1944, telling his parents, 'Please try not to worry as I am keeping my chin up and patiently waiting the great day when we can all be together again. Tell Madge I love her and am waiting to get home and be married. Your ever-loving and devoted son, Gerard.'

Shortly after Christmas, Gerard fell sick with dysentery and died of 'enteritis and malnutrition oedema' before the end of January. He was interred in one of the many shallow graves that the prisoners cut into the rocky ground of the surrounding hills, some of which were washed out again by the rainstorms. Arthur attended many short and simple funerals there.

> The officer says little more than 'Ashes to ashes and dust to dust', there's a covering of soil and a rough cross placed at the head as the guards grunt 'Speedo, Speedo!' This might seem callous but it wasn't intended to be. It was a physical ordeal to stagger over the rough ground with the weight of a body. I found myself thinking not so much of the person when he was alive but the rest of us. There was just precious little of anything to waste on the dead. We were battling to survive and we all wondered how long it might be before we were being carried up the side of that hill.

A new commander, Captain Imamura, arrived to replace the fanatical Wakiyama and conditions slowly began to improve. A treasure trove of Red Cross supplies — chocolate, cigarettes, tea, bully beef and even bacon — arrived in the camp and Imamura shared it out equally among the men. Some gorged on it, some tried to eke it out for weeks and, according to Arthur, nothing was ever stolen. The new commander delivered a lecture, too, which Arthur later wrote down because, after so many days of 'one day at a time', it was the first moment he allowed himself to believe that the end might truly be in sight.

I have endeavoured to make your life comfortable and peaceful by issuing as good a ration as is possible in my power. Thus mentally and physically we have been treating you well but it is not because the Axis countries are losing the war. Such a thought is very dangerous for you. In harmony with our kind treatment you must reward us by discharging your allotted work and also obeying faithfully to our instructions.

'Just another day,' he whispered once again.

London, 1944–1945

The men running the British war effort towards the end of 1944 knew that the end was coming, too, but had no idea when. And they struggled with many disappointments, as the promises of the summer were not fulfilled as quickly as expected. After D-Day, the hard grind of the Normandy campaign and then the successful 'Falaise pocket' battle of August, when the German army lost 300,000 men and much of its best remaining armour, the generals predicted a swift move across the Rhine. Instead there was painful defeat at Arnhem, bad-tempered disputes about strategy and finance and a frightening new rocket offensive on London.

The V2s started falling in September 1944 and, unlike the earlier V1 'doodlebugs', you couldn't hear them coming. Some landed short but those that did reach the city created appalling damage. On 25 November one struck the New Cross branch of Woolworths in south-east London, a ton of high explosive suddenly detonating in the middle of a crowd of midday shoppers. One hundred and sixty people died and 108 were injured. Britain had seen nothing like this since the Blitz of 1940 and 1941. By the end of the war more than nine thousand people, mostly Londoners, would be killed or injured by Hitler's so-called 'revenge weapons'. It did not significantly affect the economic life of the nation and nor did it stop the gradual return of evacuee children to its capital, which had been happening slowly for years now. But it did add to a gnawing sense that the war was not ending as quickly as people had hoped in those giddy days after D-Day and then the liberation of Paris. Rocket attacks, the failure at Arnhem, growing tensions between the Conservative and Labour members of Churchill's wartime coalition — it was an anxious autumn and winter and the prime minister felt it keenly. What particularly rankled was an ever-growing feeling of powerlessness. With every passing month it became clearer that wartime strategy — and the country's post-war economic prospects — were being decided not in London but in Washington.

The future financial shape of the world had been sketched out at the Bretton Woods Conference in the summer of 1944, and the American delegation set the pace. Bretton Woods established powerful new institutions like the International Monetary Fund and a prototype World Bank, both of which were set to steer the global economy for decades to come. If Britain's pound sterling had been the most important international currency in the nineteenth and early twentieth centuries it was now clear that the mighty US dollar was poised to shove it aside. Then there was the question of the huge debts run up by Britain during the war, meaning that London would require continuing 'Lend-Lease' support and the promise of a gigantic loan to kick-start its economy when peace finally came. British factories were busily turning out the *thingummy bobs* that were winning the war, but they were no longer making the exportable goods that had kept the books balanced before 1939. Just as importantly, most of the oilfields, mines and rubber plantations that had been a reliable source of national income for so long were still under Japanese control. All of this meant a crippling shortage of cash to pay for the imports that the country desperately needed, particularly food. And the strain of all this was beginning to affect relationships with Washington.

Churchill argued passionately and persistently that the two years prior to Pearl Harbor, when Britain had carried the weight of the struggle quite alone (until the Soviet Union was forced into the war in June 1941) should entitle it to a generous post-war settlement from the Americans. But the hard-headed men around President Roosevelt were not so sure about that. Many blamed the old imperial system of 'trade preference' for the economic pain of the 1930s. If the British wanted to end the war with a generous loan at a decent rate they would have to make some promises about trade, and about access to the markets that they had formerly controlled. America was doing the heavy lifting in this war now, economically and militarily, and so it would be America that set the rules for the new world, not the people who had made such a mess of the old one. This may have seemed unfair when viewed from London, but it reflected a widespread mistrust of British motives and intentions, one that stretched from the US Treasury to the Department of Defense. And in an election year there were few votes in being generous to Britain, especially if that meant relaunching and refinancing its empire. In a private State Department survey of the public's attitudes to America's wartime allies, Britain was rated as the least trustworthy.

Churchill's friend and adviser Lord Beaverbrook thought that Bretton Woods was a shameful sell-out, a craven bending of the knee to a group of avaricious Americans who had yet to give Britain the financial guarantees it needed and deserved. But in Washington they still wanted more. US Treasury officials delayed agreeing a post-war loan until more concessions on trade and commercial policy could be extracted from their ally. A large UK meat import deal with Argentina was stalled after American intervention. US airlines demanded and were promised access across the British Empire at Roosevelt's direct request. And the powerful American oil industry pressed its case for a bigger slice of the Middle Eastern oil business, all supported by senators and congressional committee chiefs in Washington. The presence of so many healthy looking American troops with money in their pockets, and magazine articles about the high standard of living on the other side of the Atlantic, thousands of miles away from the rationing and the V2s, didn't exactly cement cordial relations either.

The arguments about money mirrored those about strategy. British and Canadian troops had played a full part in D-Day and throughout the tough Normandy campaign. They were now spearheading the Allied drive into Belgium, Holland and towards north-western Germany. But the proportion of US forces fighting in Europe was growing larger every month and British influence on its direction inevitably declined at a similar rate. In a series of arguments that hinged on logistics, newly promoted Field Marshal Bernard Montgomery and Churchill himself pushed hard for what was called a 'narrow front' invasion of Germany – led, of course, by Montgomery. The overall military chief in Europe, American Dwight Eisenhower, favoured a broader and slower approach instead. The looming presidential election was also affecting thinking in Washington. American troops were leading the battle in Western Europe and even the British relied to some extent on US-made equipment and supplies. Nobody was going to take tanks or ammunition from a successful US general like George Patton only to hand them to the endlessly demanding and irritating (to US ears) 'Monty'.

The spectacular failure of Operation Market Garden, the British-planned, British-led assault on the Dutch Rhine bridges in September, set the seal on this debate. Fifteen thousand British and American soldiers were killed or captured in what many Americans regarded as an act of arrogant folly. But before the US generals could enact their 'broad front' move eastwards, they were hit by the last major German ground offensive of the war in the west when the panzers rolled forward unexpectedly in the Ardennes. The 'Battle of the Bulge' started badly for the US Army and so now it was the British generals' turn to roll their eyes at the failings of their allies. Montgomery took great pleasure in loudly boasting to the press about how he had to rush his troops south to help the Americans stem and then reverse the initial German advances. His attempt to grab credit for victory in the Ardennes caused even more bad feeling and after that – amid intense irritation on all sides – the old argument about a narrow or a broad offensive picked up once again.

These disputes became both bitter and personal. The Americans gossiped and joked about Churchill's drinking while the British happily passed on stories of Eisenhower's alleged laziness and actual infidelity. Even the normally stern Alan Brooke, Chief of the Imperial General Staff, was not above some prurient tittle-tattle, telling his fellow chiefs of staff in November 1944 (having first asked all the female secretaries to leave the room) that nobody was running the campaign in Europe with any real grip.

> Eisenhower, though supposed to be doing so, is detached and by himself with his lady chauffeur on the golf links at Rheims – entirely detached from the war and taking practically no part in the running of the war . . . [although] personally I think he is incapable of running the war even if he tries.

As Montgomery and his mentor Brooke arm-wrestled with Eisenhower over how best to cross the Rhine, Churchill worried about Italy. The campaign there was being waged with a high percentage of British and Commonwealth forces and consequently London had more strategic influence. The Allied army in Italy faced a series of defensive lines that were expertly and tenaciously defended as it inched slowly northwards – the Trasimene, the Arezzo and then the Arno. And the toughest of them all, the Gothic line between Pisa and Rimini, still lay ahead. But during the summer the Americans had insisted on taking seven of their divisions out of the Italian campaign altogether to use in the invasion of southern France. Churchill complained loudly and repeatedly and took the matter up personally with Roosevelt time after time. But once again he didn't get his way.

Holland and Germany, 1944–1945

Westerbork wasn't a death camp, but its function was to ease the path towards death. It offered false reassurance, conveying the impression to those already condemned that they were at the start of a process that, while coerced and unpleasant, was at least survivable. Detainees lived in cottages that had cooking facilities and bathroom blocks. There was a school, a café and even a camp orchestra. All this also calmed the misgivings of the many Dutch officials who delivered people to the camp and drove them to the border when it was time for their relocation. After the war Westerbork's commander Albert Gemmeker escaped the noose because of this. To many people's surprise, a court accepted that he had reason to believe that the camps he sent so many people on to would be something like his own.

But it was nothing like the life that families such as the Goslars had protected for so long. The children were cold and often hungry. The accommodation was dirty. There were no opportunities for sport. There were no friends or warm family dinners. There were no clean, comfortable beds. Hanelli and Gabi Goslar were placed in the camp orphanage because their mother had died shortly before they were detained and they were not allowed to stay in a male-only hut with her father. Their grandfather was close by, but he collapsed one day and died in the camp hospital of heart failure, or so the doctors said. A life of picnics and piano recitals was replaced by one of anxiety and loneliness. Hanelli often imagined her friend Anne Frank living happily somewhere like Switzerland or England, and the thought brought her pleasure.

Word spread in the camp that many of the earlier inmates had been sent to a place in Poland called Auschwitz. Some asked if they could go there, too, so as to be reunited with relatives. If anything proves that the inhabitants of Westerbork — and probably all their guards — did not fully understand what they were part of, this is surely it. By the middle of 1943 Auschwitz and other now notorious mass-execution sites had been receiving and then killing trainloads of people for well over a year. When a large group of families, including the Goslars, were gathered together and sent to a place called Bergen-Belsen in Germany, some were disappointed that their destination was not to be Auschwitz.

Belsen is known today as a place of horror and disease, but it was not built to be a murder camp and when this large party of Dutch Jews arrived in February 1944 it was still possible to survive for many months, as the Goslars would prove. The Nazis preferred to carry out their mass executions on foreign soil rather than in the heart of the Fatherland, which is why the true extermination camps were all built further east. Belsen, near the Saxony town of Celle, was originally set up to hold prisoners of war but it was then expanded many times over to accommodate a range of different military and civilian detainees. Officially it was known as a 'holding camp' or sometimes an 'exchange camp' because one of its functions was to house people who might one day be traded for Germans being held by the Allies. That one piece of information brought the Goslars and others in their overcrowded train some hope as they attempted to reassure their children.

More hope came from Jews already living in the area of the camp to which most of the Dutch families were directed, the so-called 'Star Camp'. They said that the food supplies were the best to be had in Belsen and that people were indeed, from time to time, taken away and sent abroad to freedom as part of prisoner exchanges.

The 'better food' turned out to be a bowl of thin vegetable stew every day with a turnip and either a small piece of bread or a potato, but it was just about enough. The suitcases they had carried into Westerbork were long gone and they only owned the clothes and shoes that they stood in, but they were able to trade with other prisoners from time to time. There were some rough blankets in the huts, each with its own occupying army of lice, and for much of the time that is what the inmates wore draped around their shoulders and tied at their waists to help keep out the cold. Life became a round of roll calls, horrible latrines and working on menial jobs such as stitching sacks or repairing boots for the army.

Belsen may not have been a death camp but its inhabitants were far from safe. In late 1943, almost two thousand Jews from Poland who had been held here in the hope of a prisoner exchange were 'cleared' and put on trains to Auschwitz when the proposed deal collapsed. The weather, the poor food, the untreated diseases and the often brutal behaviour of the camp guards also caused death, especially among the elderly. Inmates tried to steal food and clothing but the penalty for those caught with even an old pair of shoes was violent and often fatal. In the women's barracks they fantasised about dinner parties, imagining elaborate menus with soups, grilled meat, fresh vegetables, rich sauces and seven-layer chocolate cakes. Hanelli Goslar dreamed of toast and boiled eggs, a hot bath and clean sheets. The women also discussed whatever scrap of news they could pick up from the guards, stories of the great battles in France and the nightly bombing raids on Germany. In the skies they sometimes saw hundreds of British or American warplanes pass close by. Everyone clung onto the hope of liberation as they just about endured their insecure, hand-to-mouth existence in the camp. But soon even the desperate struggles of these days would feel like a happy memory.

India, 1944–1945

Nurses were taught that the bedpan contained information vital to the health of their patients and so they should examine it closely however unpleasant a task that may be. As a result Angela Noblet and Mary King had seen just about everything a human body could produce. But neither of them had ever seen anything quite like this.

Urgently seconded to the Indian civilian hospital, they came upon an entire ward full of men and women trussed up in hammocks with holes cut into the base of the fabric, suspended over bowls set to catch the continuous gushes of waste that emerged from them 'with the consistency of rice-water'. This was cholera, a local outbreak caused by drinking unboiled water, and everyone was petrified of it. Before they even approached the beds they scrubbed every inch of themselves and wrapped their bodies tight in gowns, masks and gloves. The dangerously dehydrated patients were bound tightly in their canvas cradles, writhing and groaning like human larvae inside the folds of mosquito netting, a vain attempt to keep the clouds of flies away. The intense vomiting and purging, the shrieks of pain from paralysing muscle spasms, the sweepers continually emptying the stinking bowls, the nurses fussing around trying to insert saline drips into collapsing veins so as to pump some moisture back into shrivelling bodies — this was all entirely new and frightening.

'So must the wards of Scutari have looked to the Crimean nurses,' Angela wrote later that day back in her bungalow. But of the ten cases that Mary and Angela personally nursed through this crisis, all survived. Apparently the worst infected hadn't even made it to the wards. Amid the shock and the fear, both women were proud of how they had cared for — and helped save — so many people.

> The normally silent Mary King has come to life over this traumatic episode, revealing depths of feeling that I for one had not known existed in her. Behind that calm face with its perfect features is a personality that slept like a *princesse lointaine* waiting to be awakened by the right circumstances or person into a joyous vitality. I hope that I will be around to see it happen.

In the days that followed the nurses nervously checked each other for any sign of infection, but none appeared. The only dangerous thing that happened was a leopard casually wandering across the track leading to the hospital one evening as they returned from a party. And, although it felt bizarre to move between the reality of a cholera ward and a fantastical evening under fairy lights, the busy social life of the nurses did continue apace. There being so few British women around, they were continually invited to dinner dances, picnics and numerous other events, even from army and air force bases many miles away. Military trucks were provided to ferry them back and forth and there were usually gifts and hard-to-get culinary treats on offer as further inducement. On one memorable night Angela met the 'splendid' Angelo, a Greek-born officer and 'the only man I met in India who could dance the tango properly!'

One evening, while being driven home by an off-duty ambulance driver, she faced a moment of personal crisis. As they trundled along an isolated valley road the ambulance lights went out and the driver suddenly stopped the vehicle, claiming a technical fault. 'Very well,' she said, 'I shall walk' and immediately set off by herself in the dark. At that the electrics suddenly worked again and the driver called out, *'Tik Hai,* Miss sahib, lights work now.' It might all have been true or it might, as some of her friends thought, have been a version of the 'running out of petrol gambit' used by 'pouncers' and would-be rapists the world over. Angela questioned herself intensively about her reaction. Did she panic because the driver was Indian? Would she have behaved differently with a white man? Was this in some way connected to the hospital worker she had struck in the face? Or was it part of some INA plot to kidnap a British nurse? Either way, after that 'Miss Summerfield and Colonel Cawthorn concocted a new rule that sisters should never travel alone'.

Angela hadn't seen Teddy since their trip to the tea plantation, and didn't trouble her diary with details of any letters that might have been exchanged in the weeks that followed. Yet suddenly, not long after the cholera outbreak, she wrote that they were engaged to be married. She did mention a 'charming' letter she had received from his mother, delighted that her son had found such happiness with her, but there was nothing about her own happiness, or any emotional reaction at all. Given the intense self-analysis in the earlier pages, and the great joy she had expressed at the beginning of the relationship, this is a surprise. It may have been the shock of her encounters with the cholera bacillus, the ambulance driver or the prowling leopard. Or perhaps it was a lurking doubt.

India and Britain, 1945

India had long been a key source of raw materials for factories in Britain, something that infuriated nationalists. But now, with the imperial motherland struggling to support operations stretching across five continents, and with enemy submarines prowling the oceans, India's *own* factories were encouraged to take up the slack. A new generation of business people and entrepreneurs immediately rose to the challenge. The empire needed clothes, chemicals and cement, paper, parachutes and paint, machine guns, mortars and medicines, and by 1945 India was producing as much of all this as South Africa, New Zealand and Australia combined. Railway lines and bridges were constructed, forests were felled and mines were dug. There were new airbases, weapons depots and all manner of military infrastructure, all of which needed staffing and defending. The number of military airfields alone rose from just sixteen in 1942 to over two hundred by 1945.

Ammunition became a particular Indian speciality. Over the course of the war almost a billion bullets left Indian factories en route to Allied rifles and machine guns along with nearly nine million artillery shells, five million bombs, grenades and mines and 6,250 armoured vehicles – hugely impressive from a nation that had not produced as much as a single armoured car before 1939. The Bengal and Assam Railway ran from Calcutta up into the mountainous regions of Assam and East Bengal where the

Kohima and Imphal campaign took place. Originally built to serve the tea plantations that proliferated here, its rickety infrastructure and numerous changes of gauge made it unsuitable for supplying Allied armies. But after a major effort — and an injection of American technical know-how — a carrying rate of just 600 tons a day in 1942 rose to 7,000 tons by October 1944. It was still not enough but with the addition of more military transport aircraft, and all the new airfields, it gave 14th Army a further huge advantage over its enemies.

As Indian and British businessmen alike grew rich there were new opportunities for women to enter administrative and management roles. The Women's Auxiliary Corps proved popular and was one of the first British-run institutions in which all races served on equal terms and with equal pay from the start. Back in London some worried that the idea of female Indian officers commanding white subordinates could cause trouble, but the government of India went ahead anyway, a sign of changing attitudes but also of the pressing need to keep the war machine running when skilled workers of either sex were in such short supply.

India was modernising fast. Bombay, Delhi, Madras and Calcutta bustled with hostels, canteens, jazz clubs and dance halls, even during the worst days of the famine. Troops from across the empire and, increasingly, America too spent their money playing billiards and table tennis, going to concerts and watching movies. Previously rare consumer goods like refrigerators and gramophones filled the shops and new cars jammed the roads. All this drew people away from the rural areas, creating opportunities for poorer Indians to work as bearers and personal servants, tailors, taxi drivers and rickshaw-wallahs. It also created a new demand for prostitutes, fuelling tension between locals and the sinful foreign soldiers.

Along with American soldiers came journalists. They wanted to write about the independence movement and they inevitably contrasted the continued high level of official repression (most

Congress leaders were still under arrest) with all the Allied propaganda about fighting a war for freedom. Their articles reached British servicemen and women, too. But what is surprising is that these same people were being slowly and subtly educated out of imperialism by their *own* government at the same time. In a much-discussed pamphlet from the Army Education Corps called *The British Way and Purpose*, millions in uniform were able to read that

> we no longer regard the Colonial Empire as a 'possession', but as a trust or responsibility. 'Imperialism' in the less reputable sense of that term is dead: there is obviously no room for it in the British Commonwealth of equal nations, and it has been superseded by the principle of trusteeship for Colonial peoples . . . [a concept] already passing into the more active one of partnership.

From control to trusteeship to partnership, that was the way of the future. Statements like this would have had Winston Churchill spluttering into his brandy for most of his life but they were distributed far and wide by a branch of his own government. Britain was fighting on the side of freedom now and so its empire must evolve into something else, with no mourning necessary for past glories. The maps on schoolroom walls would remain predominantly pink but the nations represented there would increasingly become self-governing 'partners' rather than colonies. This pamphlet was one of many edited by Robert Marshall, the socialist son of a Scottish mining family and a leading force in the Royal Army Education Corps. He was a man of a new type. After the war he ran the Cooperative College in Nottinghamshire and established similar educational 'co-ops' all over the English-speaking world. Some of his former students went on to rule newly independent Commonwealth nations.

And so in one sense a large number of British troops came to believe that they were in fact waging war to abolish the age of empires altogether, including their own. It was a plot twist that doubtless pleased George Orwell. Back in 1941 he'd written his famous essay on patriotism, *The Lion and the Unicorn*. In it he attacked the excesses of empire and the old class system, but found his faith in what he called a specifically English — and definitely *not* Soviet — form of socialism. In the decency of the masses Britain would find its purpose and its future. J. B. Priestley, one of the most popular broadcasters in Britain, was another left-wing intellectual yearning for a new and better world. His remarkable play *An Inspector Calls* was written during the war and first performed in 1945. It was an eloquent and passionate manifesto for change, skewering the old Britain of bigotry, inequality and deceit.

But playwrights do not generally lead governments. As with the words of the Atlantic Charter, leaflets like *Way and Purpose* could only ever articulate a *vision* of a post-colonial world. Both parties in Churchill's coalition — with his sometimes grudging assent — were indeed happy to talk about that vision, and the goal of colonial partnership, too. But as someone in the Colonial Office said at the time (apocryphally but no less tellingly) a 'partnership' could also be defined as that between a horse and its rider. What was often *meant* by all this talk was change within a family of nations still directed from London. All those pink territories on the map would be steered towards a better future, with white hands still firmly on the reins. Because Britain was not going to stop being a global power overnight, however many standing ovations J. B. Priestley might receive in the West End, and there were many bills to pay.

SECTION THREE
Every Scrap of Territory

'What's real and what's true aren't necessarily the same.'
— Salman Rushdie, *Midnight's Children*

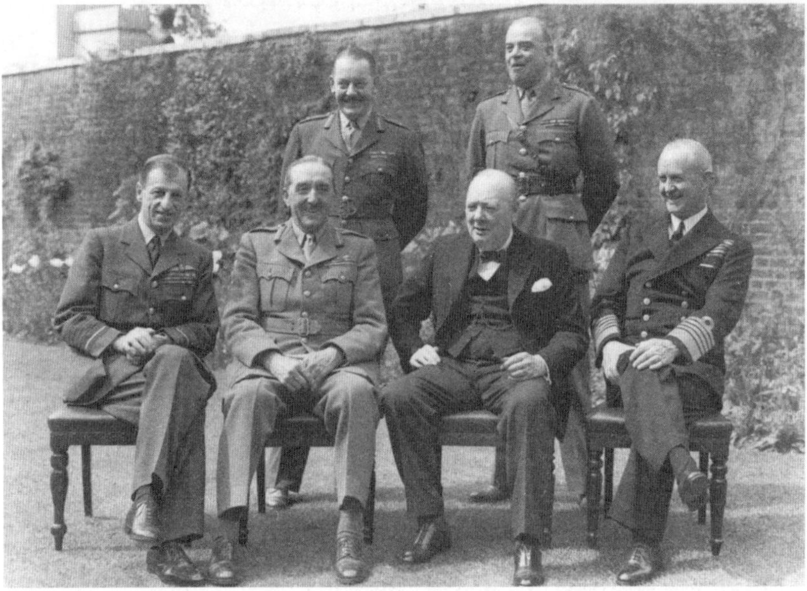

10

The Great Game

India and Burma, 1944–1945

After the long monsoon ended, fighting in Burma restarted in the final weeks of 1944 with Allied prospects looking ever brighter and the Japanese–INA position ever more difficult. Perhaps Bose and his allies had simply missed their moment. Popular anger about misrule and military failure had been running hot in India two years earlier but, since then, in military terms at least, the British had recovered their confidence and their poise. The 25th Division was ordered to return to Arakan for a drive towards Kangaw and beyond. After a month's 'monsoon leave' with his family Timmy was keen to be part of this big new campaign and he found his men rested, healthy and in a confident, combative mood. Their main role was to clear the hills between Maungdaw and Buthidaung. After his successes during the previous campaign in this region, Timmy was entrusted with attacking the first and most challenging hill of them all, codenamed 'Poland', where thousands of Japanese soldiers were waiting inside a network of deep tunnels. He studied the problem and learned what he could about his enemy, discovering that every morning a thick mist blanketed the hilltop. Perhaps the weather could mask his intention?

For days in a row he ordered an early morning artillery barrage in the hope that, when the time came to attack in earnest, the Japanese commanders would assume that any dawn gunfire meant nothing more than their daily harassment. He also instructed his men to practise silent night climbing. On the night before the attack went in, hundreds of them managed to get close to the summit without being detected and then, just when the mist was at its thickest and the morning artillery fire ended, they launched their assault, finding most of the Japanese still hiding deep in their tunnels. By the time they reacted, Timmy's *jawans* were already close enough to pick them off in their hundreds.

> As expected, when the attack began, a Japanese officer with several men came running down the trail. Corporal Man Singh leaped forward waving his kukri and screaming the battle cry. The Japanese officer drew his sword and charged. The officer also was holding a suicide grenade to his chest.
>
> Man Singh said that he did no more than touch the officer's head with his kukri, but I found that the officer's head had been neatly sliced off just above the eyebrows. In any case, the Japanese had been blown apart by the suicide grenade. Thus Man Singh would not have had his prisoner in any case, but I felt that he overestimated the brittle quality of Japanese heads.

Timmy could hear and see glimpses of the battle, but he had no idea of the result until he saw a 'success flag' on the summit of 'Poland'. Excited about joining his men in their moment of victory he jumped straight into his jeep and told his driver to head down a narrow jungle track. The next second he was lying in a ditch, his head ringing and his body aching from the impact of a huge explosion. In their haste and excitement neither the driver nor Timmy had considered the dangers of this little-used route and they had run over an uncleared Japanese landmine. All the men in the jeep survived but a clerk standing nearby lost his legs and they could not save him. It was a desperately sad way to celebrate a victory, but losses overall had been surprisingly light and he received warm notes of thanks from everyone in his chain of command, right up to the corps commander himself.

It seemed as if Timmy's brick-dropping days were well and truly over. Indeed, such was the admiration for what he'd achieved that he was quickly made acting commander of the entire brigade, the first

Indian in the history of the army to rise this far. Lord Louis Mountbatten, Supreme Commander of Allied Forces in South East Asia, was visiting nearby and asked to meet Timmy to thank him personally. Travelling with Mountbatten was his new Chief of Staff, Lieutenant General Sir Frederick Arthur Montague Browning, known to all as 'Boy' Browning and the man credited with the famous phrase 'a bridge too far'. As the photographers started snapping, Browning caught sight of Timmy and shouted cheerfully: 'You must have been with me at Sandhurst. What a delightful surprise!' Photographs of Timmy and a group of other Indian officers being feted by a British lord and a knight soon flew around the world, a dark-skinned hero of the empire accepting the gratitude of two members of its ruling elite. And it was without doubt a glorious moment for Timmy. As a boy he'd dreamed of military success and social acceptance, of being allowed the kind of life he could only glimpse from his school dormitory window: the uniforms, the medals, the admiring glances. All were his now. He was proud of himself, of his men; but most of all he was proud of the Indian Army.

As ever, Bose and Timmy make for an irresistible comparison. The Hyderabadis and all the other Indian, British and African troops now fighting across Arakan and on the Chindwin River felt more and more part of a winning team. Not far away Bose's own bedraggled troops, disappointed by their lack of success at Imphal and Kohima, and unhappy at the way their Japanese patrons were treating them, had to lick their wounds and wait for the next Allied attack. And yet today it is Subhas Chandra Bose, failed invader and ally of Imperial Japan, rather than General (as he became) Kodandera Subayya Thimayya who is celebrated as a national hero. Both wanted to create a new and free India, but which of them truly did most to bring it about?

Leaving the glad-handing behind him, Timmy turned to his next mission and, although he did not yet know it, an appointment on board HMS *Phoebe* with a hot bath and the Admiral's finest whisky.

London, Washington, Warsaw, Moscow, 1944–1945

If persistent mistrust between Britain and America was troublesome, that between Britain and the Soviet Union was downright dangerous. When Russia had been an empire it had joined enthusiastically in 'The Great Game' against the wily representatives of Queen Victoria and King Edward VII, vying for influence and opportunity wherever they were to be had. To many inside the British government it felt like that game had started up again, but this time it was being played not against an imperial family in St Petersburg but a global communist movement controlled from Moscow and backed by the ever more powerful Red Army.

That Stalin's men were flexing their muscles and looking to conquer — or at least dominate — new territory was hardly a surprise. After the horrors of Nazi occupation it was accepted in London and Washington that the Soviet Union would need — and deserve — a 'buffer zone' to its west, especially since many of the governments there had initially chosen to side with Hitler. Romania, Hungary and Bulgaria would all pay the price for that. But Poland was a very different case. Britain had gone to war explicitly in defence of Polish independence and everyone in London remembered that, at *that* time, Stalin and Hitler had carved the nation in two amid much repression and bloodshed. The Polish government-in-exile — and the tens of thousands of Polish fighting men and women serving alongside the British — hoped that their independence would be an explicit war aim for Churchill and Roosevelt. And indeed it was, until the negotiations with Stalin about the post-war world turned serious and everyone realised that in this new Eastern European iteration of 'the game' it was the Soviets who held most of the high cards.

The fate of Poland was one of many difficult issues that hovered at the margins of the numerous 'Big Three' summits in the final year of the war. Despite all the inspiring talk of a new 'United Nations', signs of a renewed global confrontation were becoming ever more visible, although in London they worried that Roosevelt's men didn't see them clearly enough. Stalin repeatedly refused to accept clear evidence of the Soviet massacre of more than twenty thousand Polish officers and intellectuals at Katyn in 1940, a massacre carried out at his command, and neither Churchill nor Roosevelt challenged him directly on it. The many euphemistic conversations about 'spheres of influence' during 1943 and 1944 meant one thing to Churchill but something else entirely to Stalin, as became painfully obvious when a citizens' army in Warsaw rose up against the German occupation in the summer of 1944. The Red Army was already on Polish soil but it was ordered to halt while the Germans slowly and remorselessly destroyed all resistance in the city. To make things worse, the Soviets did everything they could to prevent the Western Allies delivering aid to the rebels, and delivered almost none of it themselves. And so the dream of a strong, free and independent Poland was crushed by Hitler's troops, Stalin's disingenuous dealings with his allies and the Red Army's studied inaction. At the height of the uprising, Churchill wrote to Roosevelt saying that Soviet behaviour 'constitutes an episode of profound and far-reaching gravity'. But by now Stalin was openly calling the brave fighters of Warsaw 'criminals' and 'adventurers', confident that Roosevelt would not take Churchill's side with any force. This was partly because he was playing a game with the Americans, too, holding out the prospect of joining the war against Japan and offering access to airbases in Siberia which would greatly boost US air power in the region. In Washington they were already planning for an invasion of the Japanese mainland and anticipating a frightening level of casualties. Any help that Stalin could give to reduce that number might be worth a few concessions in Eastern and Southern Europe.

Churchill's long-serving — and long-suffering — private secretary Jock Colville called the events in Poland 'a black cloud in an otherwise azure sky', but it meant rather more than that. Churchill saw that Soviet intransigence about the post-war government of Poland — and Stalin's attitude towards the Baltic states — proved that he could no longer guarantee that Czechoslovakia, Austria or Greece would end the war as allies of the West. So he began some game playing of his own. When the Germans pulled out of the Balkans, Churchill enthusiastically backed the exiled King George II of Greece and ordered a reluctant Alan Brooke to prepare British forces to support the royalists in the civil war he saw coming. That war would be fought against communist partisans who had taken the lead in resisting the German occupation of their country, sometimes with British help, but who were now aligned more with Moscow than with London. As more and more units were committed to this 'policing' mission, Alan Brooke grumbled to his diary and Britain's other commanders – their own urgent supply requests going unanswered – fumed to their secretaries. When the crisis exploded into open warfare on the streets of Athens the British Labour Party and most of the Americans immediately saw the long shadow of imperialism behind Churchill's bellicose response. A prominent critic of British policy, the *Chicago Herald Tribune*, used the events of Greece to accuse the President of being under Churchill's bloody thumb.

> Mr Roosevelt's fine purpose, at least since 1937, has been to preserve the British Empire. Now that the end has been achieved, and at very high cost to us, the State Department discovers that Britain is stepping out on her own to dominate as much of the world as she can, and this apparently amazes the State Department?

The arguments about supply and shipping grew so intense at this point that the Americans threatened to stop British equipment even *going* to Greece. In response Churchill drafted – though did not send – a furious letter to Roosevelt speaking of a 'fundamental breach' between the two countries.

THE GREAT GAME

East Bengal, 1944−1945

Gliding along the wide Brahmaputra River, the stately nineteenth-century paddle boats of the Indian Hospital River Steamer Service carried the sick and wounded from one hospital to another, depositing many of them onto the special medical trains that now ran from Sirajganj to Calcutta. Although an experienced 'India hand' by now, Angela Noblet had lost none of her enthusiasm for exploring this spectacular and exotic land, which is why she had requested this very special posting. After the heroics on the cholera ward her matron gave her the welcome news that she would *not* be joining most of her friends heading east to support General Slim's army. Instead, she'd be going back to sea, or at least to a river that could be as thrilling and dramatic as any ocean.

Her steamer was a floating microcosm of empire. The doctors and nurses were a mixture of British and Indian. The master was a Muslim from Chittagong with a long flowing beard, black embroidered waistcoat and a bright red fez. Angela thought he looked like an Old Testament prophet. Many of the crew members were Muslims, too, and the smaller number of Hindus had their own separate cookhouse, although food was shared with little regard for religious sensitivities as far as she could see, in what was a harmonious and friendly little community. As they navigated their way along the river, ever alert for shifting sandbanks or drifting patches of thick vegetation that might clog the paddles, she enjoyed the sight of fishing boats and paddy fields and delighted to hear the echoing sound of temple bells.

> Sometimes, despite the Master's best endeavours − and the religious-like intoning of the crew member charged with measuring the water's depth − we drift onto a sandbank. But he always manages to free us after a great deal of shouting, clanging of bells and reversing. He showed us a paddy field where, a few

years ago, one of the steamers was left high and dry in the night, the river having whimsically altered its course.

Each steamer could take about a hundred patients. Some were dangerously ill, especially the numerous burns cases, but there was little of the drama or the pressure of battle casualty treatment and she had time to nurse the men personally, learning their names and family histories and helping them write letters home. 'They fill every available space,' she wrote in her diary, 'lying wearily on their straw mattresses gazing at the passing scenery, only too glad to be in an area where they are safe from sudden death.' Many of the casualties coming out of Burma were recovering from dysentery and she had the cooks make them simple meals of milk and eggs, knowing that their bodies could not yet tolerate meat or even fish, even if that was what they craved. In the finest traditions of the British afloat there was an evening rum ration, and often time to relax along with her colleagues and her 'boys' at the end of the day, revelling in the peace and beauty all around them, hearing stories of the very unpeaceful places where they had been just days before.

Angela made what she called her first 'native friend' here, a fellow nurse called Mary de Souza from Goa. Mary instructed her in Urdu and taught her how to wear a sari and dance to Indian music, much to the delight of the crew and the other Indian nurses and doctors on board. During the long, warm evenings the women would sit together, gazing out at the 'lights in riverside huts which look like nests at the foot of mop-headed palms and sampans silhouetted against a primrose sky'. As plunging birds dived for fish, they'd 'speak for hours under the stars of everything and nothing'.

> The evenings are delightful. I have come to appreciate Indian food, music and stories of Hindu gods and goddesses, and gradually relaxed into a slower attitude to life, removed as I am from the hospital ward crises.

And, for once, supplies were generous, too.

Face-flannels and toothbrushes, soap and razors, socks and pyjamas and even exotic things like port and brandy. Now and again we find a note tucked into the toe of a sock giving the name of the knitter and a town in the United Kingdom. This pleases everybody beyond belief.

Whenever they stopped to pick up or discharge their human cargoes it felt like a special occasion, celebrated with gangs of school children on the piers along with music and waving flags. Mary and Angela were invited to more dinners and parties than they could ever possibly attend. One evening, in a scene that could have come straight from Kipling, a friendly Scottish jute manager with a large estate near Dacca invited the entire medical staff of the steamer to a grand dinner preceded by a raucously tuneless bagpipe concert in the garden of his club.

Angela was proud of her nursing on the river and enjoyed seeing weak and desperate men transform under her care. There was a shortage of qualified doctors and so Indian 'licentiates', partly trained medical staff, worked on the steamer, too. One evening, as a soldier with cerebral malaria was slipping into a coma, one such young man had a crisis of confidence and held back from administering the intravenous quinine that Angela, from painful experience, knew was the only hope. 'As we stood there looking at the patient by the dim rays of a kerosene lamp, it suddenly dawned on me that he had never given an intravenous injection before.' She took his hand and encouraged him to try, and another life was saved. The recovering patients and the general bonhomie made it a happy ship and a hopeful time, and she was also able to learn a lot about the state of the war.

I sat with men from the Lancashire Fusiliers and the Leicester Regiment who came up to the serving hatch for a rum ration and a good 'dekko' at a genuine British female. They tell me how in the jungle it is the 'brew ups' and the fags that make life bearable . . . These men live on American 'K' rations until they hate the sight of them, although they are vastly superior to the British packs. And they long for air drops that supply them with such luxuries as canned fruit, rum and cigarettes.

The calmness and camaraderie of days and nights like these touched Angela deeply, as did the friendships and romances she witnessed between men and women of very different races, faiths and backgrounds. Her hand on that of the nervous young doctor, wheeling around the deck in her sari in front of her cheering friends, reciting Urdu poetry up toward the stars – all of it combined into a vision of a better world, an antidote to all the inequalities and abuse she'd witnessed. In her diary late one night, perhaps after one of her moonlit dances, she wrote:

> Ahead of us curves the moon, a single thread of light flanked by a single star which proclaims to the Muslim world the advent of Id al Fitr and the end of the long fast. The sky is a lucent indigo, drawing its light from the increasing stars rather than the fragile moon. Like the new fire of Easter in the Western world, this festival speaks of a fresh start in life. It is time for hope and trust in the future.

But despite feeling so hopeful and sentimental, of her fiancé she wrote nothing.

London and Athens, 1944–1945

The Greek crisis underlined Britain's rivalry with the Soviets but it also threatened the coalition that had held Churchill's own government together since May 1940. Prominent Labour MPs worried about British lives being risked to reinstall a king, irrespective of what ordinary Greeks might want. And by now Alan Brooke was losing faith in Churchill, too. He would always credit his prime minister with the astonishing leadership that had been necessary to carry Britain through the early years of the war — the backs-to-the-wall days of 1940, the disappointments and defeats that so often characterised 1941 and 1942. But now he wrote that

> I feel that we have now reached the point that for the good of the nation and for the good of his own reputation it would be a godsend if he could disappear out of public life. He has probably done more for this country than any other human being has ever done, his reputation has reached its climax, it would be a tragedy to blemish such a past by foolish actions during an inevitable decline which has set in of late, and I am filled with apprehension as to where he may lead us next.

In the end Churchill did prevail over Greece. The army delivered the troops and Roosevelt gave him his unenthusiastic approval and some ships. But Alan Brooke thought that the pressures of these months had driven his boss over the edge. Amid many 'bad' meetings he contemplated resignation time and again. One of the worst moments came after what he called a 'frightful' encounter with Churchill who was

> in a maudlin, bad-tempered, drunken mood, ready to take offence at anything, suspicious of everybody, and in a highly vindictive mood against the Americans . . . He then put forward a series of puerile proposals . . . [and] . . . it was not until midnight that we got onto the subject we had come to discuss, the war in the Far East . . . he became ruder and ruder . . . Fortunately he finished by falling out with Attlee and having a real good row with him concerning the future of India. We withdrew under cover of a smokescreen just on 2am, having accomplished nothing beyond losing our tempers and valuable sleep.

More signs emerged that the fall of Hitler would not necessarily bring peace and harmony to the European states he had occupied.

In November the communists threatened a coup in recently liberated Belgium and were met by British troops and tanks on the streets, forcing them to back down. And the fighting in Greece was growing more serious. Extreme right-wing factions, including former Nazi collaborators, fell in behind those already being supported by the British Army, whilst Moscow secretly worked with the communists. The war against Hitler was far from over but already two of the three Allied governments were waging a kind of proxy war against each other. Churchill believed that Stalin had promised him a free hand in the Balkans in return for Soviet control of other parts of Eastern Europe, but that's not how 'the game' was being played in Moscow now. On 3 December 1944 Greek police loyal to the monarchists shot dozens of left-wing protestors dead as British troops stood close by, leading to a widespread outbreak of violence. It was a vicious urban war and Churchill was determined that Britain's side should win it. In the left-wing London press there was outrage. The *New Statesman* thundered that British troops were 'still shooting our friends' in Greece and that 'with every shot we fire . . . we make it harder for any of our Allies, whether in France, America or the Balkans, to trust or respect us'.

It seemed like a Churchill-led attempt to crush a popular left-wing movement of anti-Nazi fighters in order to aid a right-wing faction that now included open Nazis. And certainly, on the night of 4 December 1944, Churchill wrote to the British commander in Athens in tones that feel redolent of the earlier wars of empire, ordering him to behave 'as if you were in a conquered city where a local rebellion is in progress . . . We have to hold and dominate Athens. It would be a great thing for you to succeed in this without bloodshed if possible, but also with bloodshed if necessary.'

Amid chaotic street fighting, massacres and roadside executions, British units were in deadly combat with their former allies in the ELAS movement, while fighting alongside men who had served in the notorious 'security battalions' that had exercised power during the German occupation. Over two hundred British troops would die, and a thousand would be injured, in this morally confusing battle for the Greek capital. Images of Lend-Lease-supplied British troops using US equipment to defend a monarchy against republican rebels sent the worst possible message to Washington and the American press. Less concerned about politics and more about logistics, Alan Brooke simply wrote that 'one thing is certain — we must get out of the mess that this Greek venture has led us in'.

When Churchill visited Greece at Christmas he narrowly escaped a sniper's bullet but he could not dodge the political explosion back home. Labour MPs, newspaper editors and numerous trade union leaders queued up to condemn what was being done in Athens. Soon the crisis triggered a vote of confidence in Churchill's own government. He argued passionately that his enemies in Greece were not democrats but mobs of gangsters trying to impose a new kind of authoritarian rule. But those who remembered the Spanish Civil War declared that, once again and despite everything that has been said about freedom, Britain was standing in the way of popular democracy. In the end only thirty MPs voted against the government and the mainstream Labour leadership remained inside Churchill's Cabinet, but the revolt was a sign of much more trouble to come.

Burma, 1945

When Burmese nationalist leader Aung San decided to abandon his alliance with Japan and switch sides at the beginning of 1945 it left the INA even more exposed. Few of Bose's men now believed that they could beat the British. But his repeated argument that a public display of resistance and sacrifice would inspire their fellow Indians motivated enough of them to put up a serious fight. When 14th Army first attempted to cross the Irrawaddy in February, Gurbaksh Singh Dhillon's 'Nehru brigade' was waiting on the eastern bank, inside bunkers that overlooked the river. Slim claimed that this was the widest opposed river crossing of the twentieth century, and opposed it certainly was. The first soldiers put onto the water opposite Dhillon's INA men were all white – a battalion of the South Lancashire Regiment – because, according to Dhillon, the British commanders he was fighting still worried that their *jawans* might decide to join the INA after all. Whatever the reason, the small rubber and canvas boats carrying the English troops made easy targets for the INA's machine guns, and the initial crossing was repulsed amid heavy loss of life on the British side (Dhillon claimed to have killed two hundred).

This was one of the few direct battles between the regular Indian Army and the INA and the rebels managed to inflict enough damage to send their enemies back to the western river-bank. But the INA had no artillery support while 14th Army had a lot of it now and in the end that, along with repeated airstrikes from 'Hurribombers' and tank fire from across the river, eventually drove Dhillon's men from their bunkers. In another opposed crossing, the INA's 9th battalion also caused casualties among the Indian troops attempting to traverse the almost mile-wide river. But in the end the khaki tide was just too strong. Dhillon had been living in a village where his men were treated as honoured guests right until the end. Even after Aung San changed sides the Burmese people living here said that they preferred to help the Japanese and their allies rather than the British. Or at least they said that to Dhillon. When it was time to withdraw he

> took a few minutes to see and thank the villagers who had turned up at the village gate to bid us farewell. Sobbing, I moved off looking at their sad faces with tears glittering in the light of the setting sun towards which our bullock-carts and men were moving silently ... Distance and time have not dimmed their image in my mind – their waving hands and full-throated good-bye of 'Jai Hind'. They made me love Hind [India] all the more and be prepared to pay any price for its liberty.

After the war Dhillon described the Irrawaddy battle as 'a sword against a needle, steel against spirit . . . but then enslaved nations have to wait for centuries for such a moment to fight for and pay the price for their liberty'. Leaving the river felt like saying goodbye to his last remaining hope of victory. Yet it did not diminish his love for Bose, who he dreamed of during the retreat, dreams that '. . . elevated my spirits. To be received by *Netaji*, even though in a dream, was auspicious' and helped him shake off 'the feelings of shame, despair, despondency and defeat'. A few days later the real-life Bose sent him a personal letter.

> I want to congratulate you on the manner in which you have stood up to face bravely the situation that is difficult. I want to express my complete confidence in you and in all those who are standing by you in the present crisis. Whatever happens to us individually in the course of this historic struggle, there is no power on earth that can keep India enslaved any longer.

The Japanese officers commanding the Irrawaddy campaign were impressed by INA field commanders like Dhillon, men whose 'close association with Subhas Chandra Bose made them very enthusiastic and eager to uphold the honour of the INA'. But they also felt that the INA's junior officers and ordinary soldiers were less well motivated and liable to give up the fight too quickly.

For all the temporary resistance of the INA, the Irrawaddy operation was a triumph. Using boats, barges and improvised pontoons, and supported by parachute drops – some real and some using dummies to deceive the enemy – tens of thousands of men and hundreds of vehicles were soon across the river and into central Burma. Within days they were spreading quickly through this flatter, drier region, ideal terrain for the type of campaign that Slim had planned – essentially a race to Rangoon before the monsoon struck in late May or June. It all relied upon a small but well-armed force being constantly resupplied from the air, fighting a numerically superior but less well-equipped enemy that Slim hoped to defeat through speed, combined arms warfare, flanking attacks and close air support. Airfields would be critical and the one at Thabukton soon fell, meaning that one of 14th Army's many innovations, an 'air transportable Brigade' could now come into play. Men and equipment poured off dozens of transport planes. High above in a 'cab rank' of ground-attack aircraft, predominantly the much-loved Hurribombers, RAF and Indian pilots awaited radio instruction. Slim's many forward air controllers could now guide these pilots to a target within minutes and the Japanese had almost no airworthy planes left to stop them.

From the ports that the British were using on the Bay of Bengal the ground distance to Rangoon was the same as that between Berlin and Moscow, but on worse roads and through much hillier terrain. So air transport was the only realistic way of supporting the men at the front. Although now much better equipped than his enemies, Slim continually faced bureaucratic battles to get the supplies — and especially the supply aircraft — that he needed most. Many of the planes he coveted were American and the men who controlled them had long been suspicious of British motives in Burma. Washington's priority in this region was getting arms, ammunition and medical aid 'over the hump' and into China, to keep Chiang Kai-shek's army in play against Japan.

Continually battered by Allied air power, and permanently low on supplies themselves, the Japanese had no choice but to dig, and to dig deep. Away from the jungles and mountains it was now a lot easier for 14th Army to see its enemy, and Slim's artillery blasted away at trench lines and bunkers. But in the end it was the tanks and the infantry that had to go in there and flush them out, such as the 9th battalion of the Border Regiment, including a young rifleman called George MacDonald Fraser.

Running across an open field, Lee-Enfield in hand, reciting poetry and fearing death, Fraser was at the sharp end of Slim's army, fighting alongside Indians and Gurkha battalions as part of the 17th Indian Division. Fraser experienced the terror of combat but also the savage joy of it. While clearing one bunker complex in a state of excitable panic he saw a friend killed right beside him. After hurling down a few grenades, accompanied by much violent abuse, he was then suddenly faced with a Japanese officer armed only with a sword and shot him dead with a pleasure he remembered for the rest of his life. Fraser loved the rough humour of the men he fought alongside — mostly from working-class backgrounds in Cumbria — and came to understand that, whatever high principles might have been at stake in this war, there was something about being in combat as part of a close-knit team that satisfied him at a level deeper than language.

When his battalion helped take the key town of Meiktila, the Japanese abandoned their dugouts and threw themselves upon the newly arrived British and Indian soldiers, in fighting as ferocious as anything seen at Imphal and Kohima. Fraser was in the middle of it all, shooting at targets only feet away, frantically trying to distinguish between Gurkha and Japanese in the dark. As the battle developed, 17th Division refused to play defence, sending groups of mechanised infantry and tanks out every day to seek and destroy the approaching Japanese columns, supported by squadrons of fighter-bombers. By defeating their enemy here, in what Slim called a 'magnificent feat of arms', Fraser and the rest of his division helped break the most effective Japanese units still fighting in Burma.

Fraser's comrades longed for home but were proud to serve under Slim. They still feared their tenacious enemy, but they no longer believed that the Japanese had any chance of beating them. He was often scared but recalled how thrilling it was to be part of a winning army, how he came to love the Cumbrians and the cheerful, brave and brutal Gurkhas, too. He was not the only one to derive great pleasure from all this. Lieutenant Colonel Hugh Pettigrew, a staff officer in Fraser's own division, called this a 'wild and exhilarating' time.

Fraser's friends spoke of black and Asian soldiers in language we would today call condescending, even offensive. To them the

Gurkhas were excitable children, funny little men twittering away in their strange language, always eager to please the white man and butcher his enemies. The Indians were scimitar-wielding harem guards, like something out of the storybook fantasies in Angela Noblet's trunk. The Cumbrians sang bawdy songs about whorehouses and rickshaw drivers, the slums and the squits. We don't have to like the lyrics to understand that they were men of their time and that none of this language stopped them respecting the black and brown people they fought alongside. If they were with us today they'd doubtless find it ridiculous that their soldierly banter would trouble anybody, and remind us that mockery and downright abuse is what they expected to get back in return. Judging by Timmy's account of his life, he'd have been unhappy at some of the racial language. But it's a certainty that, like most of the Indians who chose — and all *did* choose — to fight and die alongside men like Fraser, he'd have called these Cumbrians 'comrades' in a heartbeat, as his own Hyderabadis did the commandos at Kangaw.

Fraser also encountered many of the Burmese whose land was being contested by Japanese- and British-led armies, like the villagers who had just waved a tearful goodbye to Gurbaksh Singh Dhillon. He met community elders who just wanted to be left alone, bandit gangs that claimed to be on the side of whichever army they ran into and one angry old man who told him to take his stupid war somewhere else. The Cumbrians talked politics, too. Most were untroubled by the idea of Indian independence and planned to vote Labour in the coming election, just as he did. But mostly they talked of the families and the food that they missed, of films and film stars, of pubs and dance halls, teasing each other that their wives were probably out dancing every night and then sleeping with some wealthy American. More than anything else they just wanted to go home. Back in London the Home Office monitored letters from thousands of serving men and women and picked up hints of war weariness in Burma. Nobody wanted to be the last man to die in a war that was already all but won. They also picked up some resentment. It was obvious that the new government in London would do a deal for Indian independence, and that other colonies might not be far behind. Many had read the *Way and Purpose* pamphlet. So why were they still fighting and dying to raise a flag over places that Britain might soon be leaving anyway?

One day Fraser was on a patrol and came across four unarmed INA men who had either deserted or been abandoned by their comrades. They were sullen and resentful and he could hardly be bothered with the paperwork necessary to process them as prisoners of war. One of the Cumbrians quietly suggested to him that they discreetly shoot and bury the Indians somewhere, which is what the regular Indian units were all doing, or so he claimed. Fraser toyed with the idea for a few minutes but could not allow himself to do it.

Retreating from the British, and probably only a few miles ahead of Fraser, Bose spent most of his time now visiting the sick in hospitals and trying to travel without being attacked from the air. And war was not only raging on Burma's northern plains. In the mountainous south-east of the country British Special Operations Executive (SOE) agents had been busy, working with militias of the Karen people, long-term allies of the British and therefore much hated by Japanese and Burmese nationalists alike. As the Japanese tried to bring reinforcements into the country to help defend Rangoon, the Karen unleashed a highly effective campaign of ambush and sabotage. Working with supplies dropped from Allied aircraft, Karen fighters were key to what was called Operation Character and they wreaked havoc in areas that were supposed to be safely under Japanese control. Just over a hundred SOE men managed to marshal at least 10,000 local fighters (an army larger than the INA could now muster in Burma). They harried the enemy mercilessly and provided pinpoint information about targets for the RAF to bomb, including troop trains coming in from Thailand and numerous arms dumps. On some days there were too many targets for the RAF 'cab ranks' to handle. Modern estimates put Japanese losses to Operation Character at 11,000 men, probably more than were being killed by George MacDonald Fraser's Cumbrians and the other regular formations of 14th Army in the final months of the war.

London, 1945

Pressure was building in numerous places where the British, French and Dutch had held sway before the war. In Palestine, militants from the Stern Gang were targeting the British troops who controlled the region under the old League of Nations mandate. Although Churchill believed in creating a Jewish state in the Holy Land he was outraged when the gang assassinated his local representative – and close friend – Lord Moyne. Risking the wrath of American Zionist groups, he pulled back from earlier promises about immigration into Palestine, while British newspapers attacked America for promising Jews a new nation inside an Arab-majority area, which didn't sit easily with the language of the Atlantic Charter. But everyone was quietly backing away from the charter now. Even Roosevelt had not raised an objection when the victorious British and American armies in North Africa had essentially reimposed an old-school French colonial government across large parts of the region with no thought of a popular mandate or any of the other things that the charter had promised. As he watched both the Soviets and the Western Allies develop their own 'blocs', former President Herbert Hoover said laconically that the Atlantic Charter had apparently been 'sent to the hospital for major amputation of freedom amongst nations'.

In London, Churchill's private and persistent belief in the superiority of British rule contradicted the promise of 'global self-government' that was now at the heart of his own government's propaganda. India would almost certainly become independent – that much was accepted across British politics by 1945 – but as for the rest of the colonial empire, while progressive language was heavily to the fore, many on Churchill's side of politics hoped that life could carry on much as before. Even on the British left few believed that giving independence to everywhere straight away was possible or wise. In both the Labour and Conservative parties there was a widespread belief that it would take time to prepare for responsible handovers (the part of the argument that was said out loud) and that in the meantime the income from old colonial businesses would be most valuable (the part that was *not* said out loud). A desire to recover both economic assets and a sense of national prestige featured often in Churchill's private conversations, to stave off the steep economic and psychological decline that he feared was Britain's post-war fate. Jock Colville noticed this, too, writing in his diary that his prime minister was producing 'sombre verdicts about the future, saying that old England was in for dark days ahead, that he no longer felt he had a "message" to deliver and that all he could do now was to finish the war, to get the soldiers home and to see that they had houses to which to return. But materially and financially the prospects were bleak.'

With Washington still playing hardball about finance, and so much concern about the crippling lack of overseas income, it's not surprising that the British government wanted to recapture as many colonies as possible, especially ones that produced rubber, tin or oil that could be sold on the world market and bring in some much-needed cash. Churchill had explained to Alan Brooke back in June 1944 that

> the political importance of our making some effort to recover British territory must not be underrated. Rangoon and Singapore are great names in the British eastern world, and it will be an ill day for Britain if the war ends without our having made a stroke to regain these places.

Charles de Gaulle was also keen to see the age of empires continue for a little longer yet. As soon as he returned to France in 1944 de Gaulle looked to reclaim his nation's old colonies, publicly ruling out 'any idea of autonomy, any possibility of evolution outside the French bloc of empire'. The two old warriors, Churchill and de Gaulle, had clashed repeatedly throughout the war but now discovered that they had this at least in common. Both understood that American plans for a new world order would not necessarily be to the advantage of Britain or France. But how to persuade the Americans that a certain amount of old-school colonialism was allowable? One answer was the growing rivalry with Stalin. A new contest – between capitalism and communism – was going to dominate the post-war era, that much was already obvious, and many of the nationalist groups currently fighting in the Far East against Japan looked to Moscow – and the Chinese Communist Party – for inspiration and support. Perhaps, the argument went, it was better to have the old rulers back in their palaces than to see more territory fall to the communists. No doubt with this in mind, Churchill encouraged the French to send a mission to work with Mountbatten to discuss how formerly French-run Indochina might return to its pre-war state.

In this way the real threat of communism gave the old colonialists an excuse to review some of the promises they had made. If nationalist fighters against Japan – such as the ones currently serving under Ho Chi Minh in Indochina – could be recast as the local branch of the Red Menace then it was a great deal easier to turn on them. Or 'rat' as Churchill might have put it. And so, whether it was the result of anti-communism, national prestige, the desire to grab economics assets back or a mixture of all these things, a mostly hidden colonial agenda began to influence events in the final months of the war, even in some faraway and surprising places.

Faraway and surprising places like Borneo.

NORTHERN BORNEO

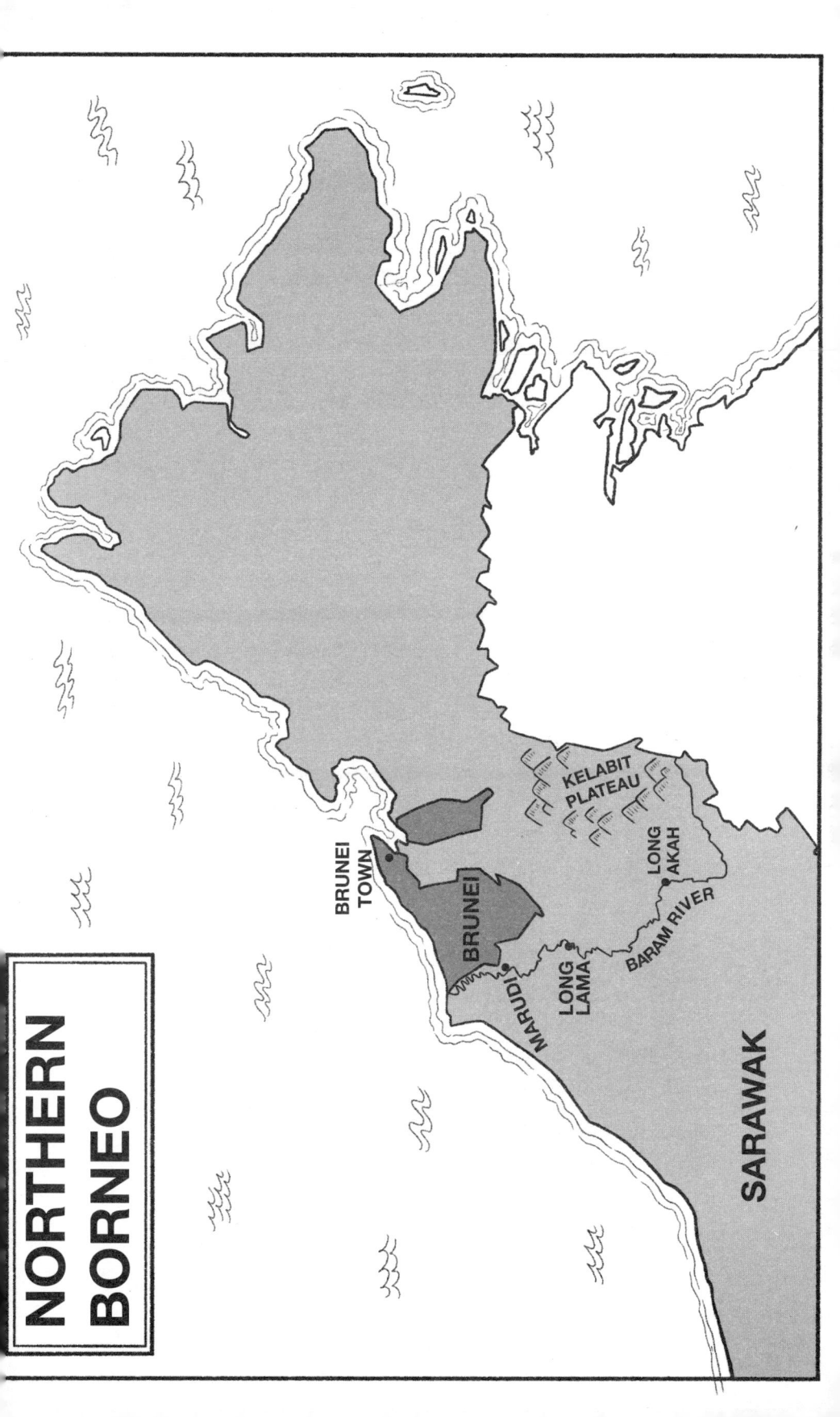

SARAWAK

- BRUNEI TOWN
- BRUNEI
- KELABIT PLATEAU
- LONG AKAH
- BARAM RIVER
- LONG LAMA
- MARUDI

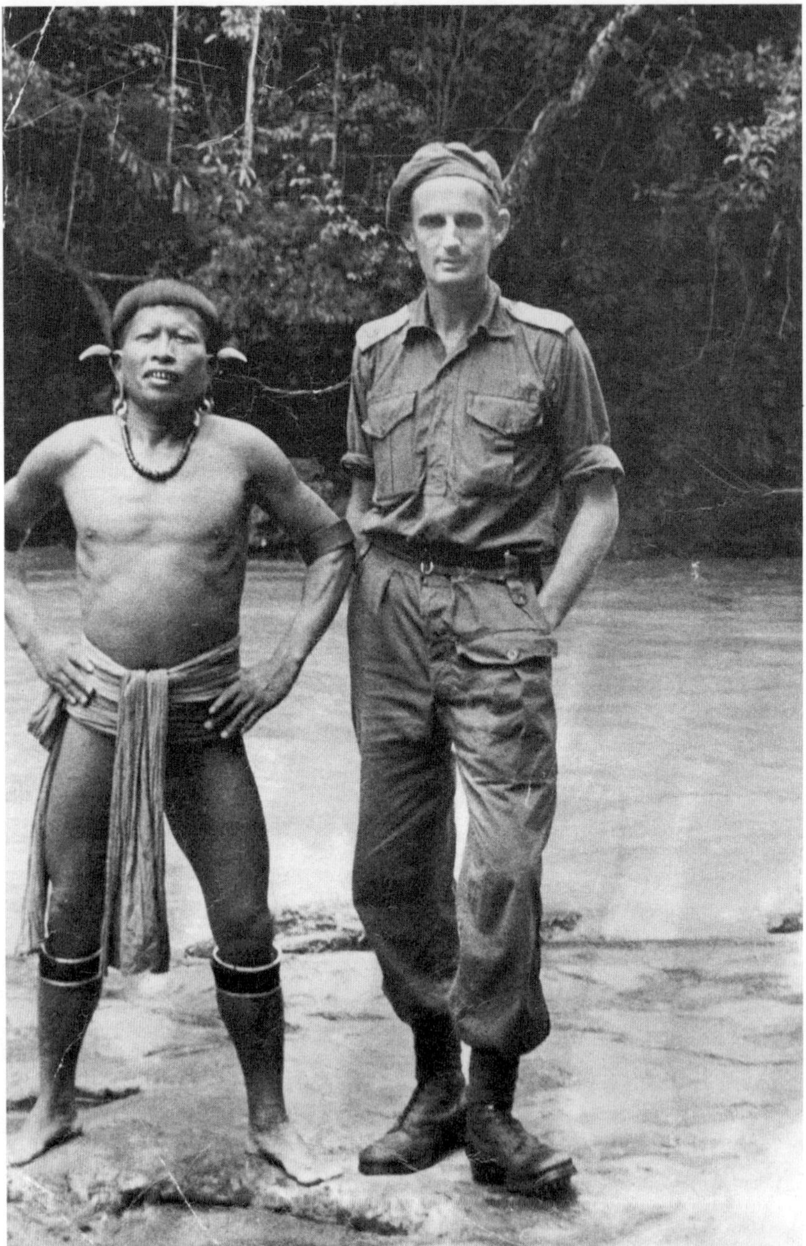

11

The Secret Agents

Borneo, 1945

Early on the morning of 25 March 1945 war came to the Kelabit Plateau with the sound of a furious anger, an unearthly rage that appeared to come from the realm of the spirits. Keling Langit heard it first, mysterious and disturbing, a rumbling ache from high above that resonated in her chest as it echoed around the paddy field. For a second she glimpsed strange shapes moving through gaps in the cloud. Two of them at first, swollen and grey, twisting and twitching, each with tiny black limbs moving jerkily on either side. Then two others, coming more clearly into view as they moved closer and lower, holding themselves upon the wind, like giant predators poised to strike.

> The big Liberator came round for the third time, rattling and juddering as its nose rose to the stall. But the cloud was back, and even thicker now, completely obscuring the valley. The pilot was certain that he was over the plateau but the drop zone was anybody's guess. And four of their mates were already down there somewhere.

Scared, Keling ran back to the longhouse. People inside had heard the noises, too, and also thought these could be spirits, angry or otherwise. Others said no, they could be flying warriors from the army of Japan, unseen so far in this isolated valley but already a potent source of fear. As the men gathered up their *parangs*, the curved machete-style sword of the Dayaks, it was quickly decided — if anyone or anything came to their home then Keling and the other women would immediately run and hide.

Jumping blind into an ocean of cloud, Jack Tredrea peered anxiously down through the wispy gloom. Then suddenly he saw a tangle of dark green rising up menacingly fast. They were nowhere near the valley floor, they were over the bloody hills. As the Australian Sergeant pulled his legs up close and braced for the kind of landing they'd all dreaded, he thought of the tiny white pill that Major Carter had pressed into his hand back at Leyburn.

'I already had a sense of how dangerous this mission was, but the cyanide brought it home to me. We knew very little of the local Dayaks. We knew that they'd had almost no contact with Europeans and that they were very primitive. And we were pretty sure that they were head-hunters.'

Lawai Bisarai was far from certain that spirits had come to his valley but until their intention became clear he wanted to greet whatever or whoever was descending through the clouds with due solemnity. As headman of the longhouse he pulled on his ceremonial robe and ordered food and drink prepared. Spirits or flying men, they might be hungry.

Another Australian, Corporal Charles 'Fred' Sanderson, was in the first group, the one that had so startled Keling Langit, and he was already safely down in the paddy fields along with his three mates. He looked up but there were no signs of the other four and, worryingly, he could now hear both of the planes droning off into the distance. Had the second section not jumped at all? Peering across the fields and irrigation ditches he identified the tiny settlement that they'd seen on the reconnaissance photos and made straight for it. Fluent in Malay it was his job to introduce the Semut team to the people of the plateau, assuming, that is, that the team still existed.

'All I knew was that we were to be dropped into enemy-controlled Borneo by parachute with no means of returning to our forces until an assault was made which would be months hence. Japanese occupied territory! And I had not been married very long.'

Hoping that the people inside it spoke Malay, and that Japanese troops were nowhere close, Sanderson walked slowly and deliberately towards the longhouse, carefully carrying his rifle low in his hand, barrel pointing back towards the jungle. He smiled and tried through his posture to be as unthreatening as a stranger armed with a lethal weapon that had just dropped out of the clouds could ever be.

Lawai Bisarai, in leopard-skin hat with feathers and dangling earrings, brass bangles on his calves, was still unsure. Was the figure a spirit after all? And if so what did it want of them? Pointing his gleaming *parang* down and away from the new arrival, he beckoned Sanderson forward with an unmistakable gesture of welcome, inviting him to step upon the ladder leading up to into his home.

Jack Tredrea smashed into the trees, his parachute tangling in the branches, his legs and backside bouncing off slimy trunks slick with thick green moss. A few cuts from his commando knife and he was slipping down to the moist, matted ground, three miles or so from Sanderson and the others; bruised, disoriented and anxious, but still very much part of Operation Semut.

As Tredrea picked the first of many leeches from his arm, Sanderson cautiously introduced himself to Lawai Bisarai, his first Dayak host, who did happily understand his Malay. At the same moment, somewhere between the northern Borneo coastline and the southern tip of the Philippines, one of the Liberators developed an unknown fault and disappeared into the Sulu Sea along with the eleven young men of its crew.

The headcount had begun.

1945: THE RECKONING

Formosa, 1945

Down the mine bonnie laddie, down the mine you'll go.
Though your feet are lacerated and you dare not answer 'No'
Though the rice is insufficient, and we treat you all like swine,
Down the mine bonnie laddie, down the mine.

Gunner Arthur Smith's adaptation of an old Scottish song that Arthur Titherington had never heard before became one of his favourites. The prisoners often sang as they worked. Hymns, ballads, even 'Rule, Britannia' from time to time, although the line 'Britons never will be slaves' always made them smile since that's exactly what they were. During their ball of rice lunch breaks and then at night back in their huts the men spoke of their homes and families, but the main subject of conversation was always food, devising imaginary meals that had them salivating in their bunks while John Marshall played Brahms's lullaby on his harmonica. They also spent hours dreaming up ruses that might win them extra nourishment. When the coast was clear they'd creep into the scrappy little farm that the guards had set up next door, stealing the pigswill from right under the noses of the animals. Treated like swine and eating like swine. But everyone understood that however bad it tasted it might give you that little bit of extra strength.

The heroic doctor Peter Seed, who had saved so many of them already, was now dangerously sick himself. His friend Ben Wheeler tried everything to keep him alive. In return for having a bad tooth pulled, one of the guards handed over a decent-sized piece of cooked pork. Wheeler fed all of it to Seed, whose body was craving protein. Then he tried a blood transfusion. Using his sole syringe he took blood from his own arm and injected it directly into his fellow doctor's veins. It worked and Seed pulled through. Then Wheeler faced a new challenge. Many of the men began to be infected with roundworm, which was very dangerous for bodies already weakened by malnutrition. Wheeler set aside an area for the worst cases and worked out inventive ways to treat them. One day he somehow managed to draw an enormous roundworm from the bowels of a suffering man by an inventive use of improvised callipers and a piece of string, a treatment that was as unpleasant as it was lifesaving. One of his patients at this time later wrote that

> sometimes the only way you could give vent to your feelings was to cover your head with a blanket and have a damn good cry . . . one night just after I had a fit of crying, Wheeler came up on the bed space and talked to me. And from then on I knew I was going to get out of it.

But how many of them would really get out of it? As the sound of American bombers came ever closer, Captain Imamura received secret orders from Tokyo to execute all his prisoners if the Allies ever landed in Formosa. Called the 'extreme disposition' plan, it called for a forced march to the mine with no one coming back. It was at this dangerous moment that Arthur Titherington suffered from the worst illnesses of his three-year incarceration: dysentery and malaria at the same time, followed shortly after by beriberi, generally a fatal combination. For the first time he felt close to giving up as 'disinclinitis' overwhelmed him. 'The time comes when it is easier to die than to go on living and now, after years of continuous hour by hour pressure, I too had reached the limit.' But with the improvisations of Wheeler, Seed and others, his own well-tested powers of recovery, and maybe a little help from all that purloined pigswill, he bounced back yet again to face another and then another in his series of 'just another days'.

By now there were only about 350 prisoners left and everybody could tell from the increasingly skittish behaviour of the guards that the end might be close. Still recuperating and covered in sores, his bones visible through his skin, Titherington was told to join a 'transfer party' about to set out for a new home deeper in the interior. Everybody immediately began to fear the worst but when they were handed farming equipment it became clear that the Japanese did indeed plan to use them for a few months more at least. And, remarkably, during the march to the new camp, he even saw guards helping prisoners who were struggling under the weight of shovels and hoes. At a small jungle clearing, they were told to halt. There were huts here for them to live in and land to clear to make ready for a sweet potato crop. The work was hard and the insects troublesome, but for Arthur it was a small improvement from the mine because at least he could spend his days in the fresh air. Fellow prisoner Jack Edwards disagreed. He thought that these weeks were, if anything, even worse than life back in the camp.

> We were walking on the narrow edge between man and animal. All of us looked ghastly, eyes sunken, mere skeletons, covered with rashes, sores, or cuts which would not heal. Others too far gone to save were blown-up with beriberi, legs and testicles like balloons.

Edwards' only pleasure came from seeing the American bombers high overhead on their way to attack Formosa's capital, Taihoku. At night they drank a kind of tea they made from a nameless root, nursed their cuts and sores and talked about their fate. Would the men who had treated them with such cruelty let them live to tell their tales? Should they run into the jungle and hide? In fact, there was still a plan under discussion back at the camp to shoot them all and dispose of their bodies in this remote spot if the Allies invaded. Unaware of this, they continued planting, weeding and hoping for the best. And after a few weeks they noticed that their guards seemed less and less interested, and that some of them were disappearing.

Yalta, 1945

The Conference at Yalta on the south coast of Crimea was the most consequential of all the 'big three summits' as the war approached its end. Stalin requested and received explicit signs from the Americans that the Western Allies would agree to his complete control of Eastern Europe. In return he promised Roosevelt that he would join the war against Japan, play a full part in the new global security architecture then being devised in Washington, with a new 'United Nations' organisation at the heart of it, and encourage all his new 'satellite states' to do the same. Churchill thought that his frail American partner had been outmanoeuvred. In fact — although undeniably frail — Roosevelt got exactly what he came for, a reduction in the blood price of defeating Japan. The more Soviet troops that could be brought to bear in the East then the lower US casualties would be. 'This makes the trip worthwhile,' he told his Chief of Staff Admiral William Leahy. Would the American president have been so keen to make this deal had he known that an atomic bomb was now only months away? Perhaps not, but at this stage nobody in Washington — of the minuscule number who had even heard about it — could be sure that the Manhattan Project would ever lead to a useable military device.

Either way there was little the British could do to change the direction of travel now, not with Soviet troops on German soil while the British and American armies were still on the wrong side of the Rhine. When Churchill did raise Soviet behaviour in Poland, Stalin immediately countered by talking about the violence committed by the British in Greece. And then conversation turned to possible future United Nations trustee arrangements for 'disputed territories and mandates'. Churchill saw this as an attempt to grab control of British colonial policy and immediately flew into a defensive rage so voluble that it astonished most of those who witnessed it, although Stalin sat through it all looking mildly amused.

'After we have done our best to fight in this war and have done no crime to anyone I will have no suggestion that the British Empire is to be put into the dock to be examined by everybody to see that it is up to their standard!'

The American note taker could not keep up with the invective that poured from the British prime minister and had to resort to note form, coming up with a sentence that perfectly captured Churchill's determination to hang onto as much colonial territory as possible, and perhaps his true feelings about the famous joint declaration he'd signed in 1941.

'Never, Never, Never . . . Every scrap of terr. over which the Brit flag flies is immune!'

When talk turned to the future of the colonies once again, Churchill tried to argue that the Atlantic Charter was aimed primarily at nations conquered by Britain's enemies and had never applied to *his* empire, which 'plainly irritated as well as bored' Roosevelt, the same note taker recorded. Back in London the prime minister defended his positions at Yalta in a parliamentary debate that ended in another successful vote of confidence in his government. Tory MP and former diplomat Harold Nicolson watched on and confided in his diary the same evening that

> he makes an extremely good case for arguing that Poland, in her new frontiers, will enjoy an independent and prosperous existence. But in his closing words before luncheon he rather destroys all this by saying that we will offer British citizenship to those Polish soldiers who are too frightened to return.

A few days later Nicolson had the chance to discuss the question privately with Churchill over a glass or two of brandy. He found that the bravado on display in the House of Commons had melted into melancholy and sad self-justification: 'He says that he does not see what else he could do. Not only are they [the Russians] very powerful, but they are on the spot; even the massed majesty of the British Empire would not avail to turn them off that spot.'

There was much official sadness and head shaking about the fate of Poland, which led Alan Brooke to a painfully embarrassing meeting with Polish General Anders, one of the heroes of Monte Cassino.

> The root of the trouble lay in the fact that he could never trust the Russians after his experiences with them whilst Winston and Roosevelt were prepared to trust the Russians. After having been a prisoner, and seeing how Russians could treat Poles, he considered that he was in a better position to judge what Russians were like than the President or PM.
>
> He said that he had never been more distressed since the war started. When in a Russian prison he was in the depths of gloom but he did then always have hope. Now he could see no hope anywhere. Personally his wife and children were in Poland and he could never see them again, that was bad enough. But what was infinitely worse was the fact that all the men under his orders relied on him to find a solution to this insoluble problem!

After so many months of frustration, success on the battlefield helped salve some of the consciences in Whitehall. Alan Brooke and Churchill were both quick to travel into Germany when the British Army finally crossed the Rhine in March.

> We walked up and down in the moonlight, it was a glorious night, and we discussed the situation we were in at the momentous moment of the crossing of the Rhine . . . He was in one of his very nicest moods and showed appreciation for what I had done for him in a way in which he had never before.
>
> I am now off to bed, it is hard to realise that within some 15 miles hundreds of men are engaged in death struggles along the banks of the Rhine, whilst hundreds more are keying

themselves up to stand up to one of the greatest trials of their life! With that thought in one's mind it is not easy to lie down to try and sleep peacefully.

On the other side of the world, a much smaller force was also keying itself up for a trial, in a shadowy operation that was very likely influenced by the arguments over colonial policy that had caused such rushed and bad-tempered notes to be recorded at Yalta.

Borneo, 1945

Long before he found himself handing out compasses, silk maps and cyanide pills in remote Australian airbases, Gordon Senior 'Toby' Carter was a proper old Borneo hand. He'd worked on the island for many years as a surveyor for the Royal Dutch Shell Oil Company's Sarawak fields, spread out along the north-west coast, about 250 miles from the Kelabit Plateau in distance but several centuries in terms of development. Carter spoke Malay, the dominant language in the populous parts of Sarawak, and he also had a smattering of some of the many dialects of the Dayak communities that inhabited the interior. The thirty-four-year-old New Zealander already knew some of the most important leaders there and had a good understanding of their culture, their lifestyle and the various feuds that existed between the different groups.

The men he commanded during Operation Semut described Carter as a diplomat who could fight. Although a proud Kiwi, he had happily served in the Royal Australian Engineers during the New Guinea campaign, which is where those planning Semut first discovered him. In an early sign that this mission was going to demand diplomacy with groups *other* than the Dayaks, Carter was first required to transfer to the British Army, which made him a major, and then join a shadowy Australian organisation called the

Services Reconnaissance Department (SRD). This was an Australian version of Britain's SOE, supposedly (but not always actually) acting independently of its bigger brother.

Carter recruited two Semut teams, each one initially made up of eight SRD men. Most were Australians but there were Britons, other New Zealanders, Malaysians and Chinese, too. His two deputies, Tom Harrisson and Bill Sochon, were both British. Normally at SRD men were selected for missions as much for their character as their expertise. 'Larrikins' were preferred, breezy, self-confident types eager for action and somewhat dismissive of military red tape or 'bull'. Men who could take control of difficult situations without waiting for orders from Canberra. But, in an early sign that Carter was perhaps not a natural fit for the SRD himself, he took a rather different approach, picking men he found responsible and reliable.

Their mission was to be challenging and unconventional. The Australian Army was planning to invade Borneo later in the year. Their job was to prepare the way by recruiting local militias, initially among the Dayak people of the interior, so as to gather intelligence about Japanese capabilities and intentions and, if possible, launch guerrilla attacks that would tie down as many enemy troops as possible and keep them away from the landing beaches. Everything they needed for this — food, communications equipment, medicine and weapons — would be delivered in the same way that they were, from the skies and through the ever-present Bornean clouds.

But behind Operation Semut lay another level of diplomacy altogether. The South-West Pacific was the domain of US General Douglas MacArthur. He had spent 1944 running a highly successful island-hopping campaign and was now busy retaking the Philippines, from which he had been rudely ejected in 1942, causing him famously to remark, 'I will return.' The US Navy's stunning success at the Battle of Leyte Gulf in October 1944 opened the way to Manila and, compared to that, some Australian Special Forces operation in Borneo seemed a rather minor consideration. But when viewed from London — where fears of post-war destitution were growing daily — there was nothing remotely small about Borneo. For many decades it had been a most profitable colony, the site of numerous plantations, mines and oilfields, offering an enviable expatriate lifestyle for the many British, Australian and New Zealand managers and their families who lived and worked there, one of whom had been Toby Carter.

The extraordinary Brooke family, the 'White Rajahs' of Sarawak, had nurtured one of the great imperial dynasties in Borneo. Until the Japanese expelled them, they had ruled a sizeable and wealthy part of the island for over a century, generation after generation, exploiting its rubber, gold, antimony and oil, running their unique little society largely along racial lines (Dayaks in the hills, Malays on the coast, Chinese dominating farming and the retail trade). There were golf and tennis clubs, squash courts and bridge evenings, with plenty of servants on hand to carry the drinks. Widely regarded as enlightened by imperial standards, the Brookes did enforce one colonial law with real vigour — a total ban on headhunting, which had been practised by some Dayak people for centuries and until recently played a significant part in their cultural and religious life.

The rich resources that first drew the Brookes to Sarawak also brought the Japanese, and now the British wanted their lost property back. But first they had to get past General MacArthur. They set out to do this with impressive sleight of hand, using the Australian military as, essentially, a cutout. The older and bigger brother of the two special operation units had ensured that it retained a powerful influence on the Australian SRD, although this fact was kept from SRD's mostly Australian volunteers and any watching Americans. British cash had set the group up in the first place and an actual British SOE officer, Lieutenant Colonel John Chapman Walker, was the SRD's most senior commander. Did he take his orders from Canberra or from London? It was never quite clear. When one of Carter's deputy commanders for Operation Semut, Tom Harrisson, was first interviewed in London for the role he was told that Britain needed to go back into Borneo to 'save some of the face' lost to the Japanese. Harrisson was a powerful character in his own right, and a genuine polymath who had helped set up Britain's Mass Observation project. But he was never an easy colleague, as many of his new Australian subordinates were to discover. As for the true power that lay behind Operation Semut, Harrisson soon took the view that the SRD was effectively the local branch of SOE.

The Americans were as suspicious of British intentions in the Pacific as they were in Burma and always ready to believe that London's priority was not the military defeat of their mutual enemies but the re-establishment of its empire. A popular joke among MacArthur's team was that their next-door neighbour, Mountbatten's South East Asia Command (SEAC), should really be called 'Save England's Asiatic Colonies'. So how was MacArthur to be persuaded to allow Operation Semut to take place on his own patch? Firstly, all political and colonial elements were excluded from the planning papers that went to the Americans. The operation was presented purely as intelligence gathering – identifying possible airbases, reporting shipping movements – so as to generate information that would be of great use to all Allied army, air force and naval units across the region. What the Americans did *not* see were the memos which spoke about the importance of 'showing the flag' in Borneo once again in preparation for a return to colonial rule, or an internal SOE document that described operations in Borneo very much in the language of the cloak and the dagger:

> . . . the real . . . objects of this mission, namely the softening of local inhabitants . . . and the arrangements for ex-Government officials to resume government of the Colony as soon as it has been liberated, have not been mentioned to [MacArthur's] SWPA as these are matters in which they would have no interest.

After some final lobbying and arm-twisting, and a well-timed reminder that fresh intelligence from northern Borneo could be very useful to the US Navy, the Americans signed the operation off. With MacArthur focused on the Philippines and Japan itself, control of Semut now formally sat with the Australians meaning, to some degree, the British. At this late stage, Carter's superiors also told him to set up groups of guerrilla fighters, something else that was never explicitly mentioned in the plan put before MacArthur. His instructions also became ever more explicitly political, looking towards a post-war scenario when there might be competition with the Americans themselves for control of regional resources. According to his own report (written in October 1945) he was instructed to

> investigate the internal political situation and ascertain the feeling of the natives towards the pre-war Government and the possible return of the [White] Rajahs and/or British Government . . . set up spheres of influence on the lines of the pre-war Government in order that the expected change over from active hostilities, to peace, could be carried out with a minimum of confusion.

Many years later Lieutenant Colonel 'Jumbo' Courtney, who was to take overall command of all SRD operations in Borneo, was cheerfully frank about what was really going on, namely 'the restoration of British rule in its Asian colonies and of its lost political influence in the Far East'. Needless to say, these aims were not uppermost in the minds of Jack Tredrea, Fred Sanderson or the other young Australians under Toby Carter's command as they parachuted down into the Bornean jungle, cyanide pills in pocket.

THE SECRET AGENTS

Belsen, 1945

As Allied bombers targeted Germany's cities and railways, food supplies ran low across the country and nobody was going to prioritise the people in the camps. Belsen's turnip stew grew thinner and thinner and its blankets more threadbare during a savagely cold winter. There were trainloads of new arrivals, too, mostly Jews evacuated from camps further east, putting yet more strain on already slender resources. Trusted prisoners drove horses and carts to meet the incoming trains, ready to pick up and dispose of the bodies of those who had not survived the long journey. The new arrivals were crammed into the existing huts, or put into temporary tent encampments, making conditions ever more uncomfortable. And that's when the typhus really started to spread. Inmate Dukie Gelber would always remember the first signs of it.

> Body lice brings a disease with it which is called spotted fever which is a type of typhoid transferred by the body lice and you get a temperature of over 40 Celsius or 100 Fahrenheit degrees and you get red spots on your body and you are so weak and you die, and most people died in the last months from spotted fever.

Belsen was still not formally a death camp, but it was about to become one of the most notorious places of death there has ever been. Inmates became so weakened by disease and hunger that they could no longer find the energy to leave the huts or even raise themselves from their filthy beds and stagger to the latrines. People who a week or so before had a modicum of energy and hope became listless and apathetic. Soon they would be laid outside the hut for the carts. Hanneli Goslar heard that there were some newly arrived Dutch in tents erected on the other side of a barbed wire fence close to her hut, and that one of them was called Anne. Could it be her friend Anne Frank? Risking severe punishment, Hanneli sneaked out at night in the cold and dark, hoping to catch a glimpse of the lively, clever girl she remembered and soon they were speaking through the fence. Anne explained that for two years she had been able to hide with her family but that now her parents were both dead in Auschwitz where inmates were being murdered in huge numbers (in fact, her father Otto miraculously survived the war). The following night Hanneli took a few scraps of food and threw them over the fence for Anne, but someone else took it, leaving her desperate. They cried together, remembering a lost life of warm food, clean beds and loving parents. Anne's sister Margot was seriously sick with typhus and now Anne was falling prey to the disease, too. 'I have no one,' she said in her utter despair. A few days later Hanneli did successfully manage to get some food to her friend but after that the tents were all taken down, the Frank sisters moved somewhere else and she lost all contact.

Everyone was now terrified of catching the typhus that was being spread by the proliferating lice. Parents tried to squeeze and smoke the insects from their children's tattered clothing. There were rumours that the Allies were fighting in France and Holland and maybe even closing in on the border of Germany, and fleets of shiny bombers crossed the skies unmolested almost every day, but could they keep themselves alive until the soldiers reached them? During February and March 1945 the typhus, along with dysentery and malnutrition, combined to kill thousands and by April the dead and dying began to outnumber the living. Guards still came occasionally to count everyone and make sure that nobody could escape, but the system for providing food, already ramshackle, was breaking down completely. Bodies lay thickly around the huts now, and just about all that the weakened people still living inside them could do was to drag them through the doors. They heard the sounds of war coming closer, and saw fewer and fewer Germans every day. But then, on 8 April, Nazi officials who looked businesslike and determined turned up with a long list of names. They told several thousand Jews that they were to be transferred to Theresienstadt in Czechoslovakia on board three special trains. They were informed that negotiations were taking place to trade them.

As soldiers shepherded them through the main gates of Belsen everyone feared that they were about be shot in some quiet forest. But the Germans had not lied. Deals *were* being made for detainees held inside the Theresienstadt ghetto. In February the SS sent over a thousand of them to Switzerland in return for a payment in gold from various international Jewish organisations. And perhaps their status as tradable Jews was the reason they received some small and unexpected kindness at the station. Women in uniform were waiting for them with water, bread, margarine and even tins of sweet biscuits. Then, as dogs barked and guards cracked their whips, they had to climb into crude wagons, sit on the bare wooden floor and hope. Hanneli and Gabi Goslar were there, but by now they were orphans. Only a few weeks earlier their father Hans had died of sickness and exhaustion. Their grandmother had also died recently and so now Hanneli, just sixteen herself, was trying to care for her five-year-old sister. She looked for Anne Frank but learned from another woman on her train that she had died of typhus in her hut, as had her sister Margot.

The train moved slowly through a nation that was falling apart. They heard explosions and air raid sirens every few hours. At one point the driver and his crew covered the roof with white sheeting in the hope that it would persuade enemy pilots that it was a hospital train. They stopped from time to time and were allowed to get out and search for water or any vegetables lying in the untended fields. Days passed like this. Sometimes they were motionless for twelve hours or more with no understanding of where they were or what was happening. Even in such a desperate situation some in the trucks did try to sound positive. 'If they wanted us dead they would have killed us already, it's going to be all right.' Sometimes they sang, sometimes they prayed. They tried to care for the sick but people were now beginning to die. They threw the bodies out by the side of the tracks when they stopped, or buried them in shallow graves when they could.

After a while the days and nights began to merge. There was a Mrs Abrahams who had done so much to help Hanneli and Gabi in the camp, a wonderfully kind woman who always went out of her way to comfort anyone who despaired, but she died of typhus on the floor of the wagon and so did her husband and her son. In her own sickness and delirium, it suddenly came to Hanneli that Mrs Abrahams had obviously been one of the 'hidden saints' that she had learned about at religious school, people called *lamedvovniks* in Yiddish, the humble men and women who enrich the world simply by their presence within it. Hannah tried to help people, too. She found herself close to a man shaking and convulsing with dysentery and attempted to steady the bucket, which resulted in her clothes getting stained with his diarrhoea. She barely noticed or cared. Some considered escaping into the trees, but who would help them there? Was it not better to stay together and hope to be traded? Nobody was quite certain. Hanneli still had her grandmother's engagement ring and she swapped it with one of the train crew for some food, including a rabbit they were able to cook at the side of the tracks during one of the longer pauses.

There's a famous set of photographs of one of these trains from Belsen, taken by a group of American soldiers who came across it, opened the trucks and set hundreds of people free. Joy radiates from the emaciated faces of the survivors as they climb unsteadily up the railway embankment, a woman's arms outstretched towards the men who have saved her. This was the 'Farsleben' train, which ran into Allied forces only two days after leaving Belsen. The people on it look wretched and desperate enough but the other two trains had it worse. One did reach Theresienstadt and its passengers joined the many thousands already living there in a state only marginally better than the one they'd left behind at Belsen, with almost no food, raging typhus and the fear that the SS would massacre them before the Allies arrived. In fact the Red

Army drove the Germans away and managed to save most of the remaining inmates of Theresienstadt. The final train, the one carrying Hanelli and Gabi Goslar, moved slowly onwards for two weeks. And every day more people on it died. After a week creeping eastwards to Berlin they spent almost two days in a railway siding on the outskirts of Hitler's shattered capital, just days before the Red Army began its final push into the city. Then they moved slowly south towards the Czech border. They heard — and felt — explosions that seemed perilously close and on 23 April came to a halt in the middle of a forest. And then they saw the train crew run.

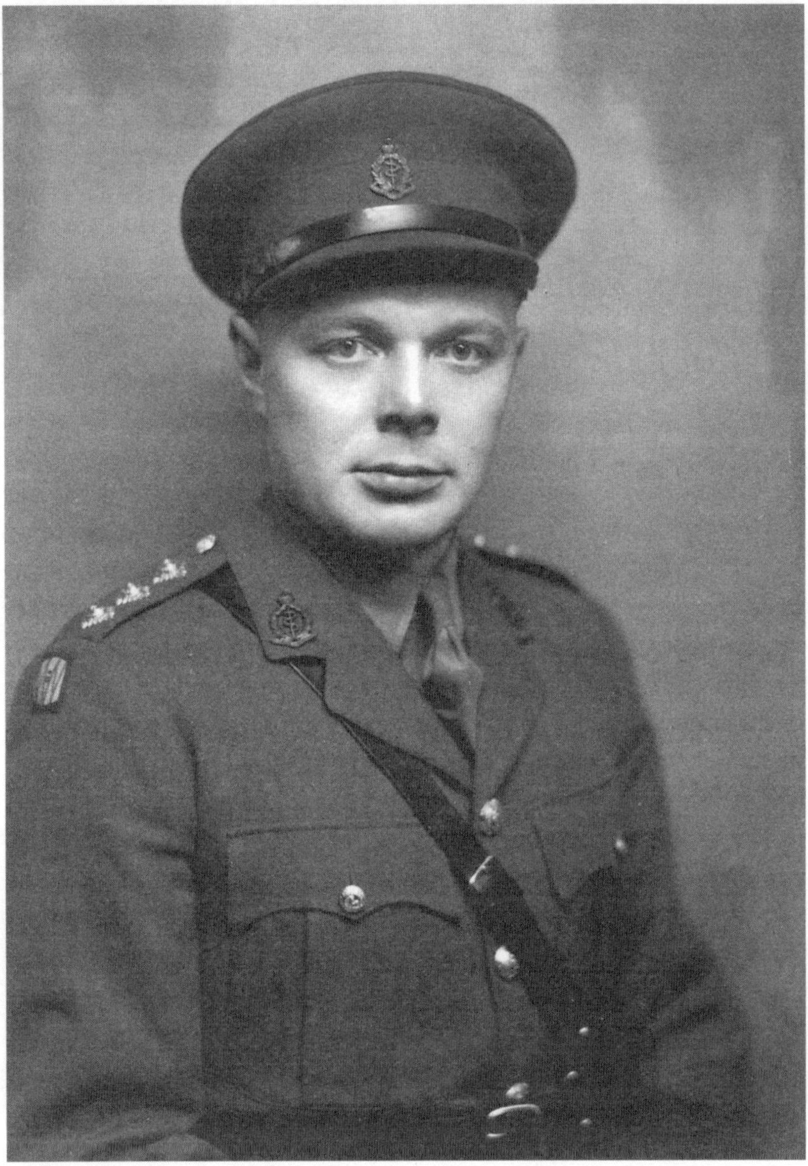

12

The Doctor

Germany, 1945

A Section:
Shovels
Stools, Camp
Tables, Camp
Containers 1 gall (tea)
Stretchers, ambulance
Lamps, hurricane
Splinting, Wire, Cramer pieces
Splints, knee
Haversacks Shell Dressing.

Contemporary observers were in little doubt that the medical support provided to British soldiers in north-west Europe in the final year of the war was the best of any army in any conflict that had ever taken place. As with the doctors and nurses on the India–Burma border, the secret lay in a blend of leadership, new techniques and treatments, and plenty of attention to detail. Number 11 Light Field Ambulance (LFA) was typical: a busy, positive and well-managed group of dedicated professionals. Its official war diary offers a window into its work, revealing the huge amount of organisation and equipment needed to create and run a forward military medical unit under the intense pressure of a fast-moving campaign.

C Section:
Hurricane lamps
Vapalux lamps
Primus Stoves
Water testing, poison and sterilization set
Two tins bleach, dubbin, canvas buckets
Trestles, stretcher pillows, blankets
Stretcher cover, anti-gas, basins
Oil stove, shovels picks
Axe, broom
Large saw.

Every fighting brigade of the British Army had an LFA attached to it, responsible for the medical needs of between three and four thousand men. Doctors and orderlies would recover and care for the less serious cases until they were fit to be returned to their own units. Others they would send to hospitals further away from the front line or back in Britain. Inevitably they were also the first representatives of British military officialdom to deal with the dead and fatally injured. A lot of care and thought went into this aspect of their work as well.

The label AF W 3371 will be attached to the peg marking the grave, which will be placed in the ground at an angle to protect the label from the weather. The label will show:

i) Army or personal number, rank, name and initials
ii) Regiment or Corps
iii) K/A (killed in action) or DW (died of wounds) or DIED.
iv) Date and place of death.

In the case of unidentified dead, any clues which may assist in establishing identity will be noted and forwarded to AD, GR and E 21 Army Group through normal channels.

THE DOCTOR

Lieutenant Colonel Mervyn Gonin, in peacetime a family doctor in Suffolk, was in charge. In his daily reports Gonin liked to highlight the performance of the doctors and orderlies under his command. Singling one man out in July 1944 he praised

> his conduct in the performance of his duties ever since the regiment landed in Normandy ... In particular on 18 July 44 at ESCOVILLE he showed great courage and example to others in recovering wounded men from a Stuart tank whilst under heavy and continuous mortar fire. His prompt action was undoubtedly responsible for those men arriving at the RAP [Regimental Aid Post] in good general condition. Recommended for award of MM [Military Medal].

Gonin came to rely upon one of the unit's doctors in particular, a young medic from Inverness-shire in Scotland, Captain Douglas Brock Peterkin. In September 1944 Gonin noted that he very much wanted Peterkin back in the unit after some unspecified leave of absence. It seems that the Scottish doctor enjoyed life in 11 FTA, too. Early in 1945 he was offered a promotion, a staff appointment at the headquarters of 21 Army Group, safely away from the front line but, according to the diary, he stated that he preferred to remain with his home unit. Peterkin played a full part during numerous battles as the British Army advanced towards and then into Germany, most notably during Operation Plunder on 23 March 1945, when the British and American divisions of 21 Army Group crossed the Rhine for the first time. According to Gonin:

> the role played by the 11 LFA in this operation was entirely novel and consisted in accepting responsibility for the evacuation of casualties which occurred with personnel of the 15 Div (S) and the crew of the assault craft while they were crossing the river ... the amount of work put into the planning and training for the crossing of the river Rhine resulted in every man of the

11 Light Field Ambulance knowing exactly what his job would be and having confidence that he could carry it out.

Afterwards a message came back to Gonin from the Director of Medical Services of XII Corps: 'Please express to your officers and men my very grateful thanks for their magnificent work at the Rhine crossing. The best of luck in your new adventures.'

Soon their normal work was being interrupted by the needs of German civilians, who they treated without complaint or surprise, including a group of children found suffering from diphtheria in the newly captured town of Holsterhausen in the Ruhr Valley. Douglas Peterkin was sent forward to look for new unit accommodation and found towns and villages 'chaotic and more or less destroyed, crammed with various Canadian and British formations'. The young doctor was sent scouting once again towards the end of March, when he managed to 'acquire' the main hotel in Hartum. Now that they were moving quickly through northern and central Germany it was clear to everyone in 11 LFA that their war would soon be over.

But none of them yet knew that their final adventure would be to hell.

Borneo, 1945

On 25 March 1945, the engines of Liberator bombers were not the only things making unfamiliar noises on the Kelabit Plateau.

Fuck 'em all, fuck 'em all, the long and the short and the tall,
Fuck all the sergeants and W. O. ones,
Fuck all the corporals and fuck all their mums . . .

Few of the men and women swaying and cheering in the longhouse understood the words, but they clearly grasped the sentiment as the men of Semut 2 celebrated a day that had gone better than any of them had expected. After many rounds of *borak*, the potent local rice wine, their hosts had stood up to sing traditional Dayak 'praising songs' in honour of their guests, each accompanied by an obligatory toast, and so it seemed like simple good manners to respond in the finest traditions of the Australian Army.

> *Cause we're saying fuck off to them all,*
> *As back to their billets they crawl,*
> *There's fuck all promotion this side of the ocean,*
> *So cheer up my lads, fuck 'em all!*

Toby Carter would surely have been proud of them. He'd worked hard to drill respect for Dayak culture into all of his men: approach a stranger with a smile, always accept hospitality, never attempt to browbeat or intimidate, make a fuss of every child, and never, *ever*, go near any of the women (although after the war some of the Dayak women did tell visiting anthropologists that they were surprised that these handsome and interesting strangers didn't even *try* to sleep with them).

Before it reached its raucous finale, this first encounter between a Semut team and a Dayak headman had begun slowly and cautiously. Lawai Bisara's command of Malay was not perfect and there were many hand gestures and drawings needed to help the communication flow. All this happened inside a rapidly filling longhouse as the community came to realise that these were not dangerous spirits after all. The Australians were struck by the noise: of children, dogs and food preparation, all reverberating along the capacious timber building under thatches of palm leaves. They had brought gifts of food and gold but what really impressed their hosts were their parachutes, immediately handed over to the women of the longhouse to turn into clothing.

The Australians told the story exactly as Carter had taught them:

1945: THE RECKONING

A war that has consumed the entire world has brought Japanese soldiers to this island. We are here now to help the Dayak people remove them. We can provide food, medicine and weapons and more men like us will soon come to join us from the air and from the sea.

When Jack Tredrea and the other three stray SRD men finally arrived, along with the cylindrical supply packages, nicknamed 'storepedoes', that the Liberators had also dropped, the atmosphere became even friendlier. The Dayak men were particularly impressed at the number and quality of the weapons these strangers had brought with them. Bisarai then asked how his people might be protected from the Japanese. Some Dayaks who had helped downed US airmen had been executed and word of this had raced around the mountains. The Australians said that their side was winning the war and the end was coming soon, so now was the perfect moment to drive the Japanese out. They also spoke of a coming invasion, bringing even more men, this time with tanks and artillery, and a sky full of aircraft, and how this would give the Dayaks the protection that they needed. In return they respectfully asked for volunteers to help them obtain information, navigate this land and – if the community agreed – to fight alongside them, too. Impressed by the story they had heard and by the rifles and machine guns spilling out of the storepedoes, and no doubt influenced by the atmosphere and the alcohol, it was soon clear that this community was willing to join the Australians' cause.

It was an impressive and persuasive pitch although unfortunately, and wholly unknown to the men singing late into the night high on the Kelabit Plateau, some of its most important points and promises would turn out to be worth . . . fuck all.

Germany, 1945

The King has been graciously pleased to give orders to the following appointments to the most excellent order of the British Empire, in recognition of distinguished services during the liberation of prisoners in German Concentration Camps.

To be Additional Members of the Military Division of the said Most Excellent Order:

Captain Douglas Brock Peterkin, M.B. (116966)
Royal Army Medical Corps (Warminster)

I began looking into the life of Douglas Peterkin for reasons that will become clear later. I had no idea that he had served in Belsen and nor did the people I first spoke to about him. So I was surprised to discover that in 1945 he received a royal honour for his work there. This quickly led me to discover a doctoral thesis that he had written at Edinburgh University in 1947.

THESIS FOR THE DEGREE OF M.D.
Submitted by Douglas Brock Peterkin, M.B., Ch.B. (1937).

OBSERVATIONS ON THE OUTBREAK OF LOUSE-BORNE TYPHUS FEVER AT BELSEN CONCENTRATION CAMP, APRIL, 1945.

Soon I was deep into this and it, in turn, led me to the records of 11 Light Field Ambulance at the National Archives office in Kew, where I discovered that Mervyn Gonin's first reference to Belsen in the unit's war diary was surprisingly mundane: '16 April – orders received to move to Belsen "at special request" of DDMS 2 Army [Deputy Director of Medical Services, 2nd Army].'

British soldiers had reached the camp the day before this 'special request' was sent to Gonin, but they had no idea how to cope with what they discovered there — tens of thousands of people in the direst distress imaginable. This was one of the very first functioning Nazi concentration camps that any Allied unit had discovered. By the time the Red Army had reached the eastern death camps most of the evidence of mass execution had been destroyed and most of the survivors had been removed. Belsen was very different, which is why the images and testimony recorded there would transfix and horrify the world.

The 11 LFA was first through the gates not as a result of a military victory but because of an ad hoc local deal done between the surviving German commanders in the area and those of the advancing British Army. All the British were told was that there was a camp for displaced people at Belsen and that typhus had broken out there beyond the ability of the local authorities to control it, hence this highly unusual invitation to drive through what was still an enemy-controlled area and take charge. To do this 11 LFA joined forces with the team from 32 Casualty Clearing Station under the command of Lieutenant Colonel H. D. 'Johnny' Johnston. He was to become the Senior Medical Officer at the camp. When they first glimpsed the fences and huts of Belsen through the surrounding trees, none of the British medics had any idea of what awaited them. Major D. T. Prescott, the deputy commander of 11 LFA and one of Douglas Peterkin's friends, described what happened next.

> The scene that met us as we entered the camp was one of utter chaos with dead and dying everywhere and an estimated 6–10 thousand people dead on site. The fitter ones seemed to be wandering about — a lot of them aimlessly — in the blue and white prison pyjamas that offered very little protection against the elements.
>
> The vast majority of the inmates suffered from diarrhoea, whatever the cause, and, of course, typhus and tuberculosis was rife. The men in our unit, clad in anti-typhus suits and liberally dusted with DDT powder, led by Capt. Douglas Peterkin and Capt. Paddy O'Donnell, went into the camp with part of our

ambulance forces termed 'contaminated ambulances' and proceeded to evacuate the illest of the inmates.

Even when sitting in Edinburgh two years later, and writing in the calm, scientific language of a doctoral thesis, Peterkin's own shock was still evident.

> Whilst serving with the 11th Light Field Ambulance the author had the dubious privilege of serving in the huts of Belsen camp from the day of liberation onwards until the last hut was burned down by the British after the complete evacuation of the camp.
>
> Few people who worked there can at any time have seen a greater wealth of clinical material. The death rate whilst evacuation was proceeding ... numbered some 13,000 in camp number 1 alone. The living had had no food or water for about seven days, after a long period of starvation. Gross overcrowding was found in every hut in the camp and the non-existence of hygiene and sanitation led to scenes of squalor and filth which almost beggar description.

Nobody was in a fit state to give a detailed account of what had happened at Belsen in the ten days since the three trains left for Czechoslovakia. But it appeared that the remaining guards, fearful of catching the typhus that was rampant in the camp, had stopped even pretending to administer the place and simply sat at the perimeter preventing anyone escaping and waited for the British to come. As Douglas Peterkin could plainly see, there had not been even the pitifully inadequate food deliveries of March and early April, just a complete absence of all services and care for an already sick and dying community the size of a small town. Wherever he looked there was disorder and hopelessness. Late on 18 April Johnny Johnson met with Peterkin and all the senior medics from his own unit and 11 LFA and together they brainstormed an emergency plan. These men had been expecting their war to end in a matter of days and yet suddenly they were now faced with an overwhelming, unprecedented challenge that would require all their energy and imagination. After the meeting Johnson sat down in front of his typewriter.

> The following is a brief account of the conditions seen on first entering these camps. It is impossible to give an adequate description on paper. A dense mass of emaciated apathetic scarecrows [are] huddled together in wooden huts without beds or blankets, in many cases, without any clothing whatsoever in some cases. The females in worse condition than the men, their clothing generally, if they have any, only filthy rags.
>
> The dead lie all over the camp and in piles outside the blocks of huts which house the worst of the sick and are miscalled 'hospitals'. Approximately 3,000 naked and emaciated corpses in various stages of decomposition are lying about this camp. Sanitation is non-existent. Pits, within only a few inadequate perch rails, are available in totally inadequate numbers, but the majority of inmates, from starvation, apathy and weakness, defecate and urinate where they sit and lie, even inside the living huts. There is no running water or electricity. All water is [now] being brought in by our water trucks.

Johnson also wrote a letter to his wife that evening:

> I have seen things which I could not have believed possible. Darling it is too horrible to describe. I have never really hated the Germans till now. Now I cannot believe they belong to the same species as you and I. This camp is over 4 miles long. It is packed with filthy, ragged, starving, people 60,000 of them. There are piles of dead 100 feet by 30 feet which have accumulated outside the huts used for the sick and dying . . . Of course there is no surgery here but there is a colossal job of doctoring, a job after my own heart.
>
> We are in tents again, near the German barracks. There are some fine houses occupied by the wives of the SS, perhaps later

we shall have those. I must get to sleep now my darling – tomorrow will be a hard day.

Hard though it was, within hours Johnson's men began to conjure some order out of the chaos as their 'colossal job of doctoring' began. Any former guards who had not fled into the woods were rounded up and forced to join emergency work parties. Although most reluctant to re-enter the camp for fear of infection – or the revenge of any inmates left standing – they were sent at the point of British rifles to clear away the dead and dying from around the huts, and then bury all the bodies in newly dug pits. By now newsmen had arrived and so this terrible process was filmed: emaciated corpses stacked in lorries, nightmarish piles of twisted arms, legs and heads pushed along by bulldozers and then tumbling into crudely excavated holes in the ground.

Basic military rations were offered to the survivors, but most were so sick and weak that they were unable to digest or even swallow them. While they awaited the delivery of special 'famine powders', Johnson and his team dreamed up what they called 'the human laundry'. Here the medics – assisted by a group of German nurses taken from nearby hospitals and pressed into service – would use hosepipes and soap to wash survivors, then burn their old rags, dust them with DDT and give them fresh, clean clothes free of the typhus-spreading lice. It took several days for the laundry to start its work, since the local water supply needed repairing. According to camp rumour, some of the fleeing guards had destroyed it in a final act of spite towards their victims. Douglas Peterkin volunteered for the worst job of them all. He was one of the doctors responsible for entering the huts, separating the living from the dead – or, rather, the dying from the dead – and deciding who had the best chance of benefiting from 'the laundry'. In his thesis he wrote:

> In places the bodies were arranged in piles up to two hundred in number but most lay where they had died, by the roadside and

pathways, in the bunks and even beneath the rotting floorboards of the huts. All the bodies were grossly emaciated showing complete absence of subcutaneous fat and little muscle tissue. Inside the huts conditions were even worse. In all there was gross overcrowding. The maximum number seen by the author was nine hundred and eighty-four persons in a hut but numbers of over one thousand have been recorded by Dixey (1945). By British Army standards of 1945 the maximum numbers in the huts should have been one hundred and twenty.

In those huts without bunks a mass of internees lay huddled together on the floors where rags, lice, faeces and urine abounded. Some wore filthy rags or blankets as clothes; others were completely naked. In those with bunks the common practice was for two or three persons to share a bunk; not infrequently the living shared bunks with the dead being too ill to be aware of or concerned with the fact. The majority were incapable of moving from where they lay. They passed urine and faeces in the bunks. With few exceptions all the internees in Camp One were louse-infested.

Peterkin had seen all manner of illness and injury, but never this extreme level of starvation and all its dreadful effects on the human body and mind. Describing it tested the cold and clinical vocabulary that he'd learned at medical school.

All the bony eminences of the trunk, limbs, extremities and face could easily be seen as well as palpated. The eyes were sunken and the cheeks hollow. The abdominal wall was atrophic and markedly retracted giving a scaphoid abdomen . . . several of these cases gave a history or signs compatible with a cardiac or renal lesion in the form of a gross valvular lesion with disturbed cardiac rhythm or casts and haematuria. Scabies and impetiginous lesions were widespread. Many bedridden patients had bedsores, all of which were infected. They occurred in the usual sites, over the sacrum, behind the shoulders, heels and elbows.

The author observed one in a bedridden female aged twenty-nine years who had lain in her own excreta for fourteen days. It measured six inches by four inches and was situated over the sacrum, which was exposed; smaller subsidiary sores were present over the ischial tuberosities.

Coupled with this abnormal behaviour was a marked loss of self-respect and loss of sensitivity to surroundings. The scene of dead bodies, of squalor and filth, of scores of people defecating in situ seemed to cause no mental reaction whatsoever. This was most noticeable in the children, the majority of whom seemed quite oblivious to their surroundings; in those whose physical state was reasonably fit there was no evidence of mental abnormality.

Peterkin did not dwell on his own role in what must have been a near-impossible working environment, but his commanding officer Mervyn Gonin singled him out more than once in his meticulous official reports.

Captain Peterkin, together with another officer of this unit, was responsible for the collection and loading on to ambulance cars of over 7,000 internees. He worked daily ... amid the most appalling hygienic conditions inside huts where the majority of internees were suffering from the most virulent infectious diseases known to man. In addition to disease and starvation I have seen Captain Peterkin dealing with mass hysteria amongst internees in a manner which is worthy of the highest praise.

Borneo, 1945

Toby Carter parachuted into Borneo on 18 April to discover that his operation was already going well. Two of the teams were now on the ground, there was no sign of the Japanese and there had been other meetings with local communities where, amid more bonhomie and *borak*, additional men and women had volunteered for the cause. The Dayak volunteer guides had already proved themselves to be indispensable, helping the Australians pick their way along tracks and across streams as they searched for newly arrived comrades or stray storepedoes.

Carter had chosen Long Akah, one of the larger Dayak villages, to be the main base for Semut 2, the team he was leading personally. It lay further down the mountains from their isolated drop zone and was much closer to where he believed the Japanese were based. He already knew some of the most important leaders in the area and was confident of a warm welcome. But getting men and supplies to Long Akah took well over a week of tough travel through the dense foliage, much harder than any training march in Queensland. Their SRD medical packs were quickly put to use to deal with a plethora of bites and stings, ulcers, sores and rashes. Intense bursts of rain turned the ground into mud and made clambering over slippery rocks an invitation to a fractured ankle, while the intense humidity sapped the energy of men struggling to keep up with their agile and apparently disease-resistant local guides.

Dayak marching songs, answered by yet more obscenity-rich Australian equivalents, helped the days pass as they navigated steep hillsides and the permanently soaking and steaming 'moss forests' of the highlands, stopping every hour or so to 'de-leech' any area of exposed flesh with lighted cigarettes. High above this strange world of entangled trees, pitcher plants and brightly coloured orchids, they occasionally saw an enemy plane flying down towards the coast. Carter sent scouts ahead every morning to check their route, but there didn't appear to be any sign of the Japanese up here in the hills. The SRD men would always remember the smells and the noises of this unique ecosystem: hot mushroom, mouldy wood, decomposing leaf matter, along with the endless cicadas, gangs of squealing monkeys and clouds of brilliant butterflies. Occasionally they saw bats, deer, pigs, orangutans and even leopards. And everywhere they heard the worrying buzz of mosquitos. 'An Eden of mixed blessings' is how one of them described it. When they could, they travelled along the rivers in canoes, reliant yet again on the skills of the Dayaks. As they half paddled, half manhandled, their way around boulders and through rapids, Bill Sochon was impressed.

> Up forward the most experienced boatman in each *prahu* balanced with the ease of years of practice, and with skill and decision signalled back to the stern paddler, warning him of rocks and submerged dangers ahead. Now travelling hell-for-leather through the foaming water, the frail craft bucked and lurched as the paddlers slewed it first this way, then that, to answer the bow-guide's signals, they shot through the boiling waters with consummate proficiency.

Along his route Carter stopped at longhouses and solicited more support, repeating his promises of protection, the coming invasion and the imminent defeat of the Japanese. News travelled through these hills faster than sweating, scratching Australians and by now they were usually expected, welcomed and feted with roasted pig and yet more gallons of *borak*. To help win even more allies they offered basic medical care in 'longhouse clinics', dispensing some of the bandages and medicines that came in their storepedoes. Carter had brought pre-war Sarawak money with him and used this to pay his boatmen. It was valued more than the currency issued by the Japanese. Despite the many privations of the trail, there was much to enjoy and numerous SRD men would later speak and write of the unearthly beauty of this place, the friendliness of its people and the privilege they felt being welcomed into Dayak settlements and homes.

Carter finally reached Long Akah, where the Akah and Baram rivers meet. It was the territory of one of the most powerful Dayak headmen of them all, Carter's old friend Tama Weng Ajeng. His support would be critical but, unlike those who lived high up on the plateau, his people had already been exposed to the Japanese and had every reason to be wary, whatever promises the SRD men might make. If the New Zealander could win this crowd over, he would have access to hundreds if not thousands of guides, spies and fighting men all along the Baram River basin. If not then Semut would become a very limited operation indeed.

With other subordinate chiefs in attendance, all dressed in their finery, there was another lavish feast and a warm embrace between Tama Weng and Carter. After the speeches and praising songs the two men spoke for hours in Malay, in the company of all the other chiefs, and it was during this conversation that Carter revealed something new, something that was to have a profound effect on his mission and the lives of many people throughout Borneo in the weeks ahead. As well as his usual promises of military aid and protection he electrified the gathering when he said that, as evidence that the Australians wanted to be trusted friends, they would from this moment on revoke the ban on headhunting, but 'for Jap heads only'.

Carter and his men had all noticed the clumps of ancient, dried heads hung high in the rafters of Tama Weng's longhouse. The opportunity to add some more could make the Allied cause even more attractive. Until the twentieth century a man returning to his longhouse with a human head was guaranteed increased status and was believed to bring spiritual protection to the community. Ancient rituals – not practised for many decades – accompanied the cleaning, smoking and displaying of a head and all triggered great celebrations. The whole process was and is shocking to most outsiders, but amid a global war in which millions of human bodies were being torn to pieces in countless gory ways – and troops from all armies were not above collecting body parts as souvenirs – perhaps it should not be.

Very little of this was ever written down, no doubt because Semut's planners knew that desecrating the body of an enemy was in breach of the Geneva Convention, but that it was discussed and approved at a high level there can be no doubt. And not only approved, financed as well, because Carter was also authorised to pay for the heads. It's not clear if any offer of payment was made in this initial conversation with Tama Weng but 'head trading' was to become an increasingly important – and troublesome – part of the operation. Although it would occupy much of his time, after the war Carter only had a single and rather anodyne thing to say about all of this: 'SRD admits to reviving the headhunting custom against the Japanese and many Long Houses have enriched themselves thereby.'

The men who planned and ran the Semut mission had a view of the Dayaks that today we'd immediately call outdated and paternalistic. Carter at one point called these people 'timid wild animals' and generally described them in the language of 'the noble savage', simple folk who had been loyal to the 'White Rajahs' and who, in his own words, 'remembered the white man and were not afraid' of his return. On the question of headhunting, Carter knew that it would be a powerful inducement, paid or not, but Tama Weng and his sub-chiefs, although impressed, still peppered him with a series of tough, pragmatic questions: 'When will the invasion come? How many guns will we receive? What is your evidence that you truly are the winning side?' Most Dayaks living along the river knew that Japan was no longer the power it had been. Nevertheless, their survival depended upon picking the right allies at the right time and it was this, rather than nostalgia for imperial rule or a passion for the old headhunting rituals, which dominated their thinking.

After the dinner, Tama Weng remained friendly but neutral, telling Carter that he needed a day or so to consult privately with the other chiefs. The SRD men went to a camp they'd established nearby and waited. Tama Weng had been wooed by the Japanese in the past and had even entertained them in his longhouse, but he had always tried to keep relations with the occupying army distant, assuming that they were more interested in controlling the oilfields and mines on the coast than anything that happened up in the hills. So far this approach had worked well. None of his people had clashed with the occupiers nor experienced the kind of brutal treatment meted out elsewhere. Did he really want to jeopardise all that for a handful of promises and the prospect of a few heads?

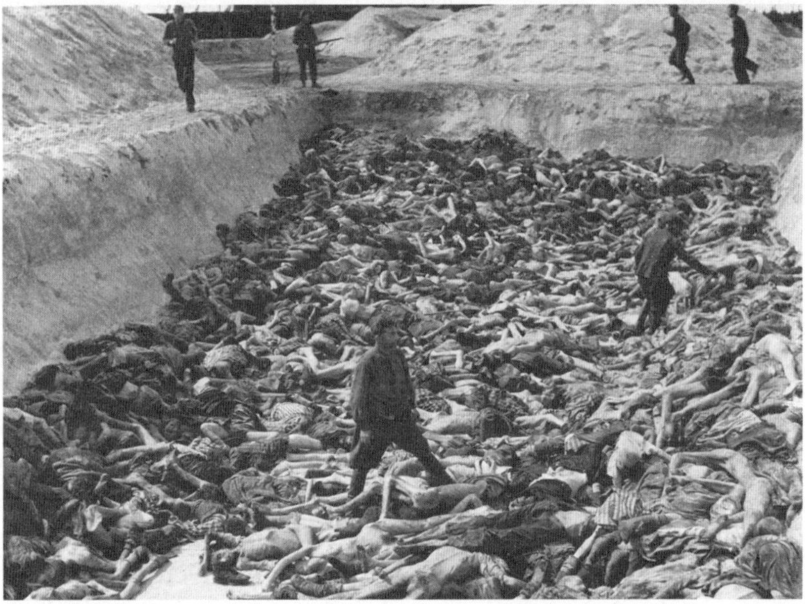

13

The Laundry

Belsen, 1945

Captain Douglas Peterkin and his fellow medics struggled to empty the huts in anything like an orderly fashion amid distressing scenes of panic and despair. They would arrive draped in their white anti-typhus overalls and carrying stretchers to discover crowds of people desperate for medical treatment and food, making the job of choosing whom to help first almost impossible. But for those who were carried to Johnny Johnson's human laundry, and able to tolerate the various food supplements now being offered, the changes could be rapid and remarkable. Three-quarters of the survivors were women and girls and most had been living in a desperate, exhausted and emaciated state for weeks now. The long and detailed equipment lists for 11 Light Field Ambulance never contained quantities of lipstick or face powder, but Peterkin and his commander Mervyn Gonin soon discovered that such things could be lifesavers, too.

> A very large quantity of lipstick arrived. This was not at all what we men wanted, we were screaming for hundreds and thousands of other things and I don't know who asked for lipstick. I wish so much that I could discover who did it, it was the action of genius, sheer unadulterated brilliance.
> I believe nothing did more for these internees than the

lipstick. Women lay in bed with no sheets and no nightie but with scarlet red lips, you saw them wandering around about with nothing but a blanket over their shoulders, but with scarlet red lips. I saw a woman dead on the postmortem table and clutched in her hand was a piece of lipstick. At last someone had done something to make them individuals again, they were someone, no longer merely the number tattooed on their arm. At last they could take an interest in their appearance. That lipstick started to give them back their humanity.

Even as they worked eighteen-hour days, forever checking themselves for the first signs of typhus, the doctors understood that they were involved in something extraordinary and historic. To use the word that Johnson had chosen in his first letter home from the camp, the challenge was truly colossal. But face to face with living – or barely living – evidence of one of the greatest atrocities of all time, they were all determined to try anything that might make a difference. Replacing tattered, lice-infested camp uniforms with proper skirts, blouses and dresses, and ensuring that there was makeup available for anyone who wanted it, was indeed an important part of the cure. Douglas Peterkin observed that once people were able to stand, eat and wash themselves, and once they were dressed in something that resembled the clothing of their former lives, 'the change was very marked as self-respect and a sense of responsibility returned'. The doctors even created a special 'store', full of clothes that the survivors could try on and choose for themselves, just as if they were out shopping back in Budapest or Rotterdam. They filled it with dresses and slacks provided by the Red Cross or else requisitioned from the German towns nearby and even put up a sign outside, on which they wrote the word 'Harrods'. Another psychological insight helped with the food powders. A bland and chemical tasting 'Bengal Famine Mixture', made largely from rice and sugar, was effective but far from popular, and just the taste of it made some of the inmates vomit. Someone suggested that a small amount of paprika added to the mix might make it taste a little like the food the survivors remembered. And it did.

It wasn't easy and it wasn't always successful, but life and hope were slowly being rekindled, even in this most lifeless and hopeless of places. People considered disposable, barely even human, and treated accordingly for years, were now receiving care from an imaginative, passionate group of men and women in the uniforms of the British Army. And then, on 20 April 1945, the Luftwaffe – or what was left of it in northern Germany – launched one of its final attacks of the war, and the target chosen for this grand gesture of defiance was Belsen. There were barely any aircraft in a serviceable condition, but a handful were scraped together for this last vindictive insult to the people most brutalised by Hitler's regime. Early in the morning three Focke-Wulf fighters streaked across the camp and headed straight for the improvised medical base that had been set up by 11 LFA. Sweeping low, they shot up equipment and transport, wounding three LFA men and killing a fourth with a bullet straight through his chest. Mervyn Gonin, whose team was working itself to the point of exhaustion day after day to try and salvage what they could from the charnel house bequeathed to them by the Nazi state, was incandescent.

> It is considered that this incident is a deliberate contravention of the Geneva Convention. The unit is located at least a 1000 yards (and probably more) from any military installation nor are any combatant vehicles of any description parked nearer than 1000 yards from my lines.
>
> This unit is located within 200 yards of 32 (Br) Casualty Clearing Station who are showing the red cross. This unit is located within 500 yards of a German military hospital marked with large red crosses on the roofs of three buildings standing

on three sides of a triangle. A red cross flag is also flying from one tall chimney of this hospital . . . At the height these planes were flying it cannot but have been seen.

As the LFA patched up the damage, more and more medical units came to assist, along with civilian volunteers from the Red Cross. Almost a hundred medical students also arrived and were quickly set to work. They had heard about Belsen on the radio and had immediately volunteered to leave the safety of their colleges in England and Scotland. All knew that they were running a serious risk of contracting typhus. A handful of American military doctors came along, too.

Throughout his long medical career Douglas Peterkin would be a keen observer of the mental as much as the physical state of those under his care. In Belsen he noticed that, even after they'd recovered some weight, many of the former prisoners remained psychologically scarred by their years of undernourishment and anxiety. 'The phobia of future shortage was very real to many internees and even some weeks after liberation they would hoard crusts, pieces of meat and other oddments of food under their pillows,' he wrote in his thesis. Another desperately sad legacy of their time in the camps came with a rash of sudden and unexplained deaths. People who were back on their feet, gaining weight and well into their recovery would suddenly collapse and die of a heart attack or develop untreatable liver failure. On the autopsy table the doctors discovered why. All that malnutrition, cold and over-work had caused these people's internal organs to shrivel and atrophy, so much so that in some cases they resembled those of young children. They were simply not strong enough to support essential bodily functions once their owners started to eat, digest, breathe and move as a normal adult once again.

It would be nice to record that Douglas Peterkin, Johnny Johnson and Mervyn Gonin arrived just in the nick of time, but they did not. Had a deal been done to open Belsen to the British

'A powerful almost loving loyalty to the men under his command.' William 'Bruno' Brown in the hills of Assam.

An amphibious DUKW of the Indian Army crosses a Burmese river. Opposed river crossings were a key part of the fighting in Burma in 1945.

How Japanese and INA propagandists wanted Indians to react to the war.

How many of them actually did react to it. Bhandari Ram, of the 6th Battalion, 10th Baluch Regiment, shows off the Victoria Cross he won in Arakan. Indian soldiers won 22 of the 34 Victoria and George Crosses awarded during the Burma campaign.

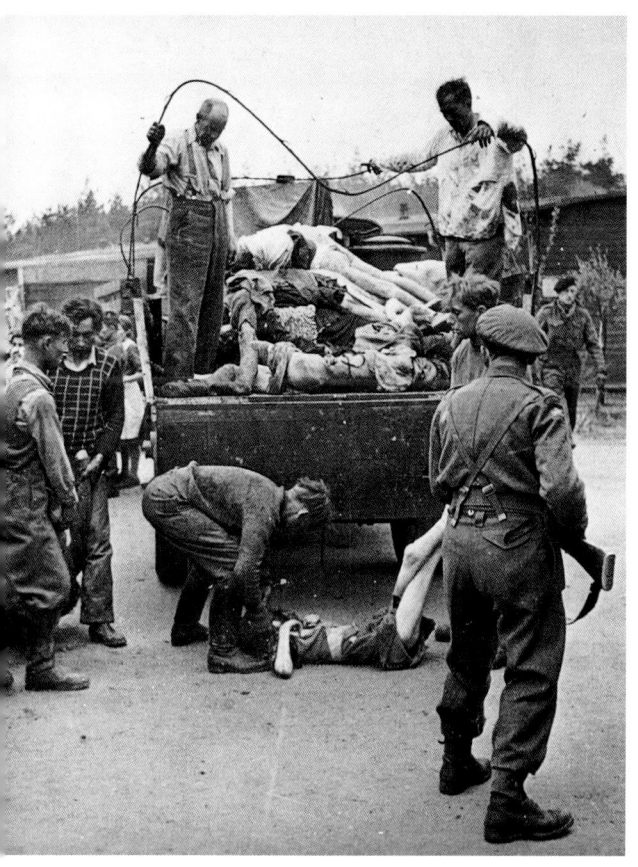

'It would be nice to record that Douglas Peterkin, Johnny Johnson and Mervyn Gonin arrived in Belsen just in the nick of time, but they did not.'

'There is a colossal job of doctoring to be done.'

Lady Wavell, the wife of Viceroy Sir Archibald Wavell, talks to soldiers in a military hospital in 1945, as a senior Indian officer looks on. The soldiers are knitting socks and scarves for comrades still at the front.

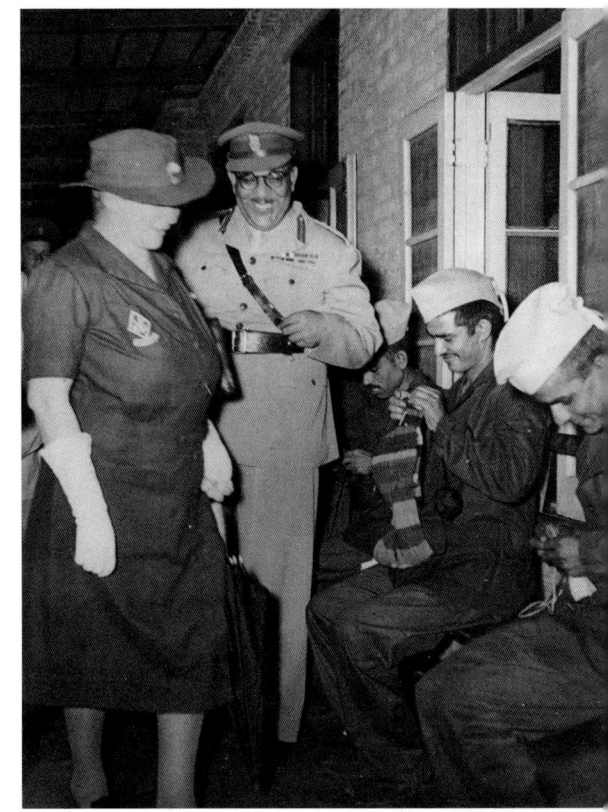

'The cavalry was coming.' Australian troops land in Borneo.

Passengers on the 'Farsleben' train are liberated by American troops just two days after leaving Belsen.

After the death of President Roosevelt, a new 'Big Three' (Churchill, Truman, Stalin) consider the fate of nations.

'Sanitary Sid' in a British prison.

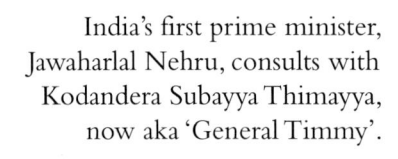

India's first prime minister, Jawaharlal Nehru, consults with Kodandera Subayya Thimayya, now aka 'General Timmy'.

'Everything was now fresh paint, professionalism and crisp command.' Mountbatten inspects Indian Army troops in Singapore after the Japanese surrender.

Indian Army troops battle nationalists in the Dutch East Indies in November 1945.

Nurse Mary King, around the time she told her friend Angela Noblet of her engagement.

Douglas Brock Peterkin marries Truda Mary Edwards in 1942.

'A quiet faraway place just living a purposeful life.' Dawlish, Devon, during the 1940s. The bay-windowed house (to the left of the shop bearing the name 'Arthur West') is the bakery where Jennifer Newberry grew up.

just two weeks earlier, when the three trains departed for Theresienstadt, so much more could have been achieved. As it was, even after twelve days of intensive work and treatment, with the human laundry working all hours, a further 9,000 inmates died, meaning that close to 14,000 fatalities occurred *after* the liberation of the camp. But almost 30,000 people who had been close to death did recover and were moved into new and decent accommodation, wearing new clothes and sometimes even lipstick. Then the last bodies were cremated and the camp burned to the ground by British Army flamethrowers, as the world's press stood around to record the final acts of the nightmare. By now footage from the first few shocking days – and the startlingly frank radio reports of the BBC's Richard Dimbleby – had been widely seen and heard all around the world. And one of the defining images of the Holocaust – disordered piles of shrivelled human beings bulldozed and heaved into mass graves – had already become fixed. At the end Johnny Johnson recorded his verdict on what the British had found in this quiet corner of a supposedly civilised modern nation, and what had created it.

> And finally I wish to make it quite clear in this official document that the conditions found at Belsen were the result of deliberate and bestial cruelty on the part of those responsible. 26,000 people were buried there during the period of our stay; it is my considered opinion that another 15,000 at least would have died within 14 days . . . but for the entry of our troops. In short the position was one of attempted mass murder.

As for Douglas Peterkin, who had been there for every day of the relief operation and who had spent more time in the huts than anyone else, the unemotional language of his thesis revealed his own health crisis: 'In addition the author, along with seventeen other members of the 11th Light Field Ambulance and six medical students working in the camp, had the misfortune to contract the disease [typhus].'

In early May he was sent away for treatment. He would be absent until mid-June, by which time the war in Europe would be over. But he had not yet finished with typhus or the survivors of Belsen, and nor they with him.

Borneo, 1945

After an anxious wait in Long Akah, Toby Carter received his answer in the form of a small regatta. A procession of decorated canoes approached the SRD camp, the first bearing a smiling Tama Weng and flying the Union flag. They had their allies and now they could start planning their war. Soon Tang Weng and two of his sons were sitting with Carter plotting the next moves. At the same time word that headhunting would be allowed – and rewarded – swept along the Baram River. In their own areas to the west and north of Carter, Bill Sochon and Tom Harrisson and their teams were making similar promises. One of Sochon's men later wrote: '[we] let it be known that we would pay the princely bounty of one Straits Settlement dollar per Japanese head.'

The story of Semut hinges on the meeting of two cultures. If the white men from Australia occasionally revealed attitudes about the Dayaks that may make us cringe today, they also quickly established a relationship of mutual trust and dependence. Their hosts needed them for weapons, but they needed their hosts for just about everything else, and to an extent few had imagined back in Australia. Plans made in Queensland – especially those involving jungle travel – were quickly amended on the basis of local advice and it didn't take long for effective day-to-day command to sit with a mixture of SRD and Dayak. With hundreds of volunteers now waiting for guns from the latest storepedo drops, Semut began to look like an indigenous guerrilla force with a handful of white advisers rather than a traditional Special Forces mission. The Dayaks' knowledge of the jungle, their understanding of river systems and weather patterns, and their remarkable resistance to disease were all perfectly suited to a campaign of intelligence-gathering, ambush and sabotage. And the growing respect was mutual. Most Dayaks enjoyed working with the SRD teams and some cross-cultural friendships were forged that would persist for life. Many years later Lipang Munan, a child in 1945, still believed that 'Japanese may be small and brown, just like us. They may have brown skin like us. And Whites may be tall with fair hair and pale skin, like spirits or ghosts. But under the skin Australians and Dayaks are linked. It is the Japanese who are alien.'

As was their practice throughout the region Japanese officials had spread propaganda in Borneo, making much of historic British, Dutch and French greed and oppression, and casting the emperor in Tokyo as the saviour of the long-exploited Asian. This was a message that some in Borneo were initially eager to hear, especially when accompanied by military victories. One Dayak leader speaking after the war said that 'He [Tojo] had already defeated the white people . . . and all the Punjabi soldiers ran away because of him. Three white people's countries were seized by him.' When it first landed in Borneo in early 1942 the Japanese army had behaved reasonably well to the non-white communities but quickly showed its appetite for extra-judicial violence by massacring the fleeing Europeans. In Long Nawang, in the north of the island, dozens of Dutch and British civilian refugees, stray soldiers, missionaries and downed pilots were rounded up and killed, including many children. Stories of rape and torture, whether true or not, were widely believed across Borneo and helped keep anti-Japanese activity to a minimum. But when it did break out the Japanese army treated their fellow Asians on the island just as cruelly as it had the old colonialists. In 1943 the occupation government suspected that Chinese and Malay community leaders in the formerly Dutch-controlled south-east of Borneo were plotting against Japanese rule. Dozens of them were publicly beheaded without even a semblance of a trial.

The SRD men made promises of security, and continually referred to the imminent Australian invasion, but everyone knew that as soon as a single Japanese soldier was hurt every day would bring the risk of a punishment patrol seeking out a longhouse and its people. Although many members of the SRD developed intense attachments to their local allies, keeping the Dayaks safe was not in fact listed anywhere in the formal objectives of Operation Semut. It's also doubtful that the people planning the invasion gave it much thought either.

After winning Tama Weng's support, Carter planned how best to guarantee order and security along the Baram once fighting began. He was driven, according to one of his men, by 'a compassion for the good-will of the natives'. Aware that it would only take a few hundred Japanese troops to devastate a small Dayak community, he asked Weng and his family to spread rumours about the size of their force. If the Japanese believed that hundreds of well-armed Australians, assisted by thousands of local warriors, were waiting for them up in the hills then it might hold them back. Meanwhile, Carter's private army grew, as did that of Sochon and Harrisson, as more local people volunteered to fight. According to Bill Sochon, 'they were apt pupils, and the mere thought of a chance to kill a few Japanese and (could they dare hope for such a wonder?) taking a head or two, drove them to heights of enthusiasm such as no regular NCO had ever dreamed he would witness'. Carter decided to recruit Iban people to the cause as well, although he knew that they had a long history of conflict with other Dayak communities. The Ibans were known to be among the most enthusiastic head-hunters on Borneo, and Carter first sought and received Tama Weng's agreement to set aside historic grievances before he approached them.

THE LAUNDRY

Carter chose the tiny river community of Long Lama as his first target. His local spies told him that it was home to about a dozen Japanese soldiers. The attack was to be led by Australian Sergeant Denis Sheppard and he spent the evening of 5 June briefing his team, three SRD men and twenty-four Dayaks, before falling asleep in a longhouse as the locals told each other stories of glorious headhunting expeditions of the past. Before dawn the group headed out for Long Lama armed with a mixture of machine guns, rifles and *parangs*.

It was just first light when Sheppard's canoes drifted quietly towards the small wharf of Long Lama. Finding it unguarded, his men set out slowly and deliberately towards the small wooden fort where the Japanese were sleeping. But someone inside was awake and suddenly there was an explosion of noise and violence. A Japanese soldier came charging out of the fort and was instantly cut down by a bullet fired from only a yard away by Sergeant Francis Pippen. Soon other Japanese soldiers were falling to gunfire and to the swinging *parangs* as a handful of others ran off into the jungle. The action was over in minutes and was a complete success. As Sheppard looked around approvingly at his casualty-free unit he noticed that two of them were now carrying human heads.

Sheppard's team discovered radio transcripts in the fort that revealed the Japanese commanders were aware of white soldiers operating in the hills, but had not yet considered it serious enough to send anyone to look for them. That could change now. They also found two frightened and wounded Japanese soldiers hiding in the jungle and took them back to their base at Long Akah. The men were petrified of the Dayaks, with good reason, but for now the headhunting had ceased and, instead of the mistreatment they feared, the prisoners were taken to a river where a Catalina seaplane flew in to evacuate them for interrogation in the Philippines. Carter could see how headhunting frightened the Japanese prisoners, but he didn't yet understand why. In Japanese burial custom the integrity of the human body is paramount, meaning that the possibility of decapitation created terror both physical and spiritual. He decided to redouble his propaganda efforts, hoping that stories about head-hungry Dayaks might be a further reason for the Japanese army to stay down on the coast.

Burma, 1945

By May the officers and men of the Indian Army started to see something entirely new: Japanese units falling apart in front of them. Formerly unquestioning soldiers began to disobey the ever-more unrealistic orders coming from Rangoon and Tokyo. Instead of fighting to the death they surrendered in the face of overwhelming odds on the battlefield and the daily harassment from their former Burmese allies and the Karen militias. On the dusty road between Meiktila and Pyawbwe, George MacDonald Fraser saw one of the reasons for this — a huge airdrop of supplies coming down from circling Dakota transport planes. Great crates fell towards him under billowing parachutes or were 'free dropped' straight into the wet, spongy paddy fields close by. One Dakota swooped so low he was able to exchange a wave with a turban-wearing transport loader as the man heaved another canvas bundle out of the back of the plane. Fraser wondered how all of this must look to the Japanese soldiers he knew would be watching from the distant hills. Most of the enemy corpses they'd seen during the advance had looked unhealthily thin and many carried the unmistakable marks of disease. Yet while they would starve again tonight the Cumbrians of 17th Division were looking forward to the finest tinned goods the American farm belt could provide.

Advancing on Pyawbwe they still faced incoming shellfire but, unlike earlier battles, here the Japanese quickly broke and ran. For the first time he was not shooting at an opponent suddenly rearing up over a trench or charging out of a bunker. Now they were several hundred yards away and he could take his time to pick them off with his Lee-Enfield as they tried to escape. Something he enjoyed more than he ever thought he would.

After the battle they shared good food, hot tea and tobacco. They were happy warriors talking about women and film stars. They took prisoners, who they robbed of anything valuable, already thinking of the war memorabilia they would show off in the pubs of Carlisle and Workington. But it was still a time of dangers and dilemmas. One day they almost blew themselves up – him included – in a mortar-handling accident. On another they came across something that challenged Fraser's idea about the war he was fighting. A small concrete building was being used to treat around thirty wounded Japanese prisoners. One night an Indian unit, which he did not name, took its turn to patrol the area. The following morning there were no more wounded men in the building but a trench running inside it, like an inspection pit at a garage, was now full of rocks. Under the rocks were the dead Japanese prisoners. This was unquestionably a war crime and as an officer he was duty-bound to report it. Instead, he grimaced and decided to forget about the whole thing.

India, 1945

The nurses floating on the Brahmaputra River were dealing with Japanese prisoners, too, Angela Noblet's first personal encounter with the enemy. Some of them cowered in fear, assuming they were being taken to a site of mass execution, which their officers had told them was the fate of all surrendered men. One had hacked away at his own tongue so he would not reveal anything under the expected British tortures. Another had a deep chest wound which reopened in the middle of the night and started to bleed at a dangerous rate. All the medical staff rushed to help and someone remembered the supply of blood plasma they had on board.

> Several weeks earlier a few bottles of the new preparation with its apparatus had been given to us. We had never had cause to use them and were inclined to look on them with suspicion, being accustomed to bottles of good red blood and the old method of blood grouping.

Within a few minutes a section of the deck was screened off, a bed prepared and the dying man placed upon it. Soon a plasma drip was flowing into his veins and they arranged to take four-hourly watches during the night, with Angela volunteering for the 4 a.m. to dawn shift. She went to her cabin feeling rather hopeless about the patient, who was still bleeding heavily, 'but we are too tired to do anything now but sleep'.

> Four o'clock came all too soon and I dressed wearily in the unaccustomed silence of early dawn. As I went on deck Captain Hennessy greeted me with a tired but triumphant smile. The patient's wound had stopped bleeding, his pulse rate had improved and he was sleeping peacefully.

The plasma had saved his life, making this fortunate man one of the very few Japanese soldiers to benefit from the new medical discoveries and techniques – and the infrastructure to support them – which the Indian Army was now able to provide to Slim's ever-healthier troops.

Everyone knew about the savage behaviour of the Japanese towards prisoners, civilians and, notoriously, the many white nurses they'd brutalised, raped, shot and bayoneted during their conquests. George MacDonald Fraser's Cumbrians, at that moment still fighting hard on the road to Rangoon, were short of pity and we know from his account that some of them considered shooting any Japanese or INA men they took alive. But they didn't. On Angela Noblet's steamer there were also men who were looking for the chance to attack the prisoners. She saw a group of Gurkhas wave their kukris at them and cry out, 'When we prisoners you starve us, when you prisoner we feed you!' But again these men didn't act on such impulses. Was it military discipline, the presence of an officer who would simply not allow his men to break the laws of war, or was it something else? Angela preferred an idealistic explanation.

> I returned to the man we'd saved. He was very young, with a delicate worn face. Where did he live? Had he a mother waiting? It struck me forcibly that never once during the whole emergency that night had the thought entered my head that this man was an enemy. He was just another patent for whose life we fought.
>
> I peeled some juicy lychees, feeding him with them one by one as he ate like a child, blinking at me nervously with dark almond-shaped eyes. 'What name?' he said in broken English. I told him and, to my surprise he nodded at the fruit, saying in English 'Chinese fruit'.

Later the senior Japanese officer on board asked to see her and called her 'honoured lady'. Later, too, to her diary she revealed, 'I shall look back to this time on the river as one of the happiest of my life. I have found the convergence of so many nationalities on one small river boat exhilarating, breaking down my stereotypes of how certain races look and behave.' Many, perhaps most, men and women serving in the Allied cause didn't share such idealistic sentiments, but there's nothing in Angela's diary to suggest any post-war soft focus being applied. She really did believe that a fairer world was not only possible but also likely, and that she'd glimpsed it on her river.

London, 1945

A better world, a kinder world, a fairer world — that's what this war was all about, or so many people liked to think. No doubt Angela Noblet's idealism, like Priestley's in *An Inspector Calls*, is exactly what motivated millions of Britons in 1945 and it's very much how we like to remember the moment today. Yet other attitudes persisted, especially among those at the pinnacle of the old system. People across the world were horrified by the footage that came out of Belsen and the other newly liberated concentration camps. But British politician and socialite Henry 'Chips' Channon had a rather different reaction.

> I took him [Channon's lover, Terence Rattigan] and Ava Anderson to see a film shown to MPs of the prison camp at Buchenwald; its horrors are too terrible to chronicle and one could scarcely take them in. The rows of dead emaciated bodies all looked like Margot [Asquith] naked! Terry and I, I am ashamed to record, enjoyed an immense tea afterwards! Our sadism is of a mild nature and I cannot understand any cruelty apart from a mild beating of a beloved.

Channon, who had long since turned snobbery into an art form, lived a life of extravagant privilege and promiscuity, and his joke about Margot Asquith, a famously thin member of London high society, was entirely in character. He had at one time been a prominent Conservative MP, but his passionate support for Neville Chamberlain and his policy of appeasing Hitler during the 1930s meant that he'd been exiled to the backbenches 'for the duration'. His world is the one that

THE LAUNDRY

Priestley so badly wanted to change, a world of gentlemen's clubs, boorishness and bigotry. Attending a party at the Savoy Hotel for his friend Harold Balfour, about to be posted overseas to administer some portion of the empire, Channon wrote, 'Harold goes to West Africa on Friday to reign over ni**ers'. On his return home from that grand affair he was irritated by the sight of underground platforms packed with his fellow Londoners trying to sleep safe from the V2 rockets, or, as he chose to call them, 'miserable heaps of dirty humanity'.

Channon lived in great style in one of Belgrave Square's finest houses, where he threw lavish parties and served the best French champagne and fine food with no apparent need to worry about rationing. He hated his wife Honor — calling her 'drab and fat' — but he took large amounts of cash from her wealthy family and enjoyed a long-term love affair with her brother-in-law, the MP and future government minister Alan Lennox-Boyd. Of the voters who sent him to Westminster he memorably said that 'I have always been bored by the poor'.

The many concessions to Stalin at Yalta caused Channon to reflect on roads not taken. Without ever stating it specifically it's clear that he meant a road that involved doing a deal with Adolf Hitler years before and letting him crush the communists in a one-front war. The news of the death of Hitler's partner in crime, Benito Mussolini, at the hands of fellow countrymen and women displeased him greatly, too: 'I don't admire the Italians for their disloyalty to their misguided leader who at one time had genius and even greatness.' The idea of a man like Channon dining luxuriously at the Ritz with Lord Linlithgow — the Viceroy of India who was so slow to react when famine struck Bengal — would not have impressed many Indians of Timmy's generation. And when Harold Nicolson wrote about the future he was no doubt thinking of people just like Channon: 'The Upper Classes feel that all this sacrifice and suffering will only mean that the proletariat will deprive them of all their comforts and influence and then proceed to render the country and the Empire a third-class state.'

Not every member of the British elite was like this. Alan Brooke moved in similar circles to Channon and the two men had friends in common, yet he was as far from being a selfish libertine as can be imagined. Conscientious, public-spirited and irritated by heavy drinking, he was much more interested in birdwatching and playing board games with his children than drinking cocktails or flogging a lover (one of Channon's many vices). Because some of the thinking behind colonial policy was never written down, we cannot know what really influenced certain decisions and strategies. But it seems likely — especially when it came to the *secret* state — that quiet conversations over dinner, soaked in both the prejudices and the priorities of the past, continued to be rather important. Conversation about showing the flag, regaining face, taking back valuable real estate and — yes — keeping the natives and the 'ni**ers' in their place. Change was coming, and many welcomed it, but this was still a deeply hierarchical world in which ideas about racial superiority remained profoundly influential. That was even true in outwardly liberal America, a nation still heavily segregated on the basis of race. And it was certainly true right across the old European colonies and, especially, deep inside Chips Channon's beloved 'clubland'.

Germany, 1945

LAMED VAV ZADDIKIM: In Hebrew the minimal number of anonymous righteous men living in the world in every generation. They are privileged to see the Divine Presence and the world exists on their merit. According to folklore these hidden saints, called in Yiddish 'lamedvovniks', are responsible for the fate of the world.

All the guards had gone and someone shouted, 'The Russians are here.' The survivors of the 'lost train' were free at last but they were still hungry and very sick. The soldiers were kind but had little food to offer and a war still to fight. Instead, they led the Jews towards a nearby German village and told them to help themselves. People were soon breaking into houses and basements and finding stores of food: jars of pickles, loaves of bread, piles of cheese and sausages. Everything they'd talked about night after night in the camps. The local Germans were terrified of them and especially of the Russians. They made no objection as starving Jews gathered food from their homes. The soldiers also found them abandoned houses. Hanelli and Gabi were put inside one that had been the home of the local major, with more cupboards full of food and – blissfully – running water that could be heated for an actual bath. The sisters luxuriated in it and felt clean for the first time in many, many months. Then they both slept in a real bed with beautiful cotton sheets. Hanneli Goslar would one day learn that, of the 2,500 people on her train, more than five hundred died during the journey. She'd also one day be able to tell Otto Frank in person of her last meeting with his daughter, and he would go on to become a 'surrogate father' to her own children and grandchildren.

But amid the joy and the relief of rescue, people were still dying of typhus. A Russian doctor handed out pills, but some families decided to seek medical care elsewhere. There were American forces close by and the rumour was that they were helping refugees. Another family of Dutch Jews from the same train, Sara and Philip Boas and their sons Samuel and Eddy, managed to cross into the American zone and met some soldiers who took pity on them, putting them into a truck for Leipzig where they were given rough mattresses to sleep on in an abandoned school building. But in the chaos of a recently conquered city there seemed to be no system to care for the thousands of refugees gathered there and soon both five-year-old Eddy and his mother were growing very weak. Samuel Boas went out into the rubble-strewn streets of the city to look — or beg — for food. And that's where Captain Douglas Peterkin came across him. The British doctor immediately asked where the boy's family were and then went with him to examine them. Realising how sick they all were, and immediately recognising what they were suffering from, he found a space for all four in a British-run hospital within hours. The entire family recovered.

The paperwork of the British Army and the oral histories of the Boas and Peterkin families are both cloudy about the details of this unlikely, no, near-miraculous, encounter. So it is unclear how or why Captain Douglas Peterkin found his way to an American-occupied city in what was probably — although not certainly — late May. His unit records state that he left 11 Light Field Ambulance to receive treatment for his own bout of typhus on 10 May then returned on 18 June and it's during this period that he happened to meet Samuel Boas in the streets of Leipzig. Was he receiving care himself nearby? Had he chosen to spend his convalescence with some of the Americans he'd met at Belsen? Are the Boas family memories geographically accurate? Was perhaps the meeting and the hospital actually some distance from Leipzig? Given how ill they were, and everything they had survived even to get to this point, none of this confusion is surprising. And whatever the answers to these questions, what really counts is that when he did come across a lone, sick child roaming the streets, one of countless thousands of lone, sick children roaming countless thousands of streets, Peterkin was not on active service and wasn't required to do anything at all. But that isn't how a *lamedvovnik* sees the world. He recognised the signs of illness. He asked questions. He understood that these strangers needed the help he was now uniquely qualified to give. He took responsibility for the fate of others. And still he wasn't done with the Boas family. He visited the hospital, put them in touch with an agency that could get them new clothes and shoes and made sure that they got proper accommodation when they were over the worst of their multiple illnesses. Peterkin also put their names on a list for a Red Cross transport back to Holland and on 13 June – just five days before he rejoined his own unit – he made sure that they got on the train.

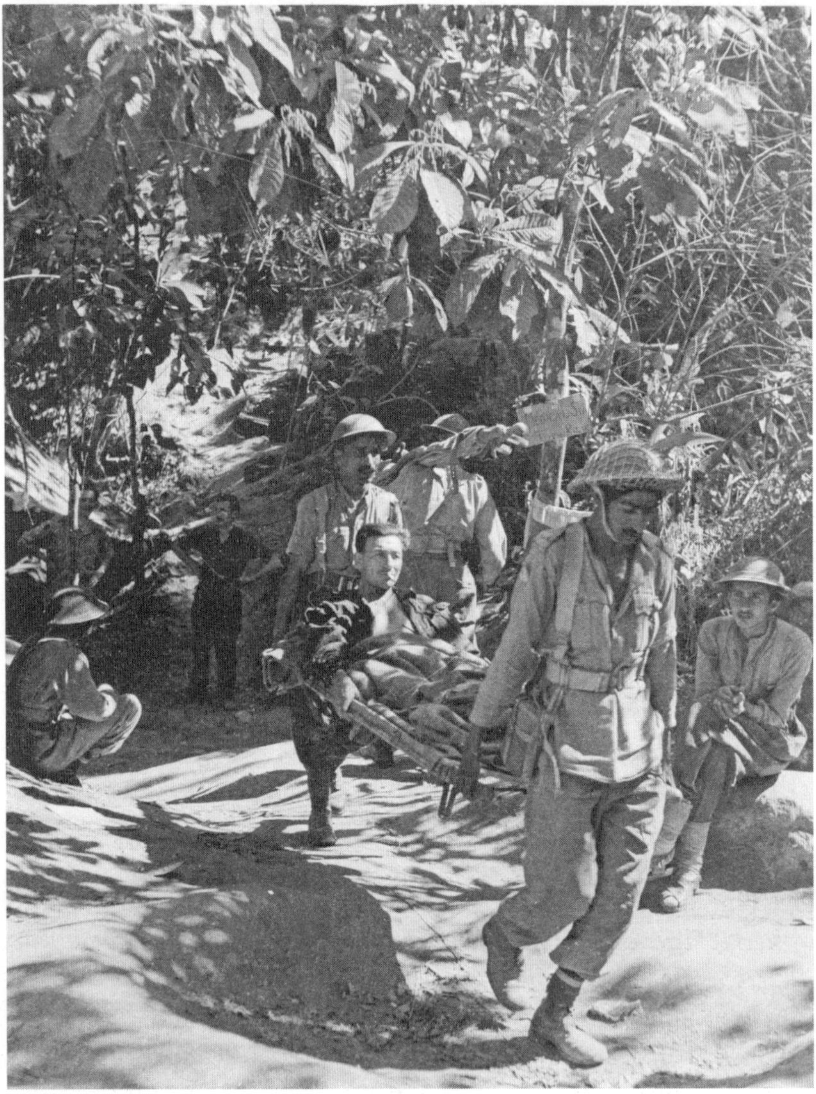

14

The Surrender

Burma, 1945

Amid the collapse of the Japanese army in Burma, the remaining commanders of the INA fought on with desperation and desire. The desperation not to yield an inch until absolutely all hope was lost and the desire to set an example that even now might inspire their fellow Indians to join them in the struggle for independence. Under the future Red Fort defendants, Prem Kumar Sahgal, Shah Nawaz Khan and Gurbaksh Singh Dhillon, 1,500 INA troops made a stand around Mount Popa in late March and early April. Laying ambushes, they managed to slow the British advance for a few days. Prem Kumar Sahgal ordered his men to be aggressive but careful: 'I told them, go seek the enemy but don't get caught. Attack, then come back.' But, amid continuing shortages of food and ammunition, he also had to approve the execution of four men caught attempting to desert.

The fighting around Mount Popa was less an attempt to change the course of the campaign and more of a political gesture. 'Madness but of the revolutionary sort,' as Sahgal himself put it later. It was an apposite comment. By the end of April the INA's war in Burma was well and truly over as fact but only just beginning as legend, and as the latter it proved to be much more successful. The many vivid tales of hard-to-confirm victories and exaggerated suffering that emerged from the final stages of the campaign have as much if not more prominence in the India of today than the *actual* victories of Timmy's Indian army of 1945, just as Bose imagined they would.

One popular story told about this time features a brave INA officer leading a small group of sick and injured men — many without boots — in a final attack on a British camp. All involved accepted that they would likely die but proclaimed that it was their sacred duty to make a final gesture of resistance. In this attack — which British war diaries failed to record — the INA men managed to kill over 500 enemy soldiers while losing just 17 of their own.

The British response to unlikely INA triumphs such as these, according to the same source, was predictably savage — bombing an INA hospital without mercy. Did any of it actually happen? Well, did Mr Oaten deserve his beating or his verb? Was Major Bird truly the tyrant of the Andaman Islands? Did the white officers of SS *Corbis* interrupt their escape from a burning oil tanker to enforce a colour bar? It depends on what you choose to believe, as Bose understood very well. And if enough people do decide to believe such stories then they become and remain influential, real even if not wholly true. As can be seen easily today at the touch of a screen.

@JungSXXXbit
Nobody cares about Mount Popa, nothing significant happened there, most of them gave up within hours (unlike where in Kohima, British Indian loyalists fought till the clothes fell off their backs).

@N07854XXX
U really need to read how 50 INA soldiers used to fight against 1000 IA soldiers, in the Burmese fields and the sacrifices of INA men will always be above the sacrifices of British slaves who strengthened British colonialism in the world.

After Mount Popa fell, Bose continued to muster his remaining resources with an eye to Indian public opinion and the media platforms of the future. He left five thousand of his best men in Rangoon with an order to maintain basic services and security in the city and then hand it to the British without a fight. He had been writing and speaking about the Indian Army, too. 'The British Indian Army is not yet prepared to take the risk and line up with the revolutionaries,' he said, but he believed that it was now full of sympathisers and he hoped that when they arrived in Rangoon they would shake the hands of the INA, hear *Jai Hind* shouted proudly and feel inspired to take the final step.

India, 1945

As Slim's army closed in on Rangoon, Angela Noblet's floating hospital was busier than ever. A group of shell-shocked Indian soldiers had to be kept in cages on the deck for their own protection but, positive as ever, Angela felt 'sure that most of these disturbed sepoys would recover once they were back in a familiar environment.' A party of friendly Americans hitched a ride upriver, laden with cigarettes, orange juice and nylon stockings. A British captain with 'the worst case of burns I have seen out here' died under her care and, as she mourned him, she wished that someone would discover 'a penicillin for burned skin'.

The Brahmaputra still entranced. She loved to lie in the just-bearable late-afternoon sun under a mosquito net watching the villages drift past, women washing clothes and naked children splashing in the shallows. But the river was not always her friend. One night they almost foundered in a sudden storm and had to gather on deck in the sheeting rain with crew, walking wounded and medical staff huddled together, lifebelts clutched nervously in their hands. On a stinking hot day she decided to take a swim but as she plunged into an appealing patch of clear-looking water between the reed beds she collided with a sari-clad but horribly swollen corpse of a woman, getting caught for a frightening moment in the hair that streamed behind her like so much waterweed. This was one, she learned, of many dead bodies that were disposed of in this way, along with farm animals of all shapes and sizes. She decided not to swim again.

On 8 May everyone on board gathered around the radio to hear that the war in Europe was over. They also learned of Belsen and what had happened in other German concentration camps. None of them wanted to believe it, or let it spoil the atmosphere of the impromptu party that broke out on deck with flags, streamers and some bottles of champagne of a most uncertain origin. This was but a prelude to a grand Victory Ball in Dacca two days later with a live band playing American swing music and everyone, as Angela recorded it, very much 'in the mood'. Exactly what kind of mood can be determined from the fist fights that broke out between British and American soldiers, apparently over 'dancing rights' to the girls. But then the atmosphere changed.

> Towards midnight everyone quietened down, the lights were lowered, couples danced cheek to cheek, and a crooner sang Vera Lynn's I'll Be Seeing You very softly. The dancers gradually joined in until all the people in the hall were singing together as quietly as they could. It was very moving and unexpected.

In the final pages of her diary, Angela Noblet gives a warm portrait of the last days of the Raj: the friendships on her steamer, the sense of a shared struggle, the understanding that change was coming and was right to come. Her interest in Indian independence, her concern for the lives of the Indian people she nursed and befriended and her anger at the racial prejudices freely expressed even by the 'nice men' she considered friends — all of it strikes us as admirable today. But people like Angela did not control the direction of the war or the fate of the empire. The hidden agenda, the broken agreement and the cynical calculation of the political officer — all of that was far from over. As was about to become very clear in Borneo.

Borneo, 1945

Tony Carter's victory at Long Lama wasn't Operation Semut's only success. All of the Semut groups were now attacking Japanese bases and supply lines, and headhunting was proving to be a powerful motivational tool. Corporal Roland Griffith-Marsh, serving under Tom Harrisson in Semut 1, sent his local volunteers into action 'informing them one dollar for the first man to bring me a Nip head'. He didn't have to wait long.

> From my vantage point up on the root of a mangrove, I saw a murderous scene enacted. A few feet in front of me was a seething mass of alternately rising and falling parangs, around a circle of khaki bolsters. I could hear the thumps of parangs, see bloody eddies and froth stain the water. A final victory howl terminated the slaughter and seven successful, pleased natives came to me, each carrying the head of a Japanese, as one would carry a fish by the gills, fingers poked through the lower jaw.

The war party then travelled back to its jungle base in spectacular if gory fashion. '[We rode in] a great flotilla of praus on the broad sluggish mangrove-lined Merapok river, the spoils grotesquely displayed over the bows, dense jungle around us resounding to the victory chant.'

For all the fingers in dead mouths, Griffith-Marsh was certain that his men treated the Japanese with less cruelty than they would have expected in return. 'Capture by the Japanese was feared the most. It would mean disembowelling by bayonet, or more often the obscenity of torture, perhaps a sliver of bamboo thrust down the urethra, or immolation by petrol, or some equally bestial death.' Corporal Brian Walpole, part of Bill Sochon's Semut 3 group, would later sum up what most of the SRD men thought about headhunting. That it was a necessary and successful idea given where they were, who they were fighting and who they had to rely upon for almost every aspect of their mission.

> What could I say? It was their culture and ... I didn't blame them at all. Besides, it would have been a brave, stupid and potentially dead man who tried to stop them. I didn't necessarily condone what they were doing, but it didn't worry me either, given what I'd seen the Japanese dish out and with my brother Denis still in their hands.

Jack Tredrea – one of the first to land on the Kelabit Plateau and a participant in the original 'fuck them all' sing-along – found that working and fighting alongside the Dayaks changed him: 'I went to Borneo thinking I'd need to teach the Dayaks how to operate and how to fight. But it turned out that it was mostly them teaching me. Without them I wouldn't have lasted a day.'

With SRD–Dayak raids breaking out throughout the interior, much now rested on the success of the invasion. Toby Carter continually feared that if it failed, or got bogged down somehow, his small groups of guerrilla fighters – and their poorly defended communities – would be horribly exposed to Japanese retribution. Carter's own group had been reinforced from the air and now numbered about seventeen SRD men and a hundred or so armed Dayaks. An ideal force to harass the enemy but pitifully small if the Japanese sent a battalion or so after them. Then on the morning of 9 June his radio crackled into life with the welcome news that the 9th Australian Division was indeed landing as planned at Labuan Island and other sites all around the Bay of Brunei. The cavalry was coming.

Based on their behaviour during previous invasions, Carter and the SRD planning team anticipated that the Japanese commanders would move inland a little rather than fight on the open coastal plain. The key thing was to have them facing back *down* towards the coast, digging in to resist the regular Australian forces, rather than pushing deep into Dayak territory. As soon as he heard about the landings Carter sent a message to Lieutenant Colonel Godfrey Courtney, in overall charge of the SRD force, recommending that the 9th Division prepare troops to send to key points in the interior such as the town of Murudi on the Baram River, to help protect the Dayaks. But it was at this point that the operation ran into its first big problem because, as Carter put it: 'Alas for the best-laid schemes of mice and men! Troops would not be available for such purposes.' Carter pushed harder, then on 19 June received the following definitive response from Courtney: 'There will be NO repeat NO army penetration inland. You are now granted freedom of action for guerrilla forces . . . Good hunting!'

Somewhere there had been 'a breakdown of communication', 'a mismatch of expectations', 'a failure to double check key mission parameters' and any number of the other smooth phrases of military bureaucracy that staff officers deploy when things begin to unravel and people start to die. The 9th Division had been told to take and hold the coastal strip, and that was all. The formal planning documents for the invasion of Borneo, reviewed after the war, contained no mention of a mission to protect the interior peoples at all. Not a single line. And so when Carter, Harrisson and Sochon suddenly started complaining that they had been left isolated, their comrades at 9th Division had no idea what they were talking about. To them the SRD men were a bunch of guerrilla fighters sent in to help − 'so, Good Hunting!' But Carter had recruited his local militias on the explicit understanding that the division would work with him to free the *whole* island from the Japanese and protect Dayak villages from any reprisals. He could see not only disaster looming but dishonour, too. 'Great was our disillusionment,' he wrote in his post-war report.

Behind all this confusion lay politics, of both the military and civilian varieties. Conventional army units had long looked upon Special Forces with great scepticism, thinking them distractions at best and renegades at worst. The SRD's private little war of ambushes in the interior was not going to do much to help 9th Division achieve its core aims, which were securing the coastal communities, ports and valuable infrastructure and then, frankly, sitting tight and waiting for the rest of the Japanese on the island to surrender. The fact that 9th Division was run entirely by Australians and that key SRD commanders — Courtney included — were British did not help at all. In their internal divisional communications 9th Division staff officers began to refer to the Semut teams as 'British units', although most of the white men fighting up in the hills were every bit as Australian as they were. Long-standing prickliness about high-handed British behaviour towards Australians also became a factor, especially when men like Tom Harrisson — hardly a natural diplomat at the best of times — started sending angry messages telling senior Australian officers what to do and what not to do. In one furious cable Harrisson wrote: 'It would clearly be an inexplicable thing if we let these Japanese do wide-scale damage inland or destroy the lives of these, our so loyal supporters and allies.' But the division did not budge. The ports, oilfields and rubber plantations were the limit of its military objectives.

When units of the regular army and SRD did finally meet, the culture clash was extreme. The 9th Division officers, unfamiliar with how the jungle campaign was being run, visited one of Harrisson's teams. They were appalled to discover that the locally recruited Ibans intended to execute a recently captured 'collaborator', an extra-judicial killing that they tried and failed to stop.

After the man was dragged out and decapitated in front of them, they attempted to put one of the SRD team up for a court martial, triggering a furious argument that was only settled when General Thomas Blamey himself, the overall commander of the Australian Army, intervened to get the charges dropped.

The politics of Canberra were also coming into play. Everyone knew that the war was almost over now and so there was intense pressure to limit casualties. Why send troops off into a pointless jungle bloodbath to help some half-arsed British adventurers when there would probably be a complete enemy surrender in just a few weeks anyway? Major General George Wootten, the Commanding Officer of 9th Division, called one message he received from the SRD 'flat impertinence' and it became clear rather quickly that important people in the Australian government and military believed that the whole Borneo campaign was a sideshow anyway.

And every day Toby Carter received new reports of Japanese forces moving his way.

India, 1945

INA commander Gurbakhsh Singh Dhillon was disappointed when he saw Burmese communities that had once welcomed his men changing sides, but he was phlegmatic about it, too. 'It is natural for the people who have the misfortune of getting themselves, their hearths and homes and their fields overrun by warring foreign armies that they side with the winner.' Then one day, when close to Rangoon, he came across a Burmese militia that had fought alongside the Japanese but was now campaigning with the British. A standoff was resolved without bloodshed after an exchange of prisoners and recognition that both groups were pursuing different routes to the same goal — a friendly future as independent neighbours. As this was happening, Prem Kumar

Sahgal led what was left of his own unit through central Burma in search of allies, food and safety.

> We moved from village to village, hiding in them during the day. I would send a man ahead with instructions to pretend that they were looking for the Indian Army and if they were told 'Yes the Indian Army is here' we would avoid that place.
>
> Then [one day] we opened fire on an approaching Gurkha battalion and soon aircraft began flying low and so the villagers came to me and said 'If you stay here and fight, they will bomb our village and set fire to it . . . Don't fight!' I had to make a decision. The bulk of my men were going to surrender in any case. For the sake of the few of us who wanted to break out was I to risk burning a village? So I said 'all right we will surrender.'

Dhillon gave himself up, too, alongside Shah Nawaz Khan, the third future Red Fort defendant. As a sign of how deeply connected men like Dhillon, Khan and Sahgal were to the Indian Army officers they had fought against, the man who received Khan's surrender turned out to be a former cadet of his in the academy at Dehra Dun. A mysterious British intelligence officer called Major C. Ore then arrived to interrogate Dhillon over several days. After the war Dhillon wrote down what had taken place in detail, revealing exchanges that highlight the curious chemistry of the Anglo-Indian relationship at this moment. Although firm to his nationalist principles throughout, Dhillon's relationship with his enemy grew surprisingly warm and emotional.

> 'Mr Dhillon, from what I know of you I am afraid you may be put on trial for waging war against the King and the trying court may have no choice than awarding you capital punishment, that is death. And when the time comes do ask for clemency and I am sure it shall be granted.'
>
> 'Ask for clemency, to whom?'

THE SURRENDER

'To his Majesty the King Emperor.'

'Ask for clemency from my enemy? Oh no I shall never do it. I cannot.'

'The King is not your enemy. He has nothing personal against you. He does not even know you . . . [in the past]Field Marshal Smuts [of Boer War fame] also acted as you have and he was awarded the death penalty. He asked for mercy and the King pardoned him. It was later that he rose to be a General and then a Field Marshal . . . and is now a world figure.'

'I am not Smuts. I am not a white man. You have different scales of justice while dealing with the coloured people. Don't you think so?'

[crying] 'You do not understand yourself. There are very few Indians like you. And India needs sons like you. India needs you, my son.'

'Thank you sir [it was the first time I had called him that].'

. . . 'Do you believe in democracy or dictatorship?'

'Democracy.'

'Do you respect Mahatma Gandhi?'

'Yes his very name is synonymous with the Indian freedom struggle.'

'Do you think he will appreciate your violent actions?'

'Well our methods may differ but our aim is the same – the independence of India.'

'What do you think will be the effect on the Indian people if some of you were tried by an open public trial? Even Gandhi won't favour you.'

'But the people will. They will immediately go in our favour and against the government.'

Ore asked me again to seek clemency. He looked moved. His eyes were wet and so were mine. Kindness had removed the sting in me.

Formosa, 1945

The prisoners in the jungle camp knew nothing of the atomic bombs that had just destroyed Hiroshima and Nagasaki, but one day they were gathered together and told that their labour would now cease, that negotiations were taking place to end the war and that they would be set free once a peace treaty was signed. Some of Arthur Titherington's friends cried with joy, but all of them remained very wary. They were still stuck in a lonely jungle clearing controlled by short-tempered men with reasons to fear a war crimes trial. In fact, Captain Imamura had decided that this was not the moment for 'extreme disposition' after all. He gave his prisoners increased rations and boxes of cigarettes and instructed his guards to leave them largely to themselves. He even allowed them to hold a Christian service of thanksgiving for the end of the war (after they first promised in writing not to sing 'God Save the King.'). In another surprise gesture he presented them with a plump bullock that they were allowed to kill, butcher and cook. Titherington tasted freshly grilled meat for the first time since 1942. As the men feasted they sang and embraced around the campfire, growing ever more certain that freedom truly was coming.

When it did, Arthur experienced a wave of conflicting emotions: joy at his survival; grief for those who had died; anger at the pointless, stupid cruelty of it all; bewilderment about why any of it had happened. Imamura made a final, bizarre speech, defending his own conduct and urging them to speak well of Japan once they were back home: 'You have received good treatment at our hands. When things were not so good you will realise that this was not my doing but because I received orders from my superiors. Go back to Britain and be good ambassadors for Japan!'

The men answered with jeers but that was all. 'During our time as prisoners we were obliged to hold our feelings in check, though the desire to strike out was very strong, to hurt them as we had been hurt, to crush them as they had tried to crush us.'

But they did not. When they finally travelled back towards the coast and a boat for home, some of the local people gathered to cheer them. Arthur wondered how many had worked as supervisors in the mine.

Allied war crime courts delivered three death sentences for the murders and abuse of prisoners on Formosa. Major Taichi Uete, the overall commandant of the island's camps, and two guards were executed in Hong Kong in 1948. Captain Imamura was tried for his time running Kinkaseki, and for an earlier role in another camp, and received a fifteen-year sentence. The Kinkaseki guards typically received sentences of between five and seven years. 'Sanitary Sid' got eight, and Dr Ben Wheeler was able to testify against him at his trial, telling the court that 'day after day I saw men who were unable to walk by themselves dragged to and from the mine by their friends and frequently beaten up by the guards'. There's little doubt that the original commander, Captain Wakiyama, would have received the death penalty but he was long gone. Unbeknownst to Arthur, he had fallen seriously ill with tuberculosis and had been sent back to Japan. Bedbound and near death, he was never brought to trial.

For the rest of his life Arthur Titherington tried to process what he had experienced. He struggled to understand the angry, overgrown adolescents who had taken power over him, and especially their need to be brutal towards other human beings who posed no threat to them. He returned to the places where he had kept going one day at a time and wrote movingly about surviving brutality and the profound, pure comradeship that he had experienced in Kinkaseki. He was not a bitter man, but he did campaign tirelessly for a formal apology from the Japanese government to the prisoners of Formosa, long after it had become Taiwan. No apology ever came. After the war he married, brought up two children and served in the British police force, until he found that life too regimented for his taste. Instead he ran a photography studio with his wife Iris and entered local politics in the town of Witney, Oxfordshire, rising to become a popular and twice re-elected mayor, initially as a Conservative and then, in his own words, 'as a bloody independent'.

Unlike many of the other survivors of the camps, Arthur reached out to the nation that had imprisoned him right up until his death in 2010, making Japanese friends and even buying Japanese cars. But he did often state that the army in which he fought – during the time that he fought – would never have been as systematically cruel to prisoners and enemy civilians as was the army that captured him. And whatever we may think of the empire that he served, across its long and sometimes brutal history, in that he was surely correct.

India, 1945

Alongside the fate of British India, Angela Noblet – now dividing her time between hospital and riverboat duties – had another and more pressing concern. Teddy wanted to set a date for the wedding and she was struggling with serious second thoughts.

> I feel moved by the suffering of my patients, I mourn bitterly at their too early deaths. I care for them as a mother might care for her children. But in my own emotional life I feel like a complete stranger. I have this fear of being in the power of someone else and this avoidance of commitment. Teddy is a dear friend and I feel safe and relaxed with him. A year ago I would have married him without hesitation.

She hadn't written anything in her diary about her fiancé for many months, and now she revealed why – an intense love affair.

> Out of the blue it came, a most powerful attraction, stronger than anything I could have imagined possible. This could not be happening to me, to steady, reliable, faithful me. But it had and what was worse was that he was a happily married man. The fact that he was in my immediate circle of friends and colleagues made it my duty to ask for a posting elsewhere – preferably to the front line in the mood I was in. But I hesitated and I was 'lost'.

Angela took care never to reveal the name, the location or even the race of this man. Given how rhapsodically she wrote about her life on the steamer and the intense relationships she witnessed blossoming there, it's nice to imagine that this is where she fell in love. But wherever it took place the experience made her realise that she could never think of Teddy in the same way again. She now described him as a 'father figure', a dear but older (by twelve years) friend who'd indulged her, educated her and fussed over her. A man who was kind, gentle, and decent, but sadly unexciting when compared to her lover, who had provoked a 'shattering, frightening passion, which destroyed all my carefully nurtured self-possession'. She knew that she could never be with this married man once the war ended but their relationship made her realise that she should not tie herself to Teddy either. In a state of sadness she travelled to Calcutta to meet her fiancé.

> I weighed up the pro and cons all night. It would be sensible to marry and have children while I was young; I would be safe and protected for the rest of my life; it would put the final seal on those youthful fantasies and poetic yearnings, which had already been sternly disciplined during my training. But when Teddy knocked on the door and entered my room I knew what my decision was.

Angela revealed everything that had happened and handed him back the engagement ring. After a sleepless night she went out the next day for a consoling dinner with a friendly brigadier, and ran into an old friend.

> While I was combing my hair and renewing my lipstick in the cloakroom halfway through the evening, who should enter but Mary King, back nursing in Calcutta, once more. She looked a different person from the retiring, self-effacing beauty with the detached expression I remembered; her sleepy blue eyes were wide and alert, and she greeted me with an enthusiasm I had never known before. It did not take me long to spot the cause of the transformation. I saw that she was wearing a diamond ring on her left hand. She told me that she had just become engaged and was at the Grand Hotel with her fiancé to celebrate. I was so pleased that I gave her a hug and a kiss, a thing I would never have dared to do in the past.

Angela wished Mary well, but could not stop herself comparing their situations with a certain sadness. And yet within days all the 'youthful fantasies and poetic yearnings' she had almost set aside to marry Teddy were to be fulfilled in a most surprising way.

Burma, 1945

CGI Philips always remembered the moment he became a 'proper fighter pilot'.

> Good news, chaps, someone said, we're getting a lot of Spitfires! Spit VIIIs. A beautiful aircraft. The handling and the flying . . . just a beautiful aircraft.

Number 8 Squadron of the Indian Air Force was saying goodbye to the old Vultee Vengeance, and its gleeful pilots were going to be glamourous 'Spitfire boys' at last. As they supported Slim's drive into Burma their immediate task was covering the capture of Akyab, from where Timmy would soon depart on his mission to Kangaw. Few Japanese fighters challenged them in the air but theirs was still a very dangerous occupation, as Philip saw firsthand when an old squadron-mate, Purnendu 'Chuck' Chakrabarty, was fatally injured in a takeoff accident.

> An anti-aircraft gunner got to the aircraft and someone said 'Cut the straps!' He didn't know how to unbuckle the straps. So they pulled him out and Chuck started vomiting. Vomiting blood. The ack-ack gunners had tears dripping down their cheeks – they were great lads! All English. I told them that it was NOT their fault.

In late January Philip flew missions over Kangaw, providing air support for Timmy's first brigade command, swooping down to attack the Japanese artillery positions that gave such trouble to the Hyderabadis and the commandos they fought alongside. Indian pilots protecting the first Indian-led brigade, while Indian warships provided fire support from the sea – unmistakable signs that the military establishment of the Raj was becoming less British in appearance and command with every passing week.

After his exploits with the commandos at Kangaw, Timmy's war ended in the most disappointing way he could imagine – in a hospital bed. Three days before 25th Division and its Indian-born Brigade commander were sent into the battle for Rangoon he went down with a debilitating bout of diarrhoea, a permanent menace despite all the many medical and sanitation initiatives of the Indian Army. When it emerged that his 'squits' were actually masking other and even more serious symptoms, those of acute hepatitis, Timmy's time in Burma was over.

Apart from the ones holding Rangoon, Timmy's remaining enemies in the INA were sent to Thailand or Malaya. Bose himself made a final address before leaving Burma.

> If you have to go down temporarily then go down fighting with the national tricolour held aloft, go down as heroes ... The future generations of Indians, who will not be born as slaves, but as free men because of your colossal sacrifice, will bless your names and proudly proclaim to the world that you, their forebears, fought and suffered ... but paved the way to ultimate success and glory.

Bose then set out on the long and dangerous journey into Thailand, dodging British air attacks and travelling only by night. While Bose slept in ditches, Slim launched Operation Dracula, a spectacular amphibious and parachute assault upon Rangoon, made all the more impressive by the fact that the monsoon came early and much of the fighting took place in teeming rain. As 14th Army seized the capital of Burma it displayed all its finest qualities of improvisation, flair and imagination. The Burmese National Army of Aung San, now allied to the British, formed part of the force that first entered the city, to a joyful welcome and surprisingly little resistance.

Timmy lay in a hospital bed listening to the air offensive that preceded his men's advance, feeling worried and frustrated. He was particularly anxious about his INA-supporting brother, Ponnappa, who, as he rightly suspected, was with the remaining holdouts of Bose's army in and around Rangoon. When Indian troops did enter the city they immediately encountered the INA. Despite all the killings, executions and defections of the last year, there was an immediate outbreak not of *fighting* but of understanding and respect.

By now the Japanese had more or less abandoned the INA and so its officers, Ponnappa included, did their best to maintain law and order in the city until the Allies formally took control, just as Bose had commanded. Timmy was not there to witness it in person, but nevertheless he enjoyed telling the story of his brother's capture for many decades to come.

My brother demanded of the English officer who arrested him that he be taken to me. The Englishman told him that Thimayya was not there, and added, 'Even if your brother were here, he would have you thrown into the clink straightaway'. 'You are wrong', Ponnappa replied. 'He would give me a cold beer, a hot curry, and then he would have me thrown into the clink.' My brother knew me, all right. That is precisely what I would have done.

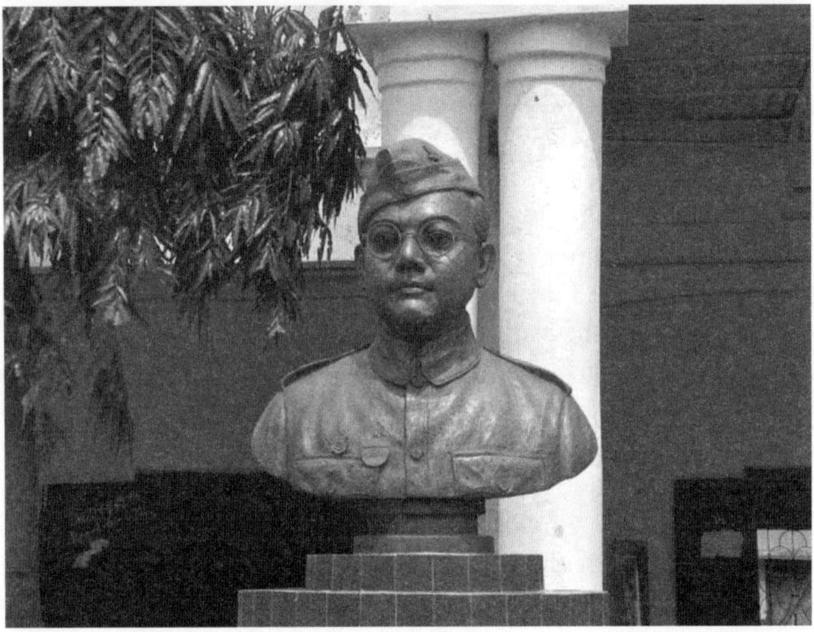

15

The Martyr

Singapore and Formosa, 1945

Bose spent July and August travelling between Bangkok and Singapore, where he approved plans for a memorial to the INA's war dead. It would bear three words: 'Faith', 'Unity' and 'Sacrifice'. When he heard that a fearsome new American weapon had been used against two Japanese cities, and that the Soviet Union had decisively entered the war with an invasion of Manchuria, he realised that his ally's surrender was imminent. He considered giving himself up to the British, believing that if the Raj dared bring him to trial it would galvanise Indian opinion in his favour. But his closest aides advised against it. They discussed him hiding in Thailand, where the large Indian population might protect him, or asking for the protection of the Russians. But in the end he decided to travel to Japan to be present at the conclusion of the war. Some believe that during this journey he was in fact quietly planning to leave his party en route to Tokyo and find his own way to Moscow, in yet another of his secret escapes. But at this point the numerous Bose legends and the documented facts do not easily align. Whatever his true intentions, he did leave in a Japanese plane and just before climbing on board he thanked his followers for their continued devotion, declaring: 'The roads to Delhi are many and Delhi still remains our goal.'

The Japanese flew him from Singapore to Bangkok, and then, after a short delay, on to Saigon. From there he travelled to

Formosa, where his plane stopped briefly in the capital Taihoku to refuel. On 18 August it crashed on take-off, the result of a propeller or engine failure. Bose survived the impact but was badly burned as he escaped. According to one witness account he attempted to run through some burning wreckage while wearing clothes that were already doused in aviation fuel. He died in a Formosan hospital within twenty-four hours. His companion Habibur Rahman survived the crash and wanted to take Bose's body back to Singapore but there were no more flights now and so he was cremated in Taihoku with little ceremony.

On learning of the death of his old tormentor, and of its manner, Edward Farley Oaten sat down to write a rather surprising tribute:

Did I once suffer, Subhas, at your hands?
Your patriot heart is stilled, I would forget!
Let me recall but this, that while as yet
The Raj that you once challenged in your land
Was mighty; Icarus-like your courage planned
To mount the skies, and storm in battle set
The ramparts of High Heaven, to claim the debt
Of freedom owed, on plain and rude demand.
High Heaven yielded, but in dignity
Like Icarus, you sped towards the sea.
Your wings were melted from you by the sun,
The genial patriot fire, that brightly glowed
In India's mighty heart, and flamed and flowed
Forth from her Army's thousand victories won!

Bose the Indian Icarus, an arresting image. From a scuffle by the school notice board to sending an army to liberate Delhi, this was a man who all his life ran towards the flame, even when doused with petrol. Someone who cared deeply for the struggling masses but who was attracted by a pseudo-spiritual language of national renewal, addicted to exposing 'traitors', intoxicated by a

THE MARTYR

call to greatness, dismissive of the petty compromises made by lesser men. And yet also beguiling, charming and admired even by some of those he hurt the most. Many years later, in 1971, Krishna Bose, married to Bose's nephew, met with Mr Oaten and found that he still only had kind words to say:

> He brought out a worn photograph of a history seminar at Presidency College. 'The was taken soon after the 1916 incident,' he told us. He chuckled and asked, 'Is it true that in India, in some of the films about Subhas, I have been shown as a fierce looking man?' . . . Mrs Oaten served a farewell round of sherry and then it was time for us to say goodbye. How to explain the old man's frank admiration of Subhas Chandra Bose, I wondered as we drove to the station. Was it his own individual magnanimity? Or was it something about *Netaji* himself that converted adversaries into admirers?

India, 1945

With Burma back in British hands, the INA dispersed and Bose dead, there was no longer any point keeping the leaders of Congress — the very men likely to lead a new India — in prison. And the Raj wasn't the only institution trying to heal old wounds. The Indian officers who met INA enemies like Kodandera Ponnappa Thimayya in Rangoon were by and large impressed by their conduct in the city and few had any desire left to punish them. As Bose had predicted, the roads to Delhi were many indeed and as they walked along them his former soldiers found themselves not shunned as traitors but feted as heroes. Allowed to return to their towns and villages, INA veterans were cheered and garlanded, even by the relatives of the men who had fought against them. And Jawaharlal Nehru himself, who had angrily condemned Bose as a dupe of fascism many times, announced that 'the men and women who had enrolled themselves in this Army and worked under Subhas Chandra Bose's guidance, have done so because of their passionate desire to serve the cause of Indian freedom'.

Popular feeling towards the INA was perhaps best summed up in a speech made by Asaf Ali, one of the Red Fort defence barristers. He had served years in the same jail as Nehru and was married to the underground nationalist heroine Aruna Asaf Ali.

> Though Shah Nawaz, Sehgal and Dhillon are no longer officers of the Indian Army, they have the whole of their lives before them to serve the country and the cause of India's freedom for which they risked their lives . . . They fought 'outside' for the attainment of Independence and, I may add, for communal harmony. I sincerely trust . . . they will become ambassadors of the unity of India.

As official censorship ended, the Indian press turned its attention to the stories behind the Bengal famine, further inflaming nationalist opinion. The very question that Motilal Nehru first raised with a young Kodandera Subayya Thimayya was being argued back and forth in barracks and officers' messes across the nation: when is the correct time to stop wearing the uniform of a foreign power? To more and more men and women the answer was plainly 'Now'.

Once recovered from his illness, Timmy was invited to attend the Japanese surrender ceremony in Singapore. The city had changed. It was no longer the corrupt and badly managed symbol of imperial malaise that he'd found so depressing. As crowds gathered to witness the spectacle, close to where Bose had announced the end of the British Empire in Asia just two years earlier, everything was now fresh paint, professionalism and crisp command. Lord Mountbatten was there, waving at the cheering crowds, and when the Japanese commanders appeared they were all loudly jeered. Later Timmy met Indian prisoners of war who had survived years of mistreatment, including half-starved *jawans* from his old regiment who had not volunteered to fight for Bose and lived to experience the consequences.

> They looked like skeletons. Many were too far-gone to know what was happening. Others could only crawl, whimpering, and try to touch my feet. To me, this was the saddest moment of the war. I was not ashamed of my own tears. Some of these men had been with the battalion for decades; seeing them now was like a reunion with members of one's own family.

His war was won and, more than that, the decisions he had made over many difficult years had proved to be correct. For all the gleaming whitewash and military pride on display in Singapore on this great day of victory, something profound had happened to the Indian Army and he had played a substantial part in it. By fighting *with* the British it had become the inevitable replacement *for* the British, as he had predicted in those first conversations with Nehru.

> We Indian officers felt the excitement of great expectations. We knew that we had made a good showing in the war. We no longer lacked confidence. We knew, also, that the British Raj was irrevocably finished. We were impatient for the day when the Indian Army finally would serve its own country under its own leaders.

Borneo, 1945

By late June the Japanese army in Borneo had burned most of the oil wells along the coast and was moving inland in search of defensible positions and food. Toby Carter decided to make a stand at Marudi on the Baram River. He had his own SRD team of about seventeen, a few dozen of Tang Weng's trained volunteers armed with modern weapons and a hundred or so other Dayaks who only had *parangs* and a few ancient shotguns better suited to hunting wild pigs. He made a camp at the small town — about forty miles from the coast — and sent spies downriver to look for signs of trouble. Marudi had been a Japanese river base before and if they seriously wanted to move deep into the interior of Borneo they would need to reclaim it. Soon word came that an attack party of about eighty soldiers was coming Carter's way and he prepared an elaborate ambush along a two-hundred-yard stretch of the river, moving his men there in the middle of the night. Apoi Anggang, one of the volunteers from Tama Weng's community, sat uncomfortably amid the thick foliage waiting for dawn to bring the enemy and a relief from insects. 'We were told to keep completely quiet. No movement, no sound. It was difficult. The place was full of mosquitos. How can you kill a mosquito without moving or making a sound?'

The Japanese arrived at the perfect moment for an ambush, silhouetting themselves against a dawn sky that was further brightened by the distant light from burning oilfields. Many of them were cut down immediately in the burst of Bren gun and rifle fire that opened Carter's attack, and those who did struggle onto the riverbank soon fell to the *parangs*. One of the SRD men exchanged fire with a Japanese soldier then saw some Dayaks 'dropping their .303s and drawing *parangs*, and his head was off before his body dropped beside my Bren'. But the battle was only just beginning and they were up against hardened jungle fighters now. From further down the river Carter heard a sound he remembered from New Guinea. The ominous 'plop' of a mortar discharging its bomb his way. As shrapnel began to fly through the foliage, and Japanese voices grew louder, it became clear that his enemies today had weapons larger than anything that could ever fit inside a storepedo. Carter quickly ordered a retreat back into Marudi where he discovered hundreds of locals preparing to flee. Unprepared to risk his men in any more fighting he pulled out of the town altogether, leaving the lower Baram Valley undefended.

Then he heard worrying reports of another force of perhaps a thousand Japanese operating nearby. As his fighters travelled upriver so, too, did most of the population of the town. Carter now had a military *and* a refugee problem on his hands and there was still no sign of any help from 9th Division. It was a deeply demoralising moment for the Dayaks and the SRD men alike.

At Carter's new temporary base at Long Murik there was a stretch of river suitable for a Catalina seaplane. On 13 July one flew in to take him down to the coast for a meeting with the commander of one of the brigades that made up 9th Division, Brigadier Victor Windeyer. As a New Zealander and a natural diplomat, he succeeded where the much pushier (and British) Tom Harrisson had failed. Windeyer agreed to send a force outside the boundaries prescribed by General Wootten to help Carter reclaim Marudi, accompanied by some armoured barges and even a squadron of Spitfires. The approach of that force was enough to persuade the Japanese to leave and, just five days after abandoning the town in panic, Carter was back in charge once again – only to discover that the handful of Malay families that had chosen to stay behind had been massacred.

The conflict was becoming unstructured and unpredictable now, as loosely organised war bands and militias fought haphazardly. There were a series of small battles in the hills around Marudi in which a handful of men from Windeyer's brigade lost their lives. At the same time, other Japanese units were moving nearby. Some were hostile and some appeared more interested in stealing food from the local people – who had precious little of it to begin with – and hiding from the fighter-bombers of the Royal Australian Air Force. Carter threw himself into an attempt to get relief aid up from the coast, seeking help for people to whom he had once promised protection with such *borak*-fuelled confidence. He also tried to organise civilian affairs in the region, with the assistance of Tang Weng and his family, even finding and reappointing some of the pre-war 'White Rajah'-era administrators and police. One day he was asked to dispense justice, just like an old-fashioned colonial officer, and delivered death sentences on two men caught informing to the Japanese, although there was hardly time for anything resembling an investigation or a trial.

Even after news of the Hiroshima bomb spread across the island, the fighting continued. With discipline breaking down and food running out, Japanese units splintered into little more than armed gangs. Some were out for vengeance; others just wanted to hide. This was a messy war of booby traps and ambushes, informers and traitors, raids and massacres. Across all the areas where the Semut teams were operating, longhouses burned and food stores were looted, while Carter's local allies collected more and more heads. The 9th Division still refused to provide the help Carter said he needed, although he did persuade the Air Force to bomb Japanese encampments in the interior. Sadly, the intelligence on which these raids were based was very poor and Dayak longhouses, along with the people sheltering inside them, were sometimes hit by mistake.

Not everything that happened in these desperate, chaotic weeks is easy to understand. Being a secretive organisation, SRD had a habit of not writing things down and there was nobody around to take minutes when the Australian officers debated the rights and wrongs of what was happening on Borneo. But we do know for certain that on 14 August Toby Carter was formally relieved of his command, or 'withdrawn' as the official document states. His second-in-command and replacement, Major Robert Wilson, put it more plainly: 'Carter has been sacked . . . summarily.' His offence? 'Jungleitis!' According to Carter himself

> one admits to having suffered from that tropical complaint commonly known as 'jungleitis', which afflicts field men with a jaundiced outlook towards their HQ unit. One also admits to having expressed views and criticism which taking the strictly military interpretation could be construed as 'insubordinate' . . . One was removed by the very people whose military careers had themselves been furthered by our efforts. Granted some of

them had rendered sterling service as well. Perhaps the trouble lay on a higher plane than SRD.

We're now deep in a world of bureaucratic obfuscation but, from what he later said, it seems clear that Wilson didn't like the way Carter was obsessing about the local people rather than pursuing their jungle war with appropriate ferocity. And that he found a way of conveying this opinion to Courtney and other senior commanders. Now that Wilson was in charge things would be different.

> Killing Japs . . . was of far more importance than the abandonment of a few hundred natives and a town to the enemy . . . Major Carter felt responsible to those natives and was worried as to what could be done for them, at least as far as feeding them . . . I felt no such responsibilities and recommended shooting a few of the more importunate to clear the air.

Given the choice between Wilson's approach and Carter's, Courtney had sided with the man who wanted to shoot the Dayaks rather than the one who wanted to feed them. Many years later Courtney effectively confirmed this when he wrote that Carter was 'not a military man . . . rather a practical idealist and man of sensibility'.

There were plenty of men left in Borneo who valued fighting more than civil reconstruction. They were on the SRD side, they were in the Dayak groups still eager to kill Japanese and take heads and they were running the more fanatical Japanese war bands. Together they continued the war that SRD had brought to this island long after the formal cessation of hostilities on 15 August and even the Japanese surrender ceremony of 2 September. In fact, the head count kept increasing well into October.

India, 1945

His public life began when he transformed a man into a verb, so what should his be?

bose
/boʊs/
rhymes: -əʊs

Verb (contested)

1. success through personal sacrifice, vindication after death

'It was hopeless but they believed they could bose their way to ultimate victory.'
Similar: **sacrifice martyr envision inspire prognosticate**

2. willing to ignore evil for sake of ambition or fanaticism

'He saw the death pits but by now he was too far bosed to care.'
Similar: **exculpate rationalise excuse mitigate overlook**

Bose could not have anticipated political and cultural change in Britain, or even the Atlantic Charter, when he decided to throw in his lot with Hitler. And the example of heroic sacrifice — truly worth a verb — that he provided throughout his life did indeed move Indian opinion, as did the Red Fort trial. To that extent he is more than entitled to the posthumous adulation he receives, and doubtless expected, but it's a shame that those who did *not* make the compromises with evil that he felt necessary — the Timmys of India — are not granted such a place in its history. Perhaps, as the historian Philip Cohen concluded, the INA and its volunteers were very much easier

THE MARTYR

to defend — and even garland — with Bose dead than ever they were with him alive.

We may look back and think this was Timmy's victory more than it was ever Bose's, and most military historians would agree, but the further we move away from 1945 the easier it is to forget about the cultural forces that shaped the players. Which is why a reckoning now can never be the same as a reckoning then. A residual loyalty to empire, even in a nationalist like Timmy, was understandable in the 1930s and 1940s in a way it simply isn't today. And, conversely, as we leave the age of European empires behind and focus our attention on their brutal and rapacious aspects, we're naturally more inclined to favour those who were implacably opposed to them from the start, whatever deals they did with whatever devils.

There's no expensive, heartstring-tugging drama series being made about Timmy's men fighting with British commandos to keep the Japanese out of India, no exciting reconstruction of the battle of Hill 170 or when Timmy pointed his revolver at the frightened pilot of his landing craft. But there is a lavish, cloyingly sentimental ten-part epic about the Indian National Army on Amazon Prime and many millions have watched it. The all-female unit that Bose created features prominently, along with numerous battlefield triumphs, but there's little or no reference to the cruelty of Bose's Japanese allies or his genocidal *Kameraden* in the SS.

Despite the many humiliations of Singapore, Malaya, Burma and elsewhere, the British and Commonwealth forces came back hard in the Indo-Pacific. Lessons were learned and new talent and ideas advanced. It may be that the British Empire's final moments in India were also its finest ones, and perhaps that is fitting. There's a sentimental account from the advance on Rangoon — one that would have drawn certain contempt from Bose — which is powerful and poignant because it captures what so many Indians of Timmy's generation felt. That this had indeed been India's war as well as Britain's war, but the army that had won it was now India's to keep.

Lieutenant Colonel John Masters was part of an old colonial family that has lived in India for many generations. As a staff officer of the 19th Indian Division he watched 14th Army columns pass along that most evocative of imperial locations, the road *from* Mandalay, moving towards Rangoon and glory, and experienced a late-imperial epiphany.

> . . . the torrent of guns and radios and trucks and machine guns swirled and rode past in one direction, south, past the bloated Japanese corpses, past the ruins of the Empire the Japanese had tried to build here, it took possession of the empire we had built and in its towering, writhing dust clouds India traced the shape of her own future. Twenty races, a dozen religions, a score of languages passed in those trucks and tanks. When my great-great-grandfather first went to India there had been many nations and now there was one . . . The Nehrus and the Gandhis and the Cripps talked in the high chambers of London and Delhi, and certainly somebody had to. But India stood at last independent, proud and incredibly generous to us on these final battlefields on the Burmese plain.

India, 1945

The VJ ball in Calcutta was a surprisingly downbeat affair, and felt most unlike the VE celebrations that Angela had enjoyed so much just a few months earlier. Most people just wanted to go home now, feeling, like her, that 'our job is done and it is time to lower the curtain'. She was also preoccupied by thoughts of love and loss, emotionally drained from breaking off both her engagement and her love affair. And her mood was not helped by the stream of slow, sentimental ballads coming from the stage.

Somewhat to her surprise she discovered that most of the

men and women she knew had voted Labour in the July 1945 general election, although she didn't reveal her own vote, or whether she voted at all. The consensus among the young officers she spoke to that night was that Attlee was a better person to build a more prosperous and fairer country than the old warhorse Churchill, and nobody wanted 'Blighty' to ever again witness the unemployment and poverty that had so scarred the 1930s.

And then within just a few weeks she was deep in love all over again. On first glimpsing Lieutenant James Bolton of the Royal Artillery on the other side of a room she whispered to a friend that this was the man she would marry. He was equally impressed and the couple were soon spending all their free time together. The fact that he was a poet and a Classics scholar (thus fulfilling the second of the ambitions of her sixteen-year-old self) could only be a sign from above, of this she was certain. And so when he proposed to her during an especially romantic picnic overlooking the Brahmaputra, forever her river and now forever theirs, she accepted immediately. At this point they had known each other for just sixteen days but it was a marriage that was destined to last and it produced four children.

'To travel abroad. To marry a poet. To write a book.'

The final ambition was fulfilled after James died in 1981, following a distinguished career teaching Classics at The Queen's College, Oxford. It was then that Angela Bolton, née Noblet, was persuaded to turn her diaries into a short book for the Imperial War Museum. Summing up both her experiences and her character, it contains this hopeful promise on its final page:

> Had it not been for the war I would have had little experience of other nationalities and perhaps would never have visited India at all. It is difficult to imagine what aspects of the past would have a lasting influence on the way I think and act in the future and yet there are certain attitudes that I am convinced will endure. I will never again put human beings into categories

according to race, colour or creed, but accept each person on his or her merits.

It's a beautiful sentiment. But even as she wrote those words into her diary while packing to leave India, in other parts of the region very different attitudes were still being forcefully applied. And they would have a lasting influence, too.

Vietnam, 1945

In September 1945 Vietnamese leader Ho Chi Minh needed some advice about the wording of a declaration of independence, so naturally he turned to his main American contact and friend, OSS chief Archimedes Patti, who later wrote:

> Of course, it was in Vietnamese and I couldn't read it and when it was interpreted to me, I was quite taken aback to hear the words of the American Declaration of Independence. Words about liberty, life and the pursuit of happiness, etc.
>
> We revamped it slightly. I could see that he had life and liberty and happiness in the wrong order and finally, we set them straight. And, that was on the very same day he invited me to attend a ceremony that he was going to hold on the 2nd of September at Place Ponier which was a square not too far away from the Governor General's palace.

The OSS — Office of Strategic Services — was the American government's principal intelligence-gathering agency, a forerunner to the CIA. Men like Archimedes Patti were Washington's eyes and ears, charged with exerting influence and building relationships. The OSS had been working with Ho Chi Minh and his anti-Japanese Viet Minh movement for many months, training guerrilla fighters, gathering intelligence for American raids on Japanese bases and transport routes and preparing the way for what Patti assumed would be a friendly US–Vietnam relationship in the years to come. Ho Chi Minh had also made some assumptions and one of them was that Patti spoke for the US government. The Vietnamese leader was well aware of the language that the Allies habitually used in their public statements, such as General Eisenhower's ringing declaration on the morning of D-Day that 'the free men of the world are marching together to Victory!' And so when he wrote to the recently inaugurated President Truman in September 1945, requesting American support for his new regime, he had every reason to expect a positive reply.

> He wanted to particularly know what the position of the United States was vis-à-vis the French and vis-à-vis the Vietnamese. Obviously, I could not give him an official position since I was not instructed, but I did indicate to him that in recent pronouncements by President Roosevelt, Prime Minister Churchill . . . had indicated that the time had come really for some sort of change in government in Southeast Asia, particularly Vietnam. French Indochina we called it in those days.
>
> And, I assured him that the precepts of the Atlantic Charter were rather valid . . . He said, 'well I can still remember the fourteen points of [President] Wilson' and he started rattling them off including the famous point about the self-determination of people who govern themselves and it seems to me, he said, that America hasn't changed, that they really believe in what they say and, although we didn't succeed in getting our independence back in 1919, after the First World War, it looks as though now you people are going to give the Philippines their independence. I hope that this will apply also, and be a good omen for the Vietnamese people, the people of French Indochina. And, during the course of conversation he told me some rather sad stories of what the colonial French had done in Indochina.

But Patti soon realised that something important had changed back home. Roosevelt had died in early April and, with a new man in the Oval Office, the words of the Atlantic Charter no longer carried the same weight. Nevertheless, he still felt that important people in Washington should know that in Ho Chi Minh there was a potential ally who admired America and very much wanted, indeed expected, to be friends. So he drafted a cable.

> Have had long conference with Prime Minister, Ho Chi Min, and he impresses me as sensible, well balanced, politically minded individual. His demands are few and simple namely limited independence, liberation from French rule, right to live as free people in family of nations and lastly right to deal directly with outside world.
>
> [The Viet Minh] are in unique advantage . . . in as much as Japs have given them independence so they consider themselves free of any sovereign power and this includes French who have been hiding behind Jap skirts, Vichy tactics and passing themselves off as friends of Americans. On whole Viet Minh has full control of situation not only in Hanoi but also the whole of three provinces.

When Patti's cable was unearthed from a dusty archive during the 1970s it was immediately held up as a classic example of a road not taken. By then millions of people had died as a result of three phenomenally destructive wars across Vietnam, Cambodia and Laos, all of them part, it could be argued, of a doomed effort to prevent Ho Chi Minh leading his people into the independence that he felt the Allies had promised him during the Second World War.

It's impossible to pinpoint the moment when American policy on the old European colonies changed, but it did so in secret and with profound implications for the future. For years General MacArthur's staff had mocked Britain's desire to grab back its lost plantations, tin mines and oilfields, and President Roosevelt himself had made no secret of his opposition to both the French and Dutch ambition to re-establish their Far Eastern colonies. As recently as April 1945 Alan Brooke wrote in his diary about Indo-China, remarking on the President's 'determination not to return this colony to France'. And yet suddenly under Truman all that was forgotten. In its place was a new doctrine, one pushed by the French and the British but by many influential politicians in Washington, too, a doctrine focused on resisting communist expansion. That resisting such expansion meant the return of valuable economic assets to their previous owners in Paris, Amsterdam and London was rarely mentioned in public but, we can safely assume, rather important behind the scenes.

And something else was happening that helps explain why politicians in Washington were dialling down the pressure on Britain and France. America was turning into a new kind of empire itself. In the Pacific US marines and soldiers had seized a series of strategic island chains that Japan had controlled since 1918. Did it really want to hand them to their indigenous inhabitants, which, on one reading, is what the Atlantic Charter had promised? The Americans had ended the war with a vastly expanded fleet. Just as the dollar was poised to replace the pound as the dominant international currency, the US Navy was set to supersede the Royal Navy as the guarantor of global trade and freedom of the seas. But to do this it needed more bases on the scale of Pearl Harbor. A new formula of United Nations 'trusteeships' would soon emerge to rubber-stamp US power in places like the Mariana Islands – and the building of huge military facilities there. For all the talk of change, this was still a colonial world, a *racialised* world, and so the idea that America should govern less developed peoples and places was seen as natural even in the Democratic Party (a party that also supported racial segregation in the Southern states and the US military). They could call it 'nation-building', they could claim to do it on the basis of principles more liberal than those of the old European empires and they could dress it up in the language of the new UN charter. But it was still about the projection of power, the securing of economic interests and the subordination of weaker people. As was to become very clear in Vietnam.

The Japanese military had been in Indochina — what we now call Vietnam, Laos and Cambodia — since 1940 but French officials loyal to the pro-Axis Vichy regime effectively ran much of the country until 1945. Then, with a new and unfriendly government established in liberated Paris, the Japanese decided to take over completely. The presence of nationalist Chinese forces loyal to Chiang Kai-shek in the north, and the outbreak of a lethal famine, left an already complex situation even more confusing to most outsiders. From Hanoi in northern Vietnam, Ho Chi Minh declared independence just days after Japan formally ended the war. Archimedes Patti had provided grammatical support and the local OSS office appeared friendly. Ho then wrote a series of studiously polite and ingratiating letters to Washington, but nobody there appeared willing to read them. Only a few months into Truman's administration, the Americans had decided that it was reasonable for their allies to use military force to help the French set the clock back to colonial times. That force was to be led by the British Indian Army in alliance with a French expeditionary unit under General Philippe Leclerc. Leclerc had led the Free French troops into Paris in August 1944 but now his purpose was not to liberate but to re-establish, in his own words, 'the future of the white race in Asia'. How the many Indian-born officers and men involved in this dangerous operation would have regarded language like that, had they been permitted to read it, is easy to imagine.

Major General Douglas Gracey, the man who had taken the surrender of the key INA leaders, still led the 20th Indian Division. He was instructed to fight alongside Leclerc's men if Ho Chi Minh's army — the Viet Minh — refused to accept their newly restored French masters. When Gracey arrived in Vietnam he immediately could see banners in the streets that read 'Welcome British and Americans but no room here for French'. Fearing anarchy and feeling outnumbered, Gracey quickly agreed to

THE MARTYR

release and rearm thousands of French prisoners who had served under the old Vichy system and together he slowly took control of Saigon, the major city of the south. But amid agitation from numerous factions, communal rioting broke out and Viet Minh guerrillas began to launch attacks on Franco-British patrols and bases. In one of these an American OSS man was also killed. The first of numerous Vietnam wars had now begun as the Viet Minh battled with British, French and Indian troops for weeks, attacking the docks and power plants, leading Gracey to call for yet more reinforcements.

And it's here that the story becomes truly astonishing. Because the reinforcements most readily available were Japanese prisoners of war, part of the army that had until recently occupied Vietnam. Some of them had fought in other campaigns and were no doubt involved in the murder of Allied soldiers, prisoners and civilians. And yet, despite all of this, tens of thousands of Japanese soldiers were handed rifles and told to serve under British command. In almost every case they did so willingly and enthusiastically. It's worth noting that numerous Japanese war crimes were being revealed during these months as the emaciated survivors of prison camps and railway gangs returned home and told their shocking stories. But none of that stopped the recruitment and arming of what were officially called JSPs, or 'Japanese Surrendered Persons'. The JSPs proved themselves most useful as guards, policemen, engineers and labourers and within weeks they were sent into combat, too. Ho Chi Minh appealed to the new United Nations, asserting that the French government had no moral right to govern its old colony again, and especially not like this. But once again nobody of any consequence noticed or ever replied.

In late October, Gracey's force of largely Indian and Japanese soldiers pushed the Viet Minh out of Saigon and into the countryside, inflicting heavy casualties. In one skirmish a single Japanese unit under British command killed fifty of Ho Chi Minh's men. Given that he had battled against the Japanese — as an ally of the

Americans — it's easy to imagine how Ho felt about incidents like this, and how they thoroughly poisoned relations that had seemed so promising only a few weeks earlier. At the cost of a hundred or so lives (it's thought that at least three thousand Viet Minh were killed) Gracey was able to turn Saigon over to full French control and, happily for him, get out of the country in early 1946. The British also reinstated the French in Cambodia, with a small force taking Phnom Penh. And, just as in Vietnam, the British commander there immediately released and rearmed Japanese prisoners to help him maintain control. It was a successful operation at a low human cost for the Allies, but the political dynamic that the British and French had now established — not least by their use of Japanese soldiers against the Vietnamese — was to guarantee decades of future conflict that would eventually drag in America and Australia, too.

Ho Chi Minh was undeniably a communist, as many nationalist leaders were. Inevitably he looked to Moscow and then later to the Maoists in China for support. But until he faced a British-led army he'd consistently tried to be a friend to the Western powers and his intense disappointment when their leaders refused to engage with him was witnessed first hand by many of his key contacts. Archimedes Patti's replacement in Hanoi was called Carleton Swift. He watched the failure of Ho Chi Minh's attempt to declare and defend the independence of his country and blamed it on the shifting attitudes to both colonialism and communism in the West, explaining regretfully many years later that

> while Roosevelt had taken an attitude toward the French that wasn't that [positive] on their re-establishing their colonial relationships, it seemed to me as Truman came in it rather changed, and that the American, the official position was pretty much capitulation to French wishes and how they returned to their colonies. And this was at odds a little bit with the American public views, the, the Atlantic Charter which the North Vietnamese knew all about.

I suspect the working level analysts had come to believe that perhaps Ho and his fellows were not puppets of the Kremlin, and that [his] cabinet was a mixture of middle, some right and some left . . . Yet at the top level, State and Truman, policies with regard to the French were pretty well set. I felt we were turning our head. We stood for principles, but we were letting the French re-establish their position in their colony as they wished to.

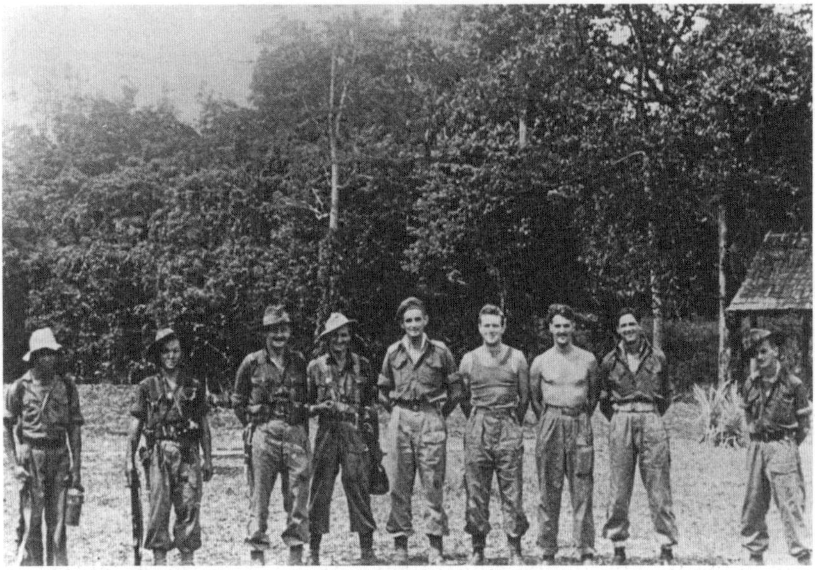

16

The Horror

Borneo, 1945

By now everyone knew the dire fate of prisoners. So when two soldiers became separated from their unit and heard foreign voices close by they tried frantically to hide. But they were soon discovered by the riverbank. Their captors tied them to trees then took turns to kick, punch and spit on them through a long and agonising night. At first light they were made to kneel and then both were beheaded with a sword. It was a sadly common story of brutality during the war against Japan in the Indo-Pacific, except in this case the soldiers *were* Japanese and their captors were in a unit commanded by an officer of Australia's SRD.

When the people who fought in the Semut operation came to reminisce about it — Dayaks and SRD men alike — some of them did so warmly. Different peoples bonded by a common cause against a cruel enemy. The drama and romance of moonlit canoe raids and great Catalinas swooping down onto still dark waters. The *borak*, the singing, the wondrous natural surroundings. It made for a thrilling story, packed with exotic colour and 'derring-do', one of those 'jolly little wars' that a young Winston Churchill had written about while serving as a cavalry officer in nineteenth-century Africa. But the stories that would dominate most post-war memories were of the horror that overwhelmed the operation in its final weeks.

That very day a white people's plane came and attacked our longhouse for about half an hour. The people all got hit by the machine gun. Many of us were hit and one died in the middle of the house, Ugap was his name. And our mother got hit in the thigh and the bullet buried itself in the ground. My uncle Gerantun got hit in the ankle and it was broken.

So many civilians died or were injured in these poorly planned and inaccurate air raids that one of the Semut teams painted a large white sign on the ground as a message to their fellow Australians flying high above. The sign read: FUCK OFF.

Had SRD's secret agents brought a jolly little war to Borneo or something closer to Joseph Conrad's *Heart of Darkness*? In one incident Iban warriors, frustrated by their failure to take a Japanese fort, came across a Chinese family sheltering nearby, killed them all and took the heads of men, women and children back to their longhouse. There's no evidence that anyone from the SRD ever paid for these particular trophies of war, but without the head-trading element of Operation Semut would the decapitation frenzy have taken hold in the first place?

There's a wider debate about whether an invasion of Borneo was necessary at this stage of the war, and in that hindsight necessarily plays its part. Nobody could be certain that the end was near and some analysts in Washington DC – unaware of their own government's nuclear programme – thought that fighting might drag on for another year. But by March 1945 the focus was on the Japanese home islands and any distant outpost occupied by the remains of the emperor's army was beyond the range of meaningful air or naval support. Some argued at the time that these places were best left to wither on the vine. And even if an invasion *was* necessary in Borneo, what purpose was served by sending in Special Forces to stir the interior communities into an armed uprising beforehand? There's little evidence that the 9th Division commanders thought that Operation Semut helped them in any way, but plenty that they considered the whole thing to be a complete nuisance. 'Over glamorised, puerile and . . . unnecessary' was the verdict of one Semut member after the war, although he did not represent the majority of the veterans.

And above all of that there was the colonial politics. Semut started life as a British-controlled political and intelligence operation carefully dressed in Australian clothes. It was meant to 'show the flag', regain 'lost face' and so help pave the way for a return to British rule. Sarawak did indeed become a profitable British crown colony after 1945 and remained so until it joined the independent Federation of Malaya in 1963. If Operation Semut helped make that happen then perhaps it fulfilled its secret purpose. But it is hard to see how it did so. Either way, at some stage inside the mysteriously opaque world of the SRD it morphed into a grand guerrilla operation with cash-for-human heads as a key ingredient. It's likely that General Blamey and the other top Australian commanders never expected it to develop in this way, and the Americans on MacArthur's staff who approved the mission certainly did not. But Special Forces were and are special, and in 1945 they carried an aura of secrecy and excitement, a cachet that placed them outside the normal hierarchy and allowed their projects to run ahead of scrutiny or control. Perhaps SRD was in fact truly run by 'larrikins', British and Australian alike. Men who enjoyed operating outside the rules, specialised in the unconventional and found the whole business of war really very jolly indeed. In her elegiac farewell to empire, Jan Morris wrote about how, during the Second World War, 'racy characters of the imperial legend reappeared from clubs or offices, to rediscover themselves in commando raids, parachute drops or weird prodigies of intelligence'. There's more than a little of this in the story of Semut.

The SRD men were brave and loyal and almost all of them came to love the Dayaks they fought alongside. The admiration and respect they received in turn from their Dayak comrades was just as intense. But, in the end, could it be that Keling Langit was right when she first saw strange grey shapes descending onto her rice paddy and wanted to warn her community about menacing spirits bringing danger from above? Not a single one of the SRD men who parachuted into Borneo lost his life, but many hundreds of others did during the events they triggered. There's no full inventory of Dayak casualties during Operation Semut, nor for the Malay and Chinese civilians dragged into the fighting and killed either by the Japanese, by headhunting Dayaks or by the poorly targeted bombs of the Royal Australian Air Force. Then there were the burned longhouses and the families driven into the jungle, prey to hunger and disease. Perhaps the Japanese army would have moved inland come what may, but it's hard to imagine they would have been quite so determined to attack Dayak communities and burn longhouses had the SRD not galvanised thousands of young men to go hunting their heads.

All former SRD men generously acknowledged that it was Dayak knowledge, ingenuity and courage that kept them alive and made their mission possible. None of these secret agents went into Borneo wanting to play the villain in a Joseph Conrad novel – with the possible exception of the messianic Tom Harrisson or the gung-ho Robert Wilson – and yet in some senses they are the accidental Mr Kurtzes of this story. And there's a final reason why Semut may have been a terrible, gung-ho, jolly little disaster. It wasn't the only special operation being considered for Borneo in the final year of the war. And for it to go ahead meant that others did not, including one intended to rescue a great many Australians barely surviving in a hellish prisoner-of-war camp on the very same island.

The Dutch East Indies, 1945

On the one hand the idealism of the *Way and Purpose* pamphlet and Angela Noblet's egalitarian epiphanies on the Brahmaputra. On the other, the self-interested manoeuvring that lay behind Operation Semut and the recolonisation of Vietnam. Both are important and both should be part of any fair reckoning. As should another late-1945 operation that's very well remembered in what used to be called the Dutch East Indies but scarcely ever mentioned today in the countries that carried it out. Because the same logic that underpinned General Gracey's bloody mission to Saigon lay behind another and even more violent expedition to a second former European colony. And here, too, Japanese prisoners of war were released, pressed into service and sent into battle by British commanders – more than 35,000 of them. Fighting alongside mostly Indian troops, these JRPs helped put the Dutch colonial masters back where they thought they belonged. Once the fighting started, one brave Japanese prisoner, a Major Kido, so impressed British General Philip Christison that he recommended him for a Distinguished Service Order. When Lord Mountbatten flew into Jakarta to help steer the operation he was startled to see just how many of the men he'd spent more than three years fighting were now serving under his command.

> I of course knew that we had been forced to keep Japanese troops under arms to protect our lines of communication and vital areas . . . but it was nevertheless a great shock to me to find over a thousand Japanese troops guarding the nine miles of road from the airport to the town.

A British aristocrat reinstalling a colonial regime guarded by saluting Japanese soldiers. This is not how the Second World War is generally taught in the West. But it is how most Indonesians remember 1945, along with the ferocious urban battles that marked this ugly coda to Allied victory. Once initial attempts to negotiate colonial control broke down, the British and Indians saw combat in the East Indies that was much more intense than anything in Vietnam. Here they were up against a determined and well-armed enemy led by charismatic men like Bung Tomo, also known simply as Sutomo. A future Indonesian government minister, he rallied his people in 1945 with the uncompromising language of popular revolution.

> The masses in their thousands, starved, stripped and shamed by the colonialists, will rise to carry out the revolt. We extremists, we who revolt with full revolutionary spirit, together with the Indonesian masses, would rather see our country drowned in blood and sunk to the bottom of the sea than be colonised once more.

In the city of Surabaya, a naval base second only to Singapore in the region, the nationalist militias attacked, killing British Major General Aubertin Mallaby. The tumultuous battle that followed lasted for three weeks during October and November 1945 and involved thousands of Indian Army troops, tanks operating in city streets, intense shelling from Royal Navy cruisers and destroyers, and hundreds of airstrikes. Surabaya was largely destroyed and somewhere between ten and fifteen thousand Indonesian guerrillas and civilians died inside it, along with at least three hundred British and Indian soldiers. It remains the bloodiest and most intense urban battle fought by a British-led army since the Second World War. And, although the casualty count was strikingly one-sided, as historian Dan Todman put it, Indian troops 'who had survived Kohima and Imphal lost their lives here in a struggle whose purpose they could not discern'.

To relieve the pressure on the Indian troops, Japanese soldiers led the way in another savage battle in the town of Semarang, where British commanders used artillery and tanks to kill more than two thousand Indonesian militiamen and civilians. According to one eyewitness there, 'Truckloads of Indonesian prisoners with their hands tied behind their backs were driven into the countryside [by Japanese soldiers under British command] and never seen again'. Gurkhas of the Indian Army fought alongside the JRPs in some of these battles and it was here that Major Kido so impressed General Christison.

THE HORROR

Britain held a large stake in the Royal Dutch Shell Company, which had operated important refineries in both the East Indies and Borneo before the war and very much wanted them back. Once their own country was free from German control, Dutch politicians successfully lobbied the new British government of Clement Attlee, stressing the economic argument but also describing the nationalists of the East Indies as dangerous allies of the Japanese. This was a clever framing of the facts and partly true. Like many other independence-minded radicals of their time, the nationalists of Java and Sumatra had indeed looked to Japan for inspiration, and had been pleased to witness the victories in 1942. The Dutch also accused their enemies of being dangerous extremists and mass murderers. There was something in this charge, too. There were some very ugly communal massacres during the fighting in late 1945. But was any of this a good enough reason to send in British troops with the order to wind back the imperial clock? British medic Harry Walker, who took part in the battle of Surabaya, did not think so and was appalled at the level of civilian suffering that resulted.

> It is quite simple, our method of 'pacifying' a country — we merely blow the town to bits with bombs & shells & kill the inhabitants by thousands until they decide they have had enough. We had two hundred odd Javanese civilians in here [his hospital] with legs blown off, arms missing, shot in the guts, head, everywhere — ranging from kids of 2 or 3 months to old men and women of 70 and 80 . . . We kill the Javanese, and the Javanese kill our lads and in the end it's the Dutch who will take over the country, and Britain's name will stink for years out here as the murderer of civilians.

The future film star Captain Derek van den Bogaerde was serving with the British Army in the East Indies. Amid the street fighting and the bombing raids he witnessed surreal scenes of late-imperial revelry, recalling how pipes and drums played on immaculate lawns while drunken officers, cavorting with their local girlfriends, fired volleys from their revolvers into the night sky.

All sides committed atrocities here. A crash-landed RAF aircraft containing wounded Indian soldiers was discovered by local militias who killed everyone on board. In revenge, Indian Army units burned nearby villages to the ground. After all this bloodshed, in battles that took place across the entire archipelago, Dutch rule was indeed re-established, but it did not last long. Nationalist forces were especially galvanised by what had happened at Surabaya, a battle still commemorated in Indonesia every year on 'Heroes Day'. So what was the new Labour government of Clement Attlee doing? In the House of Commons an MP posed the following question:

'[Had] General Christison communicated with the Government before announcing that we were not going to interfere with the political position in Java and that we were not going in to put the Dutch back into power; and whether he will state the Government's policy in relation to the overseas territories of our Dutch allies?'

Secretary of State: 'I understand that General Christison's remarks were much distorted when they were reported in the Press. The hon. and gallant Member may rest assured that General Christison is fully informed of the wishes and intentions of His Majesty's Government by Admiral Lord Louis Mountbatten. His Majesty's Government, of course, recognises no authority but that of the Netherlands Government in all the territories which are under the sovereignty of our Dutch allies.'

Unsatisfied by that, MPs called upon Attlee himself to make a statement, and his carefully chosen words revealed that his government had wholly accepted the Dutch position on the conflict.

The Prime Minister: 'With available resources of man-power and shipping strained in this way, problems such as have arisen in Java present particular difficulty. There, as indeed throughout the whole area of South-East Asia Command, it was necessary in the first instance to place responsibility on the Japanese forces for the maintenance of law and order outside key areas. But in Java we found that, outside Batavia, control had in fact been largely relinquished by the Japanese to an Indonesian independence movement. While we have had to take account of the existence of this movement we must be careful about accepting its claims at their face value. It has been sponsored by the Japanese for two or three years and during this time the people of the territory have been cut off from all outside developments.

Meanwhile, as the House is no doubt aware, Her Majesty the Queen of the Netherlands issued in December, 1942, a very liberal statement promising a large degree of self-government to all Dutch overseas territories.'

Mr Sorensen: 'Is not my right hon. Friend aware that quite a number of Members of the House are very disturbed at what seems to be the case, that the Japanese and ourselves are collaborating in using force against the actual inhabitants of Indonesia?'

The Prime Minister: 'The hon. Member and his friends, if they think that, are of the wrong impression.'

London, 1945

The 1945 Labour government is generally discussed in terms of the many changes it brought to Britain but one of the most interesting things about it, at least in terms of the empire, is the *continuity*. Imperial muscle memory in Whitehall did not suddenly atrophy because socialists now occupied the great offices of state, and in some cases the new Labour ministers could be as strong in defence of Britain's overseas interests as any of Churchill's men. While Aneurin Bevan created a new national health service and others set about nationalising great swathes of the economy, most of the people running things overseas remained in their posts and clung firmly to the ideas of the past. Foreign Secretary Ernest Bevin and Attlee himself were unlikely to challenge them because both wanted Britain to remain a great power, ideally with its own nuclear weapon as soon as possible. They were also instinctively anti-communist and, as a result, Bevin especially came to regard any agitation for independence in the colonies as the subversive work of the Soviets, writing that 'the danger to the peace of the world has been the incessant propaganda from Moscow against the British Commonwealth as a means to attack the British'. Based on private conversations with Labour politicians, the OSS office in London reported to Washington that the new government 'is as empire-minded as was its conservative predecessor'.

Under Labour, Empire Day was still celebrated in every school on 24 May, even if the visiting MP was now wearing a red rather than a blue rosette. Meanwhile influential Labour thinkers, such as those in the Fabian Society, debated whether a socialist-run managerial Britain might in fact *improve* the empire rather than disband it. During the war the British state had come to rely upon expert committees and other 'top down' agencies to organise many aspects of national life, and they had done it very well. Perhaps the same approach could be applied to the colonies, to manage them better and prepare them for future independence.

And then there was the attitude to skin colour. Like most other white British people, Labour MPs and ministers had grown up with the beliefs and prejudices of their time. Attlee was a well-meaning paternalist who believed that a strong British presence East of Suez was important to guarantee Britain's economic and security interests. But he also clearly thought that most of the people living there needed the guidance if not the control of white Europeans or Americans. In one speech he argued that colonial societies required a strong guiding hand to reach their potential. And then, when asked if Britain might take over the Italian colonies, he revealed that such a guiding hand, in his opinion, would always likely be white. 'Why should it be assumed that only a few Great Powers can be entrusted with backward peoples? Why should not one or other of the Scandinavian countries have a try? They are quite as fitted to bear rule as ourselves.'

Language like this was not as offensive as some of the things that Chips Channon might say in his club, but it reflected some of the same prejudices. And Channon himself wrote in his diary that Ernest Bevin's speeches to the House of Commons on international affairs were almost the ones he'd expect to hear from Churchill. Bevin's words, he reported one day, 'were cheered and applauded by our side'. It was 'almost a Tory speech, full of sense'. And it was under this same Labour government that the secret plotting began which would lead to the Anglo-American-backed Iranian coup of 1953, a profoundly anti-democratic act that aimed to guarantee the West's hold on valuable oilfields. And, once again, nobody ever thought it worth consulting the 'backward peoples' themselves about any of this.

In the East Indies, unlike Vietnam, it didn't take long for the penny to drop. Within months of the carnage in Surabaya the British government had shifted its position, accepting that there was indeed a legitimate government-in-waiting and that it truly was time for the Dutch to go. It was no doubt painful to see power pass to radicals who had menaced and massacred civilians, but it was much more painful to reimpose a deeply resented colonial regime whose fall had been so widely celebrated in 1942, and to do it at the point of British bayonets wielded by Indian soldiers. As Mohan Singh, the original founder of the INA, had said years before: 'Those under bonds will put others under bonds.' Echoing Singh, the Congress Party now insisted that Indian troops must never again be used to put down movements for national liberation. Before that could happen Malaya was also seized back by force and, once again, this was done with little apparent concern for the self-determination of its people. The British government was particularly keen to return to Malaya — and defend it with the Arthur Titheringtons of the future — because it helped ease the perennial shortage of tradable foreign currency. Measured in US dollars, rubber exports from Malaya to the USA soon exceeded all other exports from Britain to that critical market while the Malayan tin mining industry became one of the largest and most profitable in the world. In 1947 Arthur Creech Jones, the Secretary of State for the Colonies, informed the Cabinet that 'Malaya is by far the most important source of dollars in the colonial empire and it would gravely worsen the whole dollar balance of the Sterling Area if there were serious interference with Malayan exports.'

Few imagined that the war would end with an outbreak of global brotherhood, or that Britain would suddenly cease to think and act like a great power. Making the Indo-Pacific safe from Japanese militarism was hugely important and beneficial, and it would be unfair to define Britain's post-war role solely by intrigues over oilfields or nasty colonial wars. But the reason why what happened in Indonesia, Vietnam or Borneo is so little known today is that those stories have never sat comfortably with the nation's favourite memories of the Second World War.

Borneo, 1945

Operation Semut was far from the only SRD operation running in Borneo in 1945. For some years, under the codename AGAS, the Malay word for sandfly, a handful of SRD men had visited the island to recruit local agents and 'listeners', and it was through this network that the Australians first heard about what was happening to their fellow countrymen at a place called Sandakan.

A coastal town on the far north-east of the island, more than six hundred miles from the jungles of Sarawak, Sandakan was chosen by the Japanese as the site for one of the many camps they had to construct to house the huge numbers of men and women captured in Singapore and elsewhere. By 1944 there were about two thousand Australians there along with five hundred Britons. As in Formosa, these men were expected to work for their meagre rations and crude accommodation, and they spent much of their time building and maintaining a military airfield nearby. Discipline was every bit as brutal and arbitrary as that facing the men at the Kinkaseki copper mine, so much so that the camp commander, Lieutenant Susumi Hoshijima, would one day go to the gallows for the cruelty of his rule and the many extra-judicial murders that took place at his command.

The airfield that Hoshijima had been tasked to manage was bombed heavily and so, early in January 1945, the Japanese decided to abandon it altogether. The prisoners no longer had much of a purpose and that's when the 'forced marches' began. Some of the men in the first group to leave the camp later wrote about life at Sandakan, in terms that are instantly familiar. Lieutenant Max Carment might have been describing the feelings of Arthur Titherington in Kinkaseki when he spoke of

> the plaintive notes of the last post being played by a bugler at Sandakan and echoing from the surrounding jungle. The wonderful tropical sunsets. The sights of the whole sweep of the sky being covered by millions of flying foxes on their annual migration, and moonlight so brilliant it was possible to read by its light. I remember companionship and friendship in times of extreme stress. I remember laughter and sadness.

As the year progressed, two things conspired against the remaining prisoners of Sandakan. Firstly, there was little food left and, secondly, the Japanese commanders were growing increasingly worried about what might happen to them after the war. An order from Imperial General Headquarters in Tokyo addressed this latter problem directly.

> Whether they are destroyed individually or in groups, or however it is done, with mass bombing, poisonous smoke, poisons, drowning, decapitation or what, dispose of them as the situation dictates. In any case it is the aim not to allow the escape of a single one, annihilate them all, and not leave any traces.

The initial forced march from Sandakan was harrowing and many sick and exhausted men died by the roadside, but the subsequent ones were simply opportunities to kill and hide bodies – true 'death marches'. Hundreds of men left, supposedly on the road to a new home in Ranau, but once away from any prying eyes the guards bayoneted, shot or simply abandoned them alone and starving in the jungle. The small numbers of prisoners still in the camp were then shot in groups of a dozen and the buildings burned to the ground, with the final murders taking place after the war had formally ended. Of the 2,500 alive in January only six survived, all of them men who managed somehow to sneak away from their guards on one of the marches and found sympathetic local people to care for them in secret. The testimony of these men is the main reason we know what happened at Sandakan, and can understand why so many prisoners who had already withstood years of the most terrible treatment and ill health were not allowed to return to their homes and families. The worst of these events took place during Operation Semut, and while they were happening the leaders of SRD learned about them in detail from members of the AGAS spy ring. So horrified were they that detailed plans were made to rescue the men of Sandakan, but nothing ever happened.

As with Operation Semut itself, there's a very limited paper trail on the SRD and Sandakan. Much of what we know about SRD's activities in 1944 and 1945 is based on long-forgotten conversations that were never written down, and were open to endless reinterpretation later. And then after the war, when the truth about the prisoner massacres reached the Australian press, nobody much wanted to talk about abandoned rescue missions at all. In the 1990s New Zealand-born historian Alan Powell conducted a thorough review of available SRD papers and post-war interviews, and unearthed evidence of something called Operation Kingfisher, an ambitious combined air, land and sea plan to send Australian parachutists and Special Forces into the jungles around Sandakan, free the prisoners and evacuate them all by sea. It was closely modelled on a famous American operation at Los Baños in the Philippines that rescued more than two thousand US troops and Allied civilians, including many Australians, from a Japanese camp where they probably faced the same fate as the prisoners of Sandakan.

Training for Kingfisher began at the end of 1944 but in January, just as the death marches were beginning, a series of meetings took place to discuss SRD's priorities for the forthcoming year. Major F. 'Gort' Chester, who had spent time living undercover on Borneo, conferred with overall SRD chief, Lieutenant Colonel Chapman Walker and his deputy Lieutenant Colonel James Champion and after that Kingfisher was stopped, or, rather, in the language of the surviving documentation, it was 'de-prioritised'. A surviving minute from the meeting revealed that Chapman Walker 'saw no need to consult higher authority on this' and that 'the result was the reduction of the Kingfisher project to third place in the priority list behind the founding of an Intelligence network and a guerrilla force in north Borneo'.

By this stage SRD already had intelligence confirming the desperate state of the prisoners in Sandakan. In the following weeks more arrived, including this from one AGAS contact: 'the incidence of beri-beri among the prisoners is reported as high and those who are unable to travel are shot.' Later, when the terrible final acts were still playing out, word reached SRD of the death marches to Ranau. A Captain D. S. Sutcliffe from AGAS had spies who fed him precise details and he wrote to Chapman Walker that

'I am naturally anxious to assist them but I think if any precipitate act were taken to effect rescue and should be only partially successful it would mean immediate slaughter of the remainder.' Having reviewed this and everything else that he could find about Kingfisher, the historian Powell concluded bleakly that

> the bitter irony of this concern is that when some might have been saved, all were left to die ... it was also known that the Japanese were prone to murder those who could bear witness against them – and the excuse given for not attempting a rescue at all implies that SRD believed that the fitter men could be saved.

There is endless evasive bureaucratic language and what military officers then and now call 'arse-covering', but in the end it's clear that SRD simply had other priorities in Borneo. Lieutenant Colonel C. H. Finlay, a key SRD planner, at least had the courage to state it bluntly: 'Wars are essentially cruel and brutal and in the execution of the principal object no activity which does not contribute to the achievement of that objective [in this case the earliest possible defeat of Japan in its homeland] can be entertained.' Leaving Alan Powell to conclude that 'the men of Sandakan died because they did not have the priority to give them life'.

Given what happened during the operation that *was* prioritised – Semut – it seems especially tragic that helping the men at Sandakan slipped below it on the SRD's to-do list. Years after Powell undertook his research, writer Gary Followill dug deeper into the political pressures being put upon SRD at this time and his work led him to pose an inescapable question. 'At what stage could reestablishment of government control in Asian colonies [British, French and Dutch] become more important than the lives of Australian and British prisoners of war?'

Chapman Walker's deputy was Lieutenant Colonel James Champion. He was another British SOE man and he ran the SRD planning section before taking over the whole unit from

Chapman Walker during 1945. After the war he told a colleague that he had to prepare a 'history' and that he'd been talking to General Blamey about it.

> I pointed out to him that a true history would undoubtedly bring to light the chicanery which was necessary to maintain SRD in this theatre in the early days, particularly in regard to relations with the Americans . . . As a result Blamey agreed to prepare two copies only of the full history, one copy for the DOI and one for SOE London. Abridged copies to be prepared for the AIB, AMF records etc.

Could it be that a similar amount of 'necessary chicanery' was the real reason that Kingfisher got cancelled? And that the SOE and other powerful players in London − through a secretive Australian organisation they effectively controlled − prioritised the recolonisation of resource-rich Sarawak over rescuing prisoners? If so, was this authorised at a high level or just assumed to be the sort of thing that men like them were supposed to do? Again, we're probably in the world of conversations over brandy rather than the minutes of a Colonial Office sub-committee. But however it was rationalised, authorised and actioned, instead of a heroic Australian version of the Los Baños raid, Borneo got a messy attempt to stir up a headhunting jungle war. Nobody can ever know how well a rescue mission to Sandakan might have gone. It might have been a bloody disaster. But with near total Allied control of the air above and the water around Borneo, there had to be at least a chance that Kingfisher could have saved lives.

Whatever mixed motives and clashing agendas affected the strange and secretive world of SRD, it's only fair to the Australian High Command to point out that saving prisoners *was* high on its agenda. The Batu Lintang camp in the south-west corner of Sarawak also held some 2,500 people, a mix of military and civilian, and the 9th Division, along with the Royal Australian

Navy, set out to liberate them with real energy. When they got there they discovered printed orders to kill all the inmates over the coming week in groups: the women and children by poison, the male civilians by gunfire, the military prisoners by a death march and anyone remaining in the camp hospital by 'bayonet and fire'.

As stories about the barbarity of camps like Batu Lintang, Sandakan and Kinkaseki were made into books and films in the years after the war it became more and more difficult for the men who'd run the SRD to talk about, let alone justify, the choices they had made. Some, like Finlay, clearly believed that fighting a war meant killing the enemy until the bitter end and that was that. Others appeared to be operating to a political — and specifically a colonial — agenda that may have passed through Canberra but began its life in London.

And maybe there was another factor, one that would never appear in an official document or unit history. Semut was the kind of operation that the officers who ran SRD actually *wanted* to do. Some who served in it would recall the darker side but to others a private little war in the jungle, far away from the brass hats and tick-box-wallahs, running with the head-hunters of Borneo, swooping in and out by flying boat, gliding down tropical rivers on moonlit nights — it was all intensely exciting. It was Bulldog Drummond and Errol Flynn. It's what they'd trained for, what some of them *lived* for.

The failure to pursue a Sandakan rescue mission led to some ugly finger-pointing a few years later. In 1947 the now retired Australian General Thomas Blamey said that he had once held 'high hopes' for a rescue but blamed MacArthur for not helping him because the Americans could not or would not spare the aircraft required for the parachute drops. 'The operation would certainly have saved that death march of Sandakan,' Blamey said, but sadly 'destiny didn't permit us to carry it out.' This triggered a furious argument in Canberra with questions pouring into the office of Prime Minister Ben Chifley. Australian MPs and the relatives of the prisoners murdered in Borneo demanded to know what senior politicians in 1945 had been told about Sandakan. In a remarkably blunt response — even by Australian political standards — Chifley then slapped Blamey down publicly, pointing out that at no point whatsoever had Australia's top wartime general ever recommended that a prisoner rescue mission should proceed in Borneo nor briefed anyone in authority in Canberra about it. Which was more than a little surprising given what he was saying in 1947 about his 'high hopes' for it.

If someone important in Canberra in the early months of 1945 had truly focused upon the competing ideas for SRD missions in Borneo — and properly weighed up what might be gained from each of them — it's possible that Semut would have been 'de-prioritised' and something like Operation Kingfisher launched instead. But applying that level of hindsight to a cloudy political and military leadership group historically and, perhaps also sentimentally, attached to British ideas and British leadership is probably unfair and unrealistic. The historian Paul Ham, who wrote an excellent and very detailed book about Sandakan, doesn't think that Kingfisher was in any state to proceed in 1945 come what may. And that it would have required a much higher degree of focus — and a much higher place in the SRD's list of priorities — to have had a chance of saving those poor men's lives. And it never had either of those things.

Britain, 1940–1945

The first book I co-wrote about the Second World War challenged the once-dominant idea that Britain in 1940 was an underdog clinging on against the odds. The threat of political and popular defeatism was real enough, especially in those panicky weeks after the unexpected collapse of France, when much of the world assumed that London would be the next capital city to fall to Hitler's storm troopers. But once the decision to fight on had been made, the British state had the power, the resources and the professionalism to resist whatever Nazi Germany threw at it, especially when supported by its intercontinental network of dominions and colonies. Winning the war alone was never possible, but refusing to lose it *was*, and that was Winston Churchill's and the British Empire's greatest contribution to the twentieth century.

The end of the war has attracted much myth-making, too. Britain bankrupted itself to defeat Hitler, or so the pub wisdom goes. It sacrificed its power and its empire to bring down the Nazis, just as some of the more 'pragmatic' voices of 1940 gloomily predicted that it would. Those men — and some were in Churchill's own Cabinet — had been open to what was called a 'soft peace' after the fall of France, leaving Britain's wealth and foreign possessions intact and letting Hitler do what he liked in Europe.

But Britain didn't sacrifice its empire at all. In fact it fought hard and sometimes dirty to regain control of those parts of it that were temporarily taken over by its enemies. And it didn't bankrupt itself either. Balancing the books was painful and some form of food rationing persisted until 1954, but the *relative* economic decline that took place after the war was largely due to homegrown choices and disputes, and because rival nations grew faster and created more wealth than Britain managed to do. It was in no way the inevitable consequence of the war. In fact, as with the Malayan tin and rubber trade, income from the colonies recovered quickly as the great cities of imperial business, Hong Kong, Rangoon and Singapore, began to thrive once again. The so-called 'financial Dunkirk' that happened when America stopped Lend-Lease sooner than London expected, and attached strings to its great post-war loan, was the cause of much resentment. But the Americans could and did argue that their own wartime sacrifices in the Far East and Pacific had helped Britain get its colonies back, generating the cash to pay off the loan and rather more besides.

India was taking its independence. That had become inevitable in the final year of the war if not earlier. But Britain emerged from the war powerful by any standards, with world-class businesses, an impressive scientific and technological base, a people better educated than at any time in its history, and nowhere that looked anything like Berlin, Hamburg or Dresden. An intense national focus on making the machines of war had generated a huge expansion in technical research and produced innovations in electronics, transport, avionics, communication and chemistry that gave British companies an international head start in all those fields. That some of this was later squandered was not the fault of the wartime generation or those who led it.

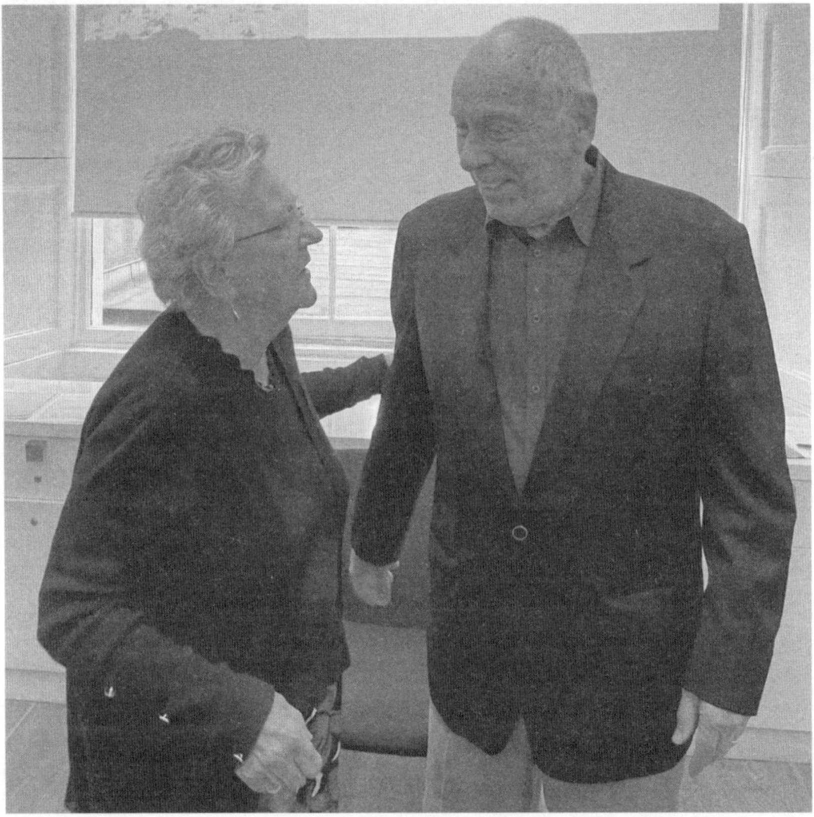

17

The Children

Dawlish, Devon, 1947

Everybody loved Dr Lees and Dr Sampson. They were the sort of family doctors you could always rely on, with easy bedside manners, a deep knowledge of the area and always time to stop for a cup of tea and a chat. The Newberry family ran the largest bakery in town and because they encountered the public every day — the sniffling, coughing public — eight-year-old Jennifer and her older brother John were always going down with something or other. One of the doctors would come around, deliver some soothing words, write a prescription and then all would be well. But this new man was a 'different kettle of fish altogether'.

> Now Mrs Newberry, do please listen. It's what we call the common cold. It lasts seven days if you treat it and a week if you don't. Let me know if anything changes but for now just keep her tucked up in bed and bring her plenty of hot drinks.

'Brusque' was the word Ethel Newberry used later to her husband Fred, 'very brusque and objectionable'. And her neighbours were similarly unimpressed. This truculent young Scot of few words always seemed to be in a hurry and if you challenged him on anything he could grow rather irascible rather quickly, even spouting Latin at you. Some said he was a socialist and, as damning evidence, pointed out that he was rarely if ever seen in the places where the town's doctors would normally be found

– the Conservative Association bar or the golf club. When they called for a doctor, the Newberrys were one of many families who started asking for 'one of the older ones if you please'. Nobody knew about his war record, or the thesis on typhus he'd just completed at Edinburgh University. Both of those subjects were on the long list of things that Dr Douglas Peterkin didn't care to discuss with strangers. But after Belsen and the streets of Leipzig it's easy to imagine him growing impatient when faced with opinionated mothers and their ill-informed questions about bunions or *viral rhinitis*.

On the surface Dawlish had weathered the war well enough. The quiet seaside town near the mouth of the River Exe was famous for its beaches, gardens and the dramatic railway line set right up against the sea wall. That line ran down towards the naval base of Plymouth and so it had attracted a few German air attacks. But the only bomb that ever exploded anywhere near the place had landed in a farmer's field, a typically entrepreneurial Devonian farmer who proceeded to charge Jennifer and the other children a thruppenny bit each to inspect the crater. One of the boys in her class was called Tony Bryant and his father was in the Home Guard, which was a lot more warlike and exciting than baking bread. One night while out patrolling on the clifftop path, Mr Bryant came across lights flickering inside a tiny cove and rushed down with his rifle, only to find it was just old Dick Rackley with his lobster pots. But below the surface other kinds of damage had been done. At the VE Day street party Jennifer was sitting next to her older cousin Babs who had just moved into the bakery along with her newborn baby.

> We all had paper hats on which was a real treat because paper had been rationed and we also had lovely fish paste sandwiches and then I saw Babs was crying and I remember saying 'Oh you mustn't cry now Babs, we've won'. But she just kept on sobbing. Her husband Richard had died in Belgium right near the end of it all you see. They were both only about twenty. As a child you don't really understand what any of that means, do you?

THE CHILDREN

Jennifer's cousin Donald came back from a Japanese prisoner-of-war camp looking happy but 'He only weighed five stone, so goodness knows what he weighed when he left it.' Yet another cousin had died in a flying accident while training for the RAF. And then there was Margaret.

> Margaret, she was a family friend, and she'd already had one little girl with her husband Stuart, but while he was away at the war she'd had a liaison with an American soldier and got pregnant. She'd had the child but when Stuart came home she had to agree to give it up for adoption and she never saw her little boy again for the rest of her life.
> And I've often thought, it's a terrible thing to come back from a war and find your wife has had a baby with another man but it's awful to give away a child too isn't it? And I don't think she wanted to. But in the end it may have been the only way to patch things up given the way people thought then, because they were happy after that and they had four more children.

Margaret might have fared much worse. The newspapers were full of stories of soldiers returning home and attacking or even murdering their unfaithful wives, amid outrage at the lenient sentences that some judges were handing out for such terrible crimes. The other thing everyone was talking about was the new National Health Service that was due to begin in 1948, a system that the government said would be based on need rather than a patient's ability to pay. As patriotic conservatives to their floury fingertips, Ethel and Fred Newberry had been very upset when Churchill was kicked out, but they were pleased that they would no longer have to hand over cash every time Jennifer or John needed the doctor. And it was this great change to the medical system — everyone assumed — that had brought Douglas Peterkin to their town. Tony Bryant's family had all voted Labour but they shared Ethel Newberry's opinion of the prickly new arrival, always asking for 'one of the older ones please'. That is until the day came when it really *wasn't* the common cold and the two older ones were otherwise engaged at the golf club.

India, post-war

It was time for Indians to take over control of the army that Timmy loved so much, and for all the poodle-fakers and brick-droppers to go back home, although many didn't seem in a particular hurry to do so. 'We Indians think that British officers whose careers had been spent in the Indian Army merely want to keep their jobs until normal retirement age,' he observed somewhat icily. But chiselling out the old guard was nothing like as challenging as what came next – the partition of India into two separate, independent countries. And that's because, as the nation split, so too did its army, with two-thirds staying with India and a third going to the new nation of Pakistan. There were numerous mixed battalions and from these the Muslim-only companies went to serve Pakistan and the rest stayed where they were. Timmy's Hyderabadis didn't escape this process and he had to say farewell to many of the men he'd proudly led into battle. By late 1947 Timmy was a major general in the Punjab, just as millions of people started to move east to west or west to east. His job – and the job of his old comrades now in the Pakistani army – was to protect refugees travelling in both directions, but it proved almost impossible as rumours led to rioting and rioting led to communal massacres on a frightening scale. Timmy spent months rushing from one trouble spot to another. 'Once we arrived we restored order quickly enough, but often the worst was over by then, and meanwhile rioting would have broken out elsewhere.'

> The most difficult part was not knowing from day to day the very size of the problem to be solved. As panic settled onto the area and the migrations began, we never knew if the movement

would stop abruptly or continue until the separate religious communities had been exchanged completely. The complete exchange would have involved so many millions of people that the mere thought of it was staggering. More than ten million people did migrate, making the largest mass movement in history. Every available means of transportation was taxed to the limit. Every plane, train, bus, lorry, and car that could be found was used. And this was only a fraction of the transportation needed. Most refugees walked.

The columns of people and the overcrowded trains attracted militants from rival communities, enraged by atrocity stories true and false. With so many weapons left over from the war, fanatics could easily obtain military-grade explosives and powerful machine guns, and didn't hesitate to use them on the people they blamed – often based on nothing more than hearsay – for carrying out massacres themselves.

> One day a refugee train from Pakistan stopped in Amritsar. Every car was crammed with horribly mutilated bodies. On the sides of the cars was written in blood, 'An inam [gift] from Pakistan.' Something beyond madness gripped Amritsar. The Sikhs, with their kirpan knives, descended on the station. A Muslim refugee train, bound for Pakistan, came along and the Sikhs went through this train and filled it with chopped-up Muslim corpses. They wrote in blood on the cars, 'An inam from Hindustan.' The attack was finished before troops could be brought to stop it.

Timmy's tireless struggles to save lives during this awful time caught the attention of the Urdu poet Faiz Ahmed Faiz, observing from Pakistan, who wrote that 'Thimayya was neither Hindu nor Muslim. Humanity alone was his sole faith.' And even amid the carnage Timmy himself managed to find some reasons for hope.

When I think of those weeks of horror I also remember the incidents of bravery and generosity that were as glorious as the violence was revolting. A mullah in Sheikhapura risked his life to protect the Sikh refugees and so did many Sikhs and Hindus risk their lives to protect Muslims. These people on both sides who were able to rise above white-hot passions, who maintained their sanity and their belief in decency, proved to me the invincibility of the human spirit.

Communal violence soon turned to actual warfare in the contested lands of Kashmir. Timmy was in command of a division that helped drive the Pakistani army back, commanding a lead tank and firing — quite possibly — upon men of his old regiment. After a few years in charge of his old military academy at Dehra Dun, where the drill sergeants no longer shouted at recruits in British accents, he was selected to organise the repatriation of prisoners at the end of the Korean War. The role required real diplomatic skill, something he'd not always displayed in his military career thus far. He did an outstanding job and earned the respect of numerous international political figures. President Eisenhower said that the commanding figure of the famous Indian general had won the 'respect of both sides by firmness and impartiality of his decisions in the face of conflicting pressures and moral viewpoints'. After this it seemed natural for Timmy to be offered the command of the entire Indian Army, the pinnacle of his life's work. During a turbulent decade he did from time to time find himself at odds with his political masters, just as he had been with his generals in Burma. On one occasion he resigned, only to have his letter refused and returned to him by Prime Minister Jawaharlal Nehru, the son of his original mentor back in Allahabad.

He kept in friendly touch with many of the British officers he had known, and he was 'honoured and delighted' when his original regiment, the Highland Light Infantry, asked him to perform a task that revealed how respect for British customs, even some of the more peculiar ones, lingered on in the army that he now led.

He received a letter from Scotland asking him to shoot some leopards to provide skins to clothe the bagpipe players of the regimental band. As a point of honour, officers of the Highland Light Infantry had always tracked, dispatched and skinned such animals themselves but, as the letter explained, the shrinking of the British Empire had made that rather problematic. Timmy, an enthusiastic tiger hunter all of his life, immediately asked his *shikari* whether he might 'beat' for leopard instead, but was told that it was not possible that season. And so, with his own money he bought 'six fine Leopard pelts' instead and had them shipped to Scotland.

Finally, after almost four decades of service to the army, he retired amid great praise and fanfare in 1961, only to be dragged back into action one last time by the United Nations, as commander of its forces in Cyprus in July 1964. And it was there, serving far away from home and family, as he had so often done before, that he died suddenly in 1965. A respected − and, yes, sometimes feared − commander of soldiers and a true hero of India right until the end.

Dawlish, Devon, 1947

Andrew Peterkin accepts that his father could be irascible.

> The thing is, he was passionate about diagnosis and really very good at it. He could spot things before even the patients knew they had them. But being so far ahead of everyone else in the room he could come across as rather . . . well, rude I suppose. I remember if people kept coming back saying they were sick and he didn't agree with them he'd just say, 'I have done all I can for you but here, please take this list of other doctors in the county!'

The Douglas Peterkin his son remembers was a practical man, a hardworking man, but hardly the 'dour Scot' that Ethel

Newberry found so disagreeable. 'He loved being a family doctor, and would read endlessly on all the latest diagnostic ideas. Catching diseases and curing people, that was his passion, not perfecting the bedside manner.' And even within his family he spoke very rarely about Belsen.

> We didn't talk about his war for many years but once I understood more about it I could completely see why he'd want to live a quiet but purposeful life in a place like Dawlish. Yes 'purposeful' is the best word I can think for him. And his purpose was making people better.

Peterkin's talent for diagnosis was put to the test when, towards the end of 1947, a new disease came to Devon and, especially, to the children of Dawlish and nearby Teignmouth. Tony Bryant was one of the first to catch it although initially his family just assumed it was a bad case of the flu. But when he began vomiting and complaining about pains in his arms and legs his mother Mary decided that the time had come to call for the doctor, one of the 'older doctors' that is. Neither was available and so, to the family's great disappointment, it was the abrupt and difficult Dr Peterkin who arrived on their doorstep. He went upstairs and spent a great deal of time examining their son, carefully manipulating his arms, legs and spine with a concerned look on his face. Then he announced that the boy must be taken to Exeter hospital immediately for some important tests. He wrote a letter for them to hand to the doctors there, and explained to Tony that he would need an injection into his back that would be rather painful, but he must prepare to be brave for his mother's sake.

The lumbar puncture was indeed most unpleasant but the spinal fluid that was extracted confirmed everything that Peterkin had feared. Tony was infected with the polio virus and needed urgent hospital treatment. The term 'polio' was rarely used at the time. Instead, another and rather more chilling phrase was common, one that perfectly described the most obvious effect of this hard-to-diagnose viral infection: 'infantile paralysis'. As her son started receiving the urgent care that would save his life, Mrs Bryant rushed to thank the doctor she'd never asked for, and she never spoke another bad word about him for the rest of her life. As with another small boy suffering from an infectious disease in a city many miles away, Douglas Peterkin had come across someone in Devon who needed the help he was uniquely qualified to give – *no*, that it was his pleasure and his purpose to give – and he hadn't hesitated for a moment.

Tony's classmate Jennifer Newberry first heard about infantile paralysis a few days later at the Dawlish cinema club, sitting next to her friend Julie Boon. The Boon family owned the newsagent's a few doors down from the Newberry bakery and Julie's sister Patsy had just gone down with a nasty illness. When she was suddenly rushed away and placed into something called an 'iron lung' the whole street began to panic, especially anyone who had been associating with the Boon family, or sitting next to one of them in a cinema.

> It was frightening but I didn't have it although my mother and father checked me for days afterwards. Poor Patsy never properly healed, never had the full use of her arms, but she was saved. In fact nobody in Dawlish died although I think someone in Teignmouth did. The worst thing was the paralysis. There were several children who had to wear callipers on their legs for the rest of their lives. I remember my friend Rosie West had to and she was never properly fit and healthy ever again. But Tony [Bryant] well he was so lucky. He was completely cured. Because they picked it up so quickly you see. And it was like a miracle, really, according to his mother, who as a good Catholic always thought it was a miracle. A miracle and a really brusque doctor!

Many years later and in a different century, as Jennifer and Tony Bryant approached their fiftieth wedding anniversary hundreds of miles from Devon, they were still getting the *Dawlish Gazette* delivered. One day there was a letter in it from Dr Peterkin. Long since retired, he was sufficiently interested in the health of the town to complain about some problem with the drains. And, as was the way with local papers, the letter was printed along with his home address.

> He must have been 90 then and we were in our 70s but Tony said to me, I don't know as a seven year old whether I ever thanked Dr Peterkin. And I said, 'Why don't you write and thank him now,' so he did. And we had a lovely letter back saying that he remembered the case very well. He remembered Tony's family. He remembered my family. And it was just so lovely to hear from him. And Tony was so glad and so grateful that he had written to thank him, because soon after that, Dr Peterkin died.
> And that man really changed lots of lives. I still like to think I would have married Tony even if he'd been crippled, but you don't know, do you?

David Olusoga reminds us that 'History is not there to make us feel good, proud or comforted' yet slotting complex lives into an easy narrative, a comfortable storyline, is always tempting. Take Dr Douglas Peterkin: the man of the future, a progressive saint, an inspector calling time on the reactionary old Tory golf club bores. But according to his son he rather enjoyed a game of golf, and hockey, too. Although when he did play he always made sure someone was left at home in case of an urgent call. Andrew Peterkin vividly remembers running down to the side of the pitch to drag his father away from his teammates and handing him the address of a family who needed him. As for his politics, nobody really knows if he was a socialist in 1947 or not, but in later life he certainly had little time for Prime Minister Tony Blair. And he wasn't as forgiving as we might expect a modern-day saint to be. Arthur Titherington was prepared to buy a Japanese car, but Douglas Peterkin would never go near a German one, 'because they had been so very cruel to those poor people in Belsen'. 'I wouldn't say my father was really scarred by the war, but he clearly relished being in a quiet faraway place just living a purposeful life helping people.'

No, not a character in a comforting story about forgiveness, or how Britain renounced an empire and embraced a health system instead. Just an unusually decent man who willingly walked into hell and tried to turn it into Harrods. A man who made things better, changing the trajectory of thousands of lives with effects that ricocheted around the world, down the generations and eventually reached even me. Because Jennifer and Tony Bryant's first child, a daughter called Frances, met me at university and married me in 1983. Some years later, when we had three children of our own, their Devonian grandparents had the clever idea of recreating a typical wartime meal of their youth, something they hoped our kids would enjoy. So they bought great piles of turnips, carrots and potatoes along with a bottle of barely drinkable 'Camp Coffee' made from chicory, some genuine old-school 'powdered egg' and other examples of 1940s culinary improvisation. The highlight was the 'Pipper Pasty' in which Marmite – and yet more turnip – replaced the traditional lamb 'because meat's rationed don't you know and we've run out of points this week!' The pasties came with 'bubble and squeak', otherwise known as potato and cabbage, and a mysterious 'wow-wow sauce' made largely, it seemed, from pickled walnuts. As we were enjoying this high-fibre historical feast, Tony suddenly produced a BBC sound effect disc that he'd borrowed from Twickenham library, put it on the record player and filled the dining room with the sound of the wartime air raid siren. 'It's a raid. Quick! Run! Girls under the stairs and boys under the table. And don't forget to grab your pasty, it might be a long one.'

Alex, Helen and Jenny (named, of course, for her grandma) found it all completely thrilling and a few days later I wrote to a friend at the BBC with an idea for something about life in Britain during the Second World War with the working title of *Finest Hour*. It became a documentary series and the first part of this trilogy.

'All of them, all the hard brave men and women, still just within reach' are the words that close the book that resulted from that fake air raid and extra fibrous pasty. And at that time they really were reachable. I sat and spoke with some phenomenal eighty-somethings, extracting deeply personal stories that were still vivid in the minds of Edith Heap, Peter Vaux, Iain Nethercott and so many others. Tears came to Edith when she told me how her fiancé Denis Wissler had died in 1940, followed by a sharp, self-reproachful 'Oh shut up!' that, for me, perfectly captured the grit of her generation. But for *this* book the only living participant I could meet in person was Eddy Boas, whose brother had so fortunately encountered Douglas Peterkin on the streets of Leipzig. And even as I was writing I could see from the obituary pages that the centenarians of the Second World War were slipping away fast. Harry Howath, who fought on D-Day, Thomas Dobie, who flew supply planes into Burma, Harry Hughes, who survived countless bombing raids over Berlin, Mike Hickie, who served on submarines in the Indian Ocean, Bob Steen, who battled all the way from Normandy to Cologne.

But *lamedvovniks* find a way to reach us still. Sitting under that dining-room table I'd never heard of Douglas Peterkin nor had any idea that my own family — my own *happiness* — was made possible by one of the heroes of Belsen. Well, we're all the consequence of innumerable accidents and surprises, I suppose, but to sit years later with Eddy Boas overlooking Sydney Harbour and hear him talk about his life and his family and how the actions of a British captain, a complete stranger, had brought them back from the brink of death, well, that was something truly special. As was introducing Jennifer Bryant, née Newberry, to Eddy when he came to speak so movingly at London's Wiener Holocaust Library. Two lives forever changed by the actions of a man who wanted to make a difference.

Of the rightness of the cause, and Britain's pivotal role, there can be no doubt. Some empires build concentration camps and some build human laundries. The British Empire built *both* those things in the course of its rise and fall, but in the time of Douglas Peterkin it should be remembered for the good that it did and the courage that it displayed. The courage of Timmy's *jawan*s every bit as much as Fraser's Cumbrians. The worst aspects of British rule – the hypocrisies and prejudices that so infuriated men and women like Timmy – doomed it in India and, with a changing world order, everywhere else in the years that followed. But it was never going to be quick, no matter how nice it may be to think that good people such as Angela Noblet booted the likes of Chips Channon out forever in 1945. They did not and nor could they have done. As the *Manchester Guardian* concluded on VE Day: 'We have solved nothing. We are no nearer the Golden Age. But at least we have stopped the onrush of evil. We have won the right to hope.'

Refusing to submit when submission seemed inevitable. Struggling on alone, fighting back the tears and gritting the teeth along every painful step of 'Fucking Hell Tunnel'. Becoming organised, professional and tough, then pressing on to the end. Shadowy figures sent Australians on questionable missions. Japanese prisoners were used to reimpose unwelcome colonialists. All of that happened and it's important that today we can see it plain and reckon with it openly. But British power, however imperfectly applied – the bayonets, the battleships and the size ten boots – put thousands of righteous, purposeful men and women into places where they could face and defeat an onrushing evil. Making the future that Angela glimpsed at twilight on her forever river – that kinder and fairer world – come a little closer. For her children and for Eddy's, for Timmy's and for Arthur's, for Jennifer and Tony's, for mine and for yours.

Acknowledgements

As noted on its final pages, this book differs from its two predecessors in one key respect. While they included numerous original interviews I had conducted with living survivors of the war, *1945: The Reckoning* relied mostly upon what historians and journalists call secondary sources. As far as I could I sought out testimony that would be unfamiliar and interesting to a general reader although in a handful of cases, such as George MacDonald Fraser's incomparable *Quartered Safe Out Here*, I allowed myself to deploy a small amount of material that will be widely known already.

I was guided through – and frequently to – my sources by a series of new and old friends. Professor Ashley Jackson from King's College London was my lead consultant and he generously shared both his time and his deep knowledge of British imperial and military history. I'm deeply grateful for his wise counsel and also to his colleague Dr Yasmin Khan, Associate Professor of Modern History at Oxford University, for recommending him to me. Her own groundbreaking book *The Raj at War* was one of my key sources too.

I have already thanked Christine Helliwell in the introduction because I simply could not have told the story of Borneo in 1945 in anything like the same way without access to her extraordinary collection of interviews. If you found that part of the book interesting then there is so much more to be discovered and enjoyed in her excellent and imaginative account, simply called *Semut*.

I didn't know Dr Robert Lyman before beginning this project, but he has become a good friend and ally. He's also introduced me

ACKNOWLEDGEMENTS

to the wonderful world of guidl.com. I am grateful to Rob for his many wise comments on my drafts, his suggestions for further reading and, of course, for his own definitive accounts of the war in Burma, notably *Slim, Master of War* and *War of Empires*. One day I'm determined to go on one of his walking tours as well! Rob also kindly introduced me to Chandar S. Sundaram, a leading scholar of South Asian military history, who very generously sent me his hugely useful and groundbreaking article *A Paper Tiger: The Indian National Army in Battle, 1944–1945*, which is a good and I think necessary antidote to many of the more florid accounts of the INA's role in the war that are readily available online.

Not every distinguished historian arrives for lunch driving a red Ford Mustang, but Robin Prior is no ordinary historian and, for me at least, the meeting we had in Adelaide in 2023 was anything but ordinary. I thank Robin for his comments and advice, and also for helping me understand something that directly affected the tone of this book. During our lunch we discussed the historian J. C. D. Clark. As a critic of what was once called the 'Whig interpretation of history', Clark was controversial when I studied the subject and remains so today. But he provides a useful lesson for anyone, academic or otherwise, trying to comprehend the past as it really was. He believes that historical figures are just as likely to be influenced by the forces of tradition – patriotic, conservative, and religious – as they are by a vision of a more liberal or progressive world to come. And he believes that historians all too often let their *own* knowledge of that 'world to come' influence their judgements, thus creating a barrier to understanding what really mattered in the times and to the people they study.

I contacted the eminent economic historian Professor Tirthankar Roy of the LSE looking for advice on some of the key Indian sections of the book and was delighted when he agreed to help. I want to thank him here for taking the time and the trouble to assist a stranger, and for his numerous very perceptive comments on my drafts. The late historian Dr Zareer Masani was also very supportive and helpful in the early stages of

ACKNOWLEDGEMENTS

researching this book and I would have loved to hear his — doubtless forthright — comments on it.

Michael Hurst is the founder and director of the Taiwan POW Camps Memorial Society, and I want to thank him for his excellent advice, for his book *Never Forgotten* and for guiding me towards the privately published memoirs of Arthur Titherington. Many other people also deserve a mention here: Craig Tibbitts from the Australian War Memorial in Canberra; K. C. Belliappa, Timmy's grandson, who gave me excellent advice and some wonderful photographs; Carol Bolton, Sylvia Hardie, Alison Evans, David Bolton, Tim Bolton and the other members of the extended family of Angela Bolton (née Noblet); Cecily Blench, the novelist granddaughter of Mary King, whose moving book *The Long Journey Home* is rich in period detail; Andrew Peterkin, Sheena Wilson and other members of Douglas Peterkin's family; Charlotte Carty, intrepid granddaughter of Lt Col William Felix 'Bruno' Brown; the formidable survivor of Belsen, Eddy Boas and his son Philip; and Karen Pollock from the Holocaust Education Trust.

Many friends from both my literary and documentary life agreed to read and comment on the early drafts of the book, or offered advice based upon their own work on this period. I particularly want to thank Tim Clayton, Giles Milton, Martin Davidson, Christopher Hale, Sue Horth, Jack Bowsher, Nick Bryant, Sir Pritpal Singh, David Wilson (who has now advised on all three books in the series), Jane Stephenson, Dr Helen Fry, Patrick Jephson, Prof. Alan Lester (for some excellent notes and a most congenial lunch), Prof. Clare Wright, K. S. Nair (for taking the time to add some much needed Indian military perspectives), Dr Samir Puri, Graham Watkins, Nick Ward, Dr Philip W. Blood, Marika Cobbold, Amanda Craig, Samir Puri, Lucy Meacock, Prof. Nigel Biggar, Prof. Jenny Hocking, Jane Caro, Dr Peter Caddick-Adams, Paul Woodadge from *WW2 TV*, Paul Bavill and Kyle Glover from *History Rage*, Andrew Lownie and Nick Short.

My family has been terrifically supportive during the time it took me to research and write this book. I want to thank my

ACKNOWLEDGEMENTS

children Alex, Helen and Jenny and especially my partner, best friend, sharpest critic and most trusted copy editor, Frances. My wonderful mother-in-law Jennifer Bryant talked to me about her wartime childhood in Devon over many family dinners and researched the mysterious origins of the war-winning Pipper Pasty.

Particular thanks go to James Holland, an early supporter of my writing, for his lovely foreword, and also to the many members of the Independent Company I've spoken, and sometimes socialised, with – all part of a remarkable community of history lovers that has formed around the hugely successful *We Have Ways* podcast that James runs with Al Murray.

There were no podcasts or social media when *Finest Hour* was written but both have now become terrific research tools. A few people I have never met in person helped me find my way to important stories after reading my request for assistance on Twitter/X. Georgy Bradders directed me to the Peterkin clan (when I had been wrongly advised elsewhere that Douglas never had any children) and Clarissa Reilly did some sterling online research to put me in touch with Angela Noblet's descendants. Nick Brittan's Twitter/X account guided me toward some great photographs and other archives of the Indian army and Mandeep Singh Bajwa used the platform to share a wonderful interview with Gurbaksh Singh Dhillon, filmed in 1995 on the banks of the Irrawaddy.

Staff at the National Archives in Kew, the British Library, the Holocaust Education Trust, the Wiener Holocaust Library and the Australian War Memorial were their usual friendly and professional selves. These institutions are national treasures and deserve the support of writers and readers alike.

Chelsea Taylor from the National Army Museum patiently guided me through the process of reproducing photographs from that excellent collection. Every reasonable effort has been made to acknowledge the ownership of the copyrighted material included in this book. Any errors that may have occurred are inadvertent

ACKNOWLEDGEMENTS

and will be corrected in subsequent editions provided notification is sent to the author.

Finally, special thanks go to my publisher and friend Rupert Lancaster for being a pleasure to work with yet again and for his excellent advice throughout. The team at Hodder and Stoughton has also been supportive and professional at every stage of the process, especially Kerri Logan, Purvi Gadia, Rimsha Falak, Priya Das, Lucy Buxton, copy editor Richard Collins, picture researcher Lesley Hodgson and mapmaker Jo Boyle.

Picture Credits

Chapter openers
Chapter 1: Image courtesy of the National Army Museum, London
Chapter 2: Public Domain / courtesy of Wikimedia
Chapter 3: Courtesy of the family of Angela Noblet
Chapter 4: © History and Art Collection / Alamy Stock Photo
Chapter 5: Courtesy of Michael Hurst
Chapter 6: © Historic Collection / Alamy Stock Photo
Chapter 7: Image courtesy of the National Army Museum, London
Chapter 8: Public Domain / courtesy of Wikimedia
Chapter 9: Courtesy Yad Vashem Archives, Image 503/4844
Chapter 10: Image courtesy of the National Army Museum, London
Chapter 11: Courtesy of Australian War Memorial, Image P01806.010
Chapter 12: Courtesy of the family of Douglas Peterkin
Chapter 13: Image courtesy of the National Army Museum, London
Chapter 14: Public Domain / courtesy of Wikimedia
Chapter 15: CC BY-SA 4.0 / Wikimedia / Arcedz
Chapter 16: Courtesy of Australian War Memorial, Image P00560.001
Chapter 17: Author's own

Insets
Page 1 top: Public Domain
Page 1 bottom: Image courtesy of the National Army Museum, London
Page 2 top: Image courtesy of the National Army Museum, London
Page 2 bottom: Image courtesy of KC Belliappa
Page 3 top and bottom: Image courtesy of the National Army Museum, London
Page 4 top: Public Domain. United States. Office of War Information.

Division of Public Inquiries. The Atlantic Charter, poster, 1943; Washington, D.C.

Page 4 bottom: Bundesarchiv, Bild 101III-Alber-064-03A / Alber, Kurt / CC-BY-SA 3.0

Page 5 top: Public Domain / courtesy of Wikimedia

Page 5 bottom: Image courtesy of the National Army Museum, London

Page 6: Courtesy of Michael Hurst

Page 7 top: Library of Congress, Prints & Photographs Division, FSA/OWI Collection, LC-USE6- D-009184

Page 7 bottom left: Courtesy of the family of Angela Noblet

Page 7 bottom right: Image courtesy of the National Army Museum, London

Page 8 top: Public Domain

Page 8 middle: © Historic Collection / Alamy Stock Photo

Page 8 bottom: © ART Collection / Alamy Stock Photo

Page 9 top: Courtesy of the family of Bruno Brown

Page 9 bottom: Image courtesy of the National Army Museum, London

Page 10 top: Public Domain

Page 10 bottom: Image courtesy of the National Army Museum, London

Page 11 top and bottom: Image courtesy of the National Army Museum, London

Page 12 top and bottom: Image courtesy of the National Army Museum, London

Page 13: Public Domain / Major Clarence Benjamin on 13 April 1945

Page 14 top: Image courtesy of the National Army Museum, London

Page 14 bottom left: Courtesy of Michael Hurst

Page 14 bottom right: Public Domain

Page 15 top: Image courtesy of the National Army Museum, London

Page 15 bottom: © Hulton Deutsch / Getty Images

Page 16 top: Courtesy of the family of Mary King

Page 16 middle: Courtesy of the family of Douglas Peterkin

Page 16 bottom: Public domain via Dawlish History Facebook Group

Bibliography

Alanbrooke, Field Marshal Lord, *War Diaries 1939–1945*, ed. A. Danchev and D. Todman, London: Weidenfeld & Nicolson, 2001.

Allport, Alan, *Demobbed: Coming Home After World War Two*, New Haven and London: Yale University Press, 2009.

Bayly, Christopher and Harper, Tim, *Forgotten Wars: The End of Britain's Asian Empire*, London: Allen Lane, 2007.

Blench, Cecily, 'East with the Sun', *Slightly Foxed*, issue 54, 2017.

Boas, Eddy, *I'm Not a Victim I Am a Survivor*, Sydney: Eddy Boas Publishing, 2017.

Bolton, Angela, *The Maturing Sun: An Army Nurse in India, 1942–45*, London: Headline, 1986.

Bose, Subhas Chandra, *The Indian Struggle*, Delhi, India: Oxford University Press, 1997.

Bose, Sugata, *His Majesty's Opponent: Subhas Chandra Bose and India's Struggle against Empire*, Cambridge, Mass.: Harvard University Press, 2011.

Caddick-Adams, Peter, *1945: Victory in the West*, London: Hutchinson Heinemann, 2022.

Calder, Angus, *The People's War*, London: Jonathan Cape, 1969.

Channon, Henry 'Chips', *Diaries 1943–1957*, ed. Simon Heffer, London: Penguin Random House, 2022.

Charmley, John, *Churchill's Grand Alliance: The Anglo-American Special Relationship 1940–57*, London: Hodder and Stoughton, 1995.

Cohen, Stephen P., 'Subhas Chandra Bose and the Indian National Army', University of British Columbia, *Pacific Affairs*, Winter 1963–64.

Connor, Stephen, 'Sidestepping Geneva: Japanese Troops under British Control 1945–47', *Journal of Contemporary History*, volume 45, no. 2, 2010.

Deery, Phillip, 'Malaya 1948', *Journal of Cold War Studies*, volume 9, 2007.

Dhillon, Gurbakhsh Singh, *From My Bones*, New Delhi: Aryan Books International, 1998.

Edgerton, David, *Britain's War Machine*, London: Allen Lane, 2011.

———, *The Rise and Fall of the British Nation*, London: Allen Lane, 2018.

Evans, Humphrey, *Thimayya of India*, 1960, hard to obtain and with a complex publication history but can be viewed here: https://archive.org/stream/in.ernet.dli.2015.111225/2015.111225. Thimayya-Of-India-A-Soldiers-Life_djvu.txt and also here https://kodavaclan.com/images/ebook/Thimayya-of-India_A-Soldiers-Life.pdf.

Fay, Peter Ward, *The Forgotten Army*, Ann Arbor: University of Michigan, 1993.

Fennell, Jonathan, *Fighting the People's War*, Cambridge, UK: Cambridge University Press, 2019.

Followill, Gary, 'Necessary Chicanery: Operation Kingfisher's Cancellation and Inter-Allied Rivalry', Thesis for University of New South Wales, 2020.

Fraser, George MacDonald, *Quartered Safe Out Here*, London: Harvill, 1993.

Gardiner, Juliet, *Over Here: The GIs in Wartime Britain*, London: Collins & Brown, 1992.

Gilbert, Martin, *Finest Hour: Winston S. Churchill 1939–1941*, London: William Heinemann, 1983.

———, *Road to Victory: Winston S. Churchill 1941–1945*, London: William Heinemann, 1986.

Ham, Paul, *Sandakan*, Sydney: William Heinemann, 2012.

Hayes, Romain, *Subhas Chandra Bose in Nazi Germany*, London: C. Hurst & Co., 2011.

Heinlein, Frank, *British Government Policy and Decolonisation 1945–63*, London: Routledge, 2002.

Helliwell, Christine, *Semut*, Sydney: Random House, 2021.
Hurst, Michael D., *Never Forgotten*, Taipei: Mei-Hua Publishing, 2020.
Jackson, Ashley, *Mad Dogs and Englishmen*, London: Quercus, 2009.
Kee, Robert, *1945: The World We Fought For*, London: Hamish Hamilton, 1985.
Keegan, John, *The Second World War*, London: Century Hutchinson, 1989.
Khan, Yasmin, *The Raj at War: A People's History of India's Second World War*, London: The Bodley Head, 2015.
Khanduri, C. B., *Thimayya: An Amazing Life*, New Delhi: Knowledge World, 2006.
Killingray, David, *Fighting for Britain: African Soldiers in the Second World War*, London: James Currey, 2010.
Kimball, Warren F., *Forged in War: Roosevelt, Churchill and the Second World War*, New York: William Morrow & Co., 1997.
———, (ed.), *Churchill and Roosevelt, The Complete Correspondence: The Alliance Emerging, October 1939–November 1942*, Princeton: Princeton University Press, 1984.
Kynaston, David, *Austerity Britain 1945–51*, London: Bloomsbury, 2007.
Lyman, Robert, *A War of Empires: Japan, India, Burma and Britain 1941–45*, London: Osprey, 2021.
Maule, Henry, *Spearhead General: The Epic Story of General Sir Francis Messervy and His Men in Eritrea, North Africa and Burma*, London: Oldham's Press, 1961.
Milton, Giles, *The Stalin Affair: The Impossible Alliance that Won the War*, London: John Murray, 2024.
Nair, K. S., *The Forgotten Few: The Indian Air Force in World War Two*, Noida: Harper Collins India, 2019.
Nicolson, Harold, *Diaries and Letters 1939–1945*, ed. N. Nicolson, London: Collins, 1967.
Overy, Richard, *Why the Allies Won*, London: Jonathan Cape, 1995.
———, *Blood and Ruins: The Great Imperial War 1931–1945*, London: Allen Lane, 2021.
Padmanabhan, Mukund, *The Great Flap of 1942: How the Raj Panicked over a Japanese Non-invasion*, Delhi, India: Vintage Books, 2024.

Pick-Goslar, Hannah, *My Friend Anne Frank*, London: Penguin Random House, 2023.
Powell, Alan, *War by Stealth*, Melbourne University Press, 1996.
Prescott, Dr D. T., *Reflections of Forty Years Ago – Belsen*, Wellcome Collection, 1985.
Prior, Robin, *Conquer We Must*, London: Yale University Press, 2022.
Raghavan, Srinath, *India's War: The Making of Modern South Asia 1939–1945*, London: Allen Lane, 2016.
Reeves, Mark, *Free and Equal Partners in your Commonwealth*, https://uwe-repository.worktribe.com/index.php/output/10464301/free-and-equal-partners-in-your-commonwealth-the-atlantic-charter-and-anti-colonial-delegations-to-london-19413.
Richards, Denis, *The Hardest Victory: RAF Bomber Command in the Second World War*, London: Hodder and Stoughton, 1994.
Roberts, Andrew, *Churchill: Embattled Hero*, London: Weidenfeld & Nicolson, 1994.
Safrani, Abid Hasan, *The Men from Imphal*, Kolkata: Nejati Research Bureau, 1971.
Skidelsky, Robert, *John Maynard Keynes, Fighting for Britain*, London: Macmillan, 2000.
Sundaram, Chandar S., 'A Paper Tiger: The Indian National Army in Battle, 1944–1945', University of New South Wales, *War and Society*, volume 13, 1995.
Titherington, Arthur, *One Day at a Time*, Worcester: S.P.A, 1993.
Todman, Daniel, *Britain's War: A New World 1942–1947*, London: Allen Lane, 2020.
Towle, Philip, Kosuge, Margaret and Kibata, Yoichi, *Japanese Prisoners of War*, UK: A&C Black, 2000.
Villers-Tuthill, Kathleen, *Patient Endurance: The Great Famine in Connemara*, Connemara Girl Publications, 1997.
Warner, Philip, *Auchinleck: The Lonely Soldier*, London: Buchan & Enright, 1981.
Wheatcroft, Geoffrey, *Churchill's Shadow*, London: Penguin Random House, 2021.
White, Peter, *With the Jocks: A Soldier's Struggle for Europe 1944–45*, London: Sutton, 2001.

Notes on Sources

As with the previous books in this series, some passages of *1945: The Reckoning* are lightly novelised. For example, Timmy's tirade at the frightened young man piloting his landing craft is not an exact quote but my own rendering of what he told us happened, pistol and all, using language adapted from the (rather numerous) other occasions in his life when he lost his temper. His eloquent defence of Indian lavatory habits to his fellow cadets at Sandhurst is similarly constructed. The excited gossip about the war being shared with Subhas Chandra Bose in the summer of 1941 was never recorded by anybody present, but the lines I use reflect what well-connected people were saying in Berlin at the time. In a handful of other sections – for example, Angela Noblet's accounts of her experiences on the Brahmaputra river – I have changed tense to increase impact. In Angela's own book about her life she mixes memories written in the past tense with present tense quotes taken straight from her diaries. From time to time, it felt more direct to put her thoughts and impressions back into the tense she used when she first committed them to paper. There are two other moments of – I hope – allowable dramatisation. Christine Helliwell only recorded the opening lines of the SRD's 'Fuck 'Em All' song in her book *Semut* and so I took it upon myself to complete it in a similar spirit. Angela Bolton gave us all the most important lines of her 'scarlet underwear song' but I added an extra one for the sake of the rhyming scheme.

I have generally used the names of nations, towns and geographical

NOTES ON SOURCES

features that were current in the 1940s, unless their modern-day replacements help improve comprehension.

Key quotations and descriptions taken from named sources are listed below.

INTRODUCTION

p. xvii   'It fell to', Robin Prior, *Conquer We Must*, p. xv.

p. xvii   'History is not there', David Olusoga, from https://www.thetimes.com/world/africa/article/david-olusoga-interview-historian-tv-book-author-00wt3fqfn.

CHAPTER ONE

p. 6   'Not far inland we came', Humphrey Evans, *Thimayya of India*, Kangaw chapter (copy referred to is un-paginated).

Almost all of the Timmy quotes in this book come from Humphrey Evans's book. As far as I can tell Timmy gave Evans the only extended interviews of his life. But when Evans published earlier than expected, Timmy and his family distanced themselves from the book. Decades later, and long after Timmy's death, an authorised biography appeared (*Thimayya: An Amazing Life*) with the support of his family. That second book reproduced all of the key elements of Evans's, with near identical quotes and details. This leads me to assume that the 'distancing' was not caused by the words that Evans recorded but rather the timing of his publication. Evans's book came out while Timmy was still a force in Indian public life and contained many of his characteristically trenchant comments about some of the leading personalities of his day.

p. 8   'The Bosch could not have stood five hours of it', from https://www.keymilitary.com/article/black-mud-green-berets-burma-commando-part-ii.

p. 9   'We invited the commandos to dine', Evans, Kangaw chapter.

p. 10   'Among the shells', David Killingray, *Fighting for Britain*, p. 158.

p. 11   'I had asked for the impossible', Slim from https://burmastarmemorial.org/view/1472417-general-sir-william-slims-biography.

NOTES ON SOURCES

- p. 12 'a young Burmese girl', Vincent Ralph from https://www.keymilitary.com/article/black-mud-green-berets-burma-commando-part-ii.
- p. 16 'You, boy. Where are you going?', Evans, Dehra Dun chapter.
- p. 18 'Blimey are you tryin'', ibid.
- p. 19 'Hockey, cricket, football', ibid.

CHAPTER TWO

- p. 22 'a picture of the real India', Bose letter from https://aadityahbti.medium.com/subhash-chandra-bose-life-of-an-indian-pilgrim-22e92308378d.
- p. 26 'The Raj could be flexible', I'm grateful for the comments of Tirthankar Roy here.
- p. 27 'promotion of liberal values', Zareer Masani from https://openthemagazine.com/essay/judging-british-imperialism-by-its-aims-and-intentions/.
- p. 29 'I don't know whether', Bose, *An Indian Pilgrim*, https://ignca.gov.in/Asi_data/2176.pdf, p. 125.
- p. 31 'Nothing less than a dictator', Romain Hayes, *Subhas Chandra Bose in Nazi Germany*, p. 14.
- p. 33 'You are Capt. P. O. de L. FAKER', this and other comic questions via Rob Lyman, https://x.com/robert_lyman/status/1602368142914863104.
- p. 34 'I don't mind it, Sir', Evans, Bangalore chapter.
- p. 36 'We are going to cut off', Evans, Allahabad chapter.
- p. 36 'First nothing would please', ibid.
- p. 37 'yogic perception', etc., Bose, *An Indian Pilgrim*, https://ignca.gov.in/Asi_data/2176.pdf, p. 138.
- p. 38 'Bose's first great speech', Sugata Bose, *His Majesty's Opponent*, p. 139.
- p. 40 'We were amused by the flap', Evans, Quetta chapter.

CHAPTER THREE

- p. 48 'My Faults: Obstinacy', Angela Bolton, *The Maturing Sun*, p. 1.
- p. 49 'The spiral stairway', ibid., p. 38.
- p. 49 'Introduced to handsome', ibid., p. 46.

NOTES ON SOURCES

p. 51   'the scarlet thread', ibid., p. 41.
p. 52   'the dusty excremental streets', ibid., p. 63.
p. 53   'There is little talk', ibid., p. 65.
p. 53   'Subhas Chandra Bose imagined', Yasmin Khan, *The Raj at War*, pp. 18–19.
p. 55   'the story of the ardour', ibid., p. 68.
p. 55   'Heroic exploits in Eritrea', Indian reactions to the war, from Khan, pp. 68–70.
p. 55   'Is not this the time', Sugata Bose, p. 169.
p. 56   'If we hate totalitarianism', 'sanctimonious hypocrisy', ibid., pp. 173–178.
p. 57   'Today I must die', Bose, *My Political Testament*, 26 November 1940, https://www.netajisubhasbose.org/political-testament-of-subhas-bose.
p. 59   'conveniently forget the imperialist character', Sugata Bose, p. 197.
p. 60   'We shall no doubt pay', Mark Reeves, *Free and Equal Partners in Your Commonwealth*, p. 2.
p. 60   'deem it right', *The Atlantic Charter*, https://www.archives.gov/education/lessons/fdr-churchill.
p. 62   'The President and the Prime Minister', ibid.
p. 62   'We must regard this as an interim', Martin Gilbert, *Finest Hour*, p. 1162.
p. 62   'When he attempted to calm', Conservative Party opposition to the Charter, from Christopher Bayly and Tim Harper, *Forgotten Wars*, pp. 97–98.
p. 62   'would only arise in such', Gilbert, *Finest Hour*, p. 1163.
p. 63   'cannot help but conclude', Reeves, p. 10.
p. 63   'when Britain won the war', ibid., p. 12.
p. 63   'you will find [the charter's] principles', ibid., p. 5.
p. 64   '[American] General Wood was present', from https://www.fabulousphilippines.com/moro-massacre-twain.html.

CHAPTER FOUR

p. 67   'At the many official functions', Bose's life in Germany, from Hayes, pp. 29–41.
p. 68   'In one sense Bose makes', Bose and the Holocaust, ibid., pp. 164–167.

NOTES ON SOURCES

p. 69   'We won't say anything', ibid., p. 80.
p. 70   'Thermometer, forceps', Bolton, p. 64.
p. 70   'the Crewe of West Bengal', ibid., p. 67.
p. 71   'depressed by defeat', 'heart sinks', 'dramatic treatment', ibid., pp. 71–72.
p. 71   'I lie awake', ibid., p. 73.
p. 71   'The sun burns like copper', 'British, Indian and Gurkha', ibid., pp. 70–71.
p. 73   'I have been out quite often', ibid., p. 81.
p. 73   'Today the rains came', ibid., p. 82.
p. 74   'It was good to talk', 'what a relief to leave', ibid., p. 85.
p. 75   'The Indian wards', ibid., pp. 86–87.
p. 76   'Many of those refugees were Indian', retreat from Burma detail, from Robert Lyman, *War of Empires*, pp. 44–47.
p. 77   'The first day [of trekking]', from https://amitavghosh.com/exodus-from-burma-1941-a-personal-account/.
p. 78   'Every day we saw', from private diary of an anonymous eyewitness.
p. 78   'Our reception in India', from https://amitavghosh.com/exodus-from-burma-1941-a-personal-account/.
p. 79   'Hundreds, if not thousands', Khan, p. 107.
p. 80   'Thus the Indian', origins of INA, from Peter Ward Fay, *Forgotten Army*, pp. 106–111, and Lyman, pp. 137–139.
p. 81   'This is Subhas Chandra', Sugata Bose, p. 213.
p. 81   'have made a deep impression', Hayes, p. 89.
p. 82   'Shaken by the fall of Singapore', Cripps mission, from Khan, pp. 132–135, and Sugata Bose, pp. 216–218.
p. 83   'If the Britishers', Sugata Bose, p. 218.
p. 84   'They called it "The Great Flap"', 'Flap' details from Mukund Padmanabhan, *The Great Flap of 1942*.
p. 84   'One fine morning', Khan, p. 107.
p. 84   'I found a change', Sugata Bose, p. 217.
p. 85   'I am engaged here', Fay, p. 113.
p. 85   'A militant campaigner', Quit India detail, from Bayley and Harper, p. 83, Khan, pp. 181–186, and pp. 191–194, and Richard Overy, *Blood and Ruins*, pp. 182–183.
p. 86   'Behind the thick screen', Sugata Bose, p. 224.
p. 87   'The sympathy of the Indian', Evans, Singapore chapter.
p. 88   'I tried to act calm', Evans, Agra chapter.

NOTES ON SOURCES

p. 88 'The younger Indian officers', ibid.
p. 89 'The consensus [of men like me]', ibid.

CHAPTER FIVE

p. 92 'I was fast becoming', Arthur Titherington, *One Day at a Time*, p. 30.
p. 93 'Our campaign was', ibid., p. 46.
p. 94 'He reached Singapore', details of campaign in Malaya and Singapore from Titherington, *One Day at a Time*, and Lyman, pp. 29–33.
p. 95 'Before long the', Titherington, p. 18.
p. 95 'From now on', ibid., p. 19.
p. 96 'Those who had barely survived', details of Kinkaseki camp, from Titherington, and Michael Hurst, *Never Forgotten*, pp. 219–262.
p. 96 'We cheered Japanese troops', from https://www.sdh-fact.com/CL02_2/Chapter-5-Section-2.pdf, p. 26.
p. 97 'my father told me', from http://www.dutch-east-indies.com/eyewithnesses.html, eyewitness number 23.
p. 100 'To us, life is', Sugata Bose, p. 231, and from https://www.nationalarchives.gov.uk/education/resources/indian-independence/bose-radio/.
p. 100 'It was a small room', etc., Sugata Bose, pp. 233–234.
p. 101 '*Netaji* would think aloud', etc., from https://scroll.in/article/1043323/abid-hasan-safrani-meet-netaji-subhas-chandra-boses-comrade-who-coined-the-slogan-jai-hind.
p. 101 For details on SS *Corbis*, https://uboat.net/allies/merchants/ship/2872.html; https://uboat.net/allies/merchants/crews/ship2872.html; https://wrecksite.eu/wreck.aspx?16749. Also, Sugata Bose, p. 234.
p. 104 'It was a great pleasure', from https://rs5hiland.blogspot.com/2015/07/subhas-chandra-to-japan-1943-45_24.html.

CHAPTER SIX

p. 107 'We took a truck', Bolton, p. 91.
p. 108 'What's that noise?', ibid., p. 100.
p. 109 'We told him about', ibid., p. 101.

NOTES ON SOURCES

- p. 109 'The calamity unfolding in Bengal', Bengal famine detail from Khan, p. 200 onwards, Lyman, pp. 248–250, and Overy, pp. 415–416.
- p. 110 'I thought I was', Khan, p. 208.
- p. 111 'The men who ran', I'm grateful for the comments of Tirthankar Roy here.
- p. 112 'I hope we can', Khan, p. 208.
- p. 113 'I feel that the', ibid., p. 213.
- p. 113 'a beastly religion', Dr Zareer Masani, *Every Effort Must Be Made*, https://winstonchurchill.org/publications/finest-hour/finest-hour-191/every-effort-must-be-made/, and Geoffrey Wheatcroft, *Churchill's Shadow*, p. 525.
- p. 113 'warriors and . . . windbags', ibid., p. 279.
- p. 114 'The starvation of anyway', ibid., p. 280.
- P. 115 'puts to blush', Kathleen Villiers-Tuthill, *Patient Endurance*, pp. 45–46.
- p. 115 'It mattered a very great deal', Kinkaseki detail, from Titherington, *One Day at a Time*, and Hurst, pp. 219–262.
- p. 118 'We now see showing', Titherington, p. 111.
- p. 119 'All time England say', 'must stop complaining', ibid., p. 131.
- p. 119 'Even the average', ibid., p. 233–234.
- p. 121 *End of Empire*, episode on Iran, https://www.youtube.com/watch?v=xhCgJElpQEQ.
- p. 122 'we were so very pious', Lyman, p. 26.
- p. 124 'If you follow me', Sugata Bose, p. 245.
- p. 124 'I was hypnotised by his personality', Fay, p. 228.
- p. 127 'Netaji Subhas Chandra Bose', from https://timesofindia.indiatimes.com/travel/destinations/this-is-where-the-indian-flag-was-hoisted-for-the-first-time-on-indian-soil/articleshow/97308286.cms.

CHAPTER SEVEN

- p. 130 'The Australians have', Lyman, p. 240, and https://theprinciplesofwar.com/quotes/list-of-australian-military-quotes/.
- p. 132 'You're Timmy, aren't you', Evans, Agra chapter.
- p. 132 'I had never seen', ibid.
- p. 133 'You are 2Lt A. BRICK-DROPPER', this and other comic questions via Rob Lyman, https://x.com/robert_lyman/status/1602368142914863104.

p. 134   'Timmy, I understand', Evans, Agra chapter.
p. 135   'Seated in the corner', Bolton, p. 107.
p. 136   'She was such a shy maiden', ibid., p. 115.
p. 137   'Can you take these', ibid., pp. 128–129.
p. 137   'I resolve', Mary King diary extracts from unpublished manuscript, courtesy Cecily Blench.
p. 139   'I was too ashamed', Bolton, pp. 137–138.
p. 140   'The responsibility', ibid., p. 136.
p. 141   'We see planes bringing', Lyman, p. 306.
p. 142   'I leapt into a trench', Evans, Maungdaw chapter.
p. 143   'In my judgement the', ibid.
p. 144   'The hands of my', ibid.
p. 144   'I got the call', ibid.
p. 145   'TO THE PRINCES', from https://stampomania.blogspot.com/2010/10/warning-and-advice-ww2-propaganda.html.
p. 146   'Thus, with plenty', Evans, Maungdaw chapter.
p. 147   'He [Niranjan Prasad] said' and other Pilot Officer Philip quotes, from K. S. Nair, *The Forgotten Few*.

CHAPTER EIGHT

p. 152   'There, there in the distance', Lyman, p. 321, and Sugata Bose, p. 271.
p. 152   INA in Mowdok detail from https://www.netajisubhasbose.org/battles-rise-and-fall-of-ina.
p. 155   'It was war against', from https://www.thetimes.com/uk/article/his-honour-judge-robin-rowland-obituary-9tjhqpgnc.
p. 156   'On foot [our enemy] was not', Abid Hasan Safrani, *The Men from Imphal*, p. 2.
p. 157   'Often regarded with suspicion', from https://www.cia.gov/readingroom/docs/DOC_0000709795.pdf.
p. 158   'We marched sustained', Safrani, p. 1.
p. 159   'I felt proud and', ibid., p. 8.
p. 159   'All preparations had', Fay, p. 309.
p. 160   'Asia is surging with', Sugata Bose, p. 286.
p. 162   'I have just been out', from https://www.reddit.com/r/tolkienfans/comments/18u44ue/in_october_1944_tolkien_saw_a_skywide_armada_on/.

NOTES ON SOURCES

p. 162   'I'm the girl that', Barbara Gordon, Basis Thomas, David Heneker, 1942.

CHAPTER NINE

p. 165   'Holland had been neutral', some detail from Hannah Pick-Goslar, *My Friend Anne Frank*, and Eddy Boas, *I Am Not a Victim*.
p. 166   'The Jews for us', from https://www.annefrank.org/en/timeline/69/seyss-inquart-warns-the-dutch-jews/.
p. 167   'The transports run', from https://www.nytimes.com/2019/09/28/world/europe/ns-dutch-railway-holocaust.html.
p. 169   'malnutrition oedema', Titherington, p. 122.
p. 169   'Those in the mine' and other Ben Wheeler quotes (and quotes about him), from Hurst, pp. 240–258, and http://www.powtaiwan.org/archives_detail.php?A-MAN-SENT-FROM-GOD-1.
p. 172   'Please try not to', Hurst, p. 257.
p. 172   'The officer says little', Titherington, p. 123.
p. 173   'I have endeavoured', ibid., p. 136.
p. 177   'Eisenhower, though supposed', Alanbrooke, *War Diaries*, p. 628.
p. 178   'Westerbork wasn't', some detail from Pick-Goslar, *My Friend Anne Frank*, and Boas, *I Am Not a Victim*.
p. 181   'with the consistency', Bolton, p. 141.
p. 181   'So must the wards', ibid., pp. 141–142.
p. 181   'The normally silent', ibid., p. 142.
p. 182   'Very well', ibid., p. 139.
p. 182   'Miss Summerfield and', ibid., p. 140.
p. 182   'a "charming" letter', ibid., p. 142.
p. 183   'India had long been', detail from Khan, pp. 82–88, and Dr Srinath Raghavan lecture, https://www.youtube.com/watch?v=lpHhvzlaLBQ.
p. 185   'We no longer regard', The Directorate of Army Education, *The British Way and Purpose*.

CHAPTER TEN

p. 190   'As expected, when', Evans, Buthidaung chapter.
p. 191   'You must have been', ibid.

NOTES ON SOURCES

p. 193   'constitutes an episode', Martin Gilbert, *Road to Victory*, p. 923.
p. 193   'a black cloud', ibid., p. 929.
p. 194   'Mr Roosevelt's fine', Robert Kee, *1945 The World We Fought For*, p. 25.
p. 195   'Sometimes, despite the', Bolton, p. 146.
p. 196   'They fill every', ibid., p. 147.
p. 196   'The evenings are delightful', ibid., pp. 148–149.
p. 197   'Face-flannels and toothbrushes', ibid., p. 145.
p. 197   'As we stood there', ibid., p. 151.
p. 197   'I sat with men', ibid., pp. 147–148.
p. 198   'Ahead of us', ibid., p. 162.
p. 199   'I feel that we', Alanbrooke, p. 581.
p. 199   'in a maudlin', ibid., pp. 566–567.
p. 200   'still shooting our friends', Kee, p. 44.
p. 200   'as if you were in', Daniel Todman, *Britain's War*, pp. 669–670.
p. 201   'one thing is certain', Alanbrooke, p. 633.
p. 202   'took a few minutes', Gurbakhsh Singh Dhillon, *From My Bones*, pp. 277–278.
p. 203   'a sword against', ibid., p. 289.
p. 203   'elevated my spirits', ibid., p. 298.
p. 203   'I want to congratulate', ibid., p. 315.
p. 204   'Running across', etc., detail from George MacDonald Fraser, *Quartered Safe Out Here*.
p. 208   'sent to the hospital', Overy, p. 616.
p. 209   'sombre verdicts about', Gilbert, p. 914.
p. 209   'the political importance', ibid., p. 834.

CHAPTER ELEVEN

p. 213   'Early on the morning', etc., detail from Christine Helliwell, *Semut*, pp. 103–108.
p. 214   'I already had a sense', ibid., p. 98.
p. 215   'All I knew was', ibid., p. 96.
p. 216   'Down the mine bonnie laddie', Titherington, p. 144.
p. 217   'Sometimes the only way', from http://www.powtaiwan.org/archives_detail.php?A-MAN-SENT-FROM-GOD-1.
p. 217   'The time comes when', Titherington, p. 174.

NOTES ON SOURCES

p. 218 'We were walking on', from https://www.ourcivilisation.com/smartboard/shop/banzai/banzai.htm, and jungle camp detail from Hurst, pp. 332–342.
p. 220 'After we have done', Todman, p. 692.
p. 220 'Never, Never, Never', ibid., p. 692.
p. 220 'plainly irritated', ibid., p. 692.
p. 220 'He makes an extremely', Harold Nicolson, *Diaries*, p. 344.
p. 220 'He says that he', ibid., p. 345.
p. 221 'The root of the trouble', Alanbrooke, pp. 664–665.
p. 221 'We walked up and down', ibid., pp. 673–674.
p. 222 'Long before he', etc., detail from Helliwell, pp. 72–84 and pp. 89–92.
p. 225 'Save England's Asiatic Colonies', ibid., p. 76.
p. 225 'the real . . . objects', ibid., p. 81.
p. 226 'investigate the internal', ibid., p. 92.
p. 226 'the restoration of British', ibid., p. 81.
p. 227 'Body lice', from https://www.yadvashem.org/articles/interviews/duky.html.
p. 227 'Belsen was still not', etc., some detail from Pick-Goslar, *My Friend Anne Frank*, and Boas, *I Am Not a Victim*.

CHAPTER TWELVE

p. 233 'A Section: Shovels', etc., and second equipment list, from War Diary of 11 Light Field Ambulance (LFA), UK National Archives, Kew WO 177/849.
p. 234 'The label AF W 3371', ibid.
p. 235 'his conduct in the', ibid.
p. 235 'The role played', ibid.
p. 236 'Please express to', ibid.
p. 236 'chaotic and more', ibid.
p. 236 'Fuck 'em all', Helliwell, p. 115.
p. 237 'Toby Carter would', detail from Helliwell, p. 109.
p. 238 'A war that has', author's précis.
p. 238 Storepedoes and other detail, from Helliwell, pp. 110–113.
p. 239 'The King has been', *Supplement to the London Gazette*, 18 October 1945.

NOTES ON SOURCES

p. 239 'Thesis for the', Douglas Peterkin, University of Edinburgh, 1947.
p. 240 'The scene that', from https://wellcomecollection.org/works/ztegksua/items, p. 4.
p. 241 'Whilst serving with', from Douglas Peterkin's thesis.
p. 242 'The following is a', from War Diary of 11 LFA, UK National Archives, Kew WO 177/849.
p. 242 'I have seen things', from https://www.bbc.co.uk/history/ww2peopleswar/stories/97/a6345597.shtml.
p. 243 'In places the bodies', from Douglas Peterkin's thesis.
p. 244 'All the bony', ibid.
p. 245 'Captain Peterkin, together with', from War Diary of 11 LFA, UK National Archives, Kew WO 177/849.
p. 245 'Toby Carter parachuted', etc., detail from Helliwell, pp. 129–148.
p. 247 'Up forward the', ibid., p. 139.
p. 248 'for Jap heads only', ibid., p. 148.
p. 249 'SRD admits to', ibid., p. 187.
p. 249 'timid wild animals', ibid., p. 151.
p. 249 'remembered the white man', ibid., pp. 151–152.

CHAPTER THIRTEEN

p. 251 'Captain Douglas Peterkin', etc., detail from War Diary of 11 LFA, UK National Archives, Kew WO 177/849, Sue Horth's notes of her research for the Channel Four drama *The Relief of Belsen*, first broadcast 15 October 2007 and 'Johnny' Johnston's testimony at https://collections.ushmm.org/search/catalog/irn503426.
p. 251 'A very large quantity', from the diary of Mervyn Gonin, http://www.bergenbelsen.co.uk/pages/Database/ReliefStaffAccount.asp?HeroesID=17&.
p. 253 'It is considered', from War Diary of 11 LFA, UK National Archives, Kew WO 177/849.
p. 254 'The phobia of future', from Douglas Peterkin's thesis.
p. 255 'And finally I wish', from War Diary of 11 LFA, UK National Archives, Kew WO 177/849.
p. 255 'In addition the author', from Douglas Peterkin's thesis.
p. 256 'After an anxious wait', etc., detail from Helliwell, pp. 143–187.
p. 256 '[we] let it be known', ibid., p. 188.

NOTES ON SOURCES

- p. 257 'Japanese may be small', ibid., p. 63.
- p. 257 'He [Tojo] had already', ibid., p. 327.
- p. 258 'a compassion for', ibid., p. 270.
- p. 258 'they were apt pupils', ibid., p. 168.
- p. 260 'On the dusty road', etc., detail from Lyman, pp. 465–474, Chandar S. Sundaram, *Paper Tiger*, and Fraser, pp. 121–132.
- p. 262 'Several weeks earlier', Bolton, p. 179.
- p. 262 'Four o'clock came', ibid., p. 179.
- p. 263 'When we prisoners', ibid., p. 181.
- p. 263 'I returned to', ibid., p. 180.
- p. 263 'I shall look back', ibid., pp. 181–182.
- p. 264 'I took him', 'Chips' Channon, *Diaries 1943–57*, p. 271.
- p. 265 'Harold goes to', ibid., p. 201.
- p. 265 'miserable heaps', ibid., p. 201.
- p. 265 'I don't admire', ibid., p. 269.
- p. 265 'The Upper Classes', Nicolson, p. 325.
- p. 267 'All the guards had gone', etc., detail from Pick-Goslar, *My Friend Anne Frank*, and Boas, *I Am Not A Victim*, and author communications with members of Douglas Peterkin's family.

CHAPTER FOURTEEN

- p. 271 'I told them', Fay, p. 343.
- p. 271 'The fighting around', etc., detail from Sundaram, *Paper Tiger*, and Fay, pp. 335–357, and Stephen P. Cohen, *Subhas Chandra Bose and the Indian National Army*.
- p. 271 'Madness but of the', Fay, p. 399.
- p. 273 'The British Indian Army', Daniel Marston, *The Indian Army and the End of the Raj*, p. 117.
- p. 273 'sure that most', Bolton, p. 154.
- p. 273 'the worst case of burns', ibid., pp. 167–168.
- p. 274 'Towards midnight everyone', ibid., p. 178.
- p. 275 'informing them one dollar', Helliwell, p. 188.
- p. 275 'From my vantage point' and 'flotilla of praus', Alan Powell, *War by Stealth*, pp. 290–291.
- p. 276 'Capture by the Japanese', Helliwell, p. 20.
- p. 276 'What could I say?', ibid., pp. 366–367.

NOTES ON SOURCES

p. 276 'I went to Borneo', ibid., p. 200.
p. 277 'Alas for the', ibid., p. 193.
p. 277 'There will be NO' and 'Great was our disillusionment', ibid., p. 201.
p. 279 'flat impertinence', ibid., p. 228.
p. 279 'It is natural for', Dhillon, p. 31.
p. 280 'We moved from', Fey, p. 357.
p. 280 'Mr Dhillon, from what I know', Dhillon, pp. 353–363.
p. 282 'You have received' and 'during our time', Titherington, pp. 180–182.
p. 284 'I feel moved by', Bolton, p. 191.
p. 285 'Out of the blue it came', ibid., pp. 191–192.
p. 285 'I weighed up the', ibid., p. 193.
p. 286 'While I was combing', ibid., p. 195.
p. 286 Pilot Officer Philip quotes from Nair, *The Forgotten Few*.
p. 288 'If you have to go', Sugata Bose, p. 292.
p. 289 'My brother demanded', Evans, Kangaw chapter.

CHAPTER FIFTEEN

p. 292 'Did I once suffer', Edward Farley Oaten, from https://www.timeslocalnews.co.uk/local-news/tunbridge-wells-academics-place-in-the-fall-of-the-british-empire-in-india/.
p. 294 'the men and women' and 'Though Shan Nawaz', Khan, pp. 304–305.
p. 295 'They looked like skeletons', Evans, Kangaw chapter.
p. 295 'We Indian officers', ibid.
p. 296 'We were told to', Helliwell, p. 215.
p. 296 'dropping their .303s', ibid., p. 217.
p. 298 'one admits to', ibid., p. 255.
p. 299 'Killing Japs', ibid., pp. 256–257.
p. 299 'not a military man', ibid., p. 259.
p. 302 'the torrent of guns', Lyman, p. 499.
p. 302 'our job is done', Bolton, p. 198.
p. 303 'Had it not been', ibid., p. 216.
p. 304 'Of course, it was', from Archimedes Patti interview, https://openvault.wgbh.org/catalog/V_3267C58E4C104A54A0AFDF230D618AE6.

NOTES ON SOURCES

p. 306 'Have had long conference', Operational Priority Communication from Strategic Services Officer, Archimedes Patti, September 2, 1945, https://history.iowa.gov/sites/default/files/history-education-pss-vietnam-operational-transcription.pdf.
p. 307 'determination not to return', Alanbrooke, p. 682.
p. 308 'the future of the white', Overy, p. 845.
p. 310 'while Roosevelt had', from Carlton Swift interview, https://openvault.wgbh.org/catalog/V_192BA69A0BD046C48872A2C4B62AAE24.

CHAPTER SIXTEEN

p. 313 'That very day' and sign for pilots, Helliwell, p. 397.
p. 314 'Had SRD's secret agents', etc., detail from Helliwell, pp. 351–360, and Powell, pp. 291–292 and p. 337.
p. 314 'Over glamorised, puerile', Helliwell, p. 15.
p. 317 'I of course knew', etc., Philip Towle, Margaret Kosuge and Yoichi Kibata, *Japanese Prisoners of War*, p. 146, and detail from Stephen Connor, 'Sidestepping Geneva'.
p. 318 'The masses in their', Bayly and Harper, p. 177.
p. 318 'who had survived Kohima', Todman, p. 804.
p. 318 'Truckloads of Indonesian prisoners', Bayly and Harper, p. 183.
p. 319 'It is quite simple', Harry Walker interview, from Wellcome Library GC/226/A5.
p. 319 'Captain Derek van den Bogaerde' and other detail, from Bayly and Harper, pp. 186–187.
p. 320 '[Had] General Christison', https://api.parliament.uk/historic-hansard/commons/1945/oct/17/dutch-east-indies-british-policy.
p. 322 'the danger to the peace of', David Kynaston, *Austerity Britain*, p. 135.
p. 322 'is as empire-minded', Overy, p. 836.
p. 323 'Why should it be assumed', Frank Heinlein, *British Government Policy and Decolonisation 1945–63*, p. 14.
p. 323 'were cheered and applauded', Kynaston, p. 135.
p. 324 'Malaya is by far', Phillip Deery, 'Malaya 1948', pp. 29–54.
p. 325 'the plaintive notes', Powell, p. 281.
p. 326 'Whether they are', Paul Ham, *Sandakan*, p. 278.

373

NOTES ON SOURCES

p. 326 'As with Operation Semut itself', etc., detail from Powell, pp. 281–286.
p. 327 'saw no need to', ibid., p. 285.
p. 328 'I am naturally anxious', ibid., p. 286.
p. 328 'the bitter irony of this', ibid., p. 282.
p. 328 'wars are essentially cruel', ibid., p. 283.
p. 328 'At what stage could', Gary Followill, 'Necessary Chicanery', p. 25.
p. 329 'I pointed out to him', ibid., p. 68.
p. 330 'The operation would', Dr Ooi Keat Gin, https://www.awm.gov.au/articles/journal/j37/borneo.
p. 331 'The first book', etc., detail from David Edgerton, *Britain's War Machine*, pp. 295–302.

CHAPTER SEVENTEEN

p. 338 'We Indians think', Evans, Jullunder chapter.
p. 338 'The most difficult part', ibid.
p. 339 'One day a refugee', ibid.
p. 339 'Thimayya was neither', from https://www.usiofindia.org/publication-books/thimayya-an-amazing-life.html.
p. 340 'When I think', Evans, Jullunder chapter.
p. 340 'respect of both sides', from https://www.usiofindia.org/publication-books/thimayya-an-amazing-life.html.
p. 341 'The thing is', personal interview with Andrew Peterkin.
p. 342 'He loved being', ibid.
p. 342 'We didn't talk', ibid.
p. 343 'It was frightening', personal interview with Jennifer Bryant.
p. 344 'He must have been', ibid.
p. 345 'Pipper Pasty', etc., from Craig-Bryant family culinary memories.
p. 346 'Oh shut up!', from https://youtu.be/ttsDDJY2U3s?si=Sc1D5EB3okvqQZmL&t=5583.
p. 347 'We have solved nothing', Kee, pp. 12–13.

Index

Abrahams, Mrs 230
Admin Box, Battle of the 141, 158
AGAS spy ring 324, 326, 327
al-Gaylani, Rashid Aali 68
al-Husayni, Hajj Amin 68, 165
Ali, Aruna Asaf 85, 294
Ali, Asaf 294
Ambedkar, B. R. 26, 27
Amery, Leo 60, 62, 82
Amritsar massacre 25, 28
Andaman Islands 97–8, 127
Anderson, Ava 264
Apoi Anggang 296
Arakan 140–5, 146–9, 152
Ardennes offensive 176–7
Army Education Corps 185
Atlantic Charter (1941) 60–5, 208, 305, 306, 307, 310
Attlee, Clement 38, 63, 320–1, 322–3
Auchinleck, Sir Claude 15, 131
Aung San 77
Auschwitz concentration camp 178–9

Bakshi, Pushkar 98, 99
Balfour, Harold 265
Bangalore United Services Club 17
Barber, Gerard 172
Basu, Satyen 110–11
Batu Lintang camp 329–30
Beaverbrook, Lord 175
Bengal famine 107–15
Bergen-Belsen concentration camp 179–80, 227–31, 239–45, 251–6
Bevan, Aneurin 322
Bevin, Ernest 323
Bird, Alfred 98–9, 127
Bishop Cotton School 17

Black, Gunner 117
Blamey, Thomas 315, 329, 330, 331
Boas family 267–9, 346
Bogarde, Dirk 319–20
Bolton, James 303
Boon family 343s
Borneo 213–15, 222–6, 236–8, 245–9, 256–60, 275–9, 295–9, 313–16, 319, 324–31
Bose, Anita 100
Bose, Krishna 293
Bose, Subhas Chandra
  and Burma campaign 151–3, 156, 157–60, 207
  at Cambridge University 28
  and Congress Party 30, 37, 38–9
  death of 291–2
  early political activism 29–31
  and Gurbaksh Singh Dhillon 203
  image of 292–3
  and Indian National Army 85–6, 123–7, 273, 300–1
  Jawaharlal Nehru on 293–4
  journey to Japan 99–105
  leaves Burma 287–8
  in Nazi Germany 58–9, 67–70, 81–3, 165
  and Mahatma Gandhi 38, 84
  political activism in 1930s 37–9
  revered in modern India 13–14, 191
  and start of Second World War 55–6
  as a teenage rebel 21–4
  view of Nazi Germany 39
Boughey, Jim 169
Boxer Rebellion 53
Branson, Clive 110
Bretton Woods Conference 174, 175

INDEX

Britain
  changing view of Empire 185–6
  dislike of 122–3
  influence on war in Europe 173–7
  post-war attitudes to Empire 321–4, 331–3
  tensions with Americans 174–7, 193–4
  tensions with Soviet Union 192–4
British Way and Purpose, The (Army Education Corps) 185, 186, 207
Brooke, Alan 177, 194, 198–9, 266, 306
Brown, William 'Bruno' 154
Browning, Frederick Arthur Montague 'Boy' 191
Bryant family 336, 342–3, 345
Burma
  and Burmese opposition to British campaign 11
  George MacDonald Fraser in 204–7, 260–1
  Kodandera Subayya Thimayya's role in campaign 3–10, 140–5, 189, 190, 286–7
  Indian Army in 3–11, 140–5, 146–9, 189–90, 202–3, 260–1, 286–7
  Indian National Army in 11, 151–61, 201–4, 271–3, 279–81, 287–9, 293–5
  Karen people in 207
  and Operation Character 207–8
  and principles of Atlantic Charter 63
  refugees from Japanese advance 76–9
  support for Japanese in 77
  volunteer soldiers in 10–12
Burmese Independence Army 77

Cambodia 306, 308, 310
Cariappa, Nina 40–1, 42
Carment, Max 325
Carter, Gordon Senior 'Toby' 214, 222–3, 224, 226, 237–8, 245–9, 256, 258–9, 295–9
Cater, Sir Norman 41
Chakrabarty, Purnendu 'Chuck' 287
Chamberlain, Neville 264
Champion, James 327, 328–9
Channon, Henry 'Chips' 264–6, 323
Chester, F. 'Gort' 327
Chicago Herald Tribune 194
Chifley, Ben 330, 331

Chindits 131–2
Christison, Philip 318–19, 320
Churchill, Winston
  and Atlantic Charter 60, 62, 63–4, 305
  belief in continuation of British Empire 208–9
  and Bengal famine 111, 113–14
  condemns Amritsar massacre 28
  and creation of Israel 208
  falling confidence in 198–9, 201
  and French colonies 210
  and Greek intervention 194, 199, 200, 201
  Indian self-government offer 82
  on Indian support during Second World War 55
  and Italian campaign 177
  joked about 177
  and Mahdi rebellion 53
  and post-war settlement fears 174–5
  tensions with Americans 193–4
  tensions with Soviet Union 193–4
  at Yalta conference 219–21
Clayton, Tim xii, xiii, xviii
Cohen, Philip 300
Colville, Jack 209
Congress Party 14, 15, 30, 37, 38–9, 55–6, 84
Conquer We Must (Prior) xvii
Corbis, SS 101–3
Courtney, 'Jumbo' 226, 299
Craig, Phil xii, xiii, xviii
Creas, Jeti 140
Cripps, Stafford 82
Cullop, Len 168
D-Day 173, 174, 176
Davies, General 'Taffy' 133–5, 142, 143–5
de Gaulle, Charles 209–10
de Souza, Mary 196
de Valera, Éamon 31, 38, 126
Dhillon, Gurbaksh Singh 13–14, 158, 201, 202–3, 271, 279, 280–1, 294
Dimbleby, Richard 255
Dobie, Thomas 346
Dutch East Indies 316–21
Dyer, Reginald 28

Edwards, Jack 218
Eichmann, Adolf 167

376

INDEX

Eisenhower, Dwight 176, 177, 305
End of Empire (TV series) 121
Essen 161–2

Falaise pocket 173
Fields, Gracie 162–3
Finest Hour (Clayton & Craig) xii, xiii, xviii
Finlay, C. H. 328, 330
Followill, Gary 328
Formosa 115–20, 168–72, 216–18, 282–3
Forster, E. M. 24, 43, 51, 78
Frank, Anne 166, 167, 178, 229, 261
Frank, Otto 261
Fraser, George Macdonald 204–7, 260–1, 263

Gandhi, Indira 120
Gandhi, Mahatma 281
  and Bengal famine 114
  and Churchill's offer of self-government 82
  as figure of independence movement 13, 25
  and Kodandera Subayya Thimayya 36–7
  and 'Quit India' campaign 84
  and race relations 26
  and refugees from Burma 79
  and Subhas Chandra Bose 38, 84
Garewal, B. J. S. 156
Gelber, Dukie 227
Gemmeker, Albert 178
George VI, King 63
Germany
  bombing raids on 161–2
  Douglas Peterkin in 268–9
  Mervyn Gonin in 233–5
  Subhas Chandra Bose in 58–9, 67–70, 81–3, 165
Goebbels, Joseph 81–2
Gonin, Mervyn 233–5, 239–40, 245, 251–2, 253–4
Gorman, Sergeant Major 18
Goslar family 166–7, 178, 179, 180, 227–8, 229–30, 231, 267
Government of India Act (1919) 26
Gracey, Douglas 308–9, 317
Greater East Asia Co-Prosperity Sphere 96–7

Greece 194, 198, 199, 200–1
Gurumurthy, Krishnan 77

Halifax, Lord 38
Hamilton-Britton, Colonel 35
Hardy, Campbell 5, 6–7
Hargreaves, Kenneth 51
Harrisson, Tom 223, 224–5, 256, 258, 297
Hasan, Abid 100–2, 104, 156, 158–9
Heap, Edith 346
Helliwell, Christine xviii
Herbert, John 112
Hickie, Mike 346
Hill 170, Battle of 6–9
Hitler, Adolf 39, 81, 83, 99
Ho Chi Minh 210, 304–5, 306, 308, 309–11
Holocaust, The 165–7, 178–80, 227–31, 239–45
Homfreyganj massacre 127
Hoover, Herbert 208
Hoshijima, Susumi 325
Howath, Harry 346
Hughes, Harry 346

Imamura, Captain 172–3, 217, 282, 283
Imphal, Battle of 153–4, 155–8, 159–60
India
  in the 1920s 25–7
  and Bengal famine 107–15
  caste system in 26–7
  effects of Red Fort trial 13–15
  independence of 332–3
  modernisation of 183–5
  post-Independence 120, 338–40
  'Quit India' campaign in 84–5
  and refugees from Burma 76–9
  support for Second World War 54–5
Indian Air Force 146–8, 286–7
Indian Army
  in 1920s India 25
  Arakan advance 140–5, 146–9
  Australian training of 131
  in Burma campaign 3–11, 140–5, 146, 189–90, 202–3, 260–1, 286–7
  in independent India 338–40
  Kodandera Subayya Thimayya joins 18, 35
  and Red Fort trial 14–15
  reorganisation of 132–3
  at start of Second World War 53–5

377

INDEX

Indian Civil Service 26, 28–9
Indian Independence League 124–5, 127
Indian National Army (INA)
   in battles at Imphal and Kohima 153–4, 155–8, 159–60
   in Burma campaign 11, 151–61, 271–3, 279–81, 293–5
   creation of 79–80
   image of 300–1
   and Irrawaddy campaign 201–4
   Kodandera Subayya Thimayya's view of 88–9
   as prisoner of war guards 94
   propaganda by 145–6
   and Red Fort trial 13–15
   and Subhas Chandra Bose 85–6, 123–7
   surrender of 293–5
Indian Pilgrim (Bose) 37
Indian Struggle, The (Bose) 30, 37, 101
Indonesia 317–18, 319, 320–1
Inspector Calls, An (Priestley) 186, 264
Irrawaddy campaign 201–4
Israel 208
Itote, Waruhui 10, 11

Jinnah, Mohammed Ali 120
Johnston, H. D. 'Johnny' 240, 241, 242–3, 251, 252, 255
Jones, Arthur Creech 324

Kangaw, Battle of 4–10
Karslake, Sir Henry 41
Keling Langit 213–14, 315–16
Khan, Shah Nawaz 13–14, 124, 271, 279
Kido, Major 317, 318
King, Mary 136, 137–8, 180–1, 286
Kinkaseki Camp 115–20, 168–73, 216–18
Kipling, Rudyard 51, 64
Kittermaster, Mr 16
Knowland, George 8
Kohima, Battle of 153–4, 155–8, 160
Kripalani, Sucheta 114

Laos 306, 307
Lawai Bisarai 214, 215, 237, 238
Leahy, William 219
Lennox-Boyd, Alan 265
Lethbridge, John 'Tubby' 130–1
Leyte Gulf, Battle of 223

Linlithgow, Lord 76, 85, 265
Lion and the Unicorn, The (Orwell) 186
Lipang Munan 257
Lossing, Edward 'Teddy' 72–3, 107–8, 135–7, 139–40, 182–3, 198, 284–6
Luther, Martin 165

MacArthur, Douglas 223, 226, 306, 330
Mahdi rebellion 53
Malaya 93, 96, 323–4
Malaysia 103,
Mallaby, Aubertin 318
Manhattan Project 163
Mariana Islands 307
Marshall, John 216
Marshall, Robert 185
Masani, Zareer 27
Masters, John 302
Mau Mau 11
McNally, Mary 70, 72
Meiktila, Battle of 205
Midnight's Children (Rushdie) 187
Milligan, Spike 47
Montagu, Edwin 28
Montgomery, Bernard 176–7
Mountbatten, Lord Louis 191, 210, 294, 317
Moyne, Lord 208
Mukherjee, Abir 1, 28
Musenberg, Werner 101
Muslim League 15, 76
Mussolini, Benito 31, 265

Nanking Massacre 126–7
National Health Service 337
Nawaz, Shah 160, 294
Nehru, Jawaharlal
   as anti-authoritarian 31
   education of 120
   as figure of independence movement 13
   on Indian Civil Service 26
   on Indian National Army 293–4
   and 'Quit India' campaign 84
   and Red Fort trial 14
Nehru, Motilal 35–7
Nethercott, Iain 346
Netherlands 165–7, 178–80
New Guinea 130
Newberry family 335–7, 341–4
New Statesman 200

INDEX

Niblock, Major 138
Nicobar Islands 97–8
Nicolson, Harold 220–1, 265
Nizamuddin, Khwaja 111, 112
Noblet, Angela
  in Assam 135–40, 181–2
  arrival in India 47–53
  and Bengal famine 107–9
  end of relationship with 'Teddy' Lossing 284–6
  on hospital ship 195–8, 261–4, 273–5
  life in India 70–5, 107–8
  life after Second World War 303–4
  treating Japanese prisoners 261–4

Oaten, Edward Farley 22–4, 292, 293
O'Donnell, Paddy 240
Office of Strategic Services (OSS) 157, 304–5, 322
Olusoga, David xvii, 344
Operation Character 207–8
Operation Kingfisher 327–9
Operation Market Garden 174, 176
Operation Plunder 235
Operation Semut 213–15, 222–6
Orwell, George 186
Overy, Richard 112

Palestine 208
Passage to India, A (Forster) 24, 43, 51
Patti, Archimedes 304–6, 308, 310
Peterkin, Douglas Brock 235, 236, 239–45, 251, 254, 255–6, 268–9, 336, 337–8, 341–5
Peterson, Lance Corporal 117
Pettigrew, Hugh 205
Philip, Pilot Officer CGI 146–8, 286–7
Philippines 64, 125, 215, 223, 226, 259, 305, 327
Phoebe, HMS 3, 4, 5, 7, 191
Pippen, Francis 259
Poland 192–3, 220
Powell, Alan 327, 328
Prasad, Niranjan 146–7
Prescott, D. T. 240–1
Presidency College 22
Presidency Jail 57
Priestley, J. B. 186, 264
Prince of Wales Royal Indian Military College 16–17, 18–19

Prior, Robin xvii

Quetta earthquake (1935) 41–2
'Quit India' campaign 84–5, 87–8

Rackley, Dick 336
Rahman, Habibur 292
Raja Nong Chik Raja Ishak 96
Ralph, Victor 12
Ram, Sarup 98
Rani of Jhansi Regiment 125, 301
Rattigan, Terence 264
Reading, Lord 18–19
Red Fort trial 13–15, 271
Ribbentrop, Joachim von 83
Roosevelt, Franklin D.
  and Atlantic Charter 60, 61, 62, 63–5, 305
  and Bengal famine 111
  and European re-colonisation 306–7
  and French colonies 208
  relations with Britain 194
  relations with Soviet Union 192, 193
  at Yalta conference 219
Rowland, Robin 155
Rushdie, Salman 187

Saha, Gopinath 29
Sahgal, Prem Kumar 13–14, 271, 279–80, 294
Sandakan 324–6, 327–31
Sanderson, Charles 'Fred' 214–15, 226
Sandhurst 32–3
Schenkl, Emilie 37, 67, 100
Seed, Peter 168–9, 216, 217
Semut (Helliwell) xviii
Sen, Amartya 111–12
Services Reconnaissance Department (SRD) 222–3, 224, 225, 226, 246–9, 256–60, 275–9, 295–9, 313, 314–16, 324, 326–30
Sewell, Captain 117
Seyss-Inquart, Arthur 165, 166
Sheppard, Denis 259
Singapore 76, 79–80, 81, 82, 85–8, 91, 92, 94, 98, 124, 126, 158, 209, 291–2, 294–5, 318, 325
Singh, Dirwan 98, 99
Singh, Mohan 79–80, 101, 323

379

INDEX

Slim, William
  and Arakan advance 148–9
  and battles at Imphal and Kohima 153
  belief in volunteer army 10
  and capture of Meiktila 205
  and Chindits 131
  and Irrawaddy campaign 203, 204
  and refugees from Burma 78
Smoke and Ashes (Mukherjee) 1
Sochon, Bill 223, 247, 256, 258
Soviet Union 31–2, 192–4
Special Operations Executive (SOE) 207, 225
Stalin, Joseph 31–2, 192, 193–4, 200, 219
Steen, Bon 346
Stern Gang 208
Sutcliffe, D.S. 327–8
Sutomo 317–18
Swift, Carleton 310–11

Tama Weng Ajeng 247–8, 249, 256, 258, 295–6, 297
Tashiro, Sergeant ('Sanitary Sid') 168, 170, 283
Theresienstadt concentration camp 229, 231, 255
Thimayya, Bonappa 42
Thimayya, Kodandera Ponnappa 12
  capture of 288–9
  childhood encounters with the British 17
  in Indian National Army 12, 88, 145
Thimayya, Kodandera Subayya 'Timmy'
  in Burma campaign 3–10, 140–5, 146, 189, 190, 286–7
  and capture of brother 288–9
  childhood encounters with the British 17–18
  death of 341
  early military career 33–5
  joins Indian Army regiment 18, 35
  and Indian National Army 88–9, 145
  and Mahatma Gandhi 36–7
  marriage to Nina Cariappa 40–1
  meeting with Mountbatten 191
  meets prisoners of war 294–5
  and Motilal Nehru 35–7
  at North West Frontier 39–42
  in post-independence India 338–40
  at Prince of Wales Royal Indian Military College 16–17, 18–19

  and 'Quit India' campaign 87–8
  and reorganisation of Indian Army 132–3
  at Sandhurst 32–3
  in Singapore 86–7
  support for Indian independence 12, 35–6
  and 'Taffy' Davies 133–5, 142, 143
Times of India 127
'Timmy' *see* Thimayya, Kodandera Subayya
Titherington, Arthur
  in Kinkaseki Camp 115, 117–18, 119–20, 168–9, 170, 172–3, 216, 217–18
  liberation from camp 282–3
  life after Second World War 283–4
  taken as prisoner of war 91–6
Titherington, Iris 284
Todman, Dan 318
Tojo, Hideki 101, 123
Tolkien, J. R. R. 162
Tredrea, Jack 214, 215, 226, 238
Truman, Harry S. 306, 307
Twain, Mark 64

U Saw 63
Uete, Taichi 283

V2 rockets 173
Vaux, Peter 346
Victoria, Queen 21
Vietnam 304–11

Wakiyama, Captain 95, 115, 117, 118–19, 172, 283
Walker, Chapman 327–7
Walker, Harry 122
Walker, John Chapman 224
Wavell, Archibald 113
Westerbrok camp 166, 167, 178–9
Wheeler, Ben 169–72, 216–17, 283
Wilson, Robert 298–9
Windeyer, Victor 297
Wissler, Denis 346
Women's Auxiliary Corps 184
Wootten, General 297

Yalta conference 219–21
Young, Peter 8–9

About the Author

Phil Craig is a bestselling author and multiple-award-winning film-maker.

A former RAF cadet pilot, he studied history at Cambridge University, was a BBC graduate trainee and built his career working for iconic British TV series *World in Action* and *Panorama*. Later he held senior positions at the prestigious Brook Lapping production company, at the Discovery Channel and at ABC Television in Australia where he ran the entire factual output including its high-profile ANZAC centenary project. Throughout his TV and writing career, Phil has spent many years researching and reinterpreting the story of Britain and its Empire during the Second World War, including his definitive and bestselling account of 1940 – *Finest Hour*.

He also hosts *The Scandal Mongers Podcast*.